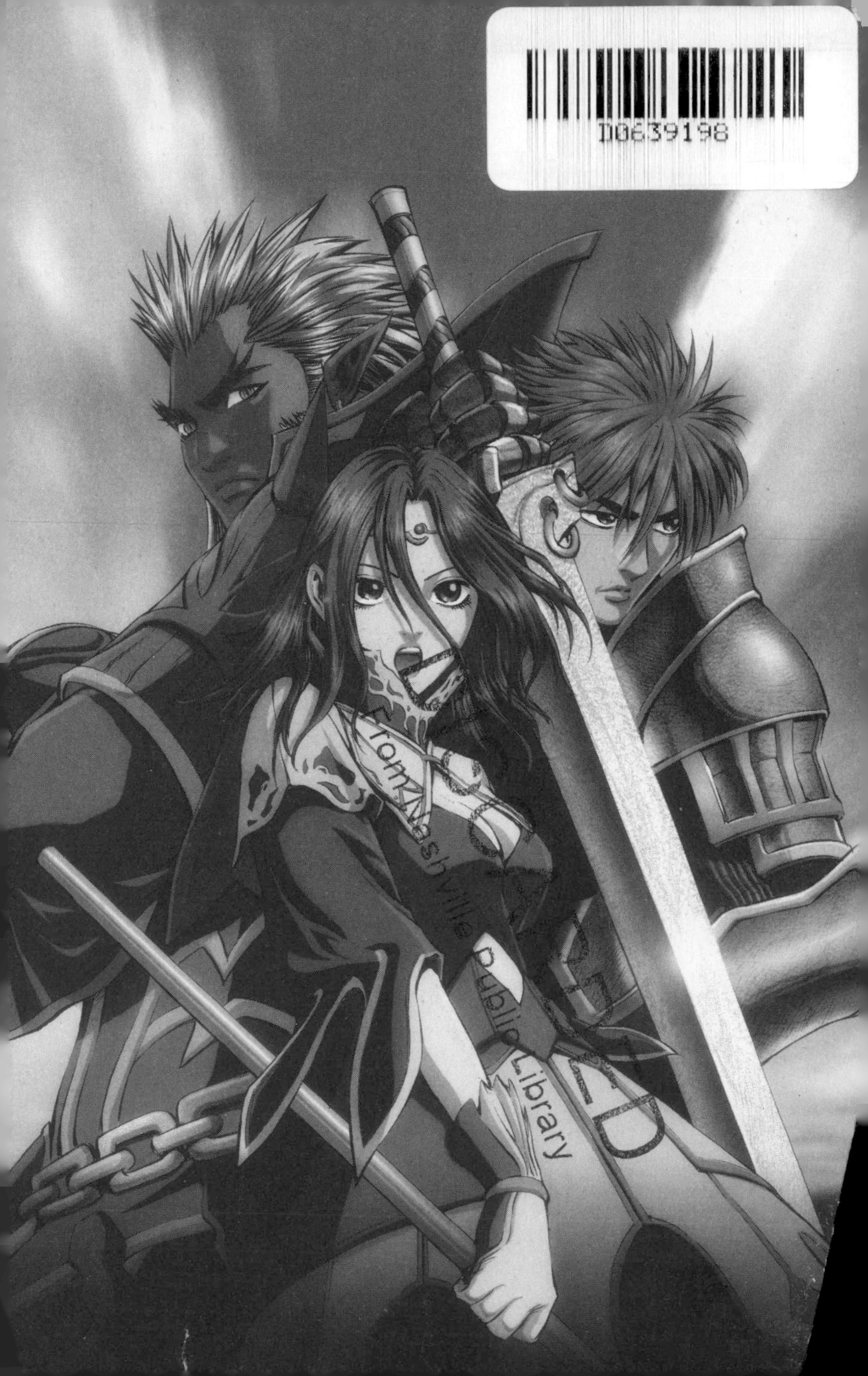

Archlord Vol. 1
Created by Jin-Hwan Park

Translation - Jennifer Hahm
English Adaption - Nathan Johnson
Layout and Lettering - Star Print Brokers
Production Artist - Mike Estacio
Cover Layout - Jason Milligan

Editor - Luis Reyes
Digital Imaging Manager - Chris Buford
Pre-Press Supervisor - Erika Terriquez
Art Director - Anne-Marie Horne
Production Manager - Elisabeth Brizzi
Managing Editor - Vy Nguyen
VP of Production - Ron Klamert
Editor-in-Chief - Rob Tokar
Publisher - Mike Kiley
President and C.O.O. - John Parker
C.E.O. and Chief Creative Officer - Stuart Levy

A  Manga

TOKYOPOP and ⟨logo⟩ are trademarks or registered trademarks of TOKYOPOP Inc.

TOKYOPOP Inc.
5900 Wilshire Blvd. Suite 2000
Los Angeles, CA 90036

E-mail: info@TOKYOPOP.com
Come visit us online at www.TOKYOPOP.com

ISBN: 978-1-59816-967-6

First TOKYOPOP printing: February 2007
10 9 8 7 6 5 4 3 2 1
Printed in the USA

by
Jin~Hwan Park

HAMBURG // LONDON // LOS ANGELES // TOKYO

Archlord History – The Chronicles of Chantra

Long ago, the Elementals infused their power into the very stones of the continent of Chantra, creating a land of magic and mystery whispered about in legends around the world. The most seductive story was that five of the gemstones --Archons-- bestowed unimaginable power upon their bearer. Adventurers from many lands sought to make this power their own -- including humans and Orcs from the western continent. But though they were in a new land, they brought their old racial hatreds with them.

Two heroes emerged in Chantra around the year 7 BD -- the human warrior Nathan and the Orc magician Walcure. Both set out on their own quest to find the Archons. Their paths crossed in the heat of the Windrill desert as they searched for ancient ruins. Their instinctive hatred gripped them and they launched into a fierce battle, magic against strength and steel, clashing for hours on end. But they were evenly matched, and finally they collapsed from exhaustion. Recognizing each other as formidable fighters, both worthy of respect, they shared their water and formed a lasting friendship.

Together they continued the quest for the Archons, finally finding the old ruins. The tumbled rock and broken roads of the ancient city were not entirely abandoned, however. Destiny had one final trial for them. As they explored the remains of the city they discovered a great hall. Wandering deep into it they saw before them a throne richly decorated with carvings of warriors in fierce battle. As they stood there marveling, a man stepped from behind the throne. He was dressed in armor matching the carvings and he raised a menacing sword. This was Salamander, the last remaining guardian of this once amazing city. He was left by the ancients to defend their treasures to the end. He launched into a ferocious attack. It took the skill of both heroes to defeat the great Salamander.

As the mighty warrior fell, a huge door at the rear of the hall slid back revealing two incredible weapons. Both carried an Archon, infused with primordial Elemental power. The sword held the Archon of Fire, the staff held the Archon of Earth. Moving forward each claimed one -- Nathan chose the sword and Walcure took the staff.

Their adventure finished, they knew it was time to return to their own people. As the battle brothers parted ways they lifted a ring from the fallen Salamander and split it between them as a reminder of their shared journey and newfound allegiance to each other.

Nathan earned a reputation as a righteous warrior and built a great castle on Chantra called Manas. Walcure came to be called the greatest magician in all of Orc history. Countless tales of their achievements were told for generations, and over time, even their weapons took on names of their own. Nathan's sword became known as Brumhart, while Walcure's staff acquired the name Gaiahon. But the most important event of their lives would happen six years later.

One night six years later, Nathan and Walcure were both awakened by an eerie sound -- a wailing cry only they could hear. It seemed to come from their magical weapons. Mystified, they both traveled to Serend to consult Gracia, a wise archer of the Moon elves. They arrived at the same time, and Gracia knew why they had come. Her own bow, Evengarda, contained two Archons and was also wailing. She explained that a magician called Cyripus had gained an Archon of his own, and was calling the weapons -- trying to unite all the powers of the Elementals in one person. Trying to become an ArchLord.

With all five Archons, Cyripus would be nearly invincible, and the three heroes knew that one person could not be trusted with such enormous powers. Nathan, Walcure and Gracia banded together to find Cyripus and defeat him. At last they confronted him and a battle ensued in the same ancient, desert ruins where Walcure and Nathan had gained their Archons. All three fought tirelessly, but finally it was the Moon elf Gracia who took down Cyripus with her bow. It cost her a deep wound from his magic, but the heroes triumphed. They had no respect for the power--hungry magician, so they abandoned the body in the ruins, Gracia's arrows still piercing Cyripus' chest. Afraid of being tempted by the power of five united Archons, the heroes decided to hide the one they gained from Cyripus. At the time, a great city named Dulan was being constructed -- at its heart a mighty castle. Together they buried the final Archon under the castle's foundation stone and sealed it with magic.

The secret of its resting place was never revealed, but Nathan had witnessed the full extent of the power of the Archon, and he became cautious of the Archon inside Brumhart. He asked the Noum to craft a magical scabbard, which would seal in the power of the sword as long as it was sheathed. From then on, he drew his weapon only when absolutely necessary, and strong cautions were handed down as the sword passed on through generations of his descendants.

CONTENTS

ARCHLORD

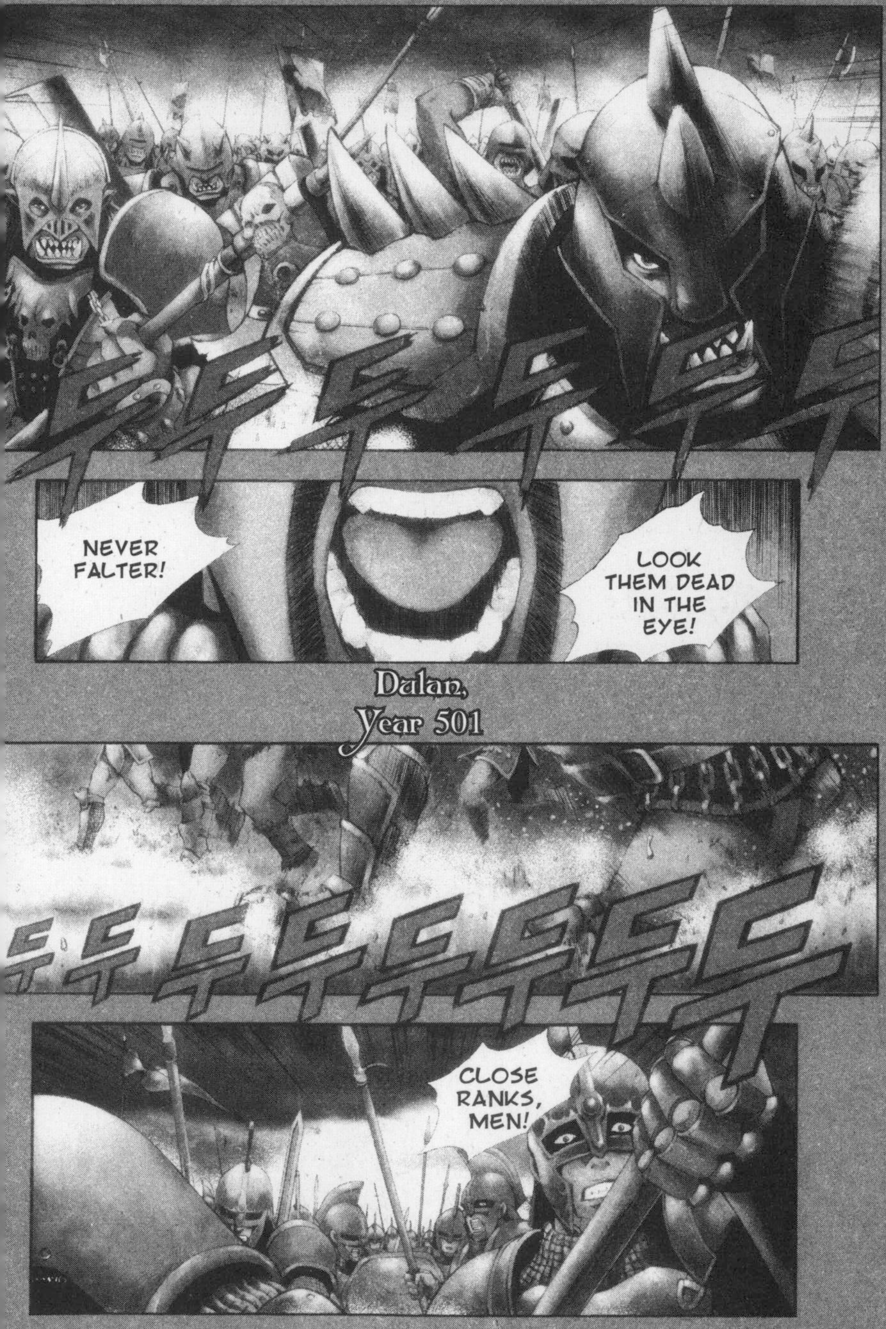
NEVER FALTER!
LOOK THEM DEAD IN THE EYE!
Dulan, Year 501
CLOSE RANKS, MEN!

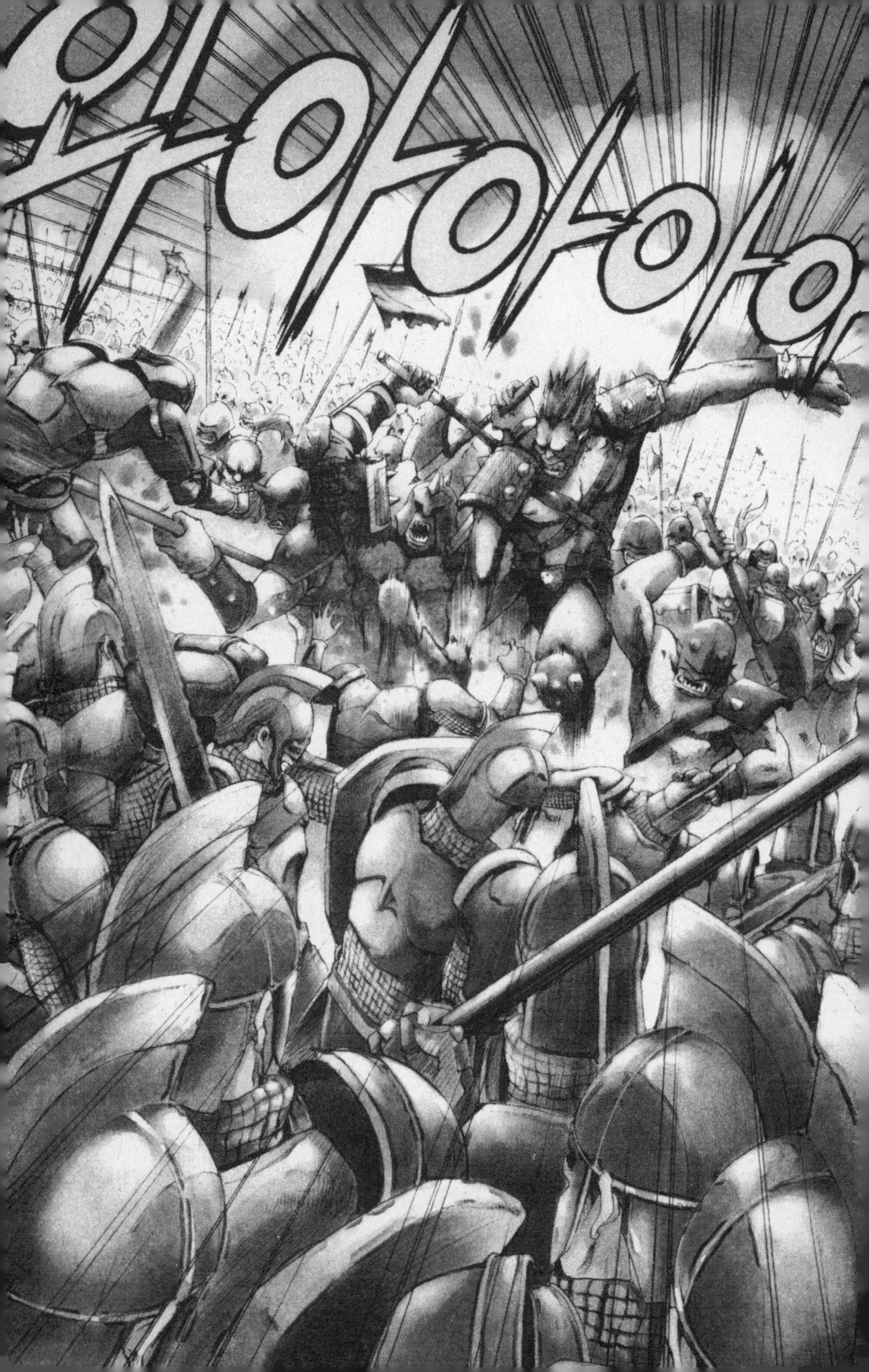

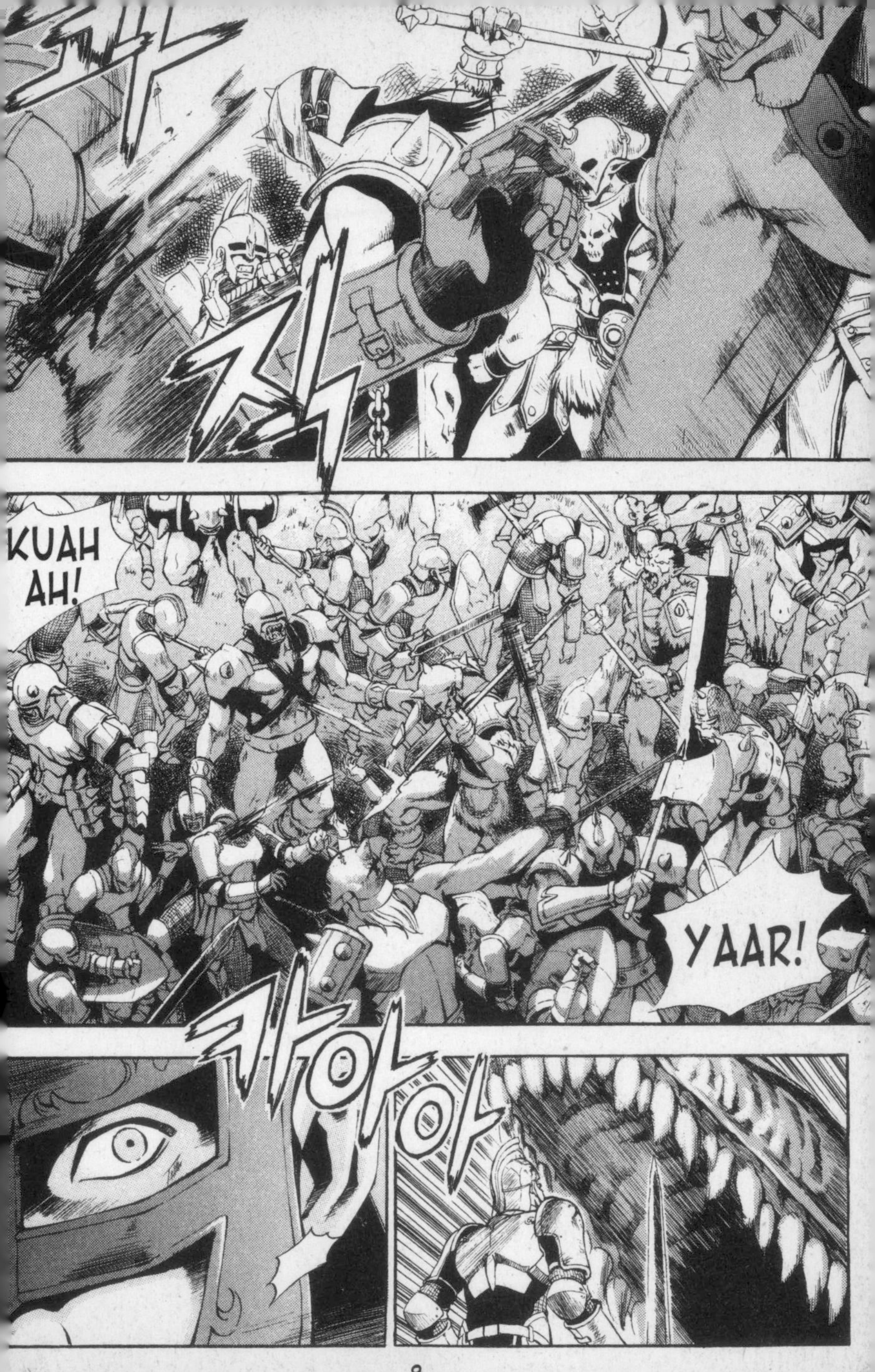
KUAH AH!
YAAR!

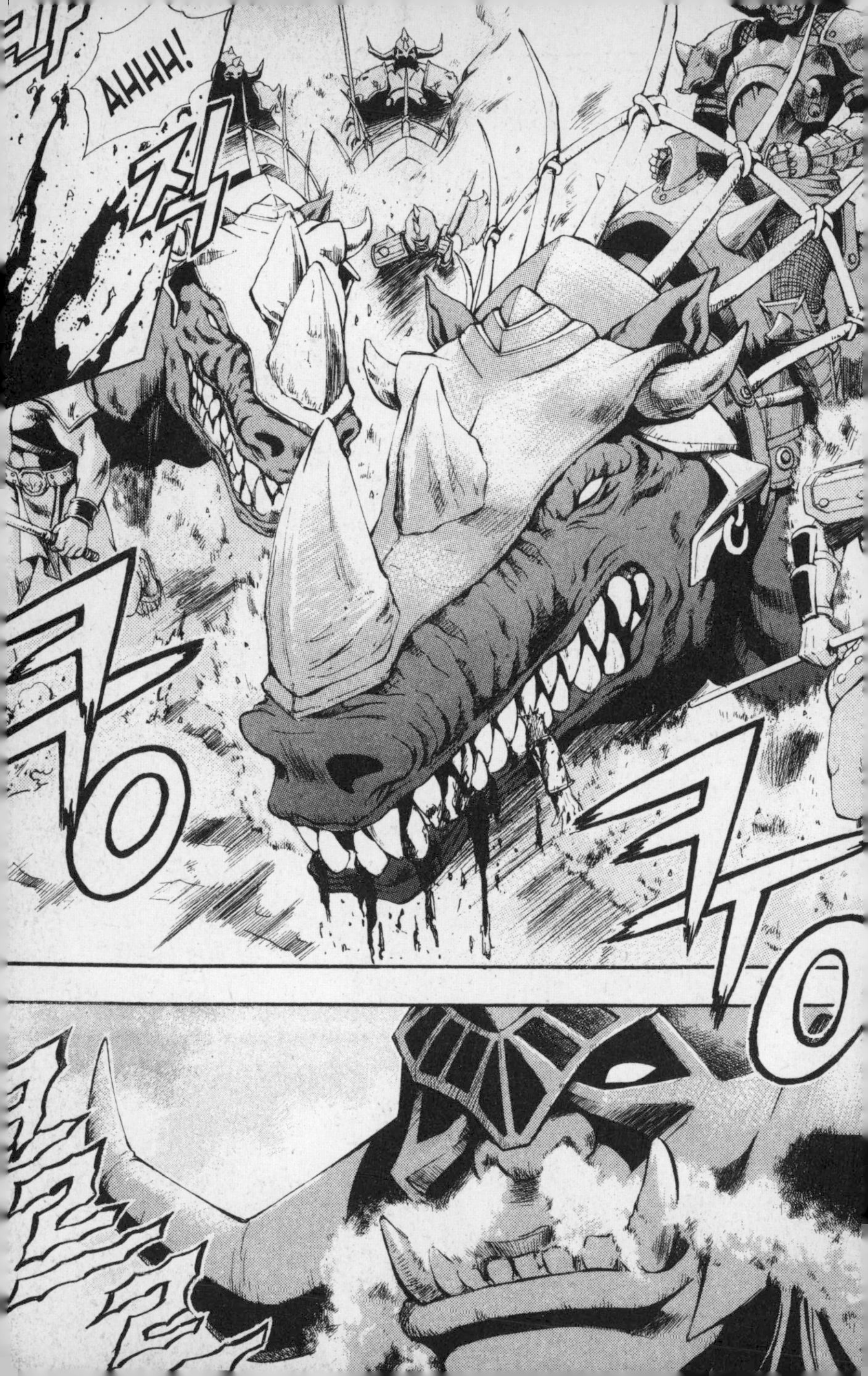

AHHH!

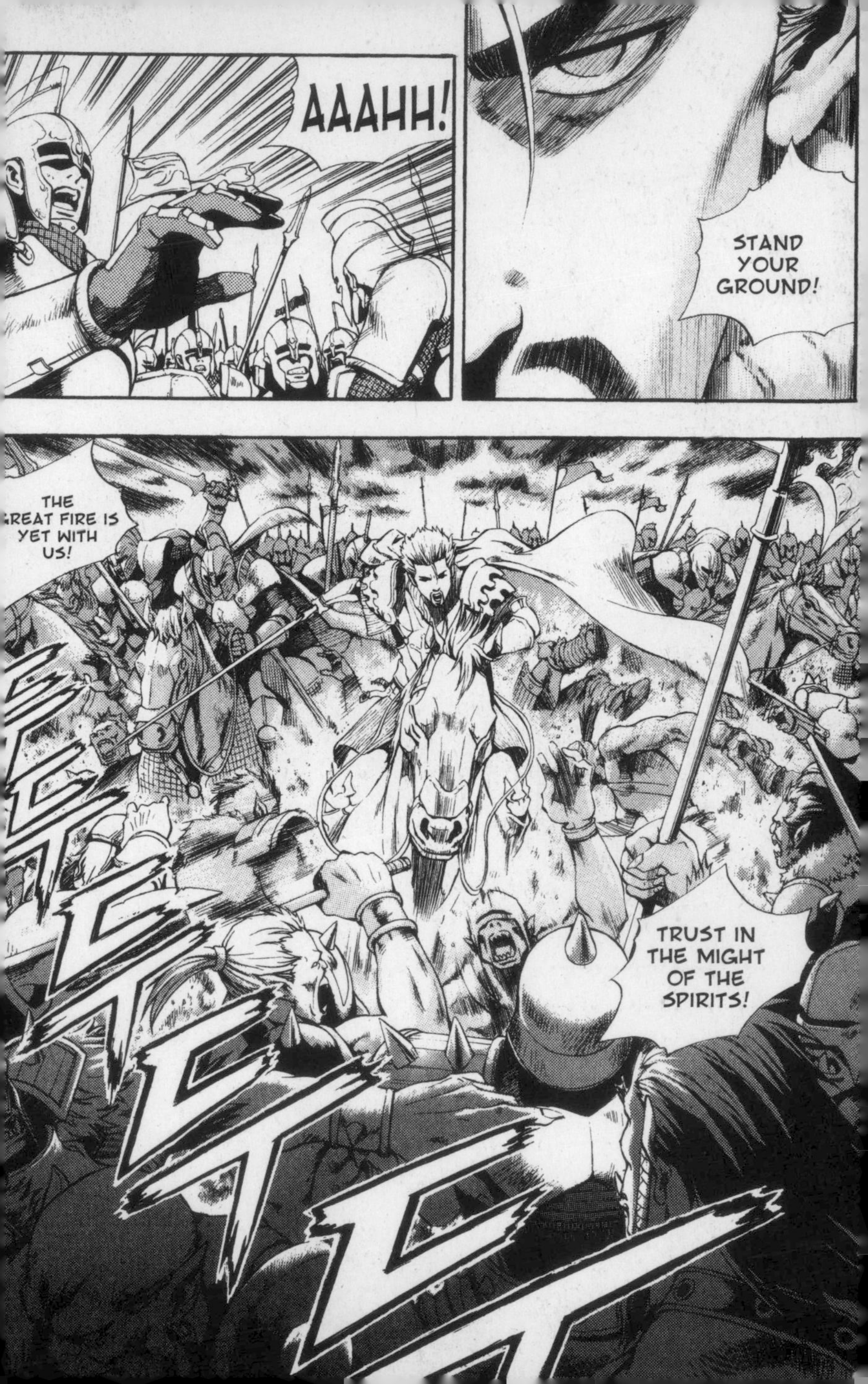
AAAHH!
STAND YOUR GROUND!
THE GREAT FIRE IS YET WITH US!
TRUST IN THE MIGHT OF THE SPIRITS!

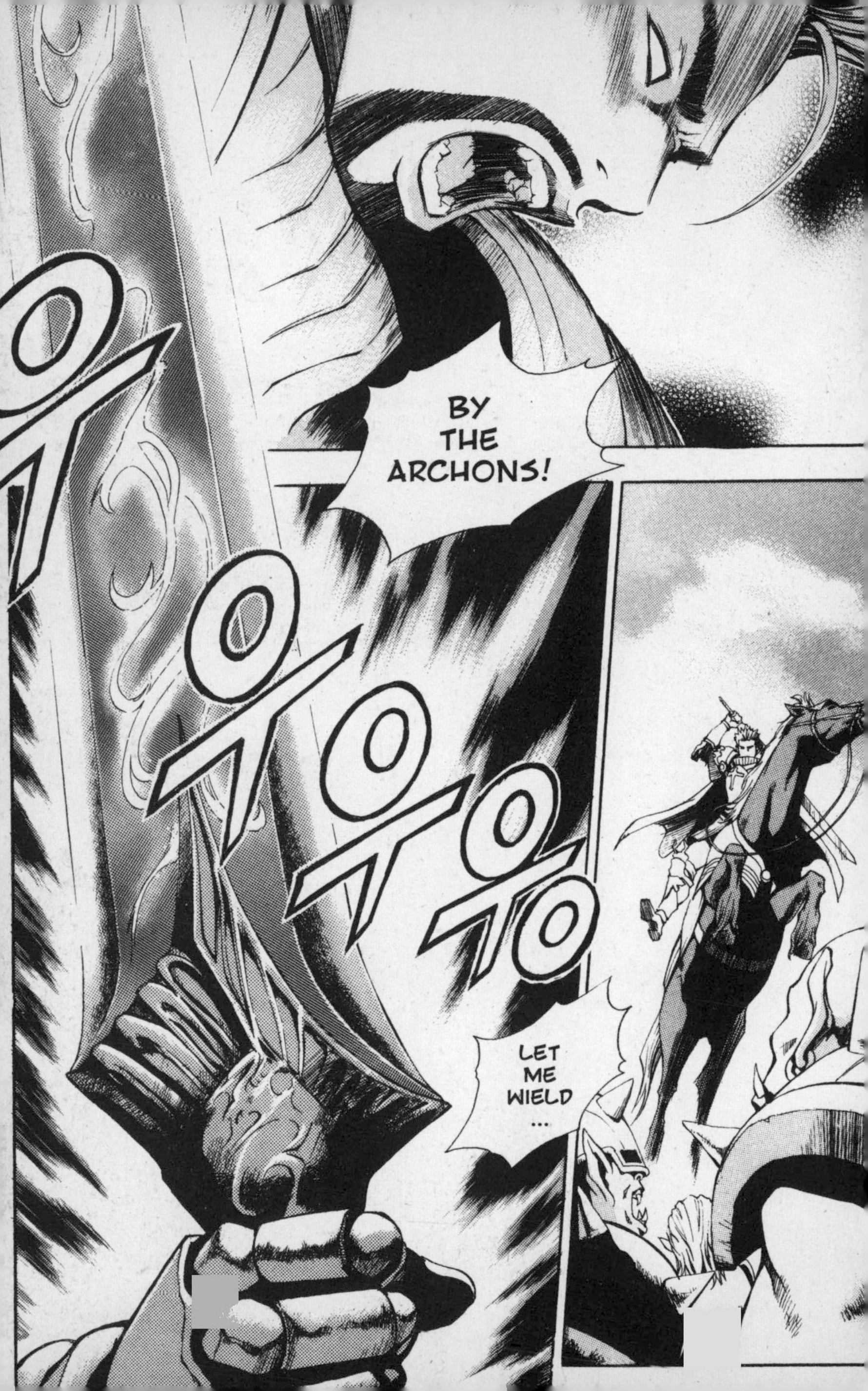
BY THE ARCHONS!
LET ME WIELD ...

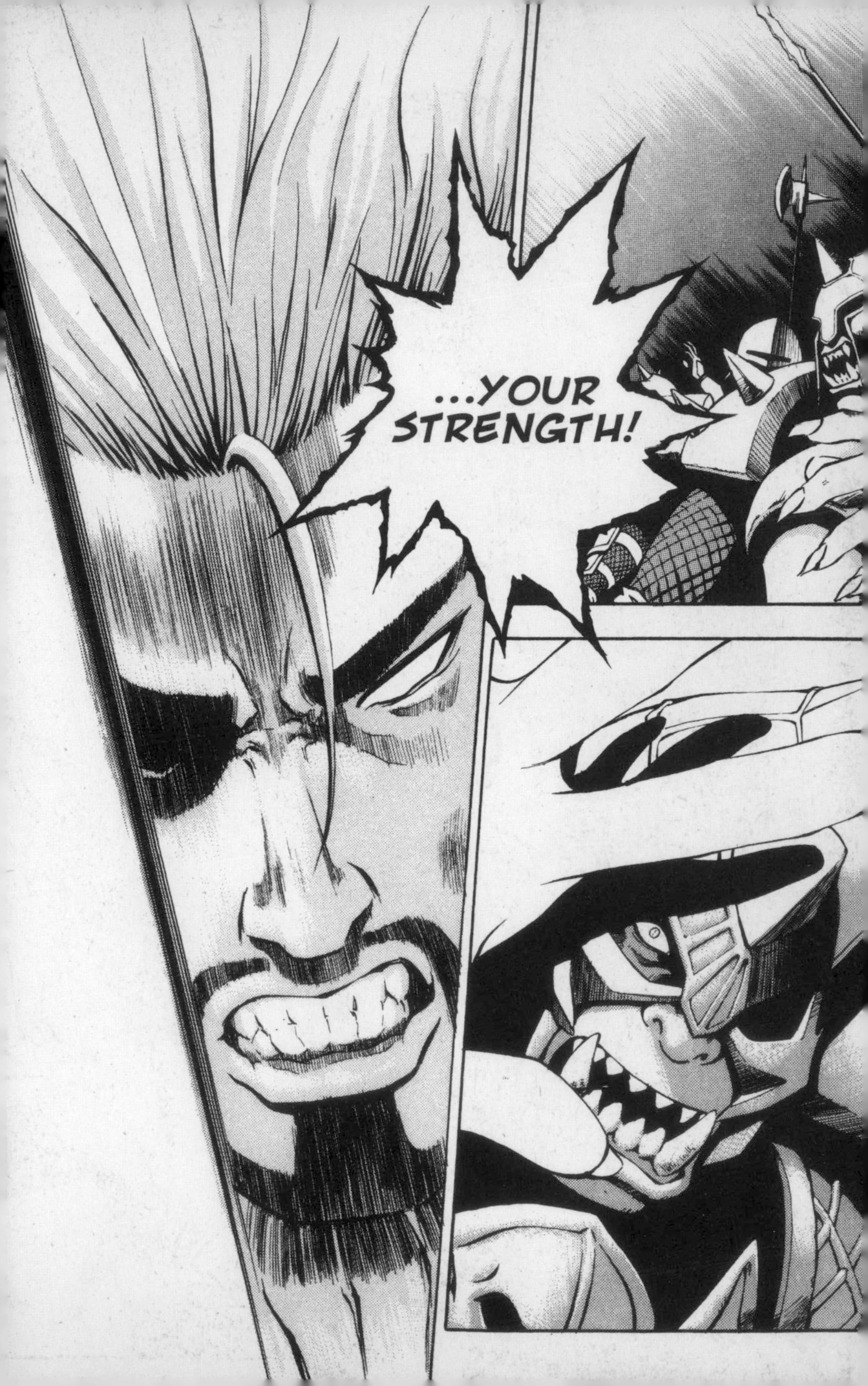
...YOUR STRENGTH!

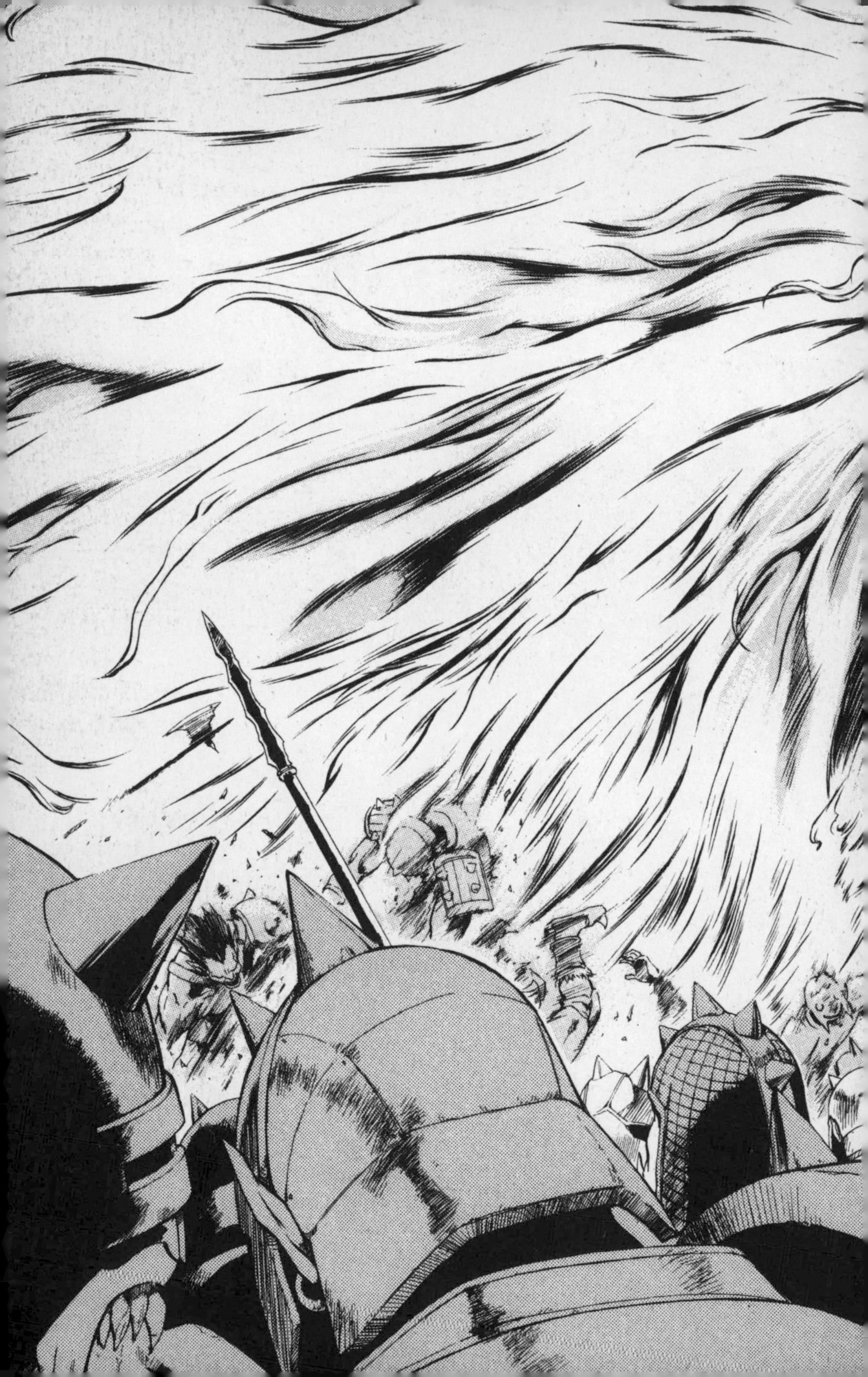

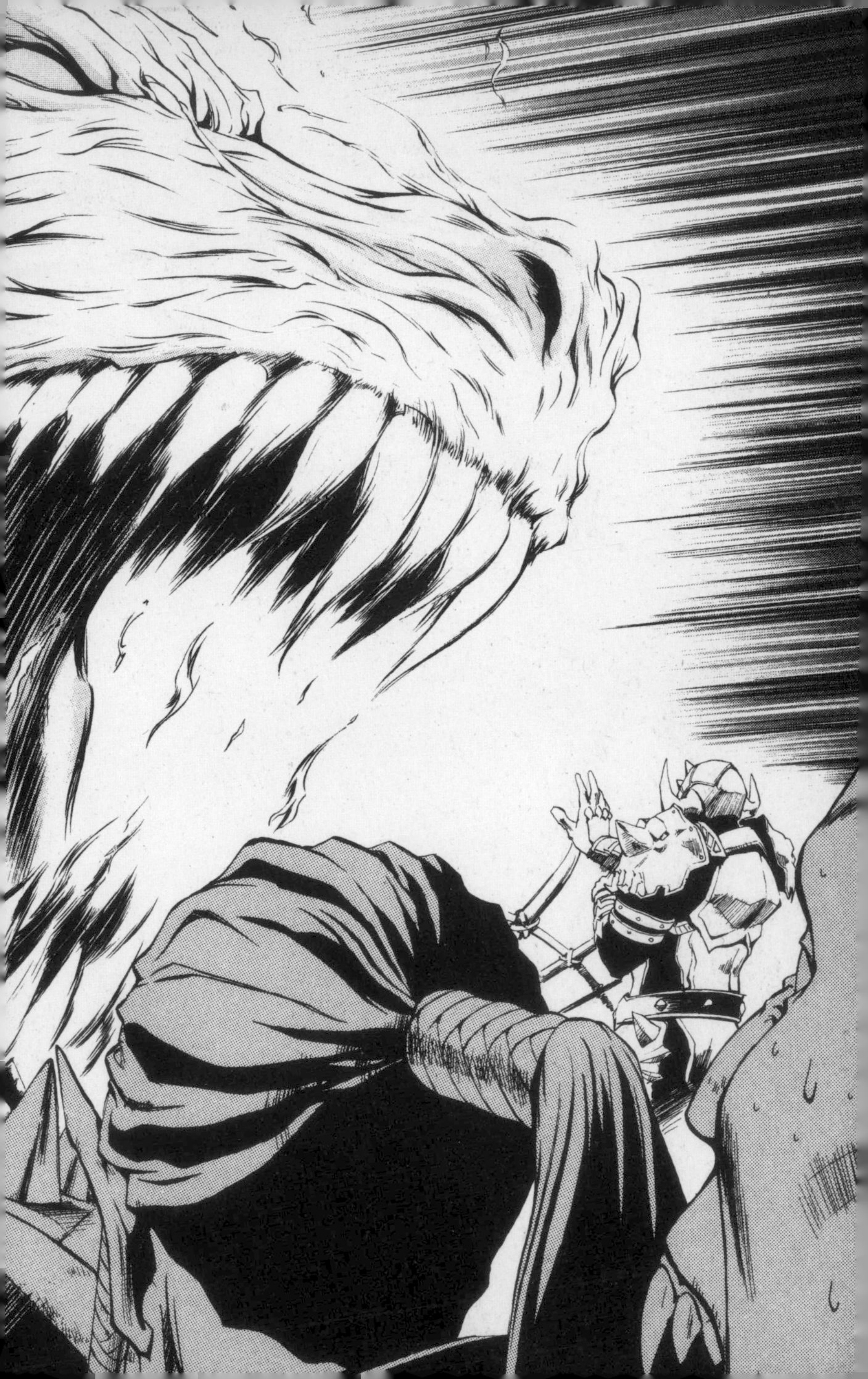

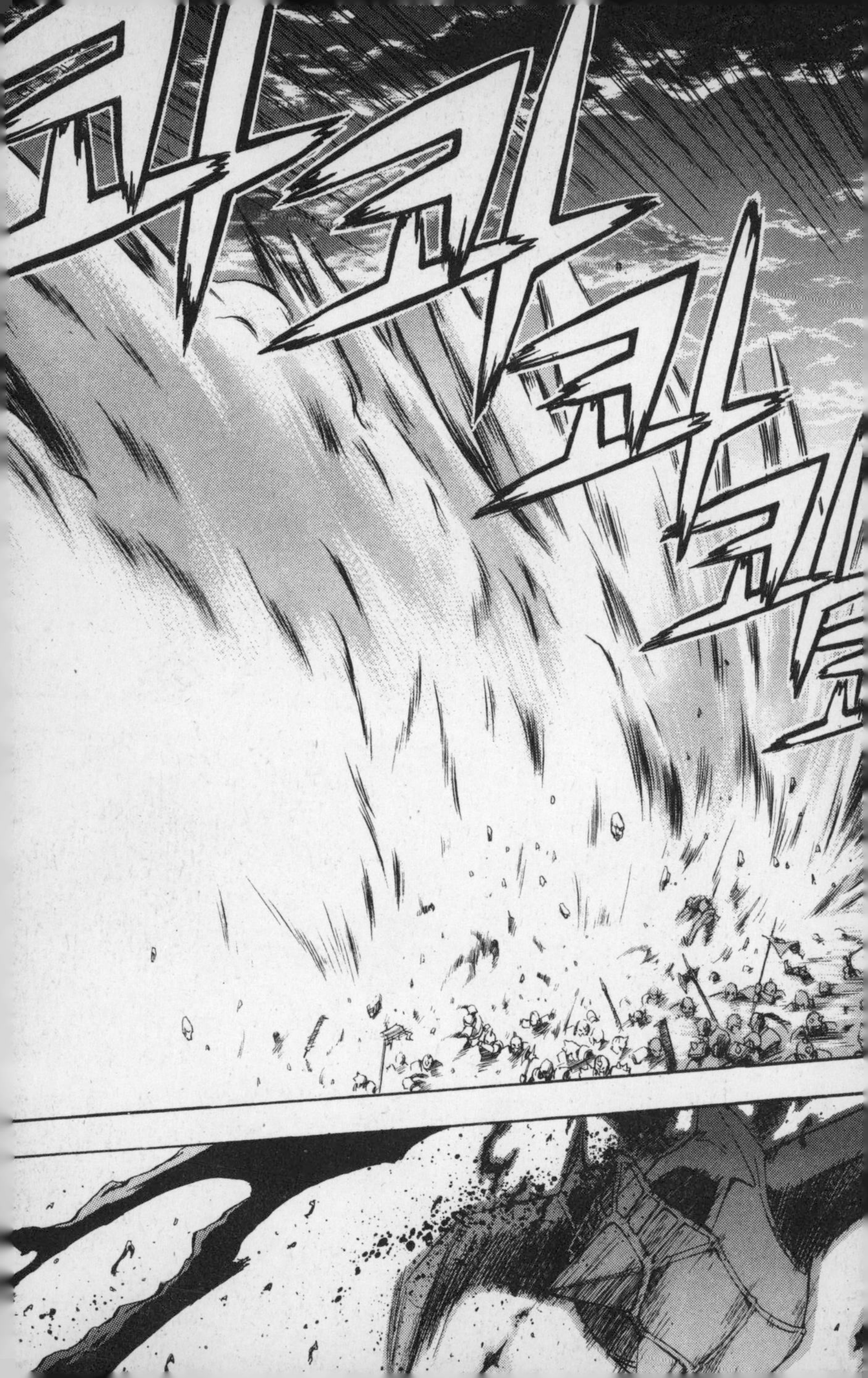

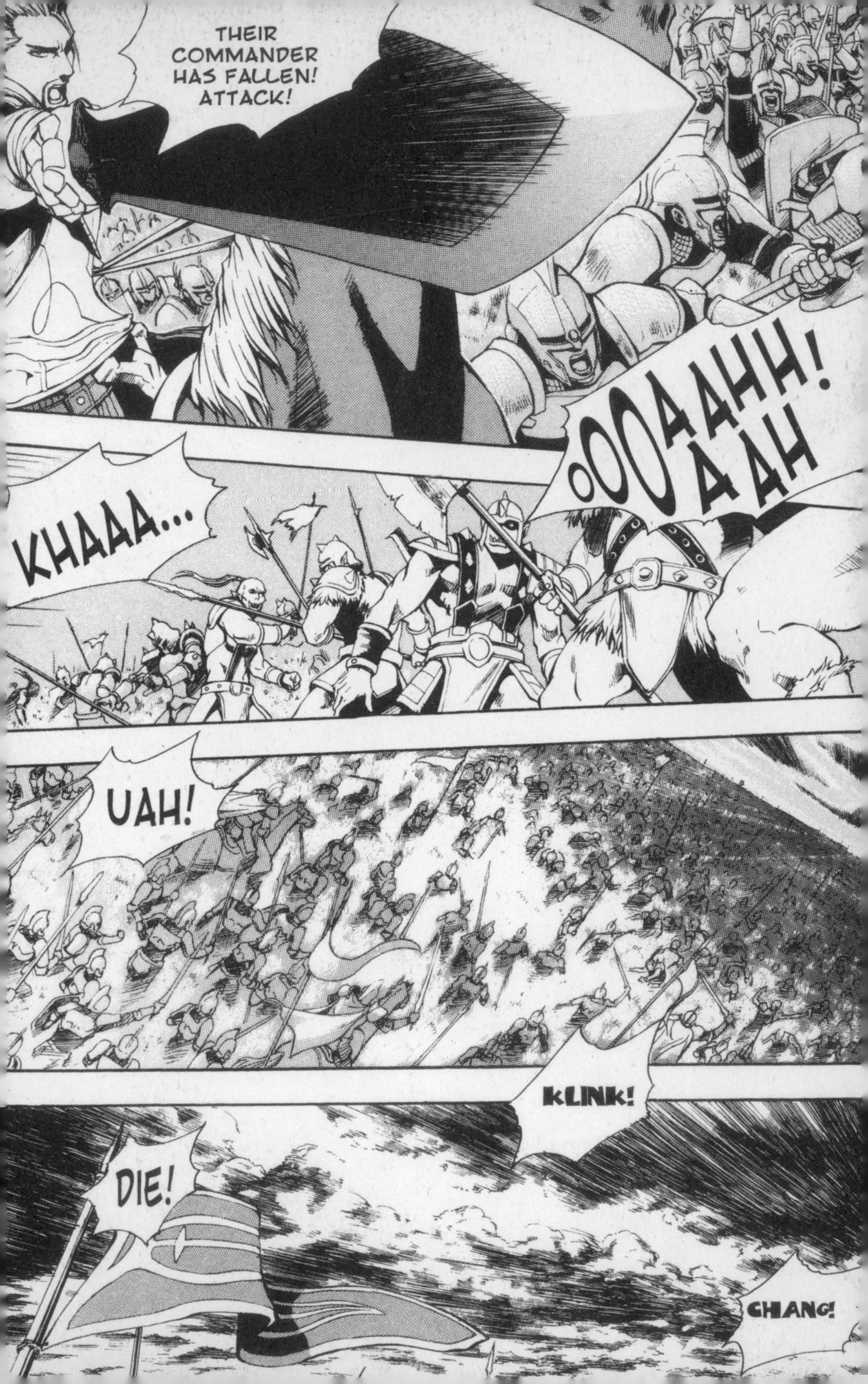
THEIR COMMANDER HAS FALLEN! ATTACK!
OOOAAHH! AAH
KHAAA...
UAH!
KLINK!
DIE!
CHANG!

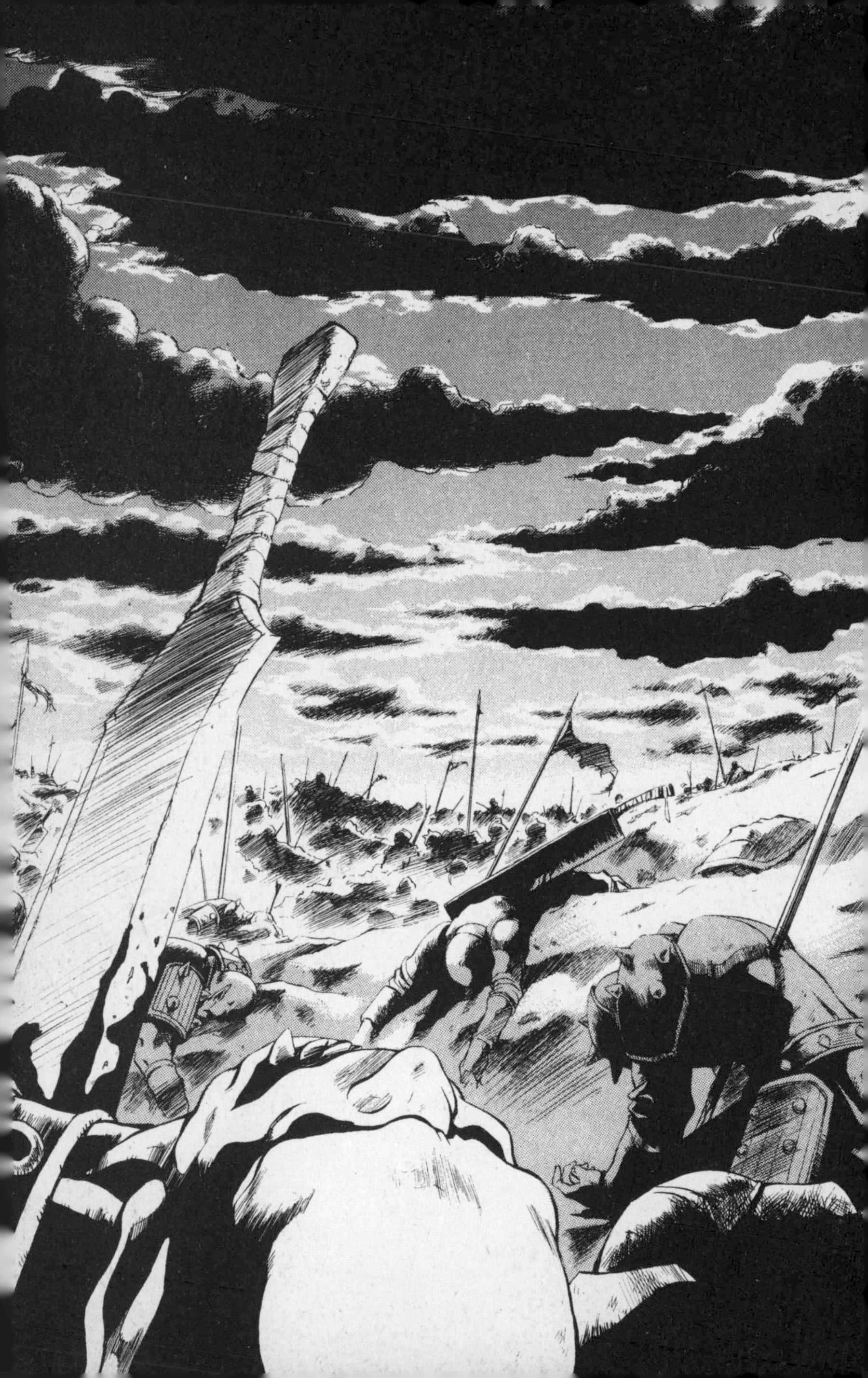

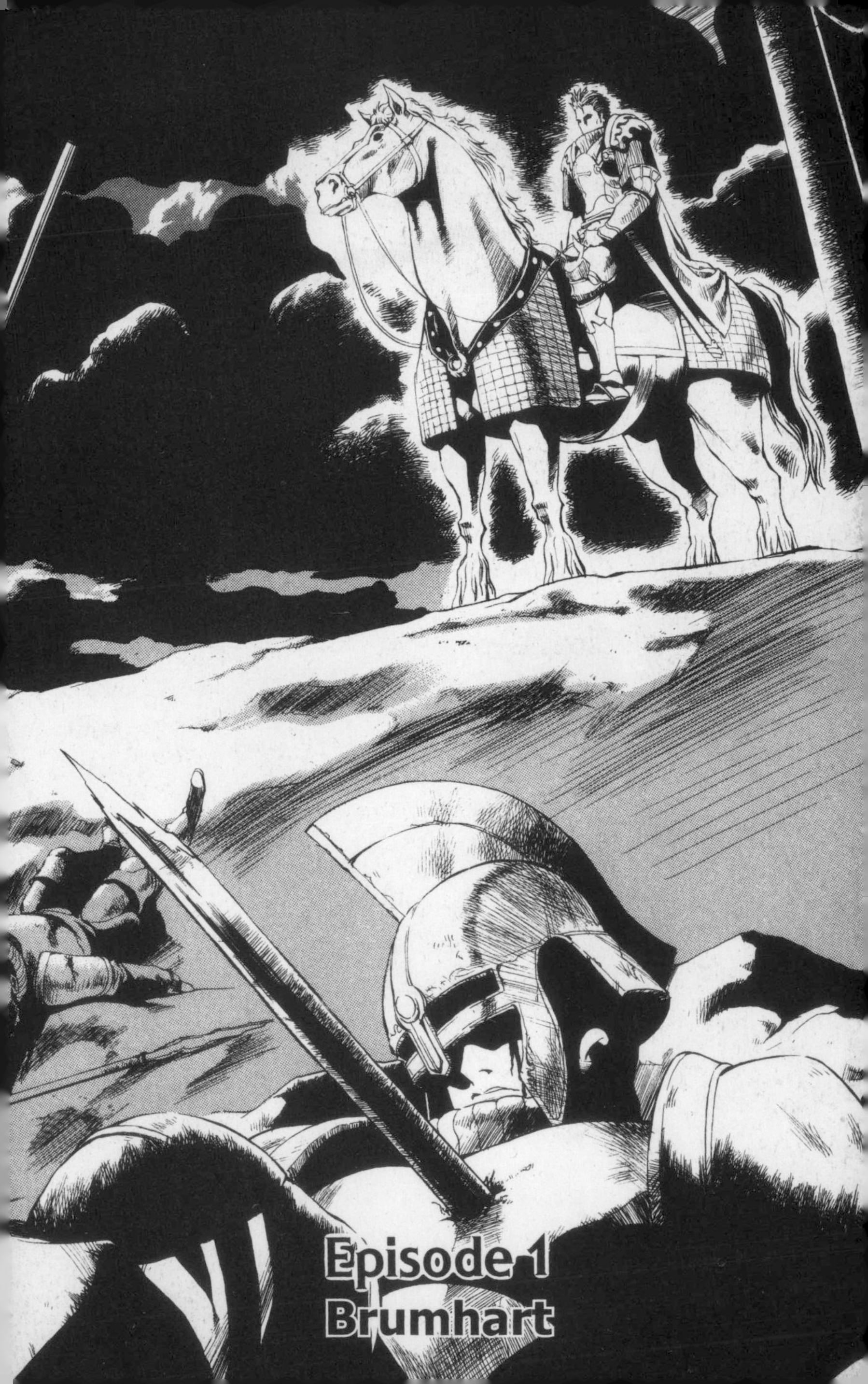
Episode 1
Brumhart

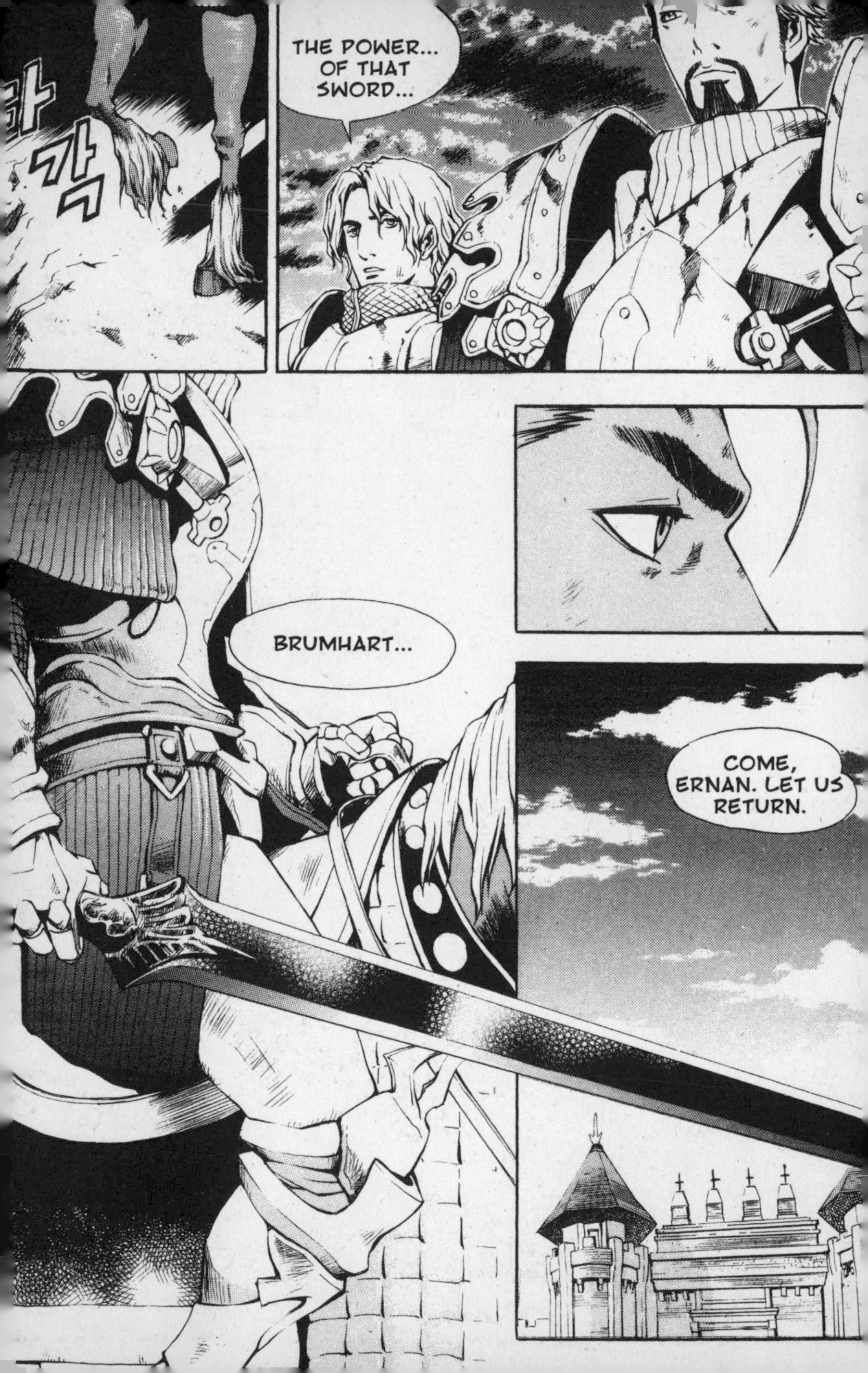
THE POWER... OF THAT SWORD...
BRUMHART...
COME, ERNAN. LET US RETURN.

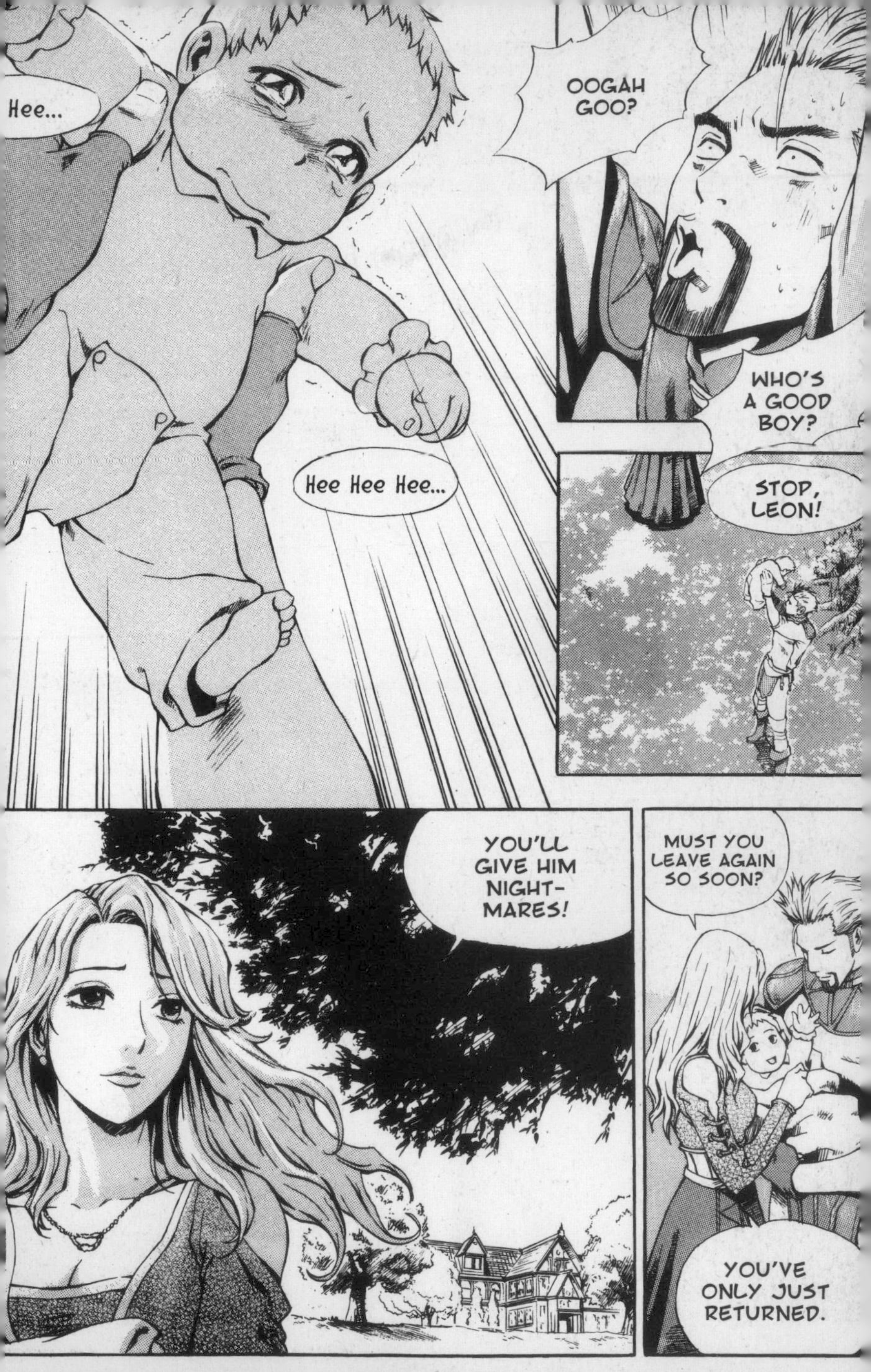
Hee...
OOGAH GOO?
WHO'S A GOOD BOY?
Hee Hee Hee...
STOP, LEON!
YOU'LL GIVE HIM NIGHT-MARES!
MUST YOU LEAVE AGAIN SO SOON?
YOU'VE ONLY JUST RETURNED.

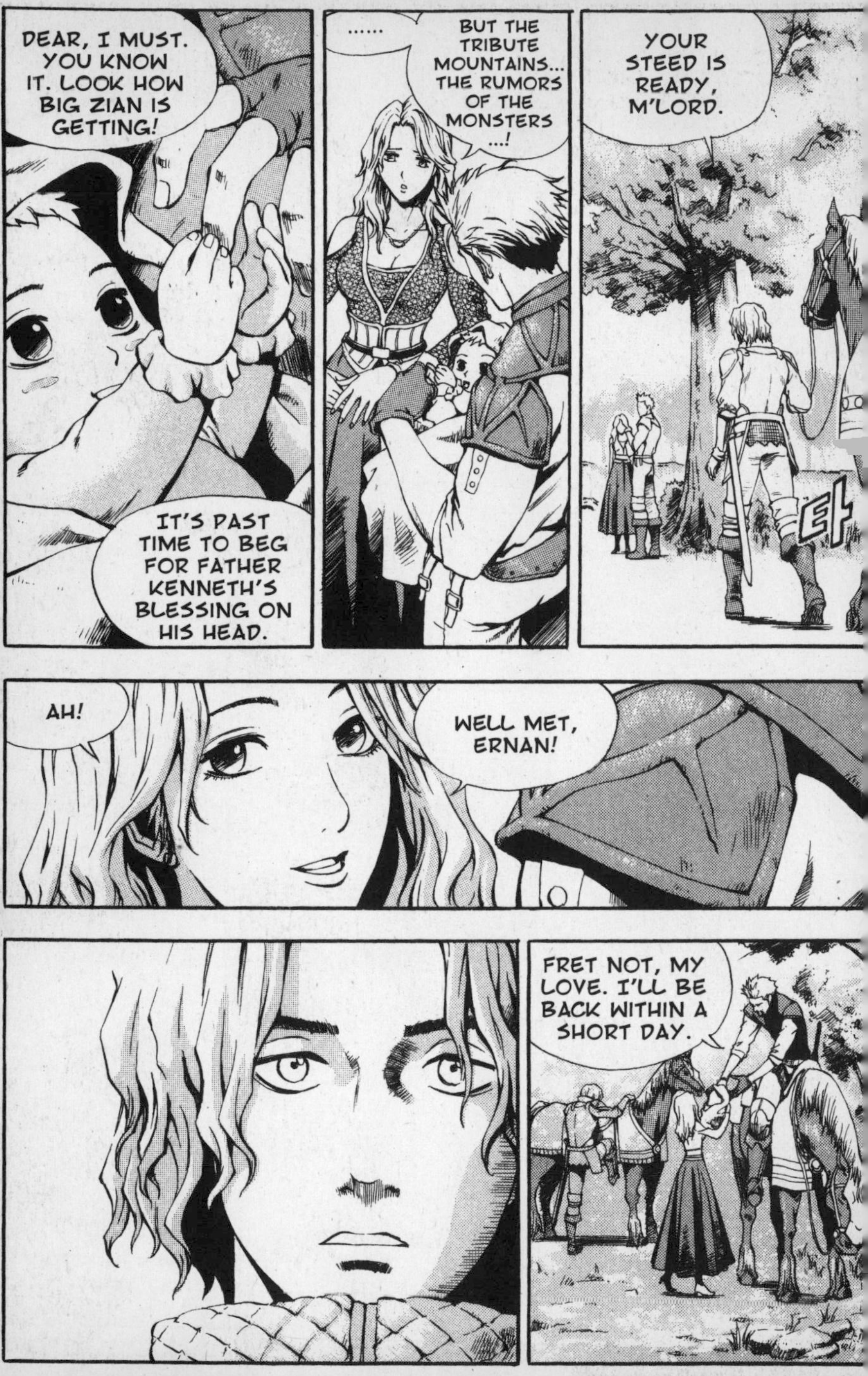
DEAR, I MUST. YOU KNOW IT. LOOK HOW BIG ZIAN IS GETTING!
IT'S PAST TIME TO BEG FOR FATHER KENNETH'S BLESSING ON HIS HEAD.
......
BUT THE TRIBUTE MOUNTAINS... THE RUMORS OF THE MONSTERS ....!
YOUR STEED IS READY, M'LORD.
AH!
WELL MET, ERNAN!
FRET NOT, MY LOVE. I'LL BE BACK WITHIN A SHORT DAY.

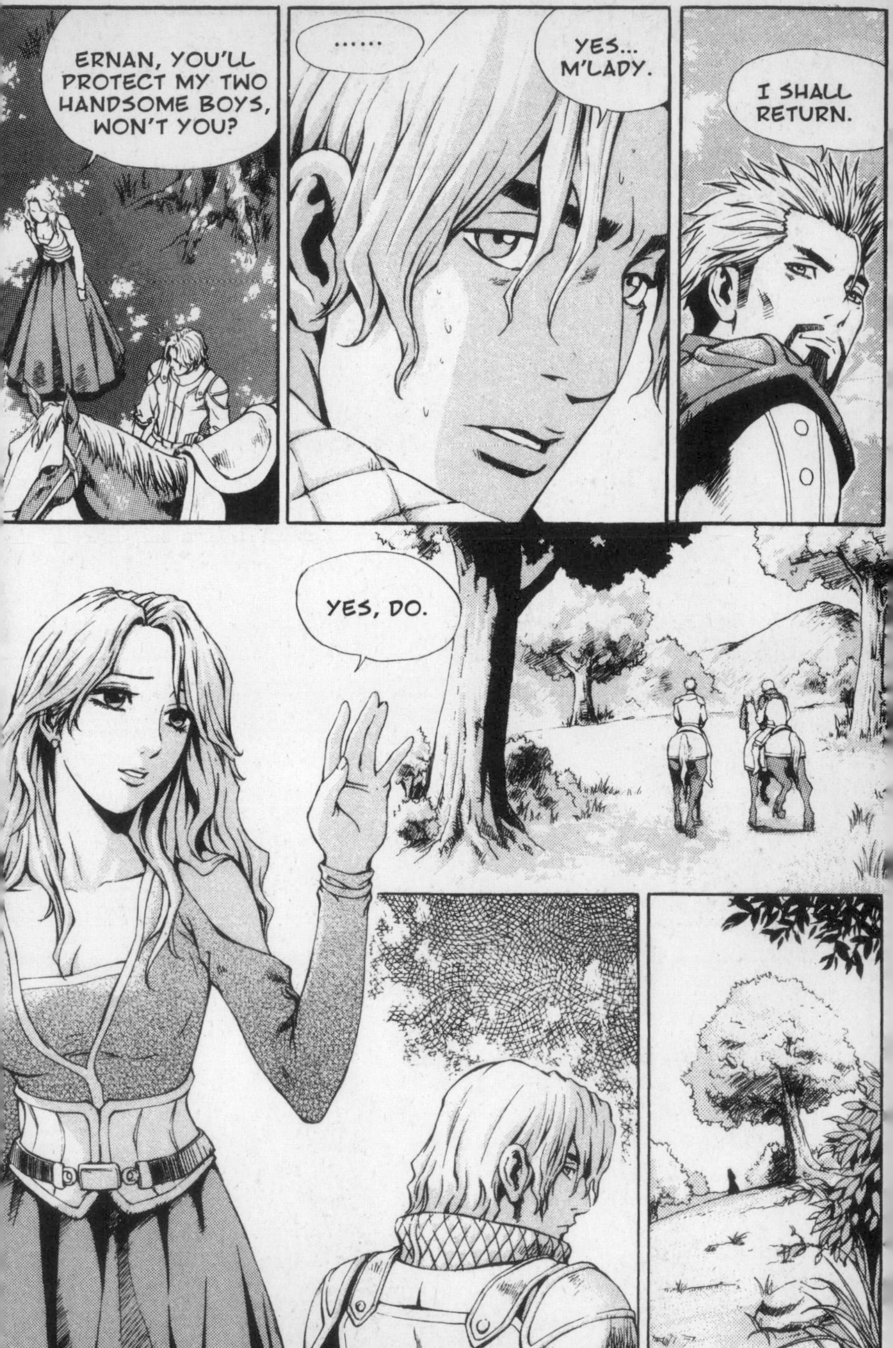
ERNAN, YOU'LL PROTECT MY TWO HANDSOME BOYS, WON'T YOU?
......
YES... M'LADY.
I SHALL RETURN.
YES, DO.

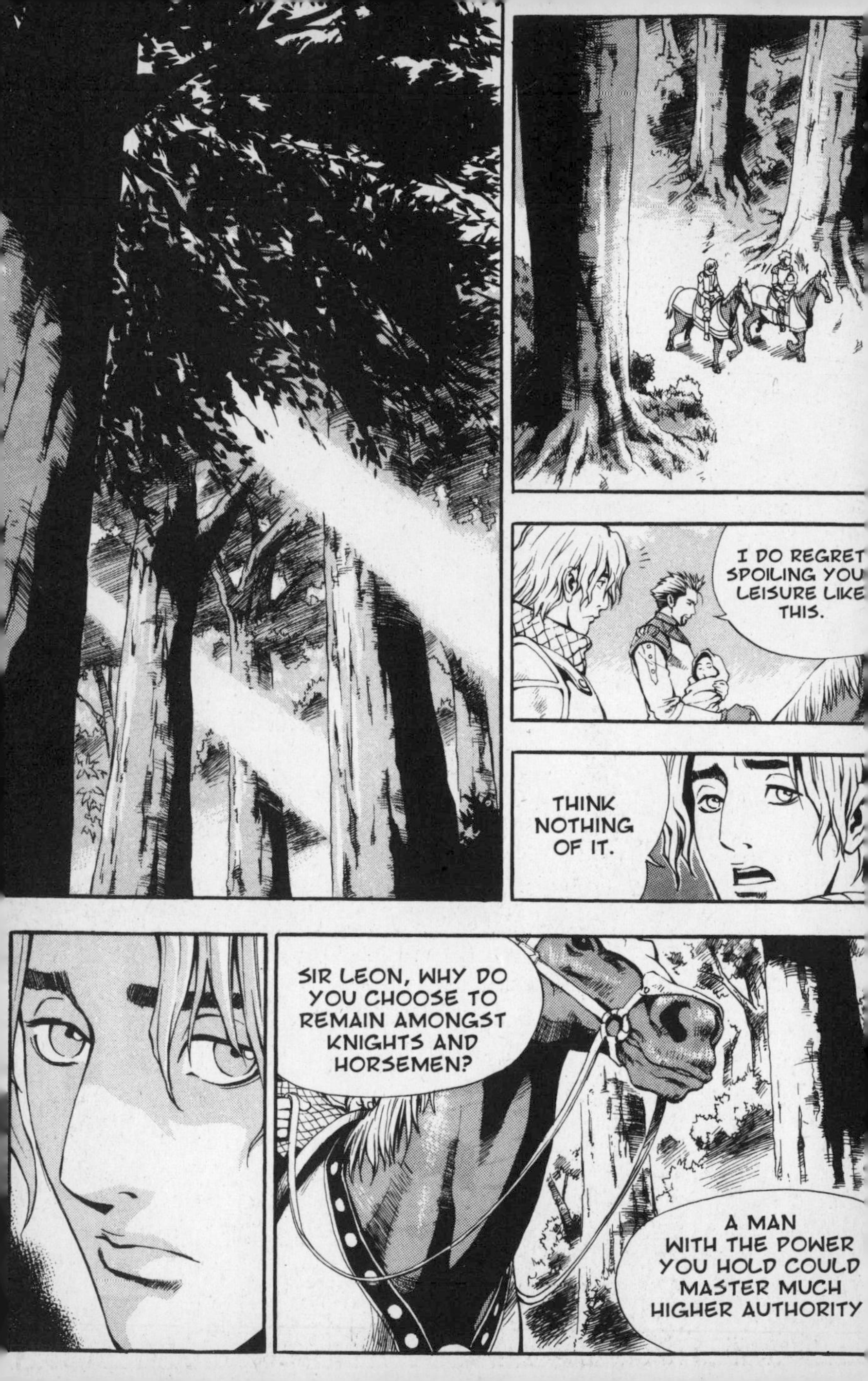
I DO REGRET SPOILING YOU LEISURE LIKE THIS.
THINK NOTHING OF IT.
SIR LEON, WHY DO YOU CHOOSE TO REMAIN AMONGST KNIGHTS AND HORSEMEN?
A MAN WITH THE POWER YOU HOLD COULD MASTER MUCH HIGHER AUTHORITY

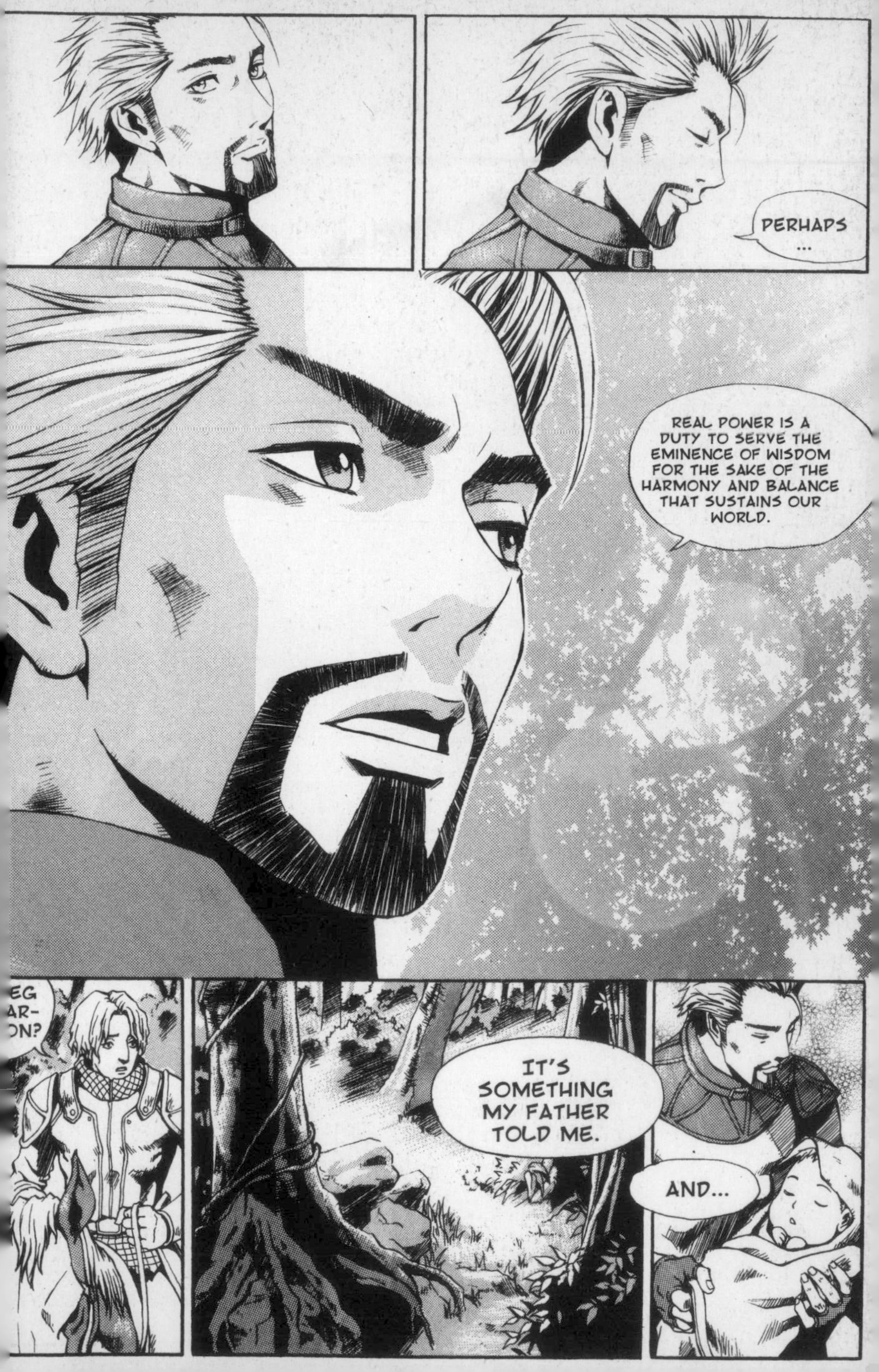
PERHAPS ...
REAL POWER IS A DUTY TO SERVE THE EMINENCE OF WISDOM FOR THE SAKE OF THE HARMONY AND BALANCE THAT SUSTAINS OUR WORLD.
EG AR- ON?
IT'S SOMETHING MY FATHER TOLD ME.
AND...

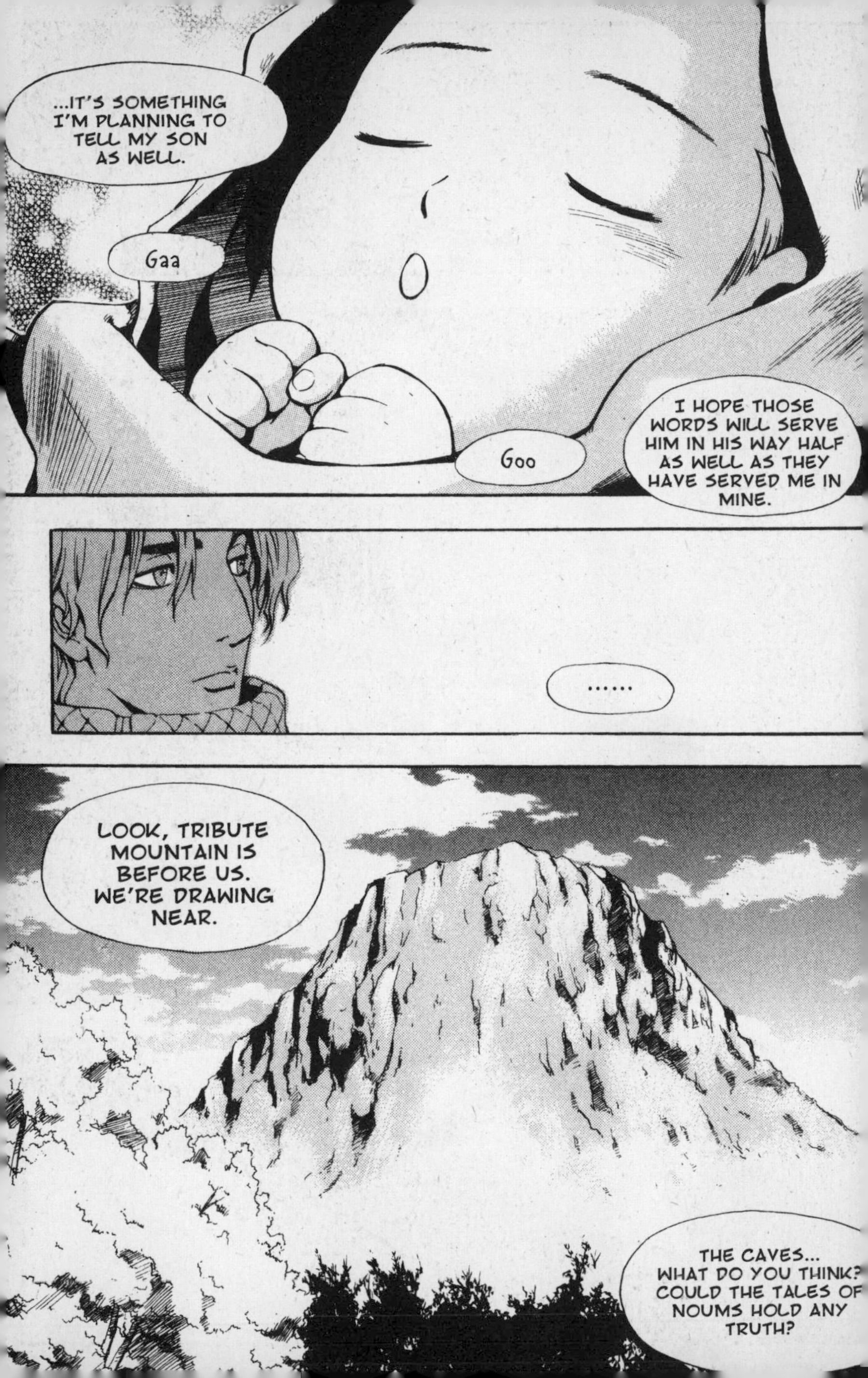
...IT'S SOMETHING I'M PLANNING TO TELL MY SON AS WELL.
Gaa
Goo
I HOPE THOSE WORDS WILL SERVE HIM IN HIS WAY HALF AS WELL AS THEY HAVE SERVED ME IN MINE.
......
LOOK, TRIBUTE MOUNTAIN IS BEFORE US. WE'RE DRAWING NEAR.
THE CAVES... WHAT DO YOU THINK? COULD THE TALES OF NOUMS HOLD ANY TRUTH?

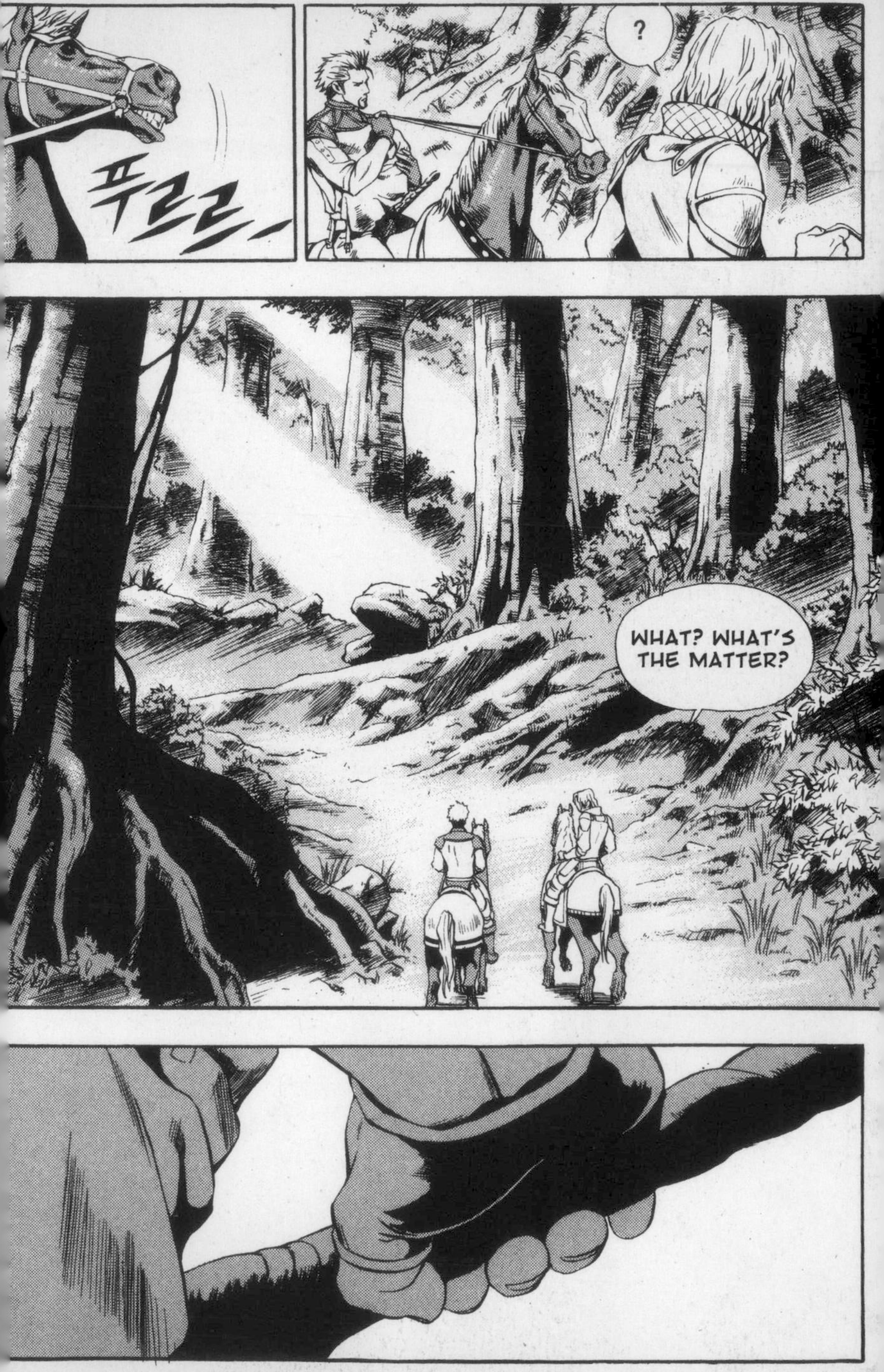
푸르르
?
WHAT? WHAT'S THE MATTER?

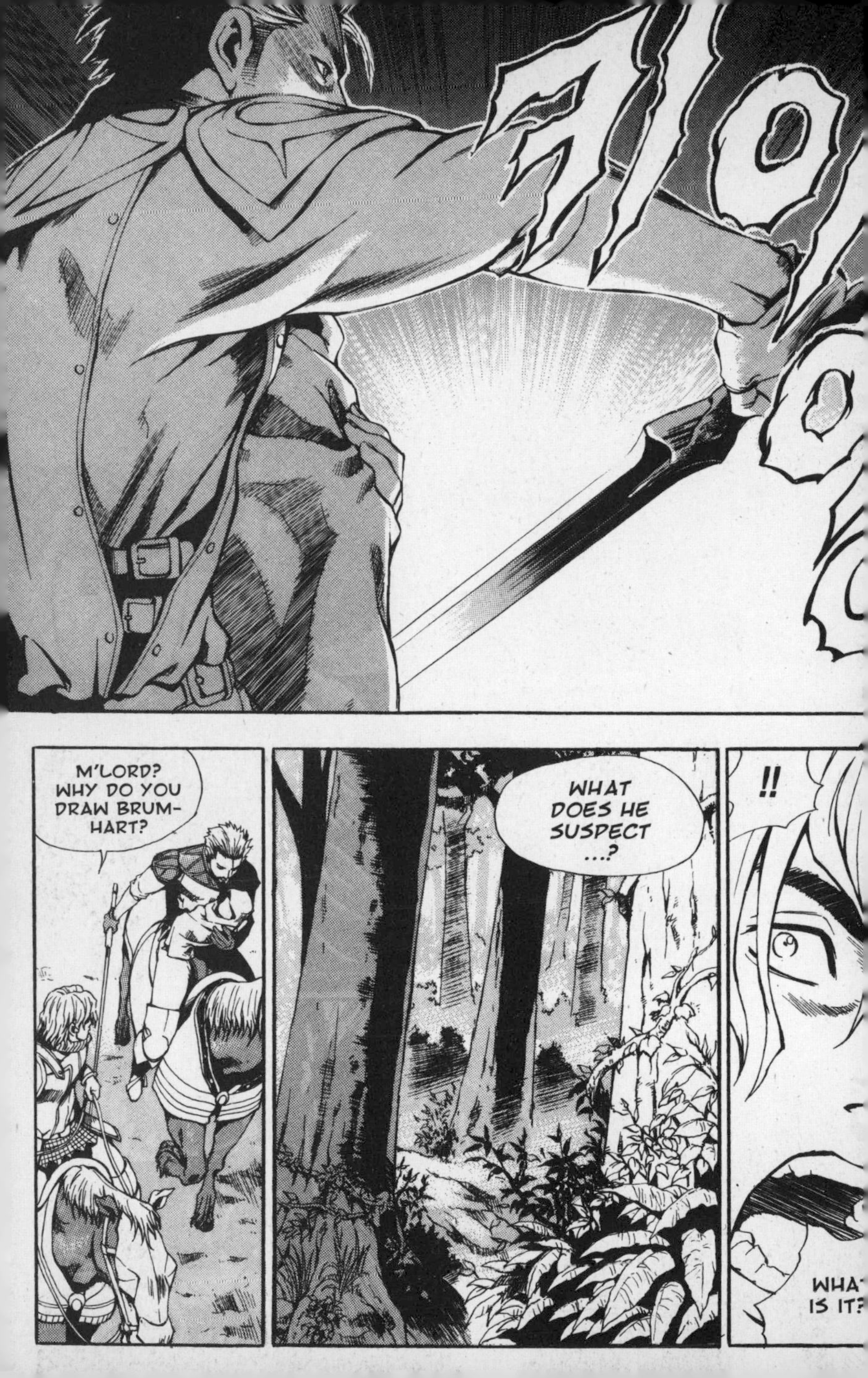
M'LORD? WHY DO YOU DRAW BRUM-HART?
WHAT DOES HE SUSPECT ...?
!!
WHAT IS IT?

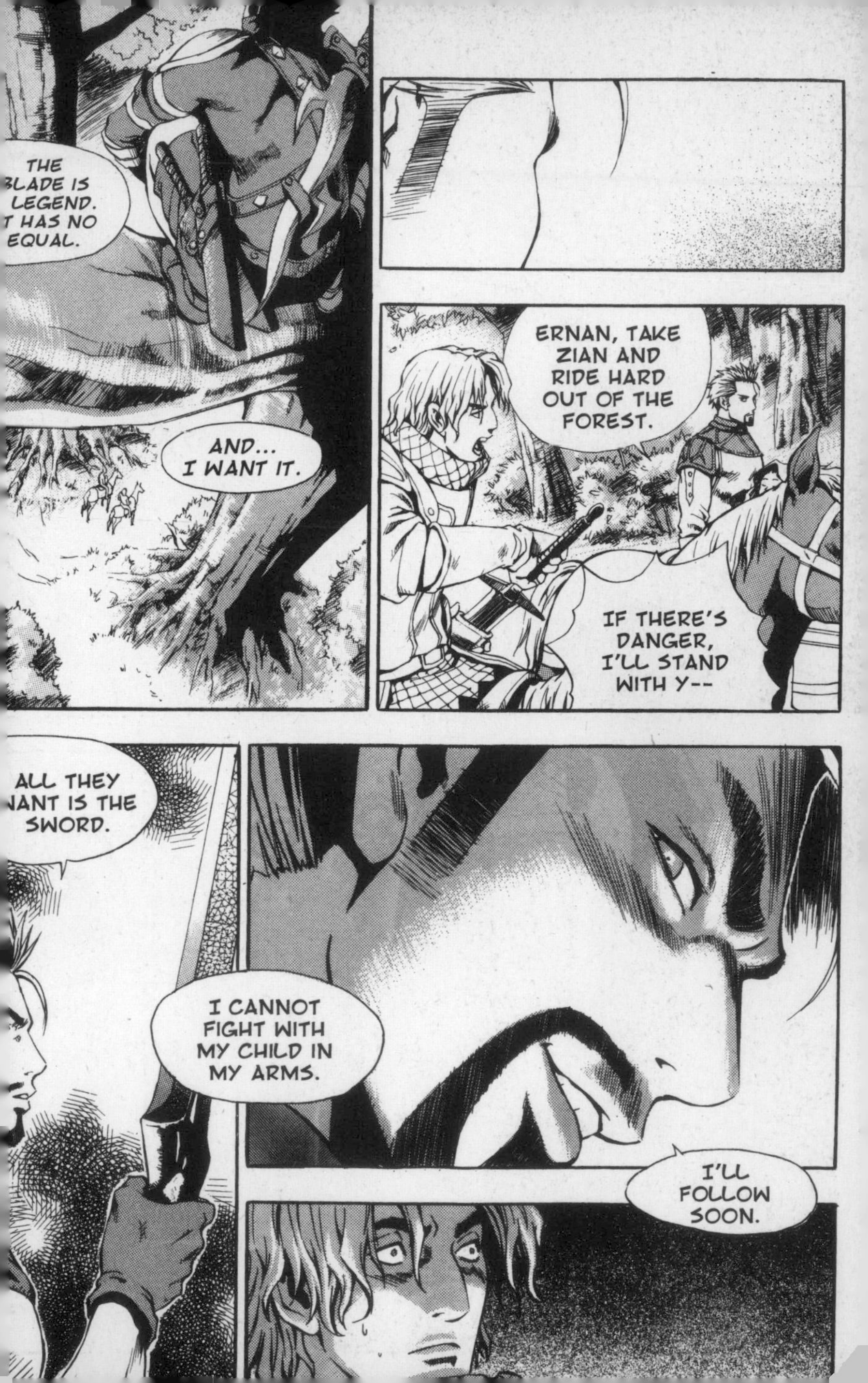
THE
BLADE IS
LEGEND.
T HAS NO
EQUAL.
AND...
I WANT IT.
ERNAN, TAKE ZIAN AND RIDE HARD OUT OF THE FOREST.
IF THERE'S DANGER, I'LL STAND WITH Y--
ALL THEY
WANT IS THE
SWORD.
I CANNOT FIGHT WITH MY CHILD IN MY ARMS.
I'LL FOLLOW SOON.

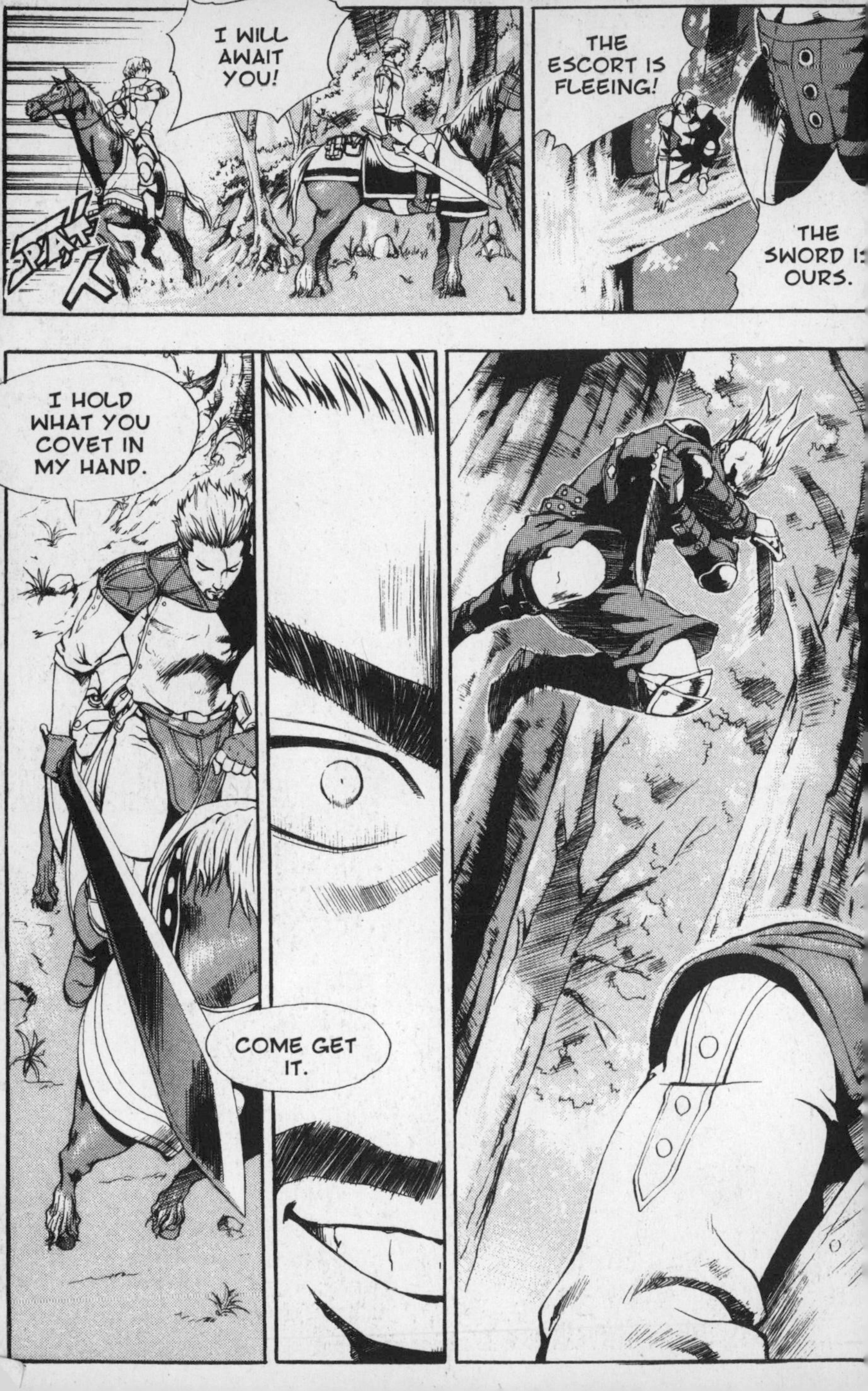
I WILL AWAIT YOU!
SPAK
THE ESCORT IS FLEEING!
THE SWORD IS OURS.
I HOLD WHAT YOU COVET IN MY HAND.
COME GET IT.

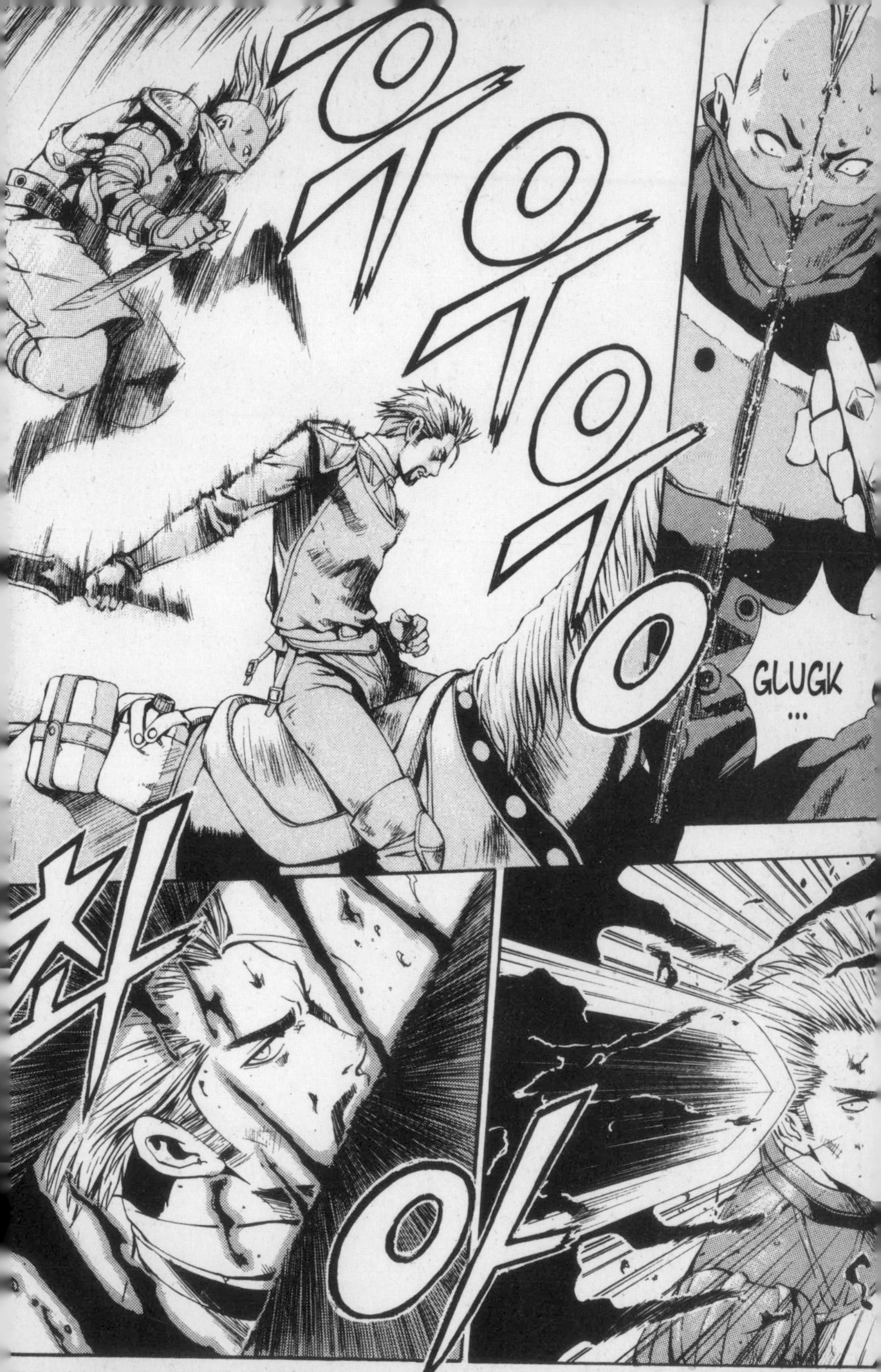
GLUGK
...

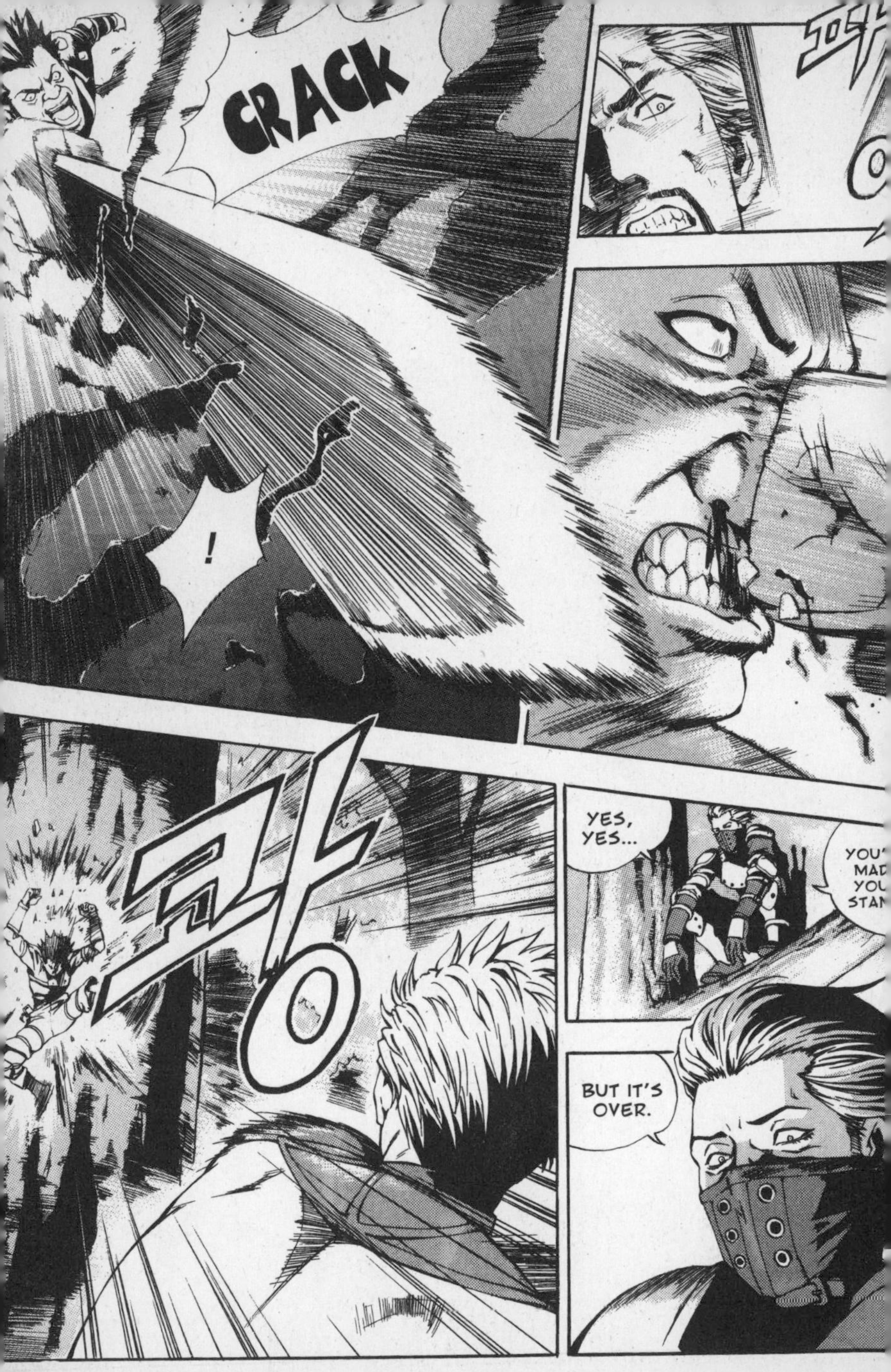
CRACK
!
YES, YES...
YOU'
MAD
YOU
STAN
BUT IT'S OVER.

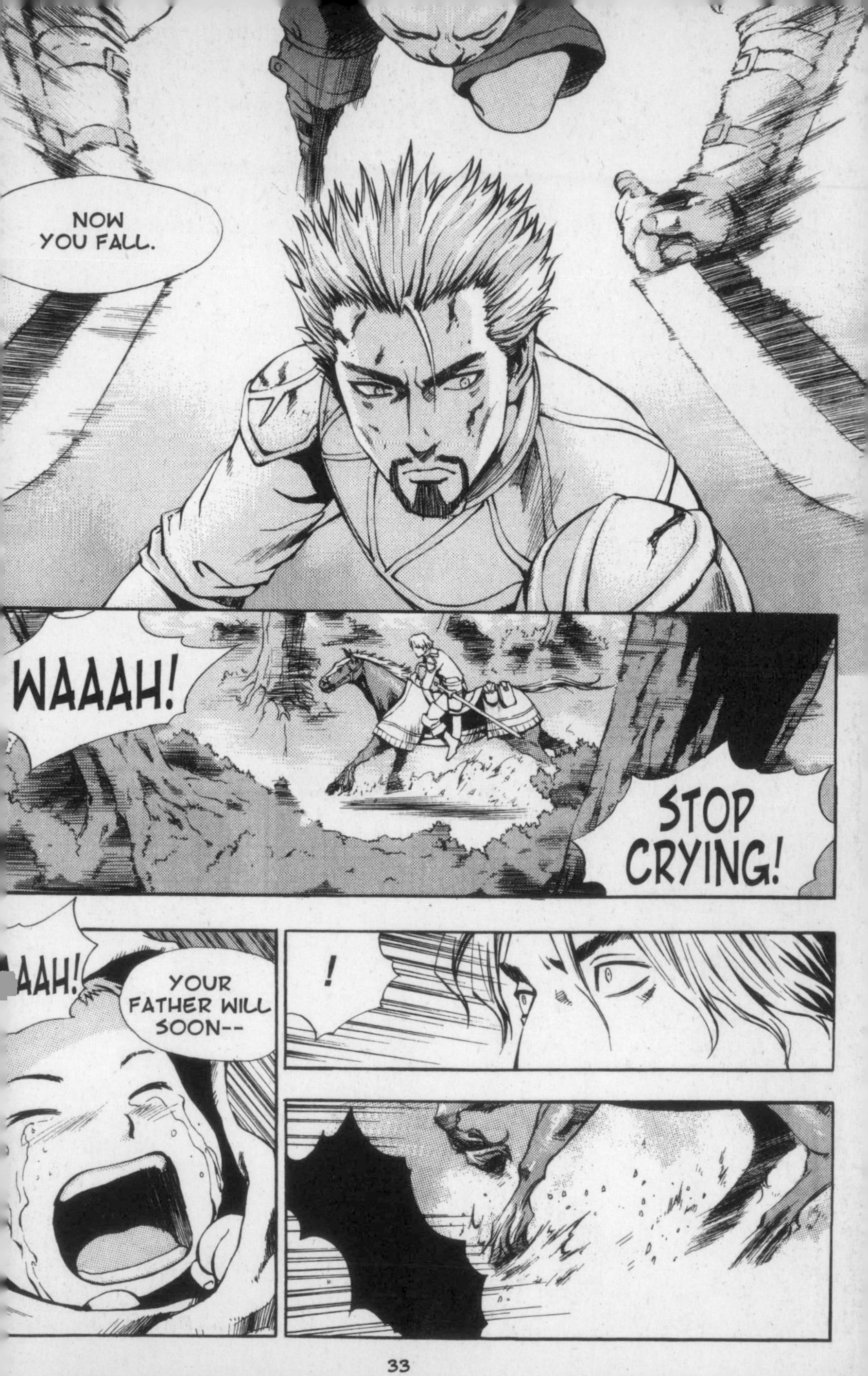
NOW YOU FALL.
WAAAH!
STOP CRYING!
AAH!
YOUR FATHER WILL SOON--
!

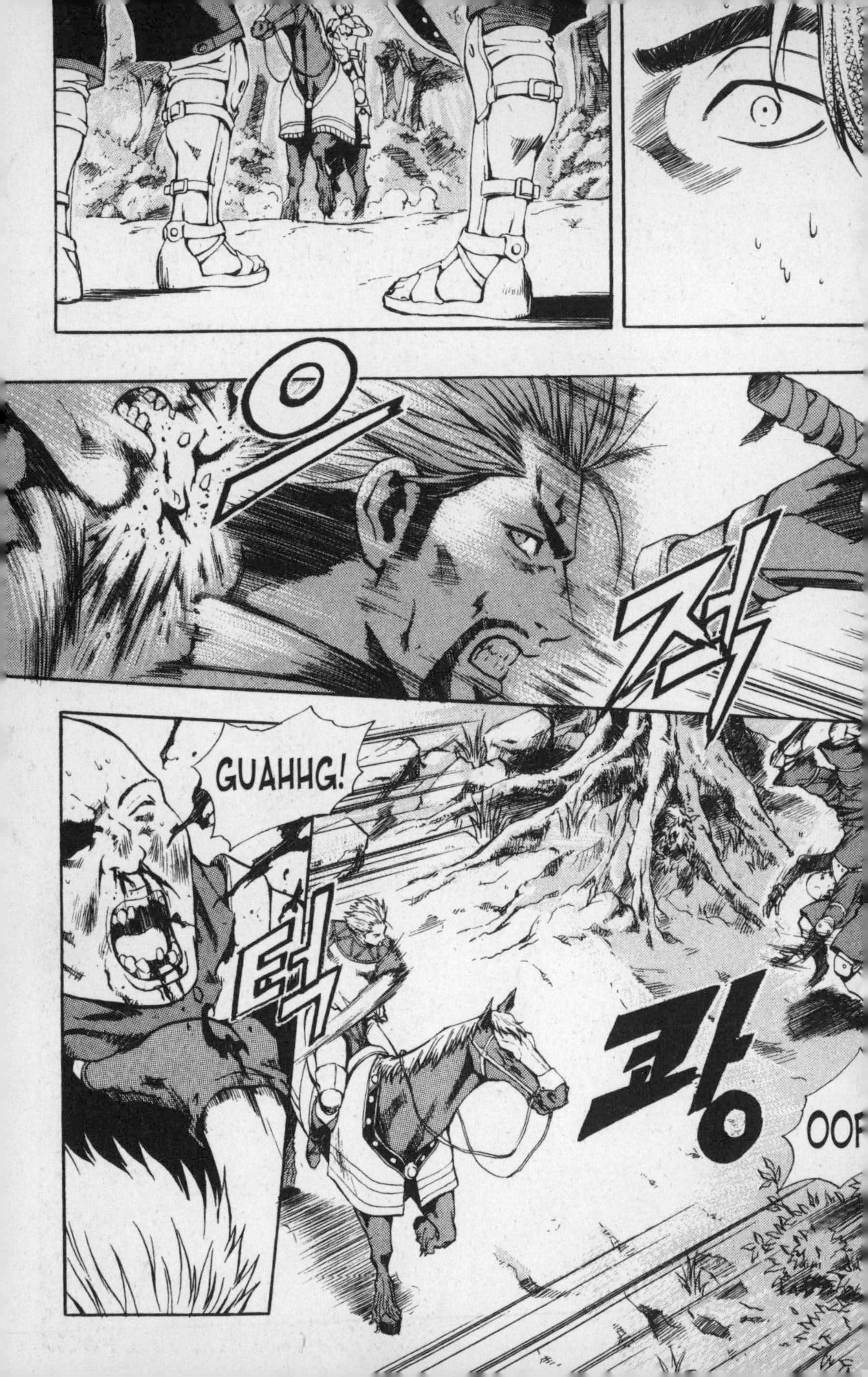
GUAHHG!
OOF

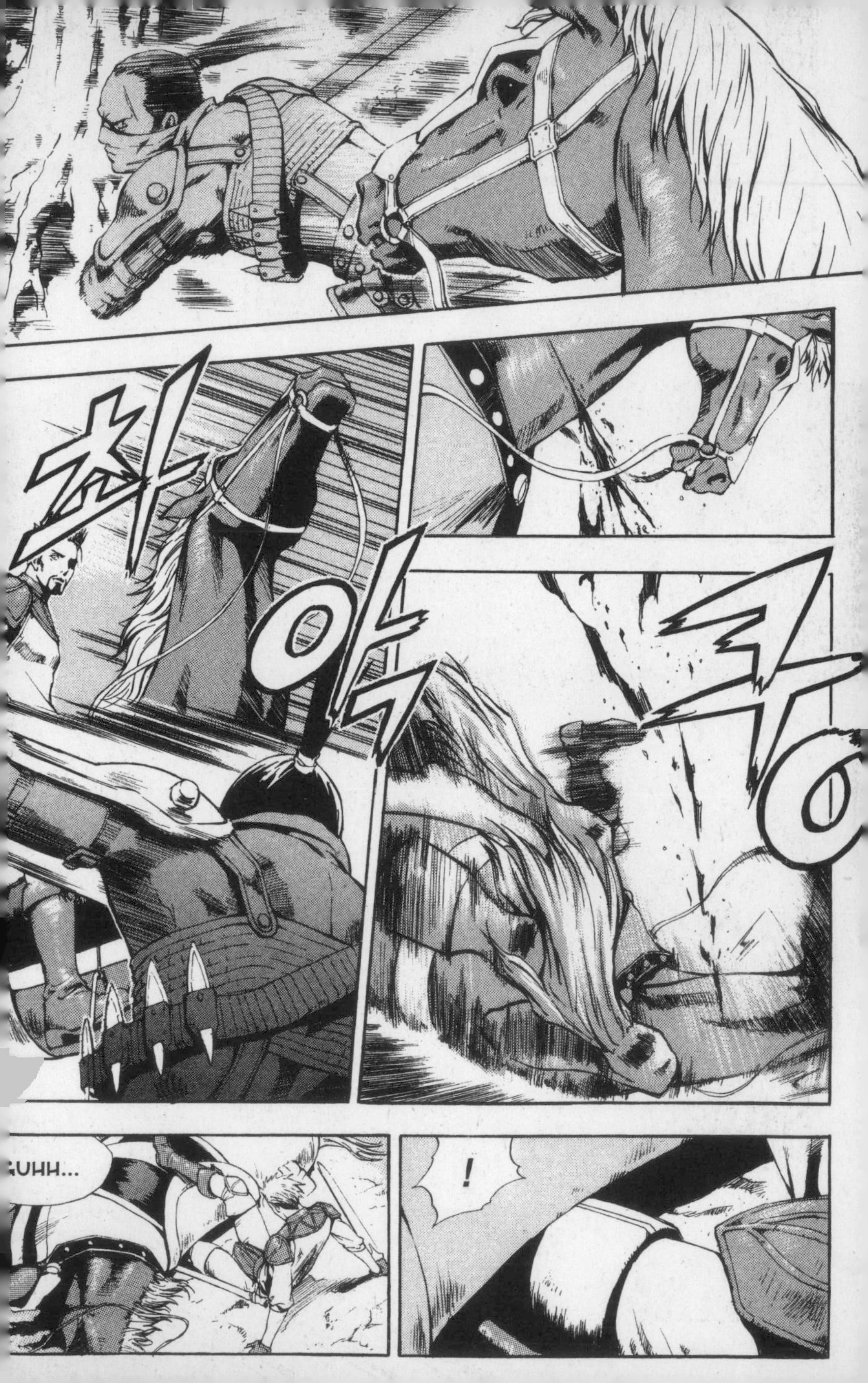
처
악
쿵
GUHH...
!

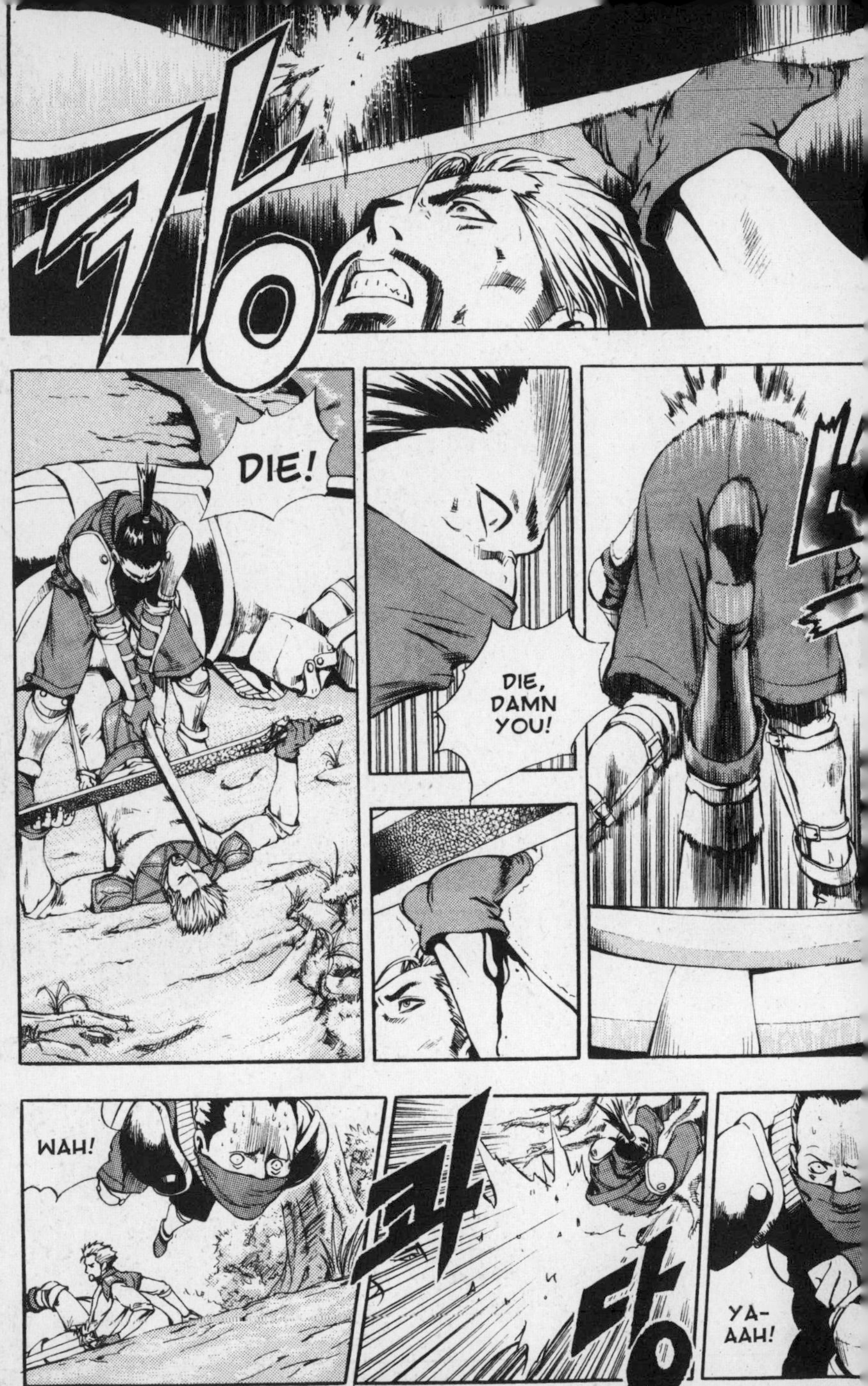
DIE!
DIE, DAMN YOU!
WAH!
YA-AAH!

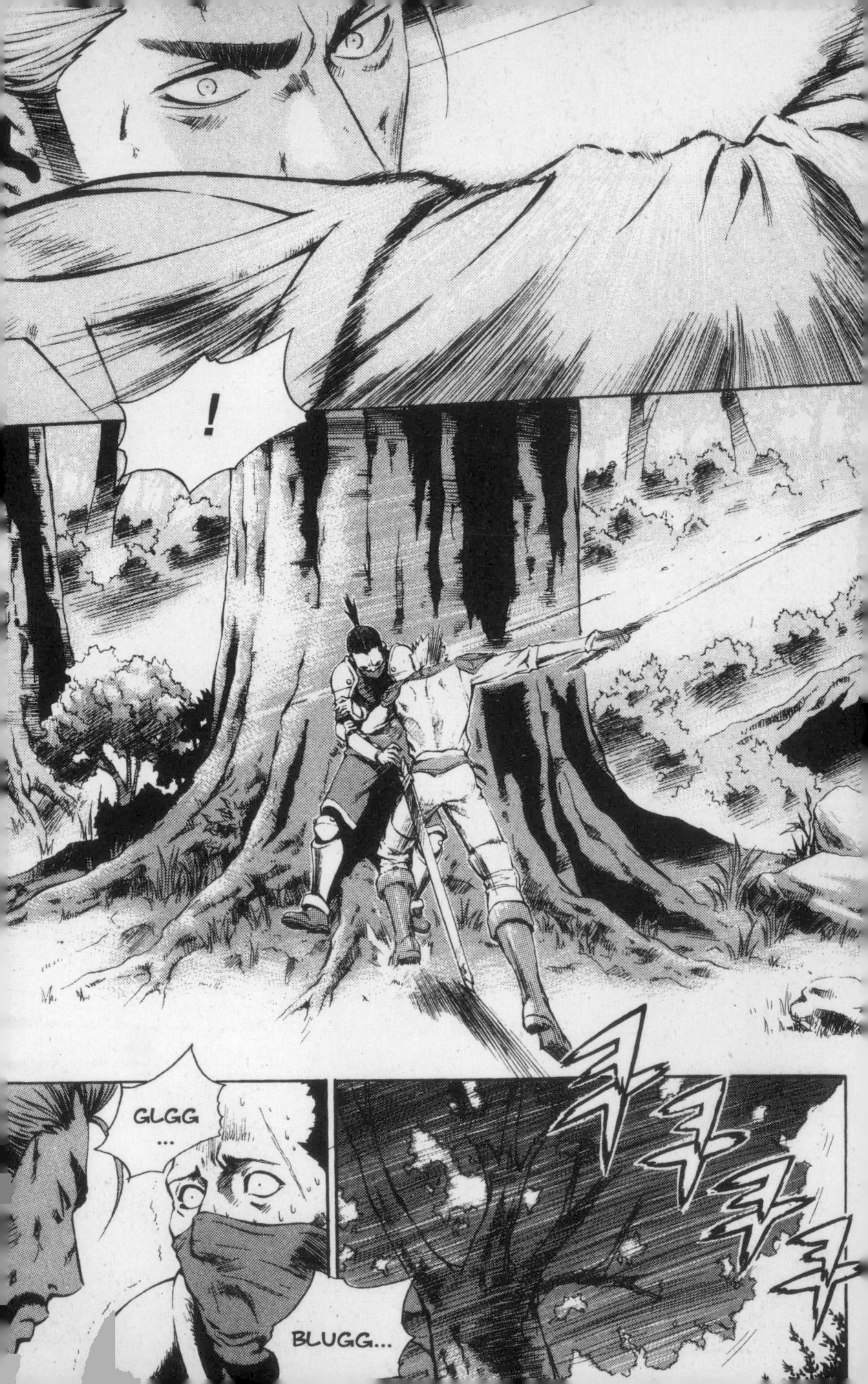
!
GLGG ...
BLUGG...

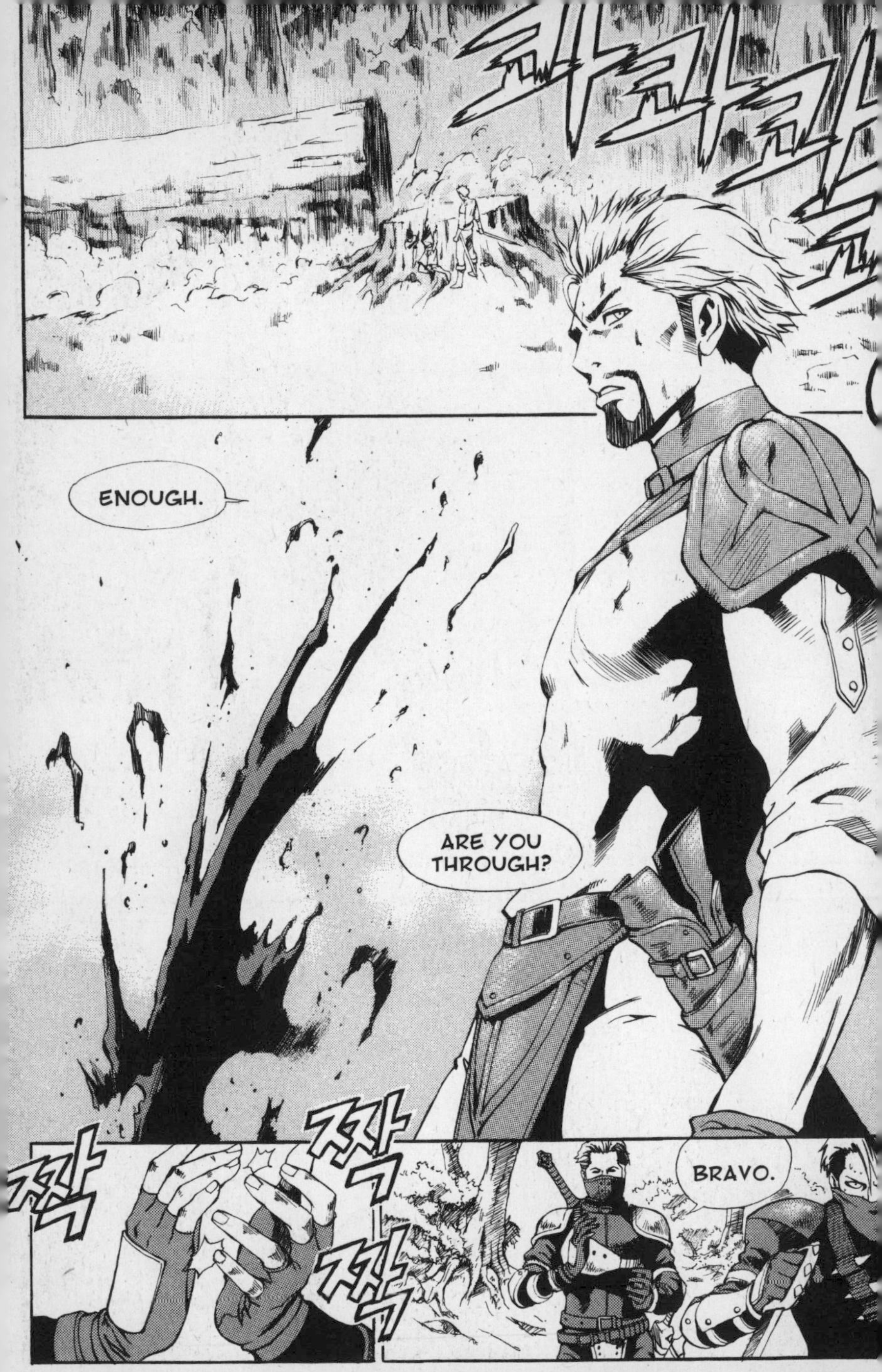
ENOUGH.
ARE YOU THROUGH?
BRAVO.

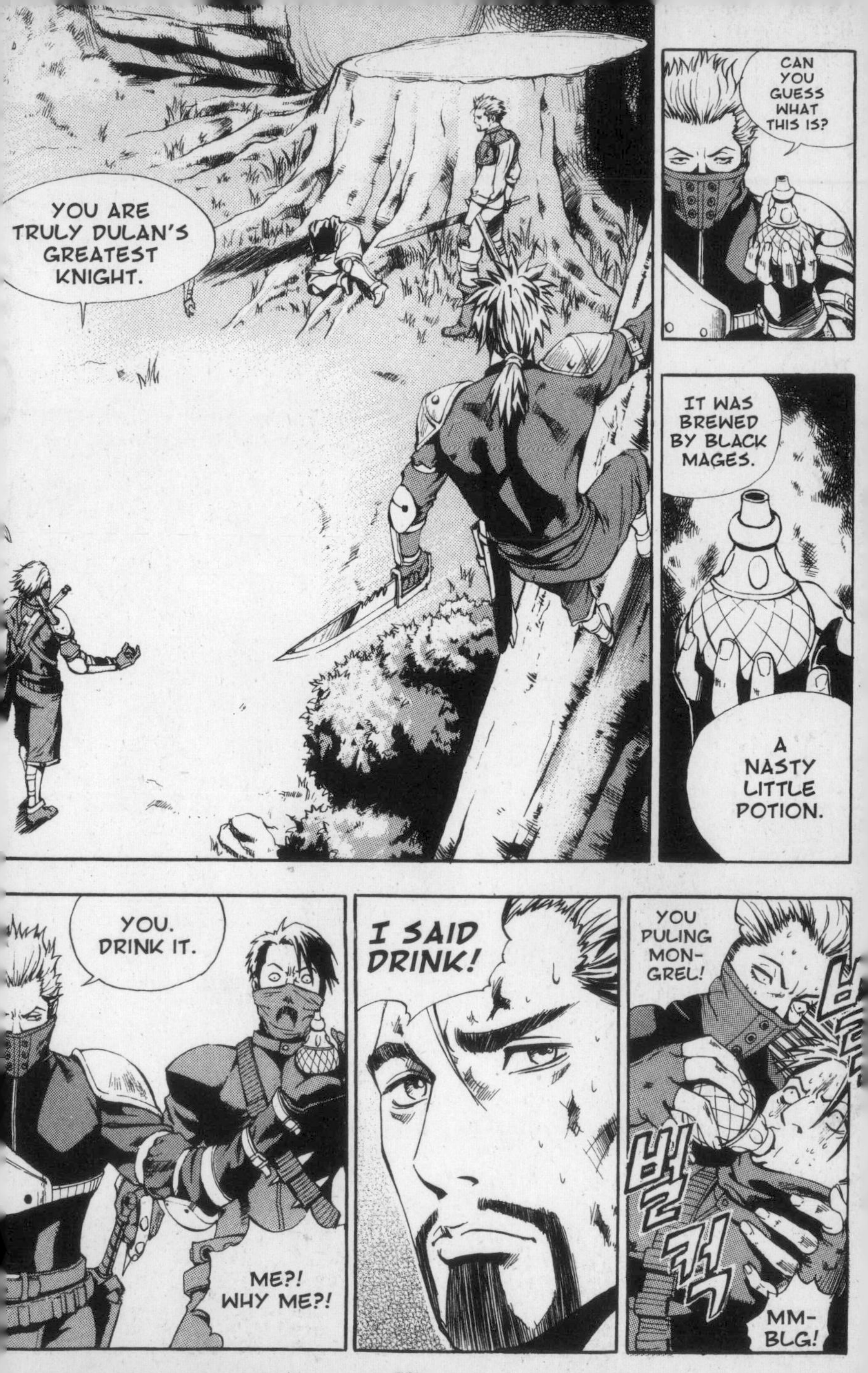
YOU ARE TRULY DULAN'S GREATEST KNIGHT.
CAN YOU GUESS WHAT THIS IS?
IT WAS BREWED BY BLACK MAGES.
A NASTY LITTLE POTION.
YOU. DRINK IT.
ME?! WHY ME?!
I SAID DRINK!
YOU PULING MONGREL!
MM-BLG!

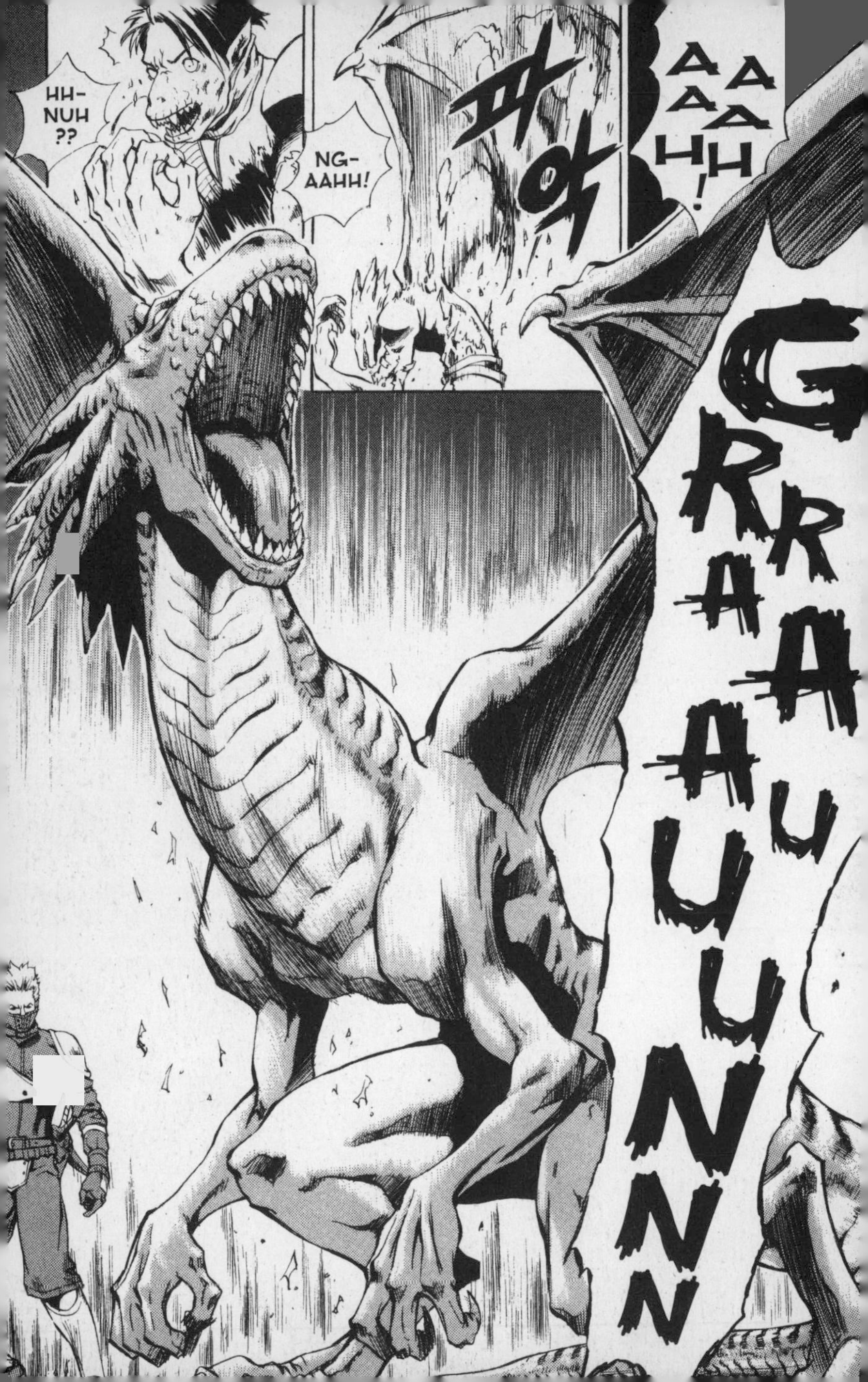
HH-NUH??
NG-AAHH!
파악
AAAAHH!
GRRAAAAUUUNNNN

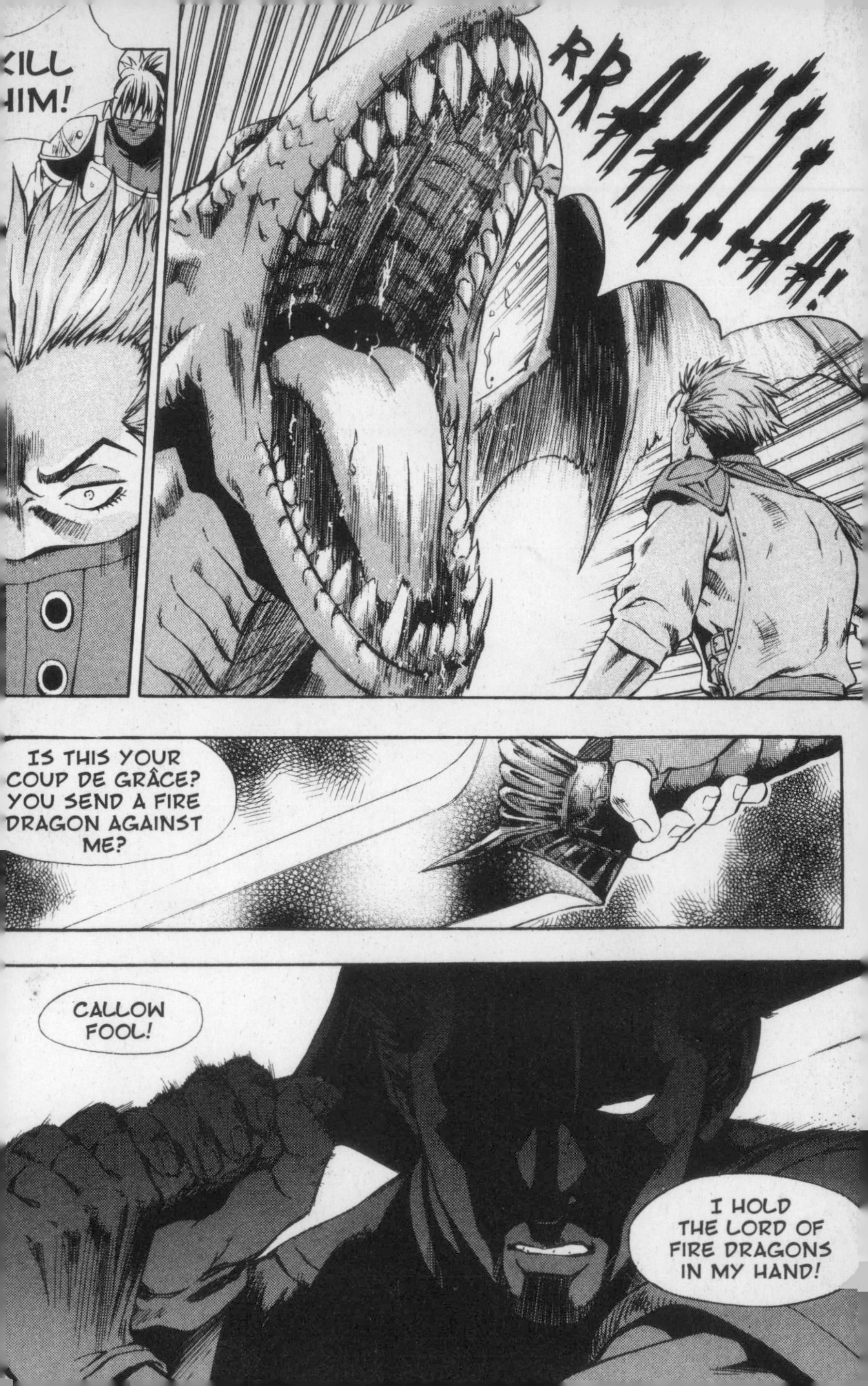
KILL HIM!
RRAAOOAAAA!
IS THIS YOUR COUP DE GRÂCE? YOU SEND A FIRE DRAGON AGAINST ME?
CALLOW FOOL!
I HOLD THE LORD OF FIRE DRAGONS IN MY HAND!

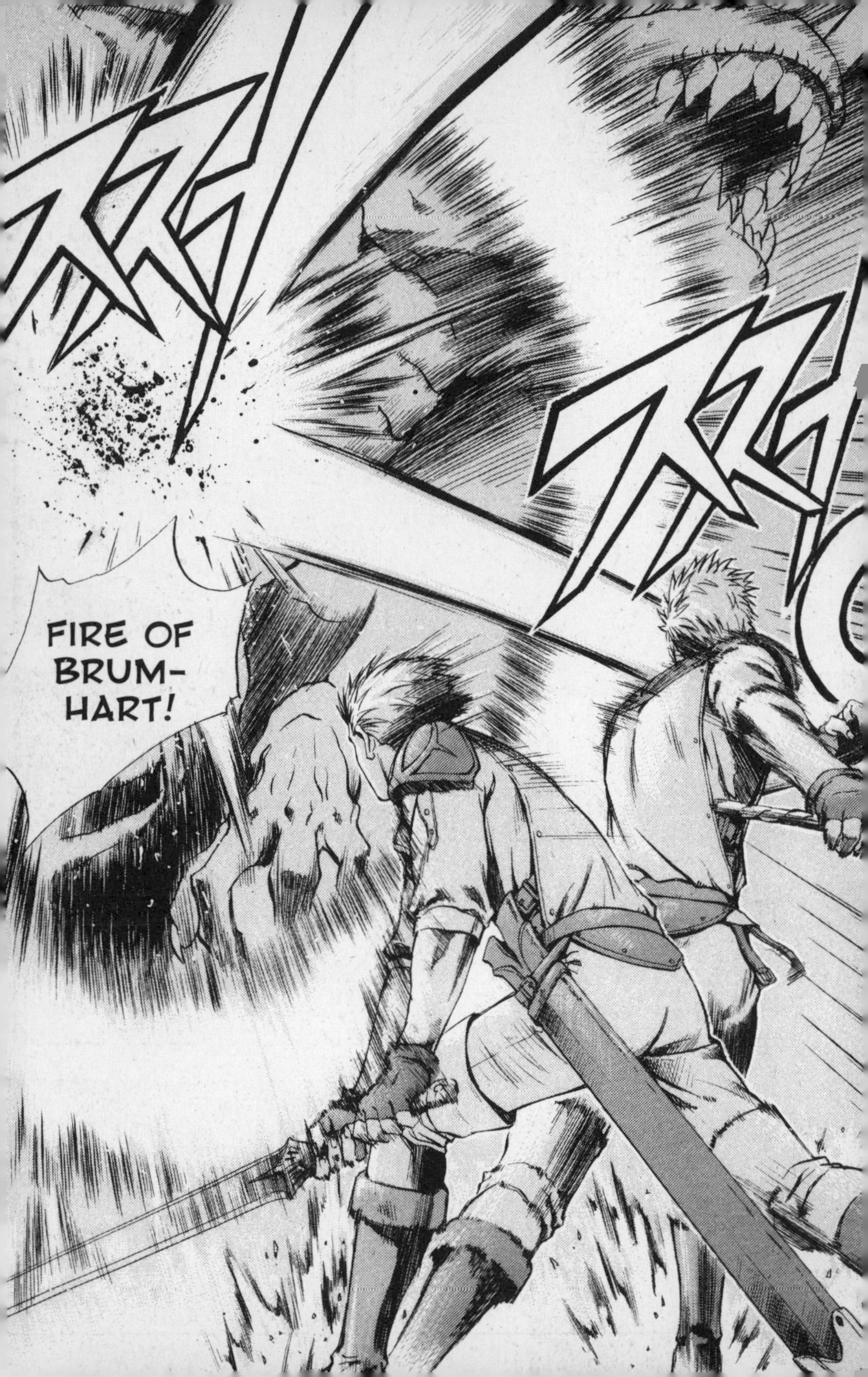
FIRE OF BRUM-HART!

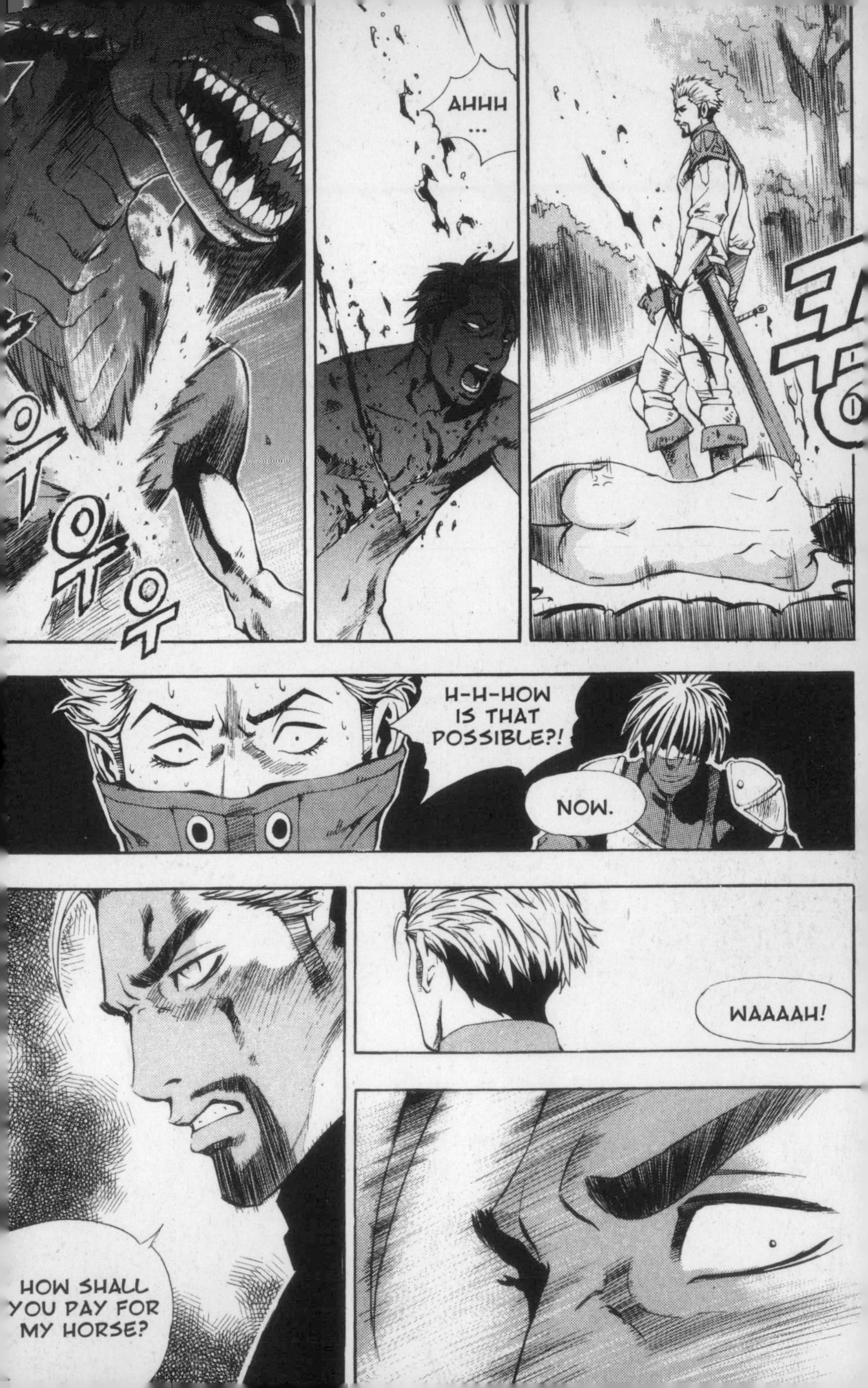
AHHH ...
H-H-HOW IS THAT POSSIBLE?!
NOW.
HOW SHALL YOU PAY FOR MY HORSE?
WAAAAH!

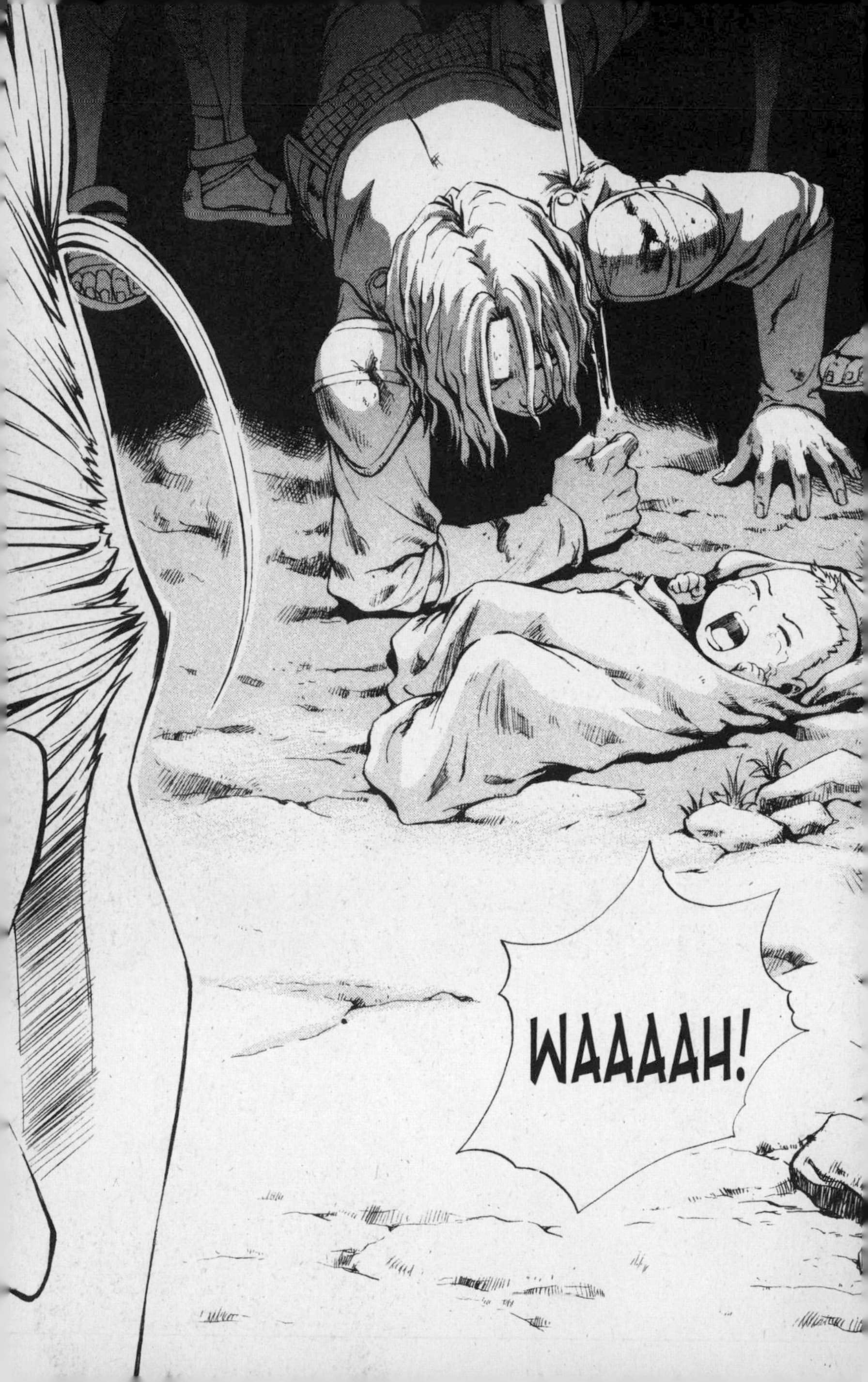
WAAAAH!

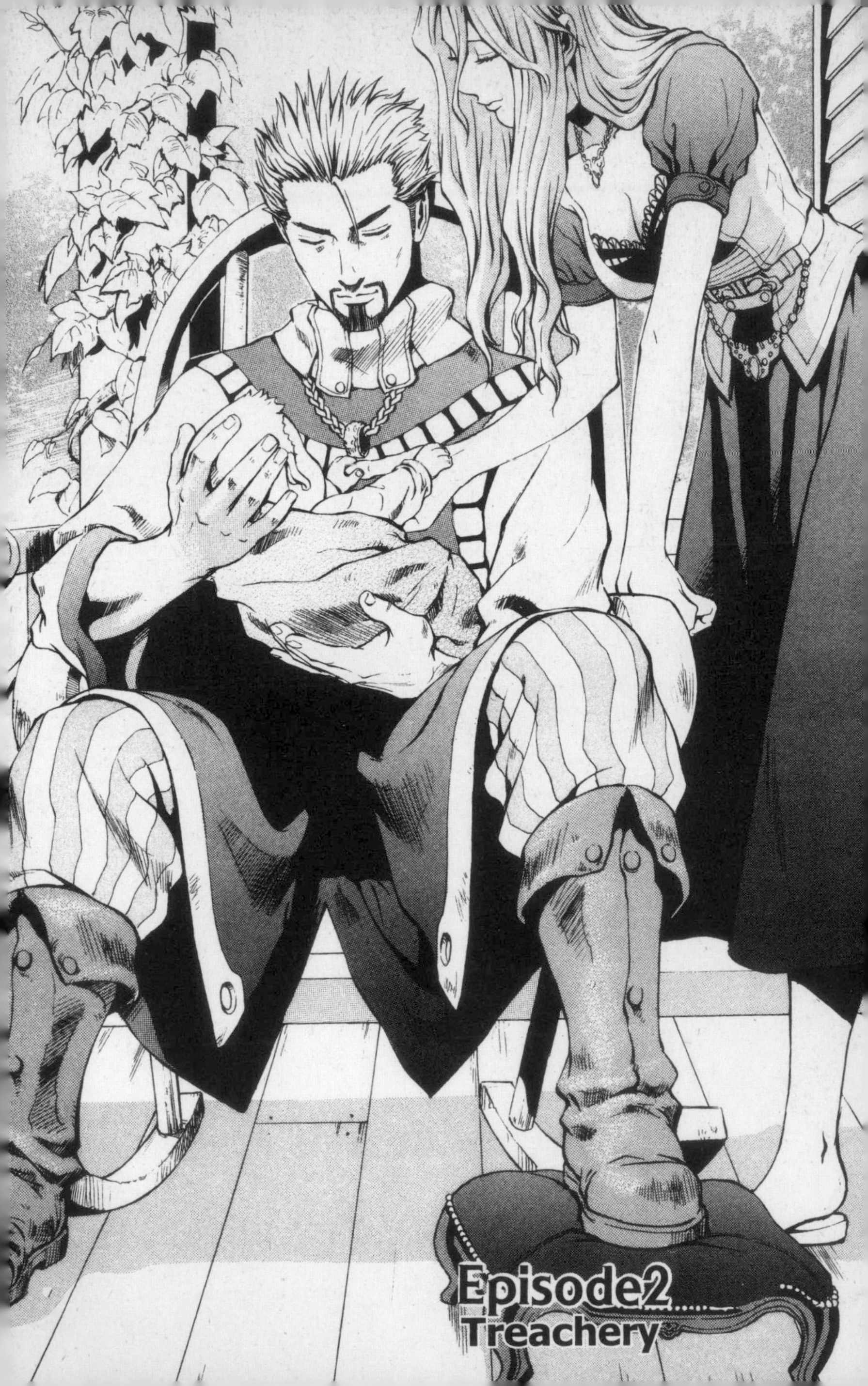
Episode 2
Treachery

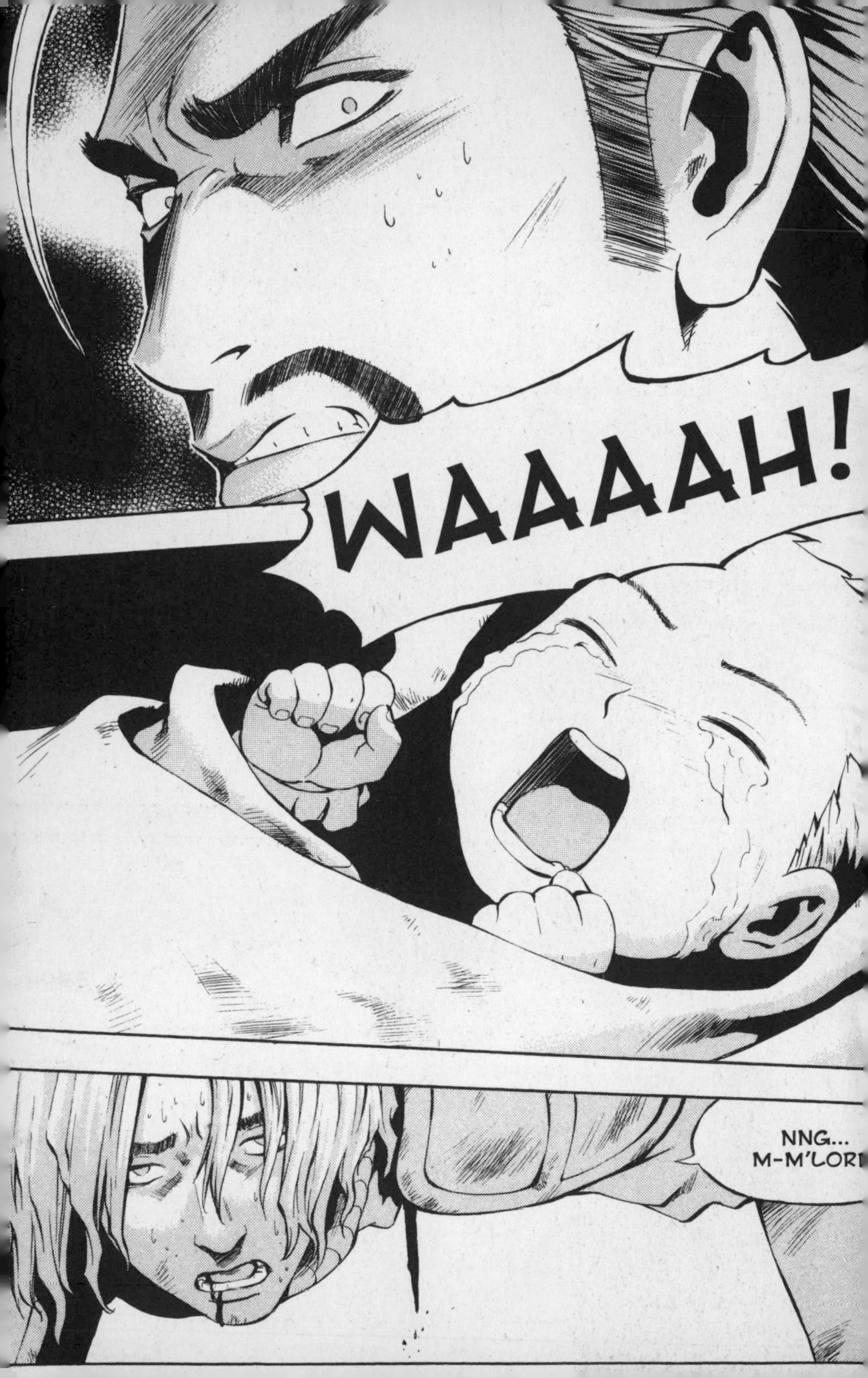
WAAAAH!
NNG...
M-M'LORD

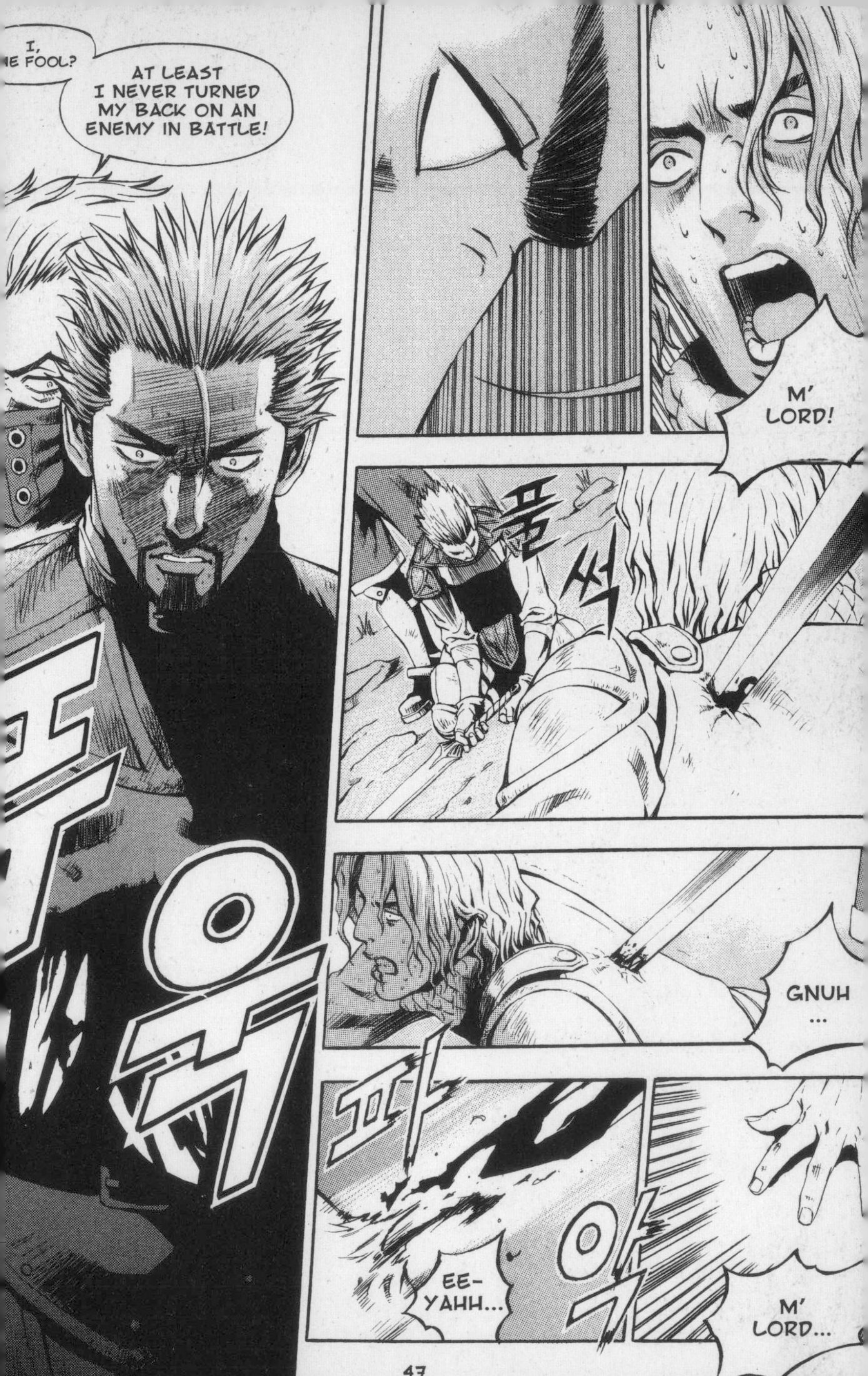
I,
HE FOOL?
AT LEAST I NEVER TURNED MY BACK ON AN ENEMY IN BATTLE!
M' LORD!
GNUH ...
EE-YAHH...
M' LORD...

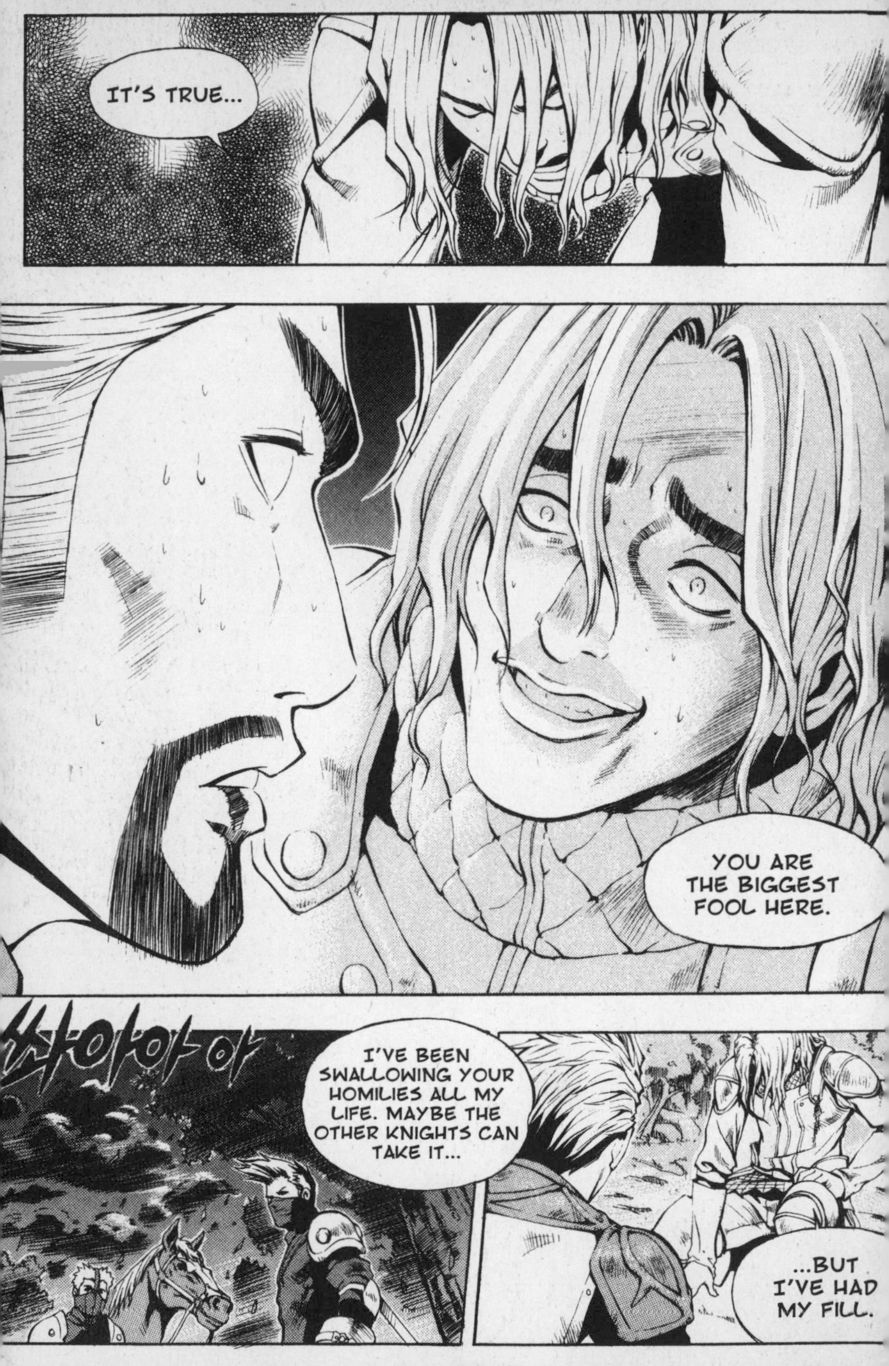
IT'S TRUE...
YOU ARE THE BIGGEST FOOL HERE.
I'VE BEEN SWALLOWING YOUR HOMILIES ALL MY LIFE. MAYBE THE OTHER KNIGHTS CAN TAKE IT...
...BUT I'VE HAD MY FILL.

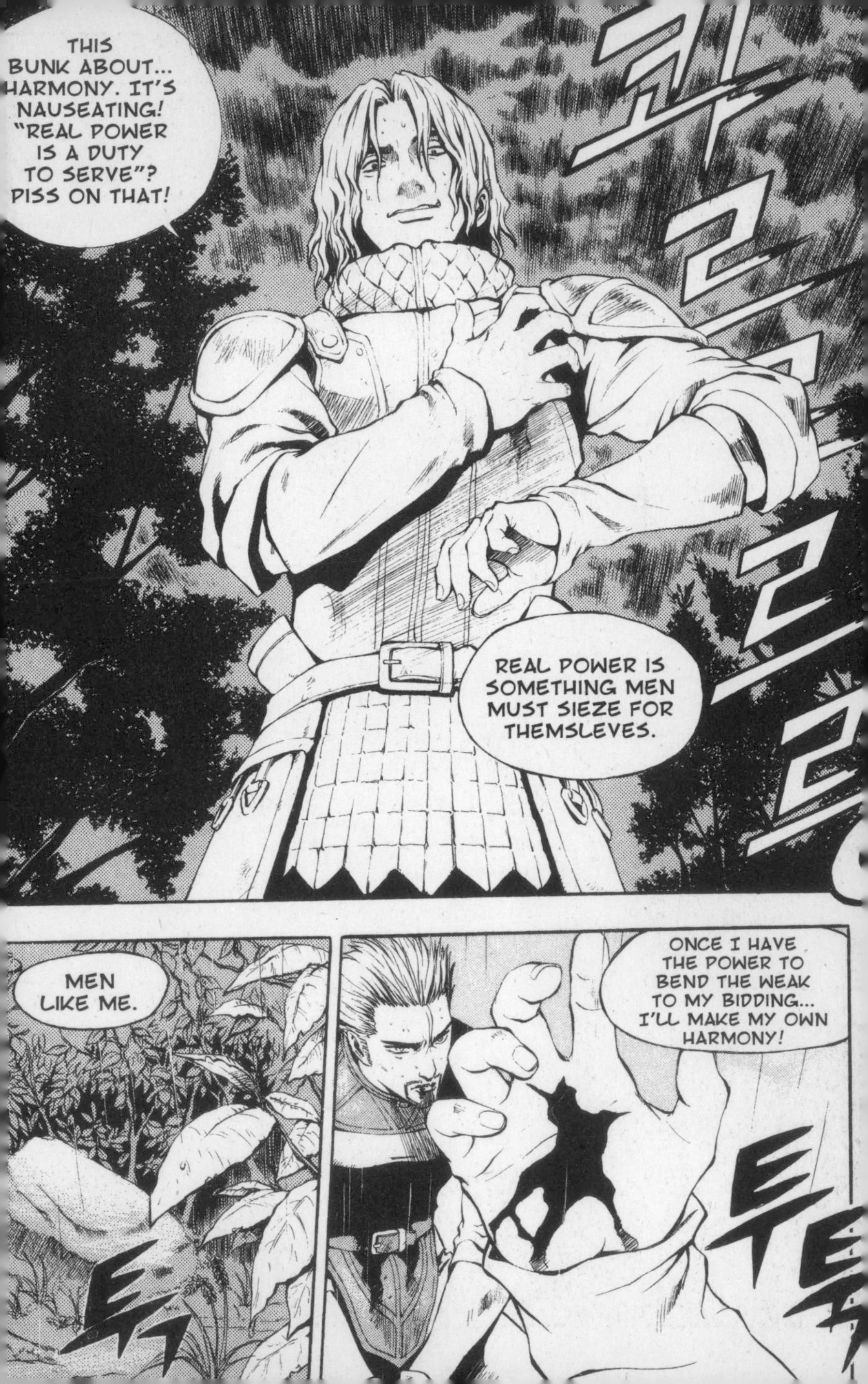
THIS BUNK ABOUT... HARMONY. IT'S NAUSEATING! "REAL POWER IS A DUTY TO SERVE"? PISS ON THAT!
REAL POWER IS SOMETHING MEN MUST SIEZE FOR THEMSLEVES.
MEN LIKE ME.
ONCE I HAVE THE POWER TO BEND THE WEAK TO MY BIDDING... I'LL MAKE MY OWN HARMONY!

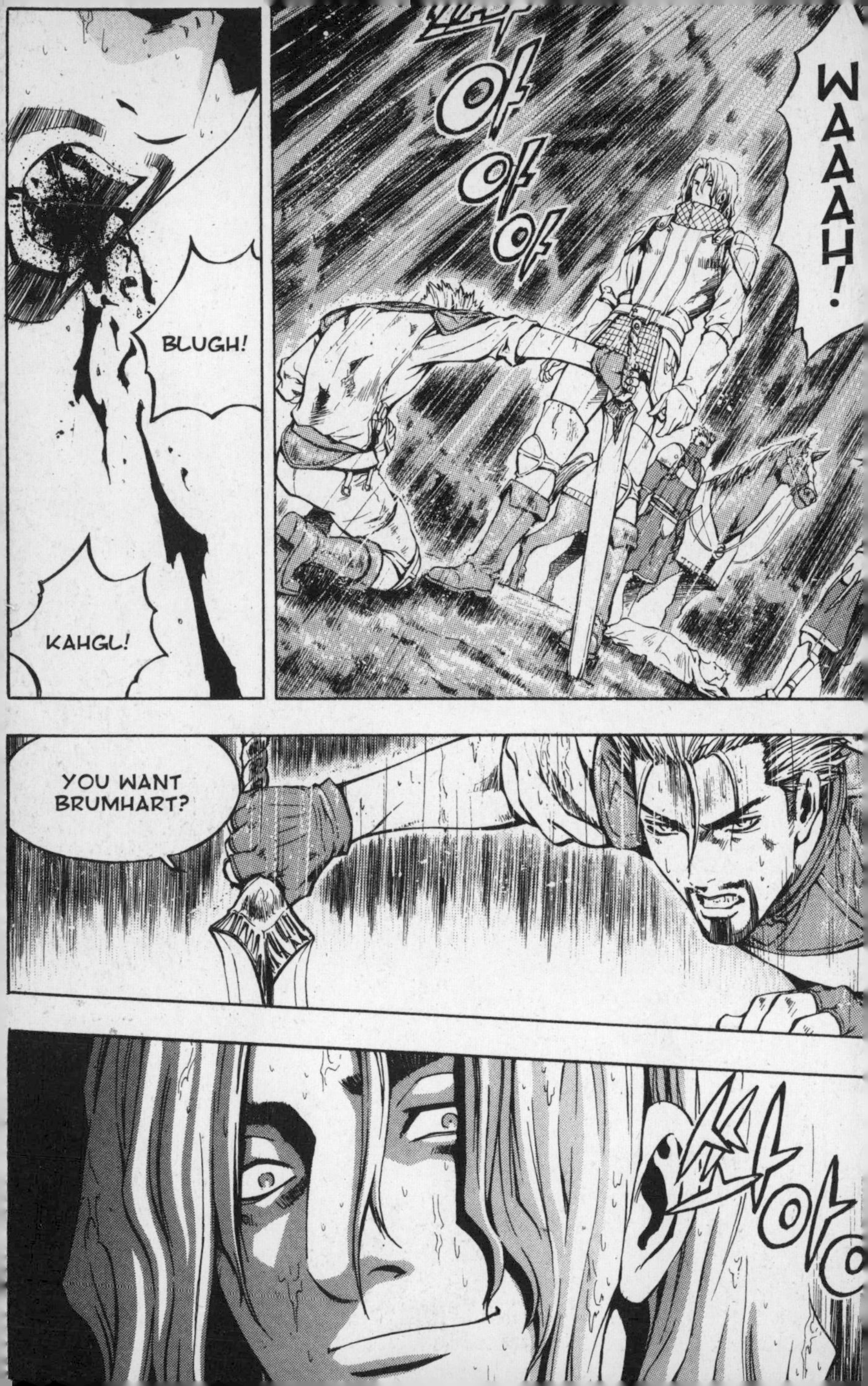
BLUGH!
KAHGL!
WAAAAH!
YOU WANT BRUMHART?

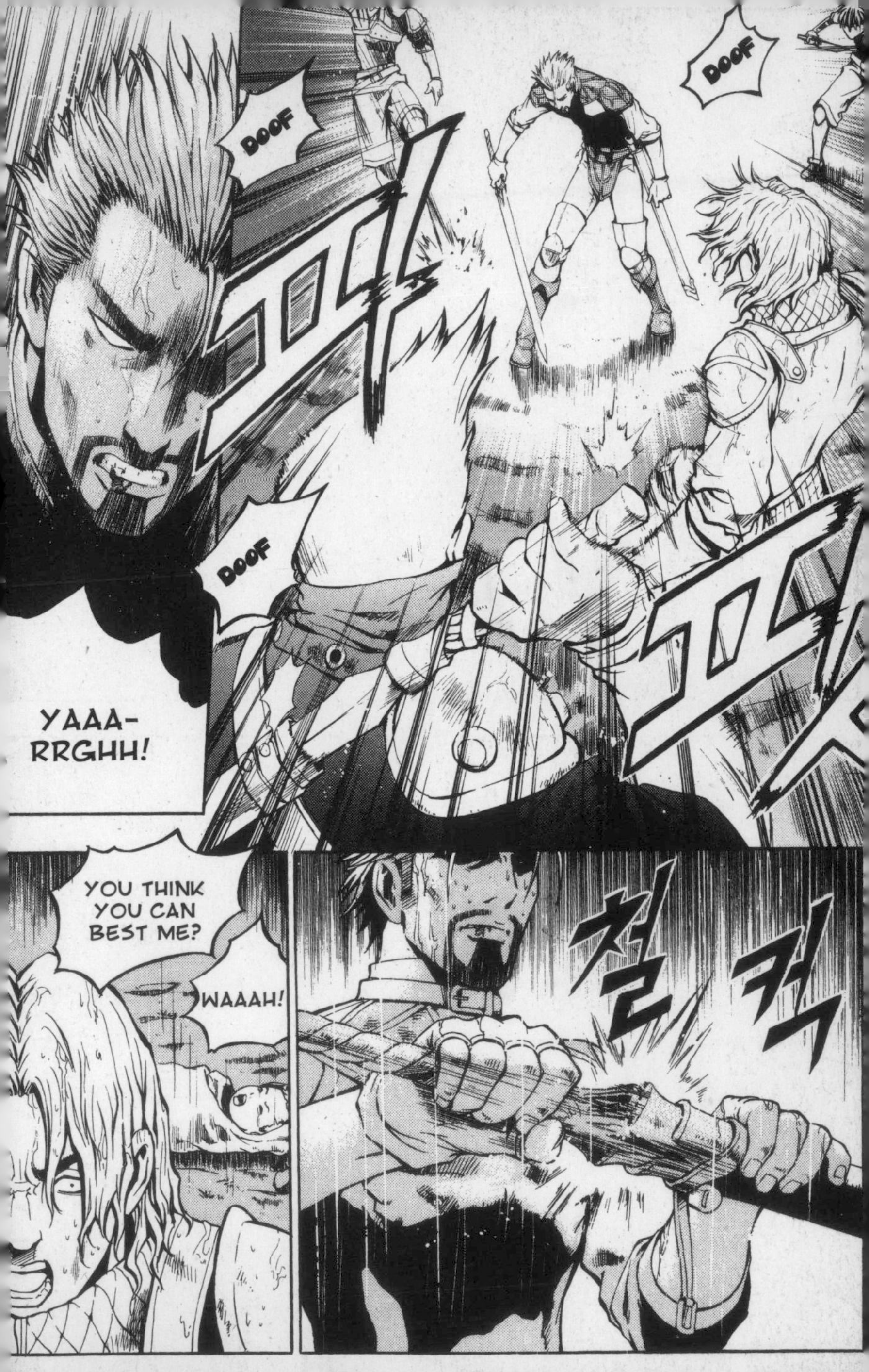
DOOF
DOOF
DOOF
YAAA-RRGHH!
YOU THINK YOU CAN BEST ME?
WAAAH!

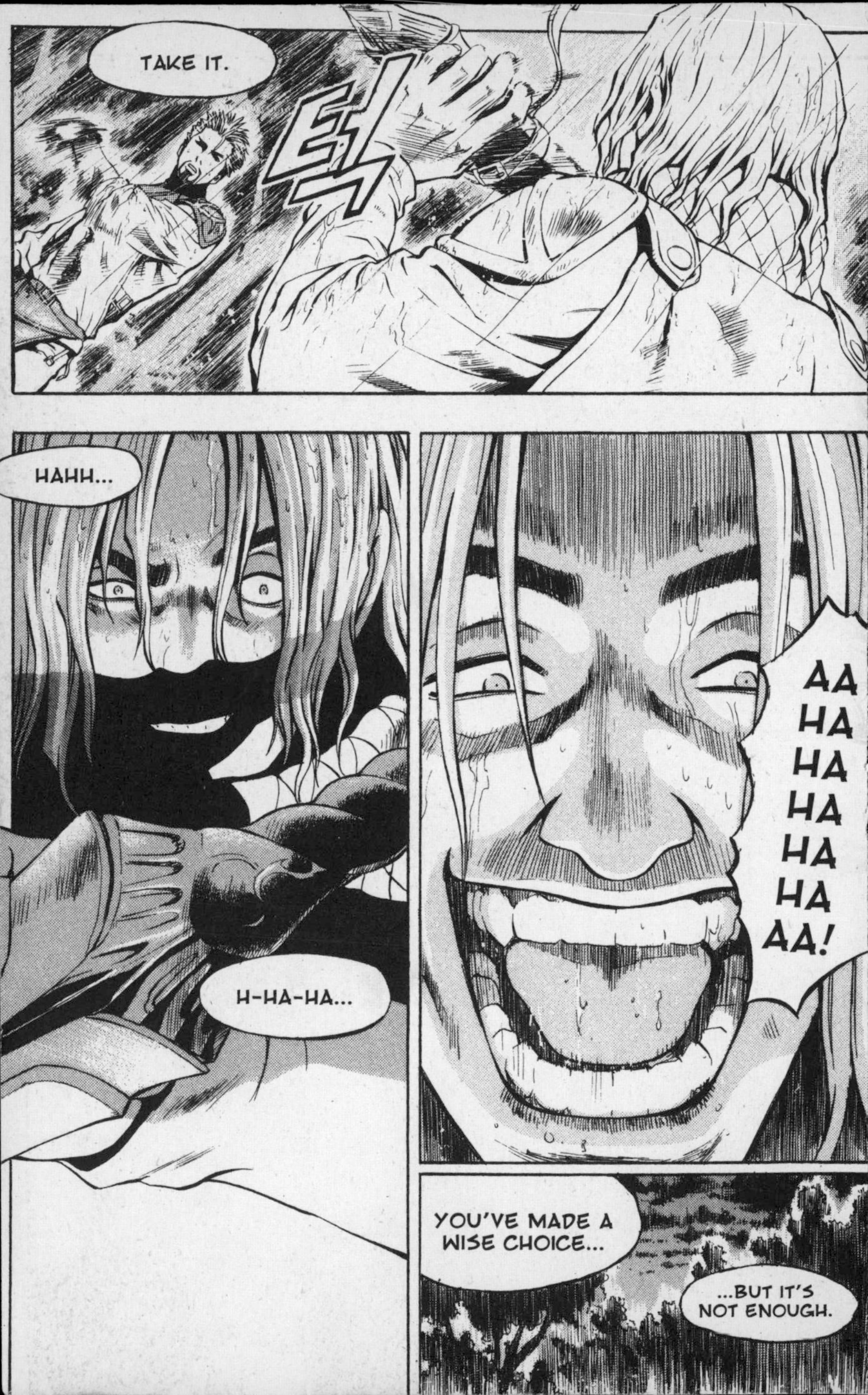
TAKE IT.
HAHH...
H-HA-HA...
AA HA HA HA HA HA AA!
YOU'VE MADE A WISE CHOICE...
...BUT IT'S NOT ENOUGH.

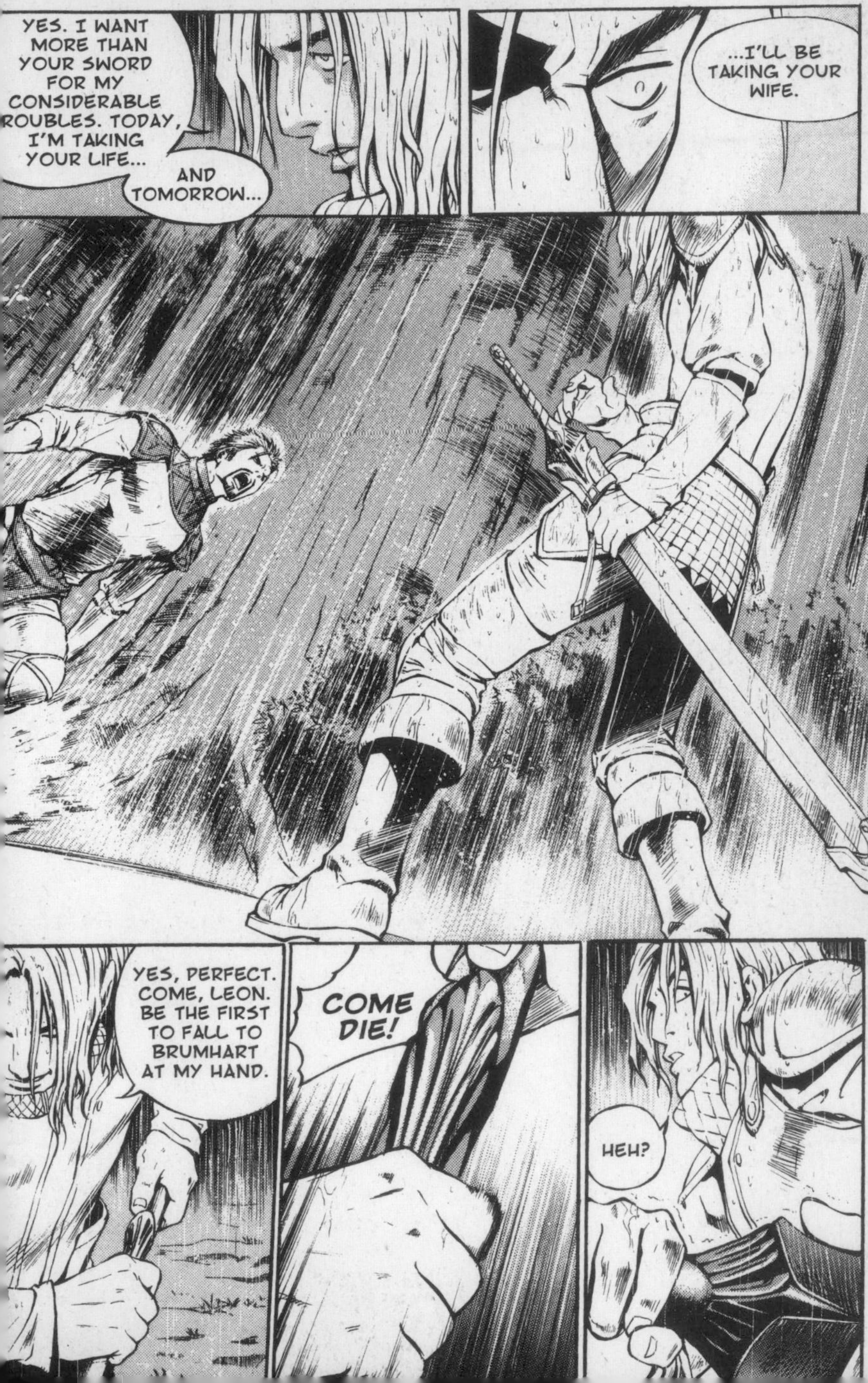
YES. I WANT MORE THAN YOUR SWORD FOR MY CONSIDERABLE ROUBLES. TODAY, I'M TAKING YOUR LIFE...
AND TOMORROW...
...I'LL BE TAKING YOUR WIFE.
YES, PERFECT. COME, LEON. BE THE FIRST TO FALL TO BRUMHART AT MY HAND.
COME DIE!
HEH?

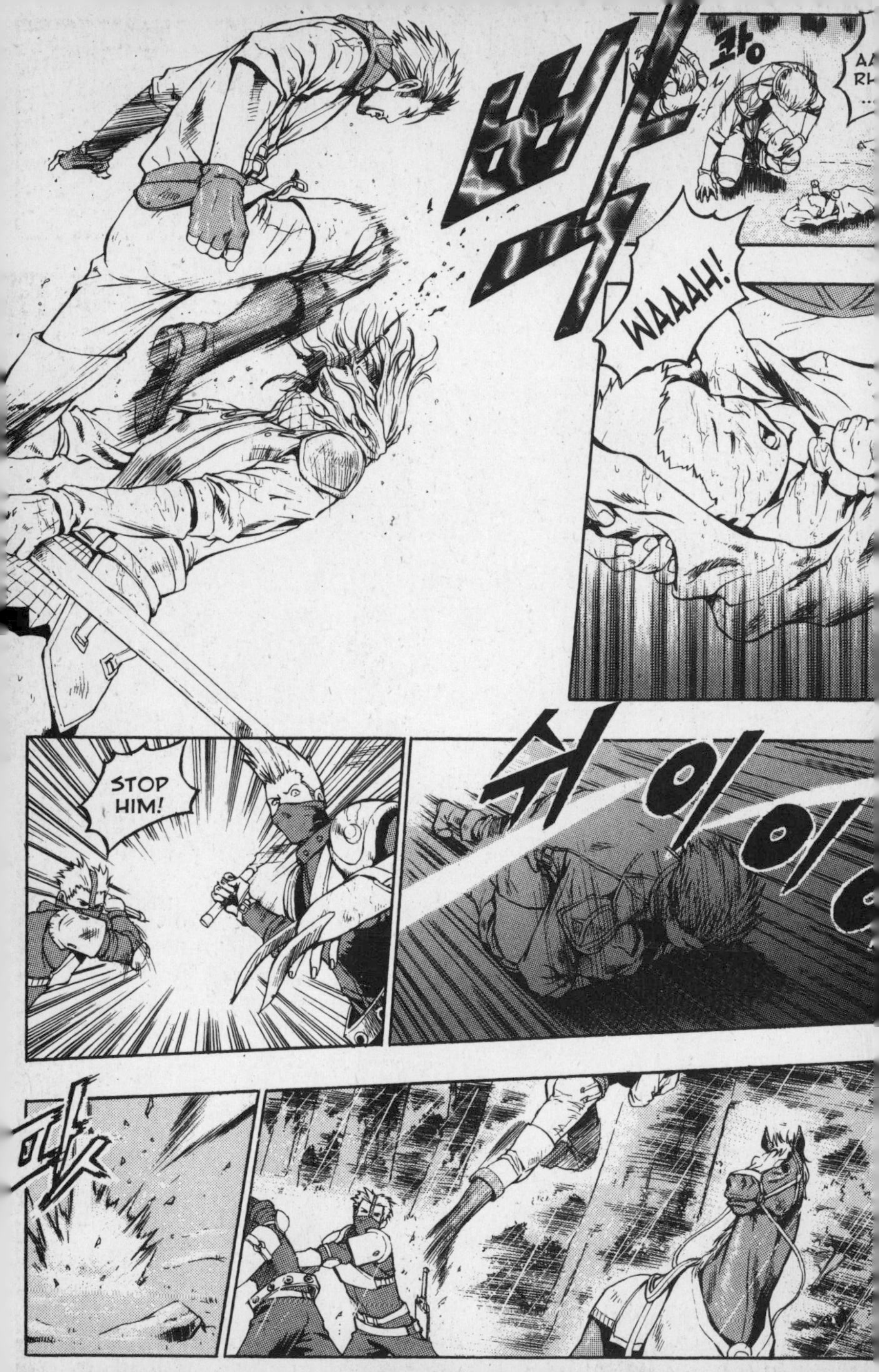
빡
쾅
WAAAH!
STOP HIM!
쉬이이

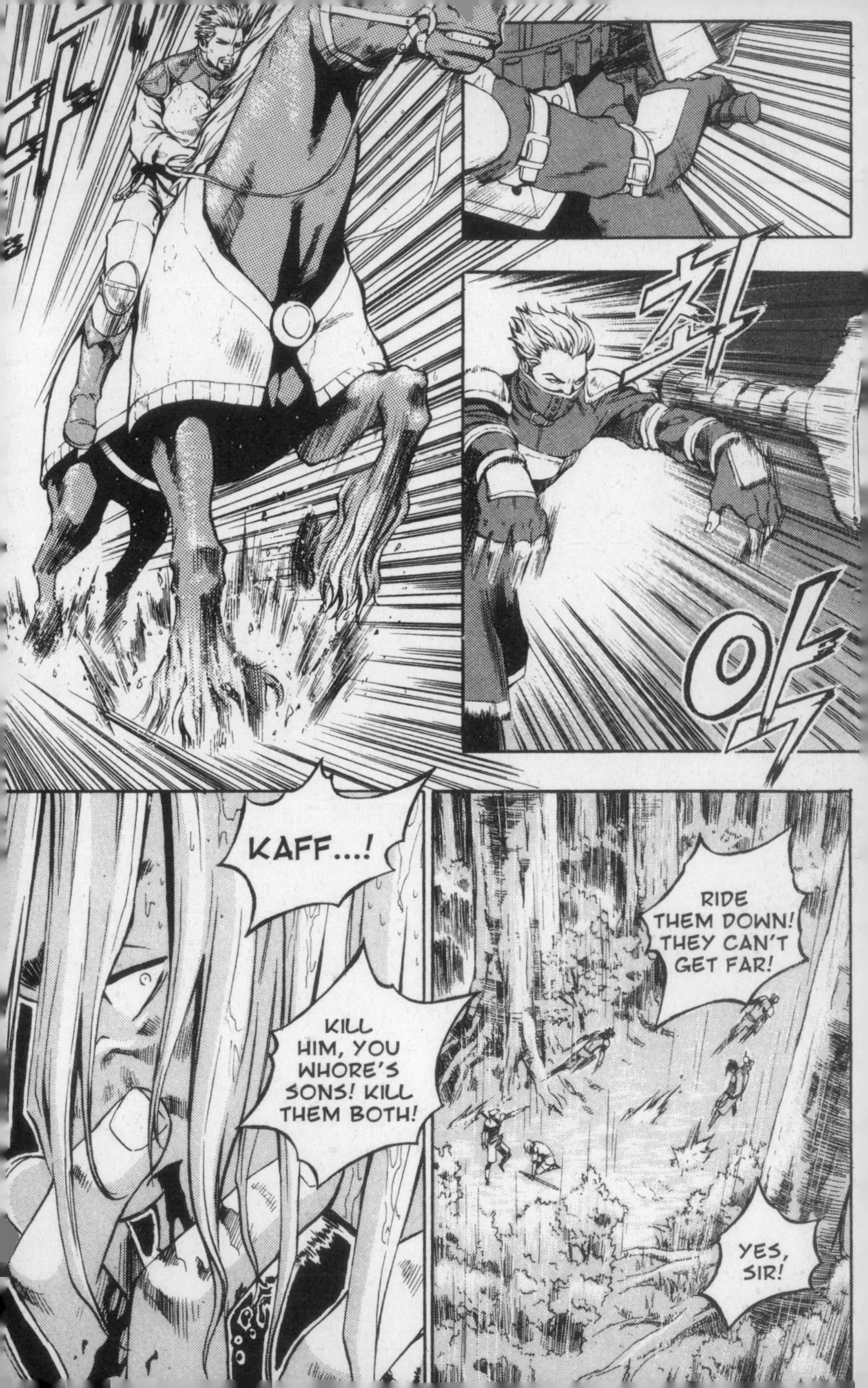
KAFF...!
KILL HIM, YOU WHORE'S SONS! KILL THEM BOTH!
RIDE THEM DOWN! THEY CAN'T GET FAR!
YES, SIR!

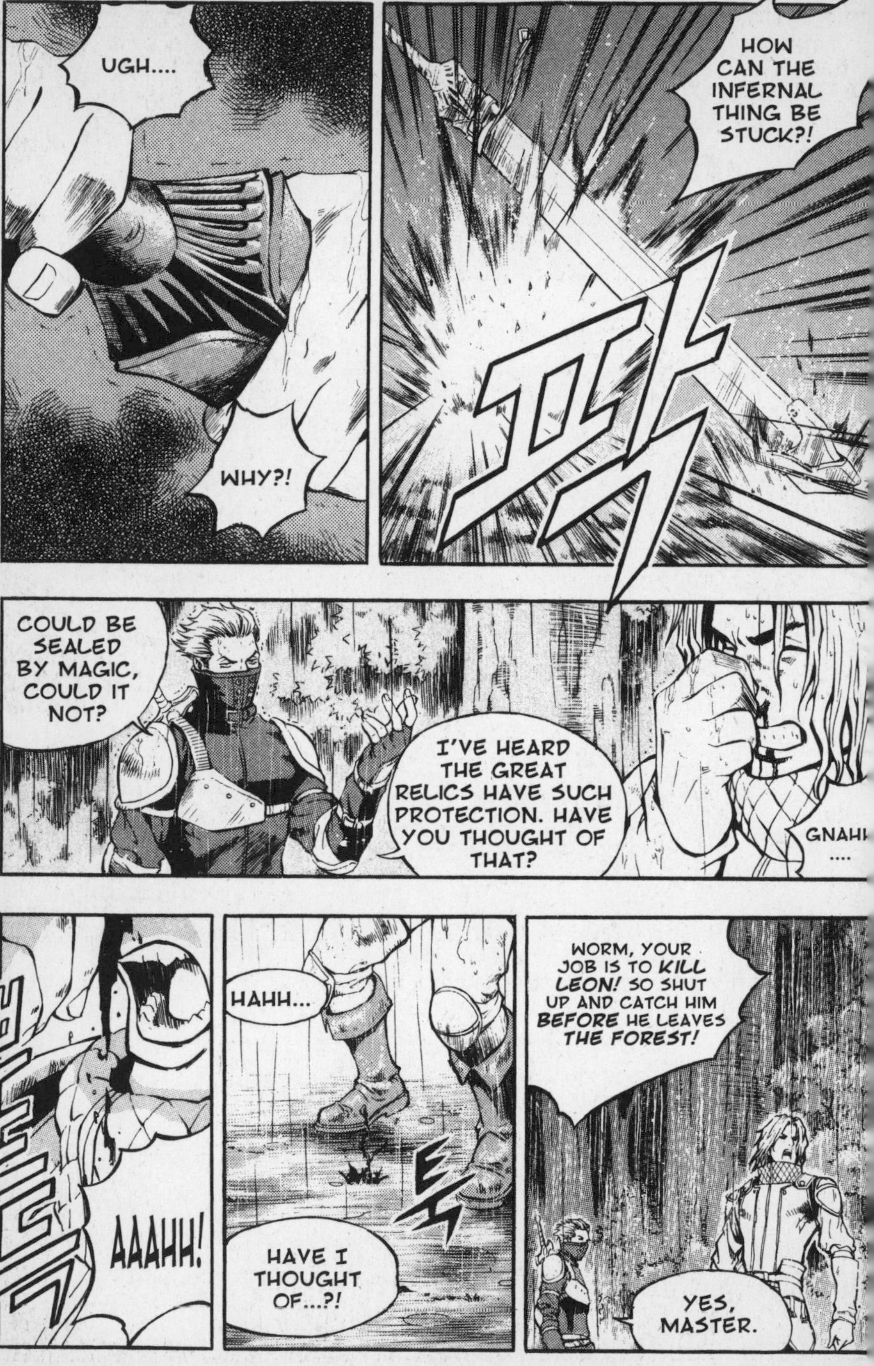
UGH....
WHY?!
HOW CAN THE INFERNAL THING BE STUCK?!
COULD BE SEALED BY MAGIC, COULD IT NOT?
I'VE HEARD THE GREAT RELICS HAVE SUCH PROTECTION. HAVE YOU THOUGHT OF THAT?
GNAH ....
AAAHH!
HAHH...
HAVE I THOUGHT OF...?!
WORM, YOUR JOB IS TO KILL LEON! SO SHUT UP AND CATCH HIM BEFORE HE LEAVES THE FOREST!
YES, MASTER.

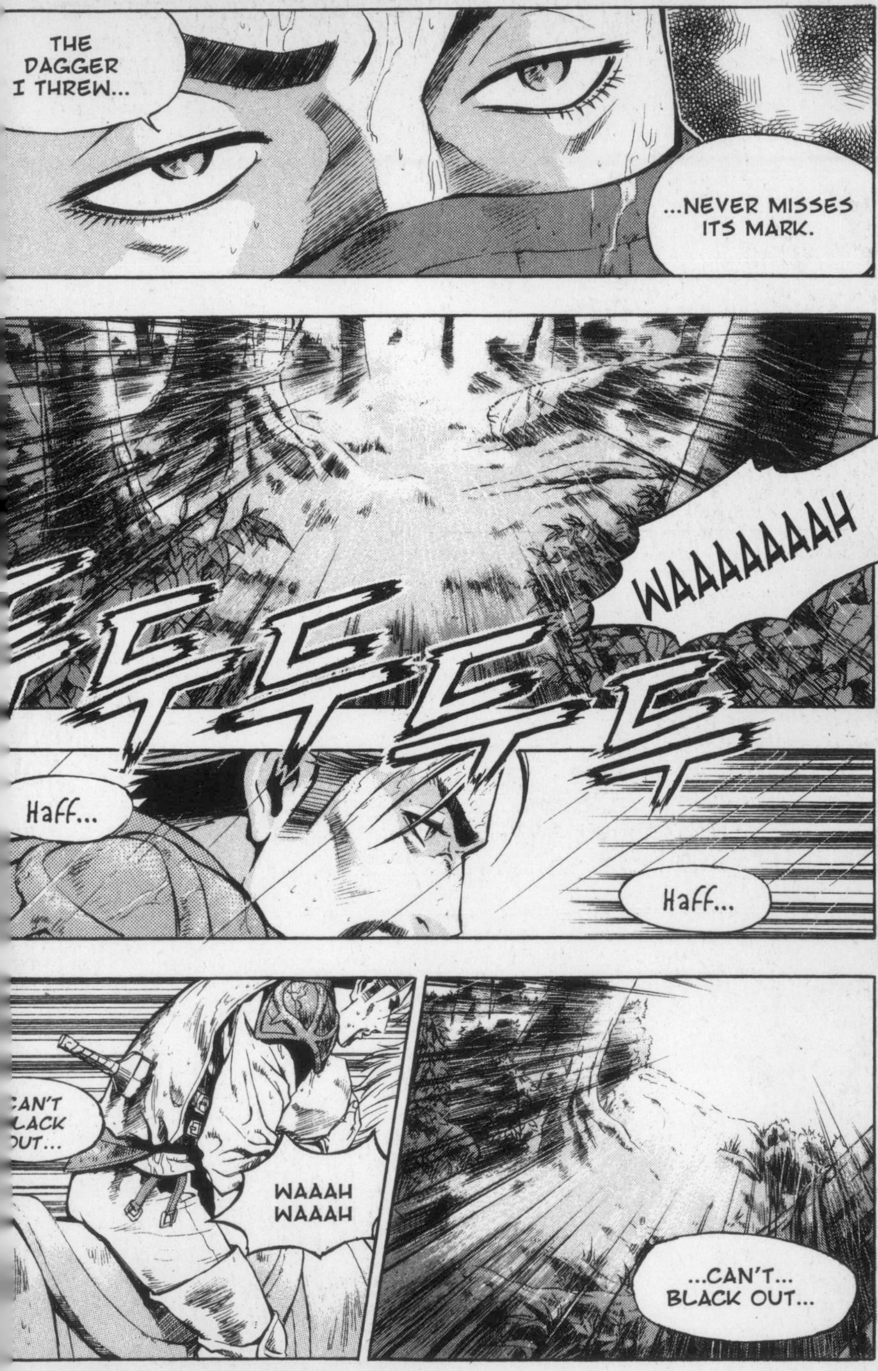
THE DAGGER I THREW...
...NEVER MISSES ITS MARK.
WAAAAAAAH
Haff...
Haff...
CAN'T
LACK
OUT...
WAAAH WAAAH
...CAN'T... BLACK OUT...

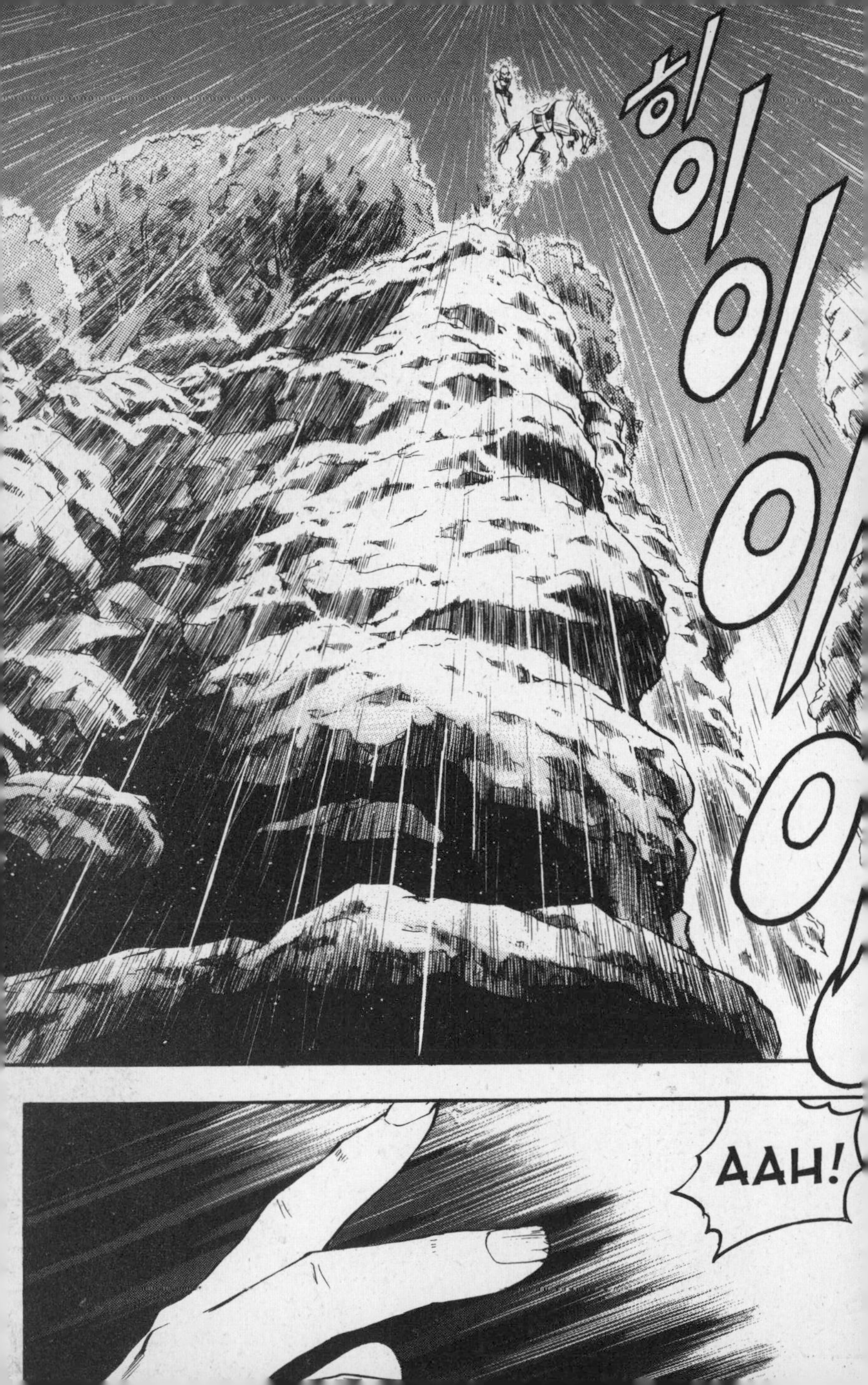
히이이이이
AAH!

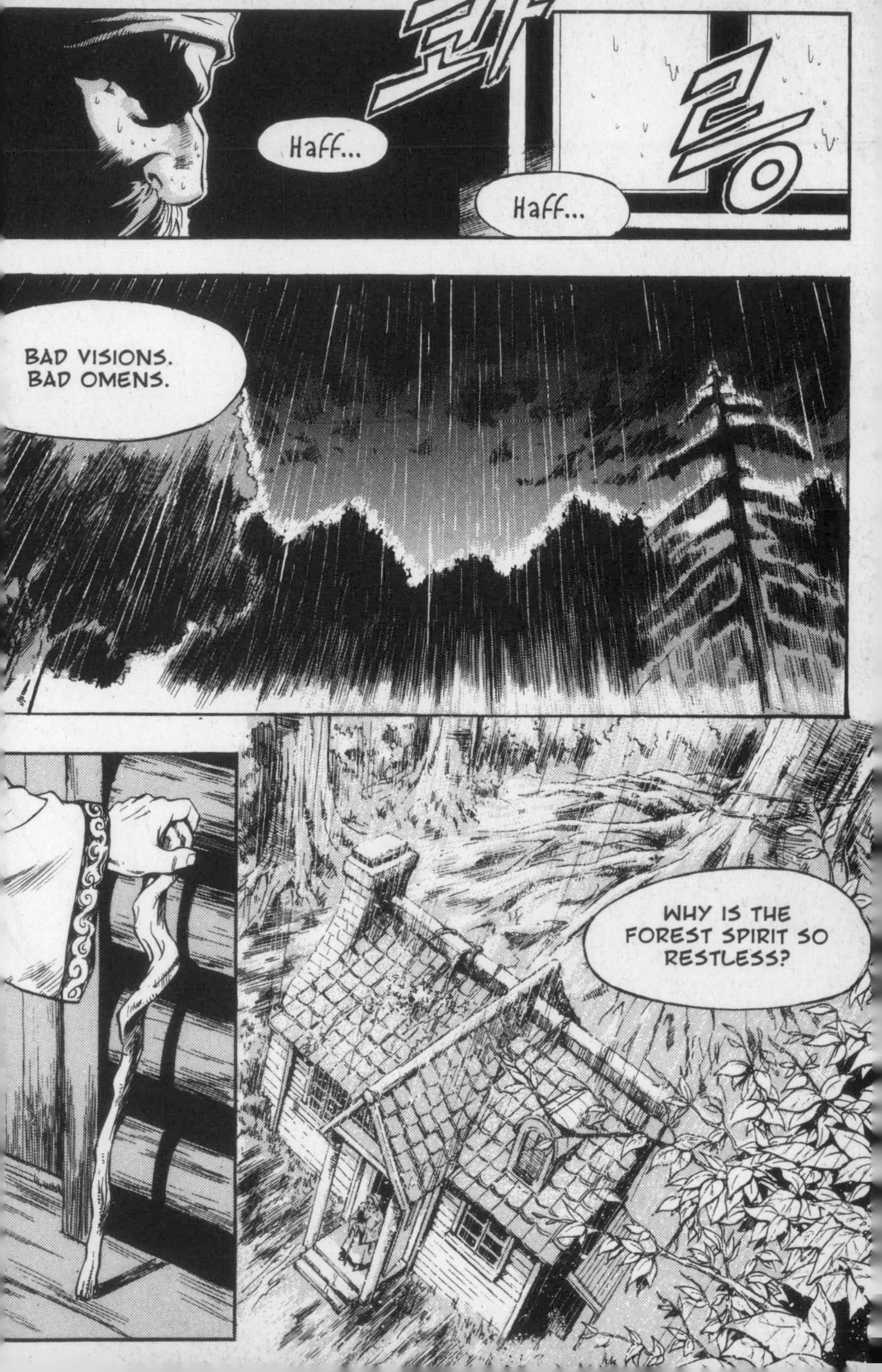
Haff...
Haff...
BAD VISIONS. BAD OMENS.
WHY IS THE FOREST SPIRIT SO RESTLESS?

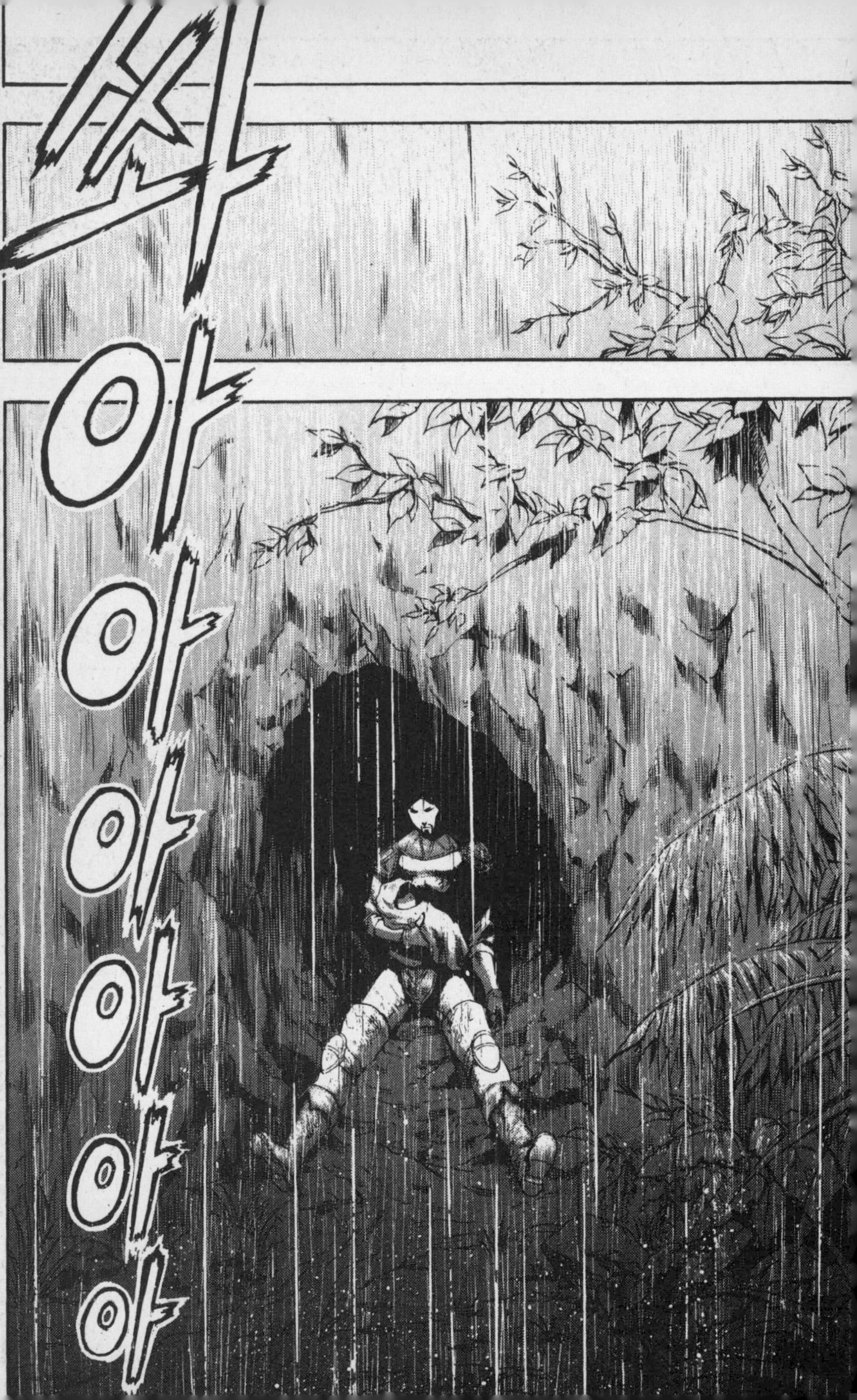
쏴아아아아아아

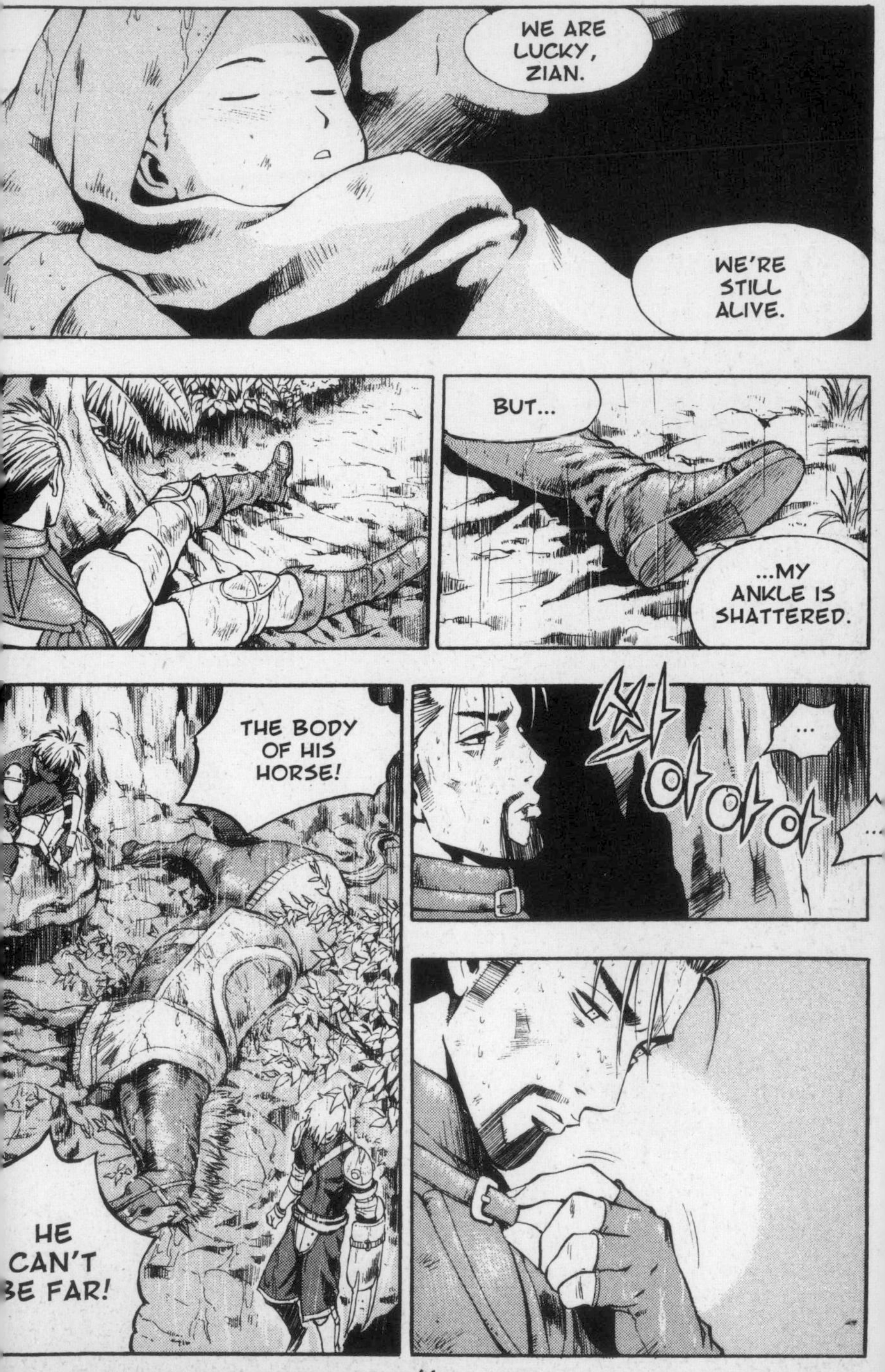
WE ARE LUCKY, ZIAN.
WE'RE STILL ALIVE.
BUT...
...MY ANKLE IS SHATTERED.
THE BODY OF HIS HORSE!
HE CAN'T BE FAR!
...
...

THE OLD ORC'S RING... THE OLD SYMBOL OF FRIENDSHIP BETWEE THE ORCISH MAGICIA WALCURE, AND MY ANCESTOR, NATHAN OF MANAS...

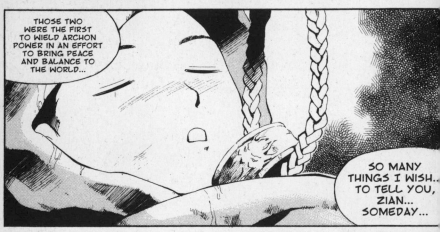

THOSE TWO WERE THE FIRST TO WIELD ARCHON POWER IN AN EFFORT TO BRING PEACE AND BALANCE TO THE WORLD...

SO MANY THINGS I WISH.. TO TELL YOU, ZIAN... SOMEDAY...

MAY THE FOREST SPIRITS WATCH OVER YOU, MY SON...

IF THE GODS WILL IT, I SHALL RETURN.

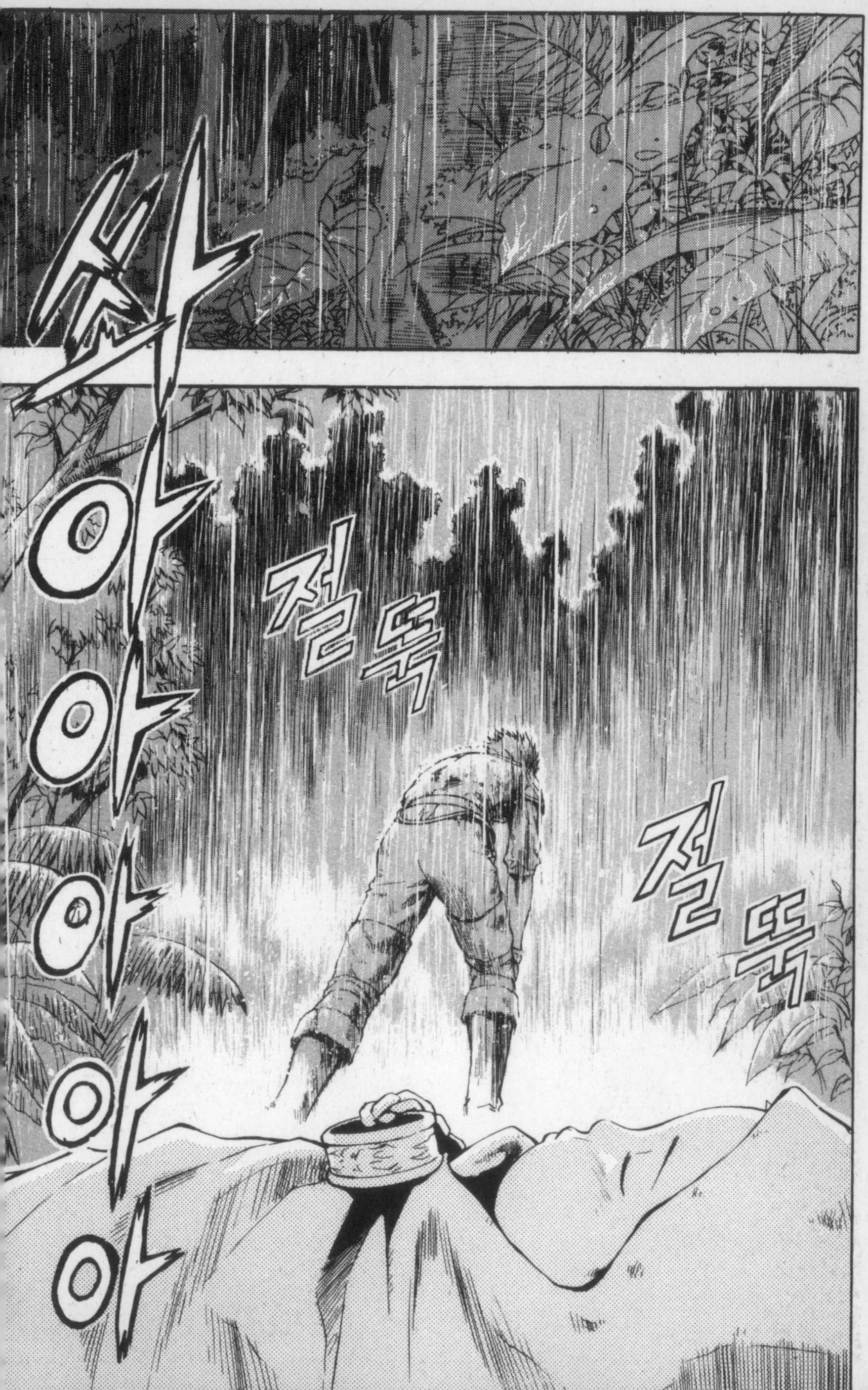
쏴아아아아아
절뚝
절뚝

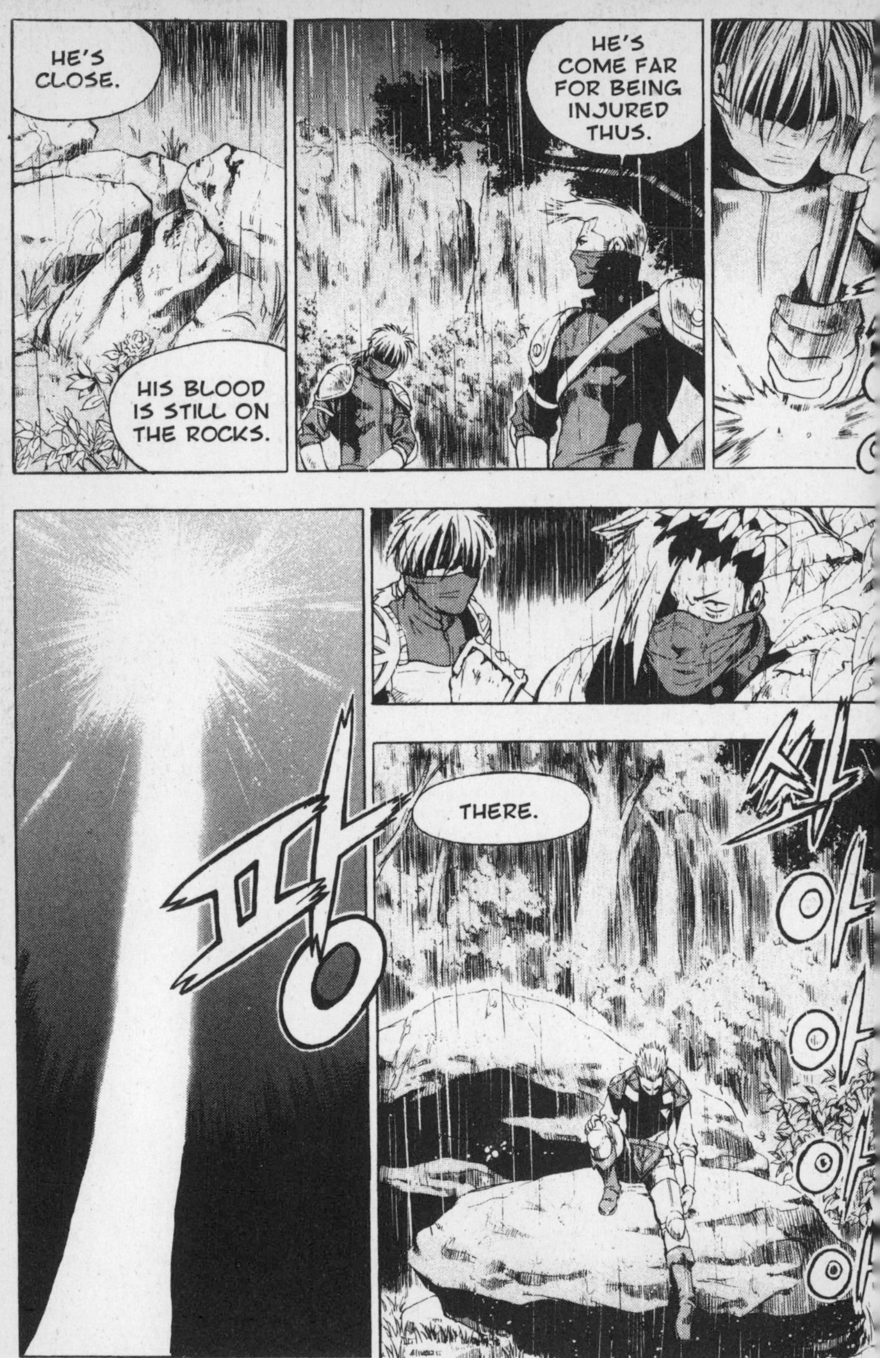
HE'S CLOSE.
HIS BLOOD IS STILL ON THE ROCKS.
HE'S COME FAR FOR BEING INJURED THUS.
팡
THERE.

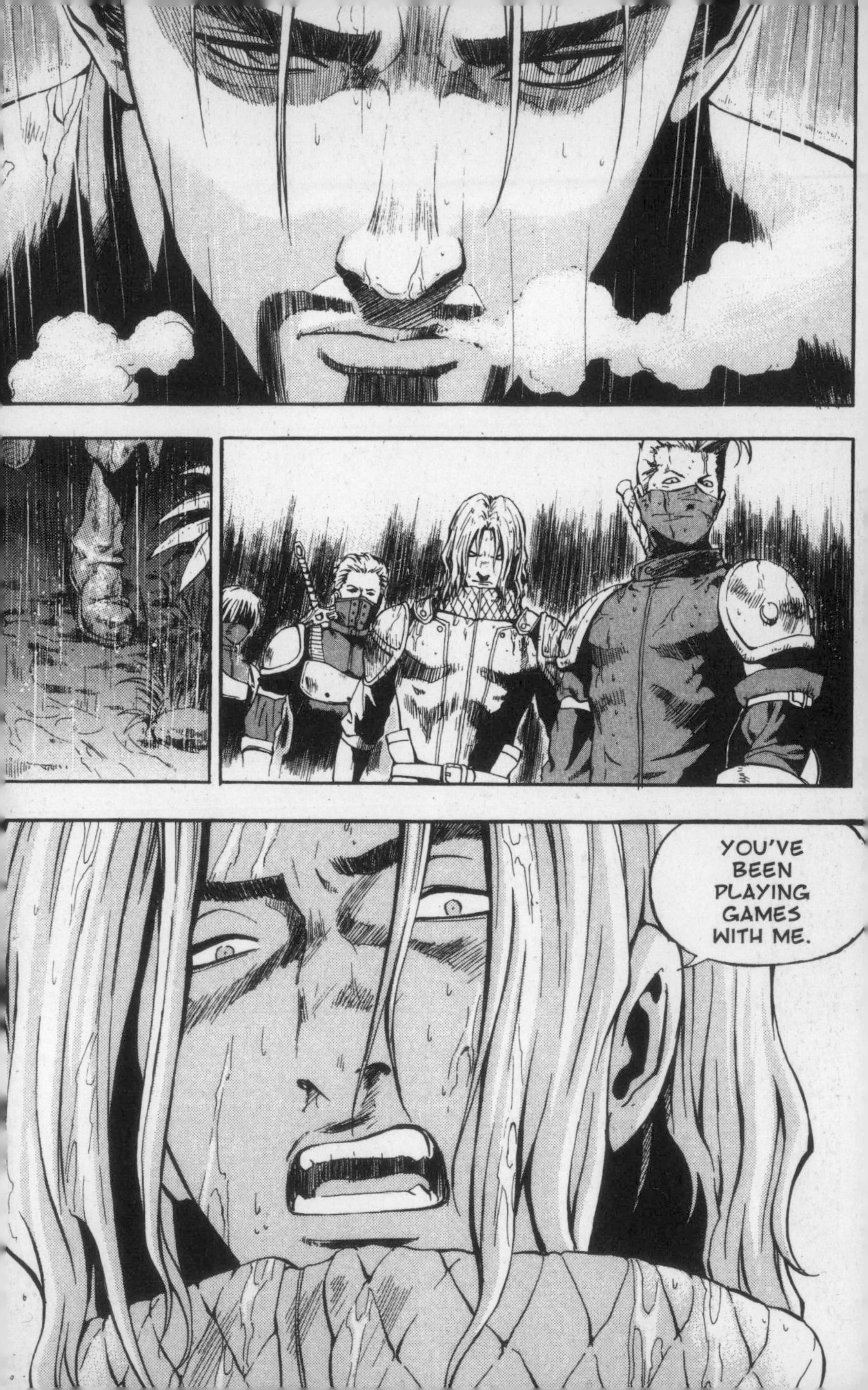
YOU'VE BEEN PLAYING GAMES WITH ME.

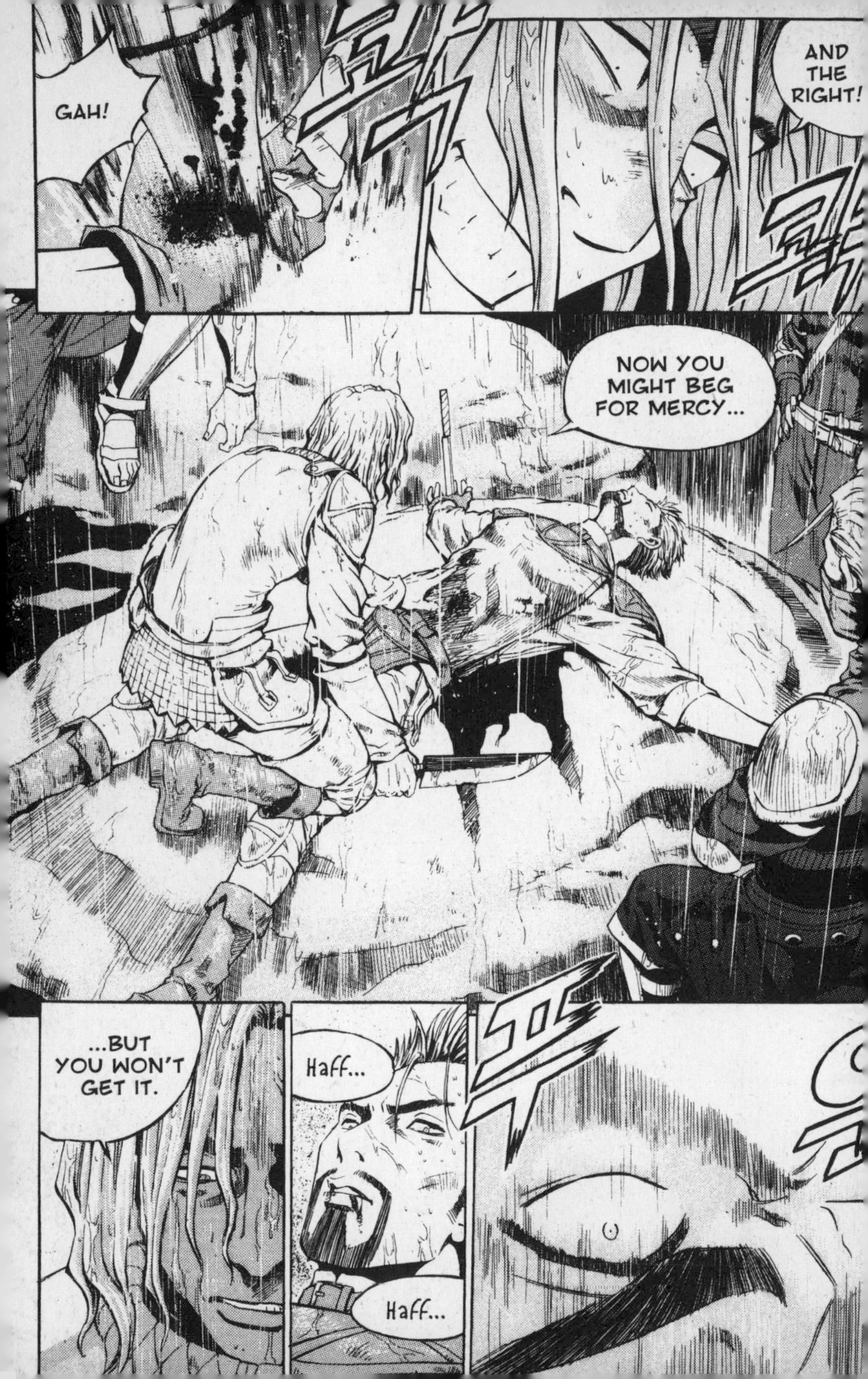
GAH!
AND THE RIGHT!
NOW YOU MIGHT BEG FOR MERCY...
...BUT YOU WON'T GET IT.
Haff...
Haff...

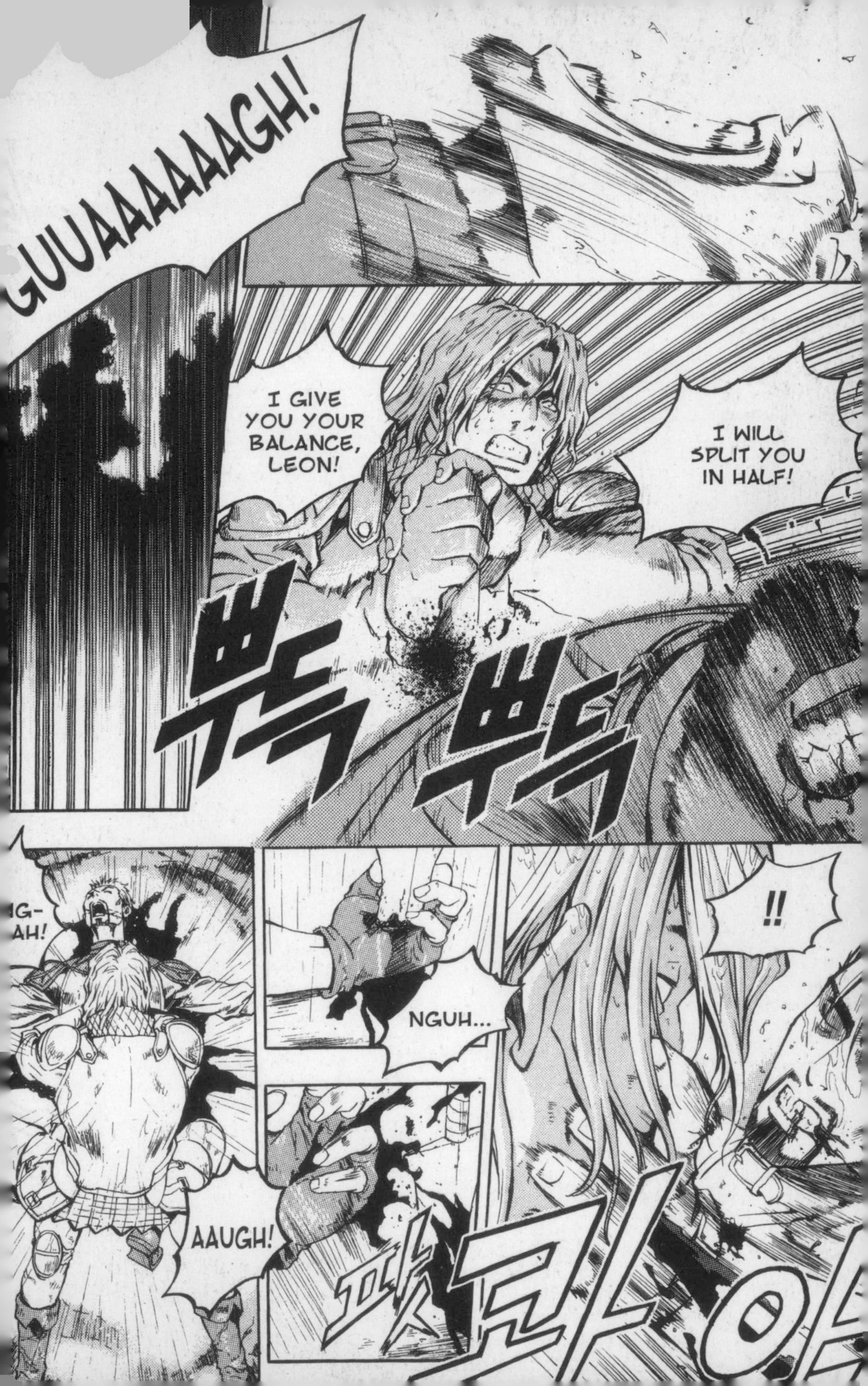
GUUAAAAAAGH!
I GIVE YOU YOUR BALANCE, LEON!
I WILL SPLIT YOU IN HALF!
뿌득 뿌득
G-
AH!
AAUGH!
NGUH...
!!

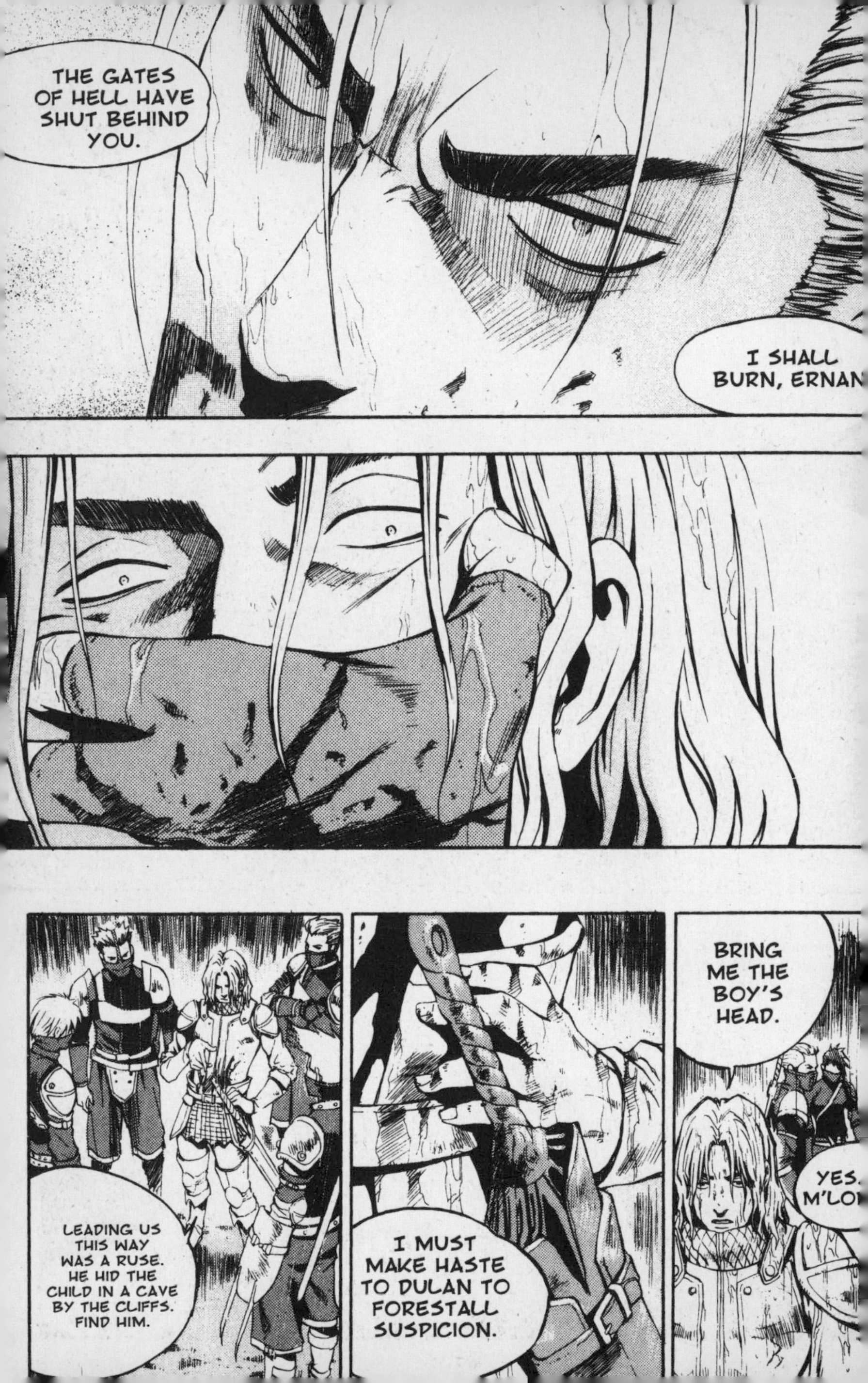
THE GATES OF HELL HAVE SHUT BEHIND YOU.
I SHALL BURN, ERNAN
LEADING US THIS WAY WAS A RUSE. HE HID THE CHILD IN A CAVE BY THE CLIFFS. FIND HIM.
I MUST MAKE HASTE TO DULAN TO FORESTALL SUSPICION.
BRING ME THE BOY'S HEAD.
YES.
M'LO

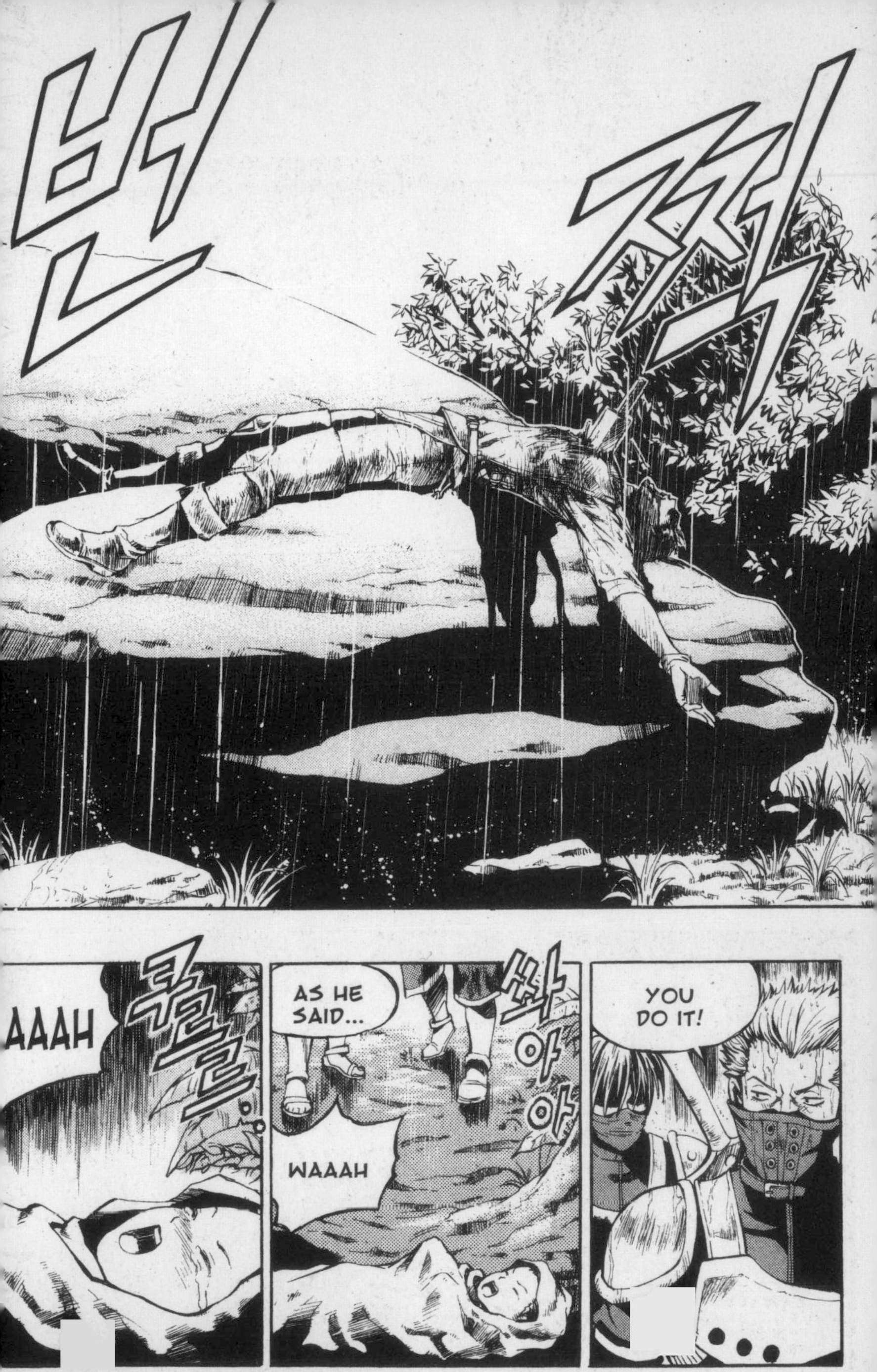

번쩍
AAAH
AS HE SAID...
WAAAH
YOU DO IT!
...

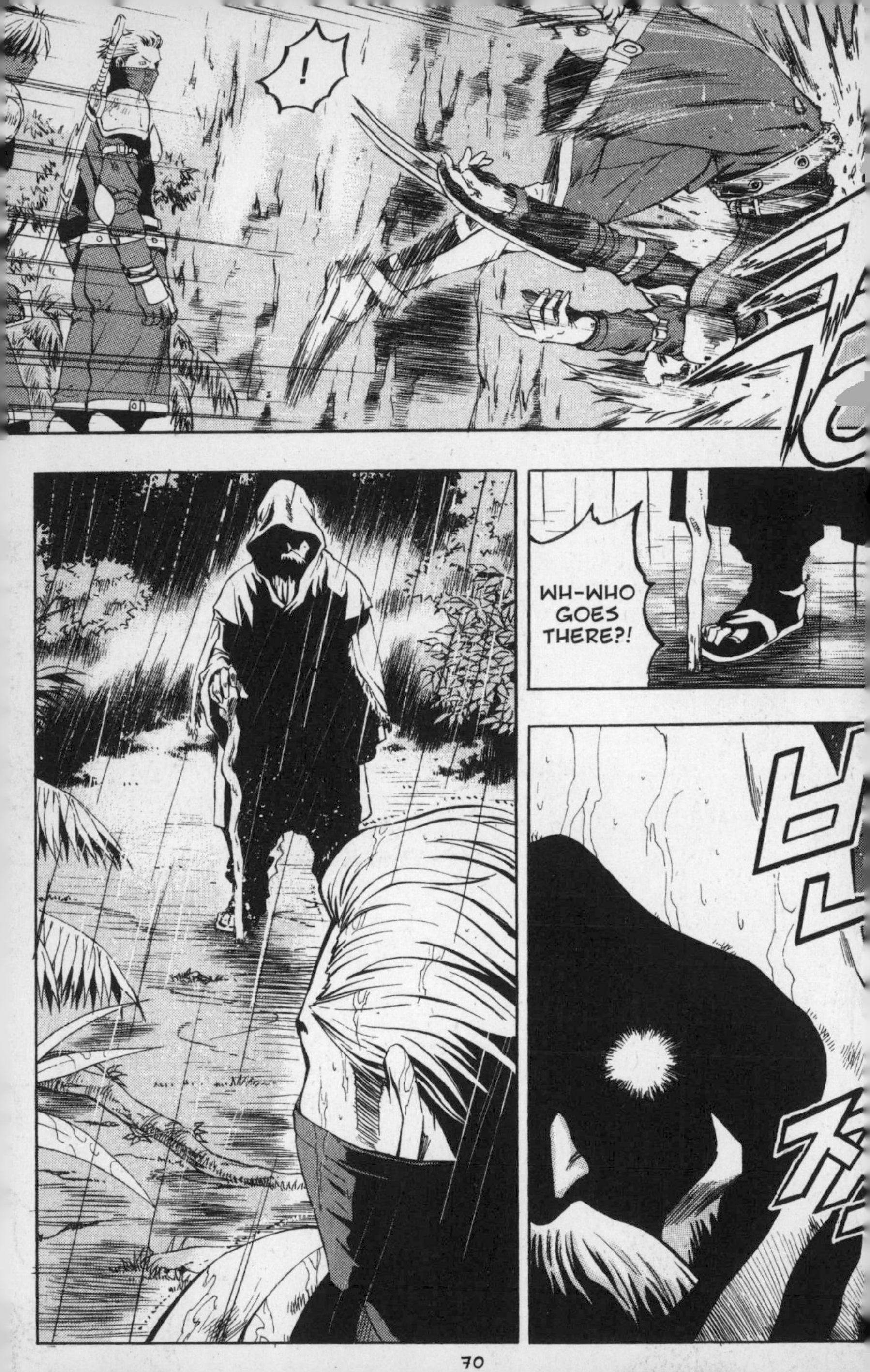
!
WH-WHO GOES THERE?!

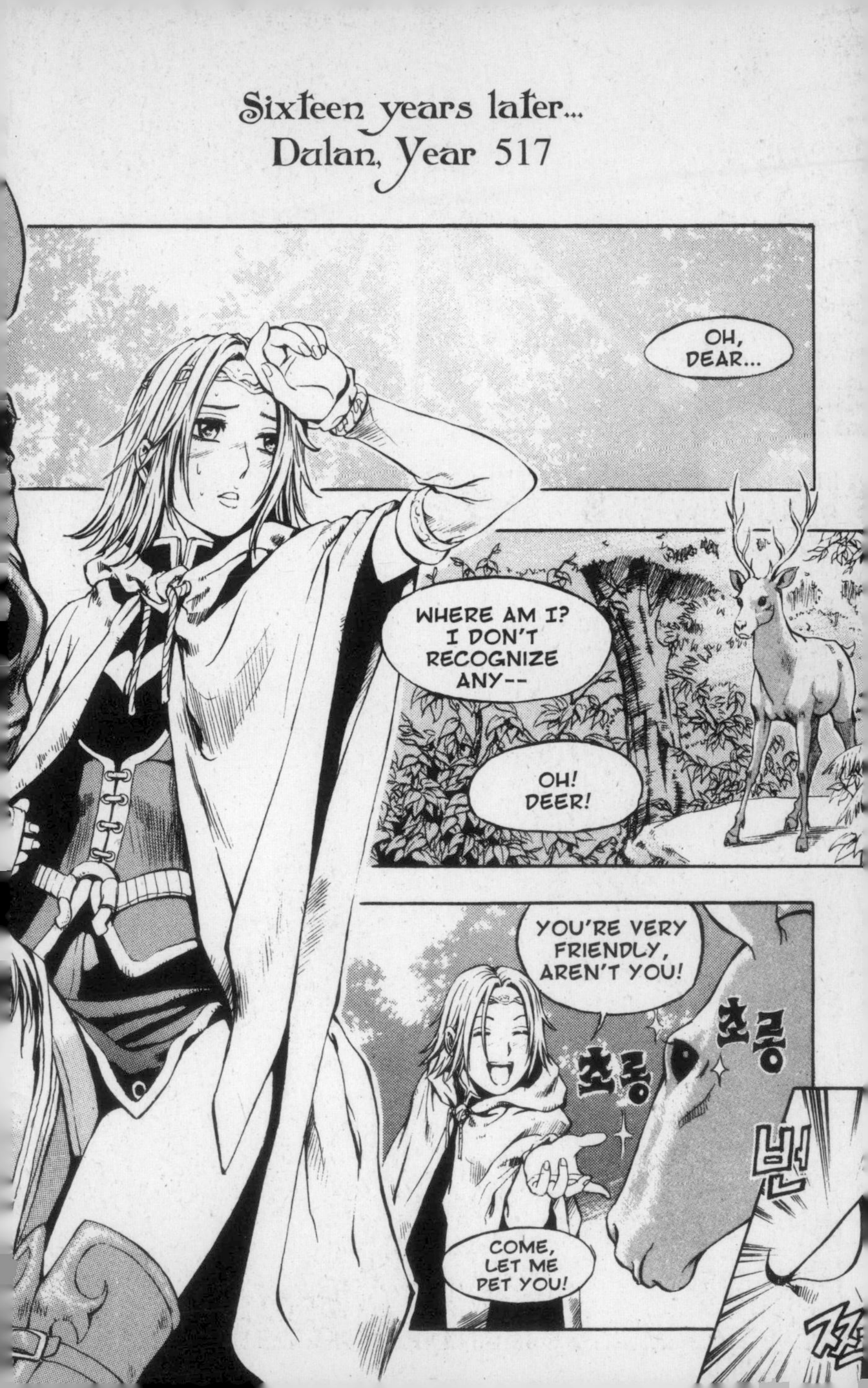
Sixteen years later...
Dulan, Year 517
OH, DEAR...
WHERE AM I? I DON'T RECOGNIZE ANY--
OH! DEER!
YOU'RE VERY FRIENDLY, AREN'T YOU!
초롱
초롱
COME, LET ME PET YOU!
번

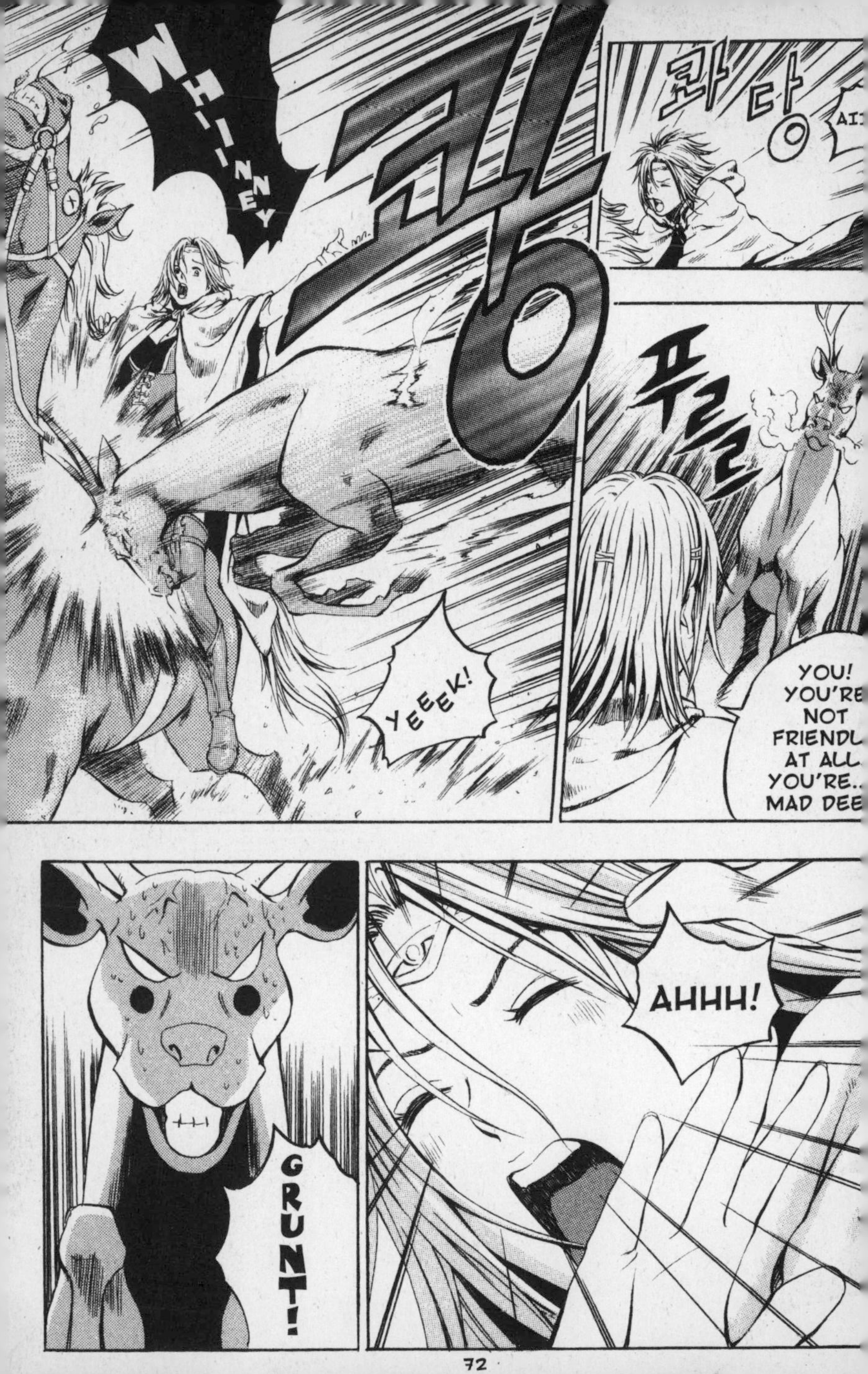
WHIINNEY
YEEEK!
콰당
AII
푸르르
YOU! YOU'RE NOT FRIENDL AT ALL. YOU'RE.. MAD DEE
GRUNT!
AHHH!

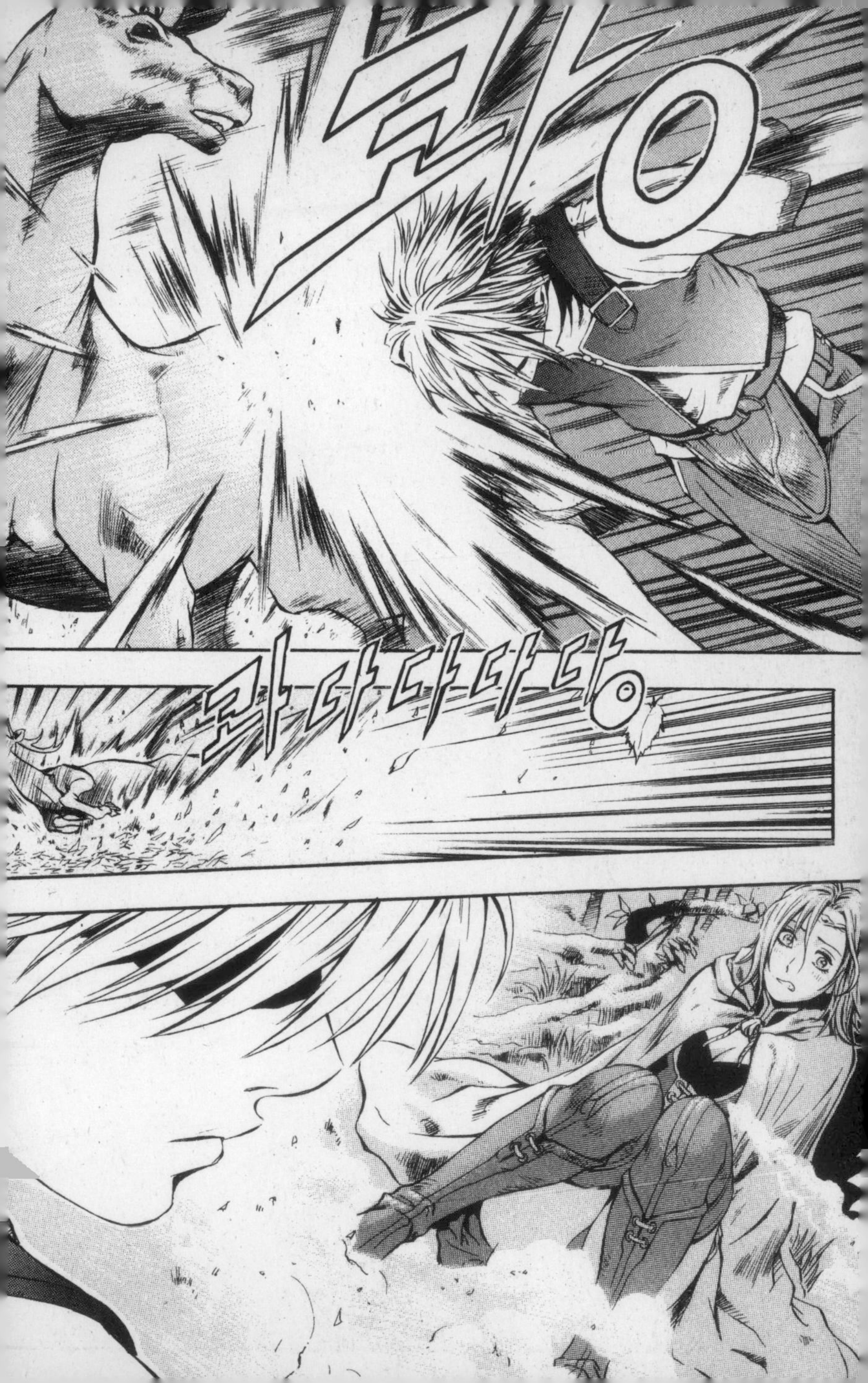
쾅
콰다다다당

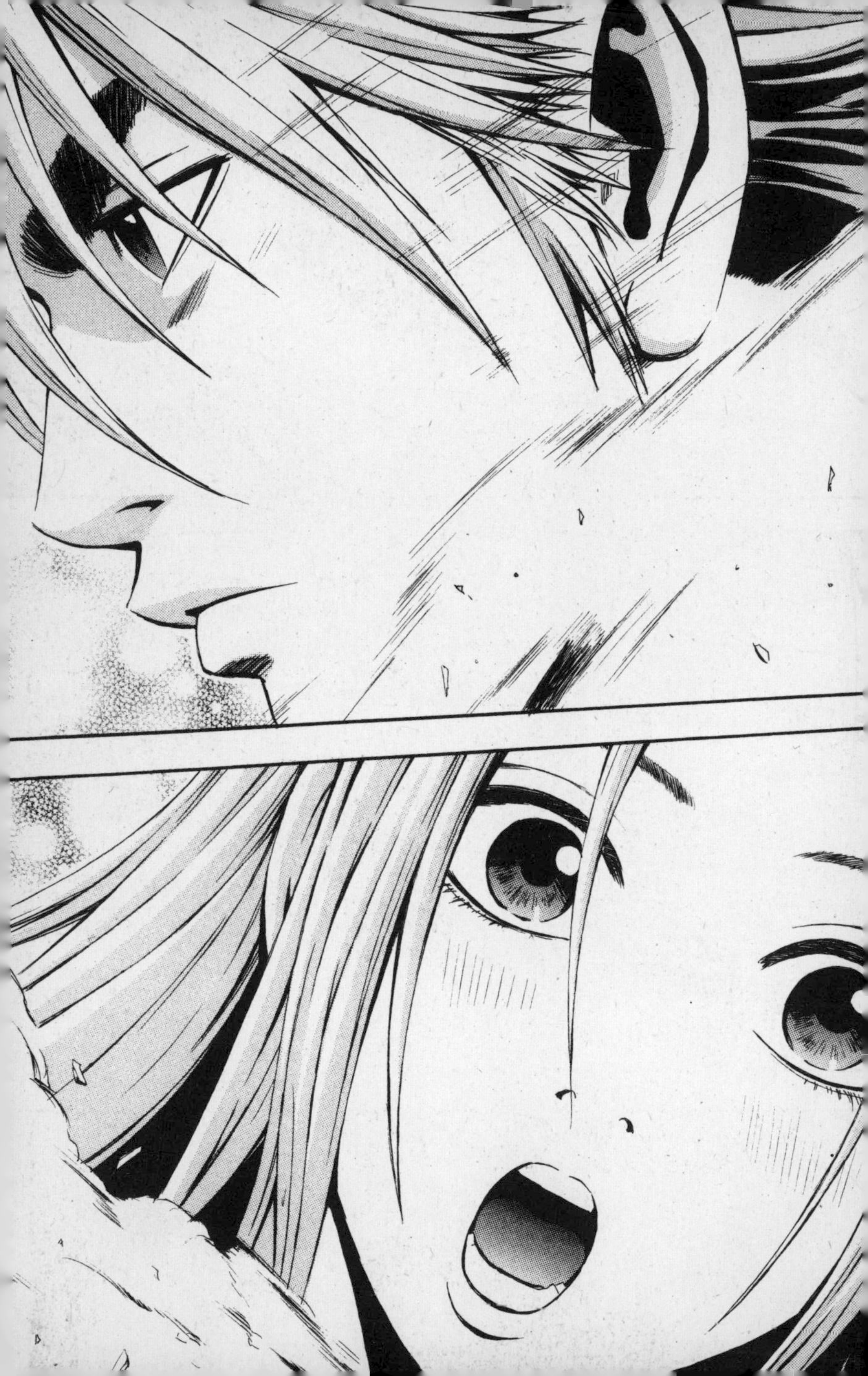

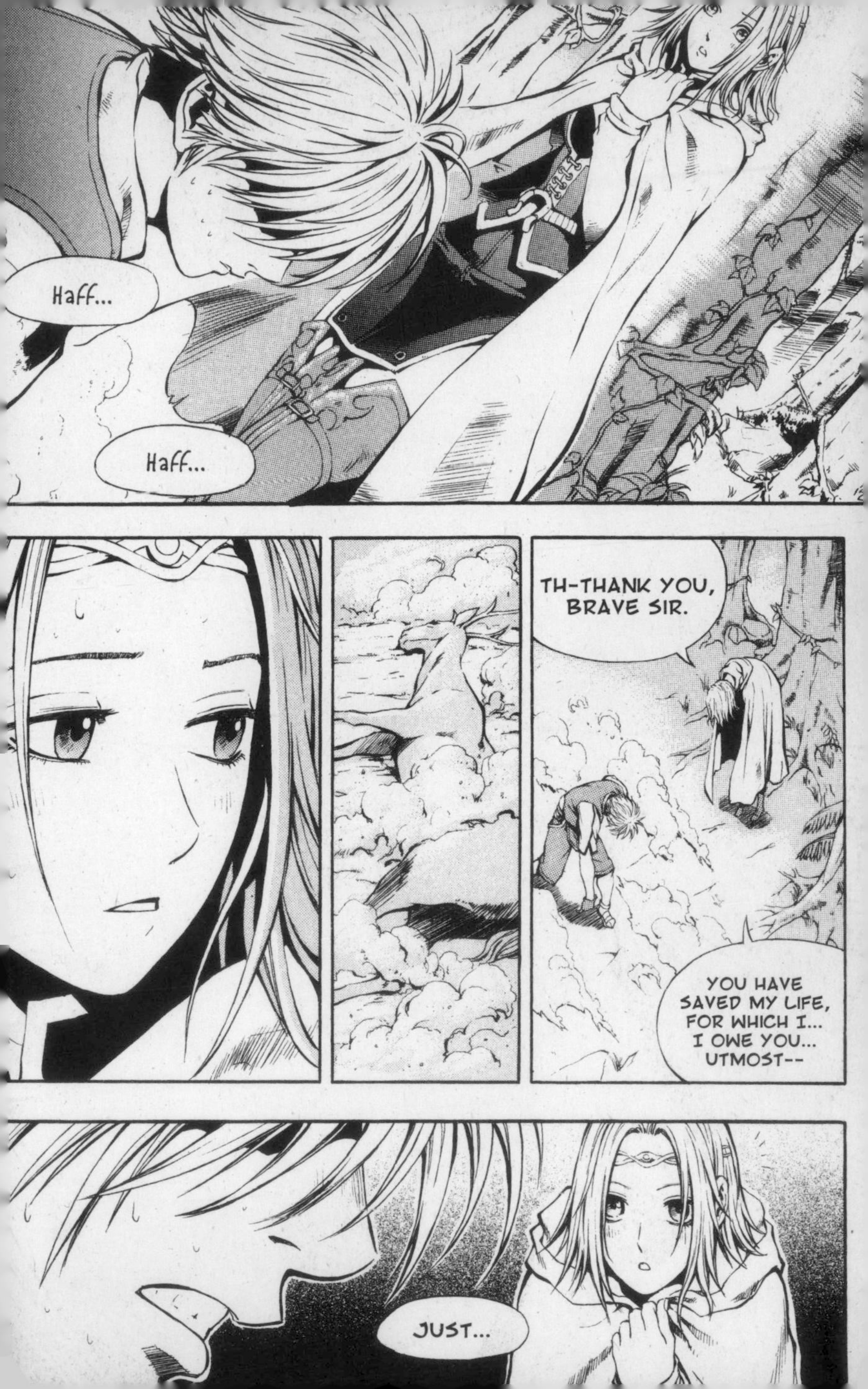
Haff...
Haff...
TH-THANK YOU, BRAVE SIR.
YOU HAVE SAVED MY LIFE, FOR WHICH I... I OWE YOU... UTMOST--
JUST...

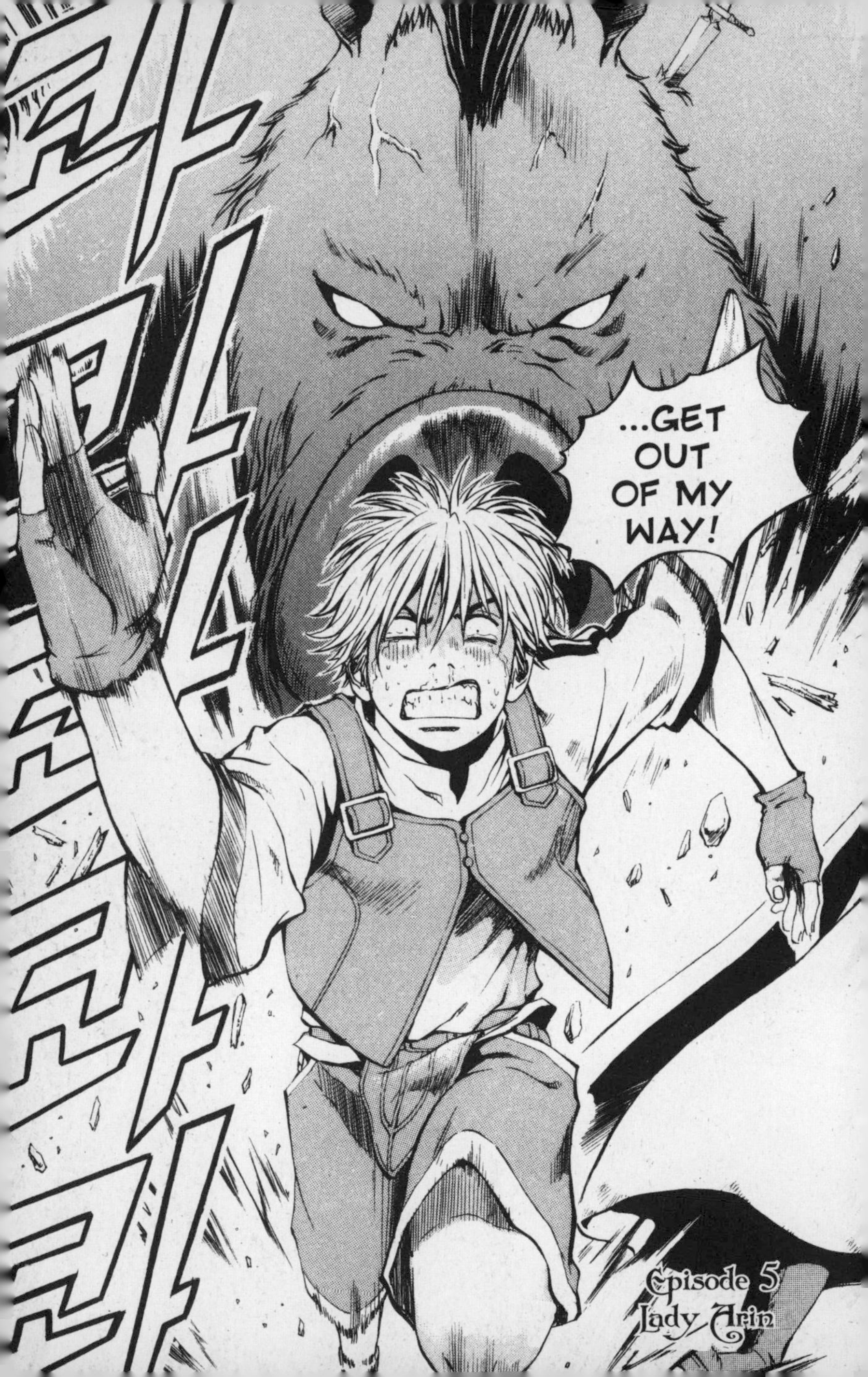
...GET OUT OF MY WAY!
Episode 5
Lady Arin

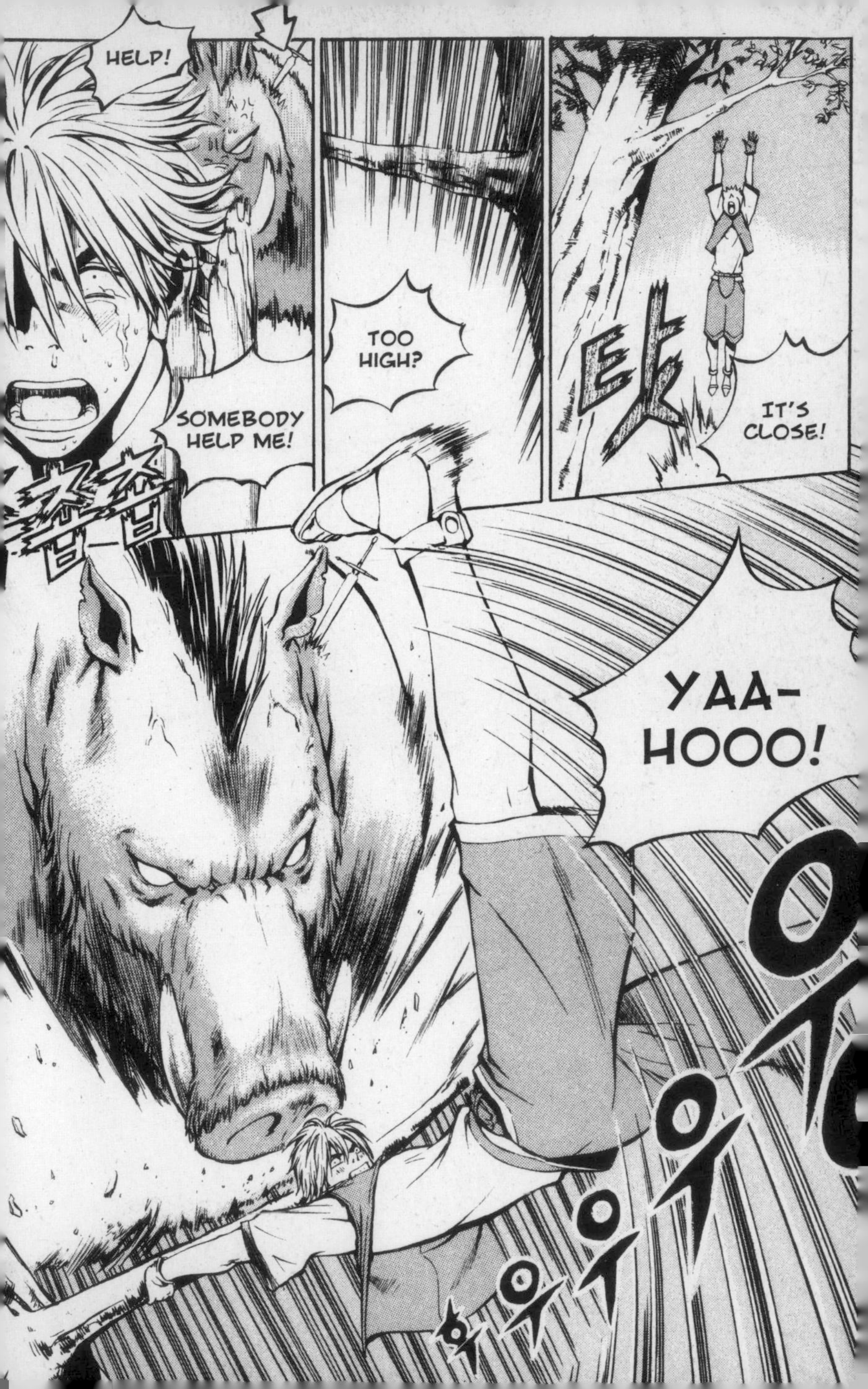
HELP!
SOMEBODY HELP ME!
TOO HIGH?
IT'S CLOSE!
YAA-HOOO!

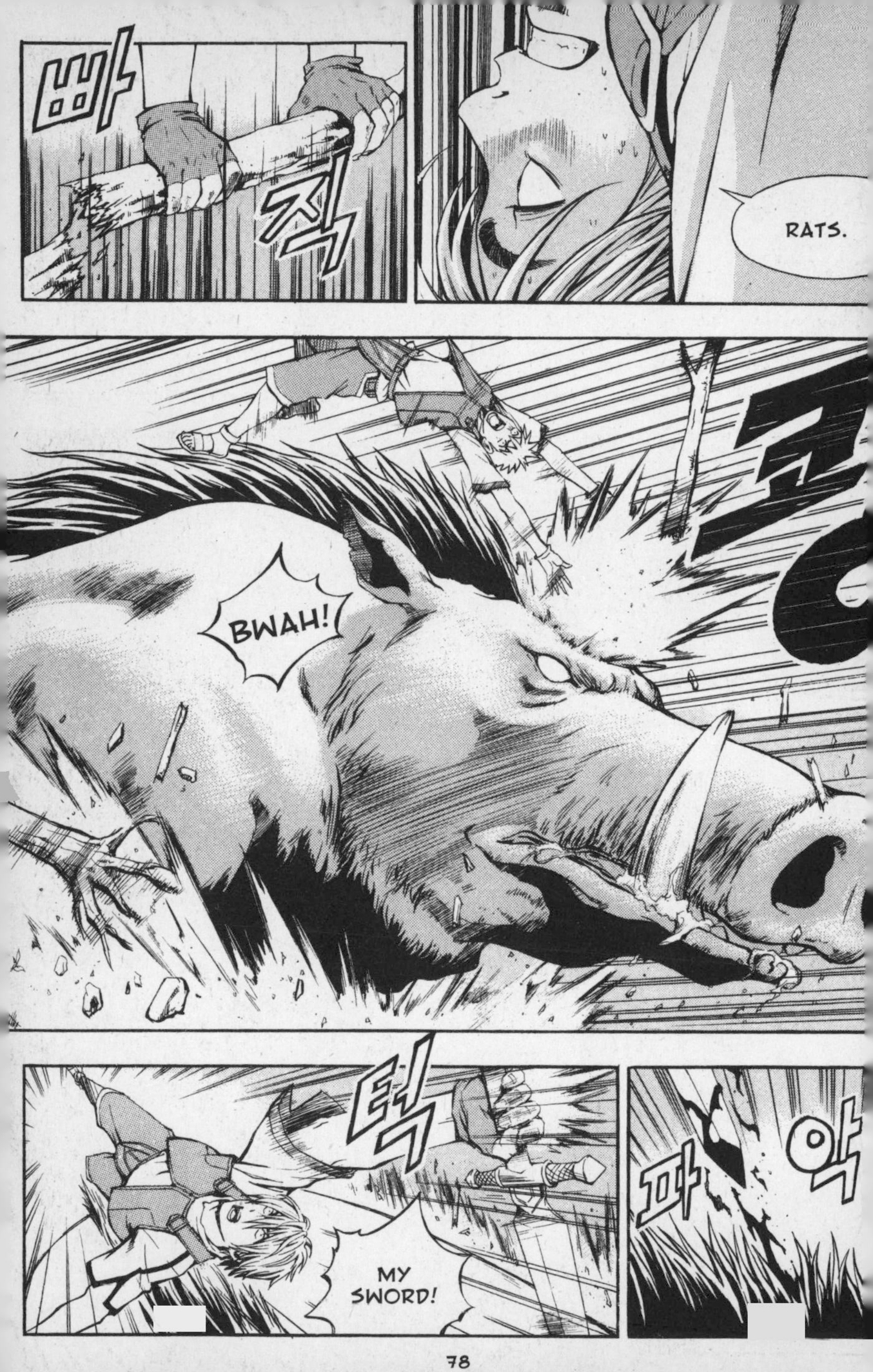
빠직
RATS.
BWAH!
턱
MY SWORD!

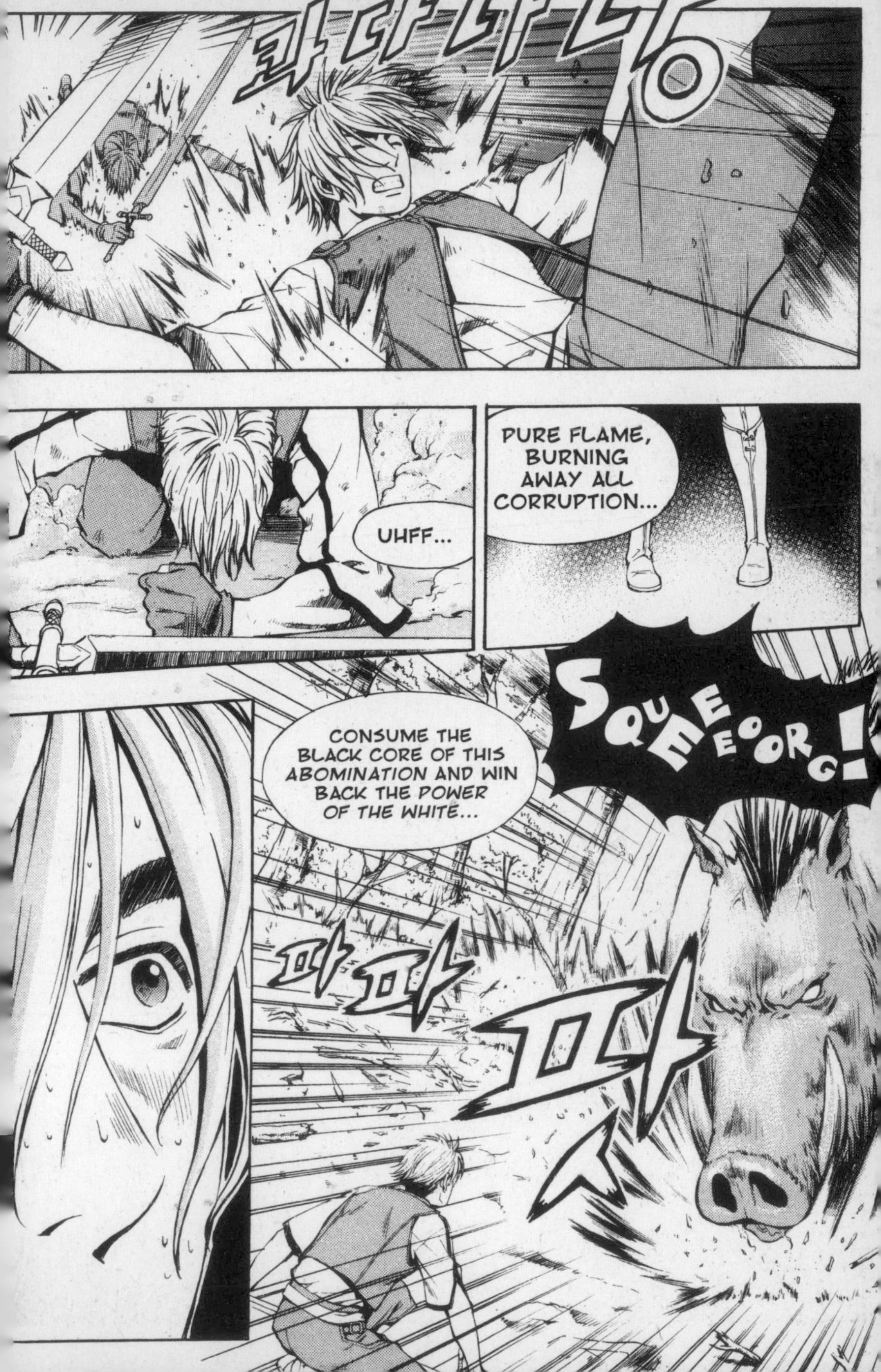
콰다다당
UHFF...
PURE FLAME, BURNING AWAY ALL CORRUPTION...
CONSUME THE BLACK CORE OF THIS ABOMINATION AND WIN BACK THE POWER OF THE WHITE...
SQUEEEOORG!
파파파

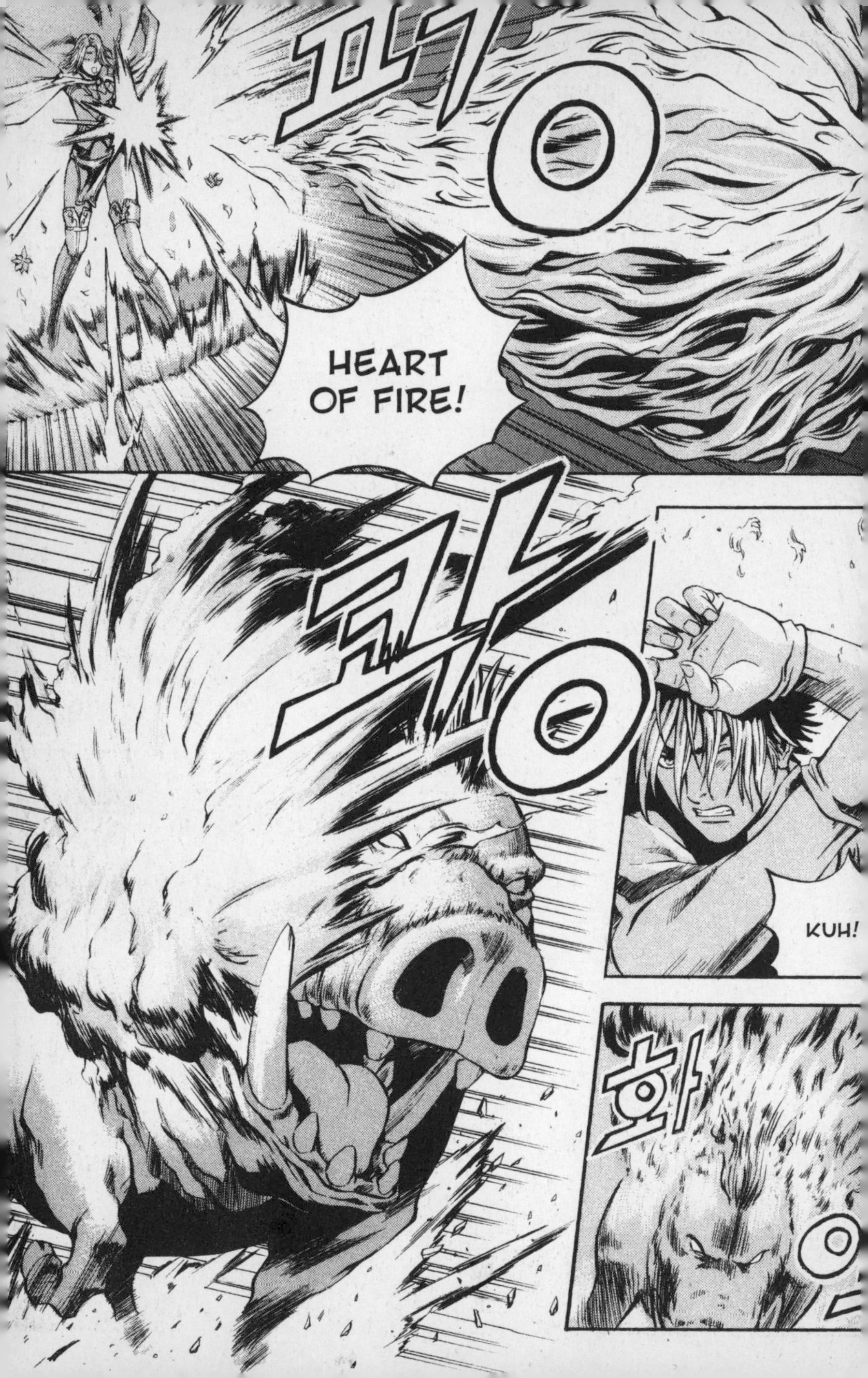
HEART OF FIRE!
KUH!

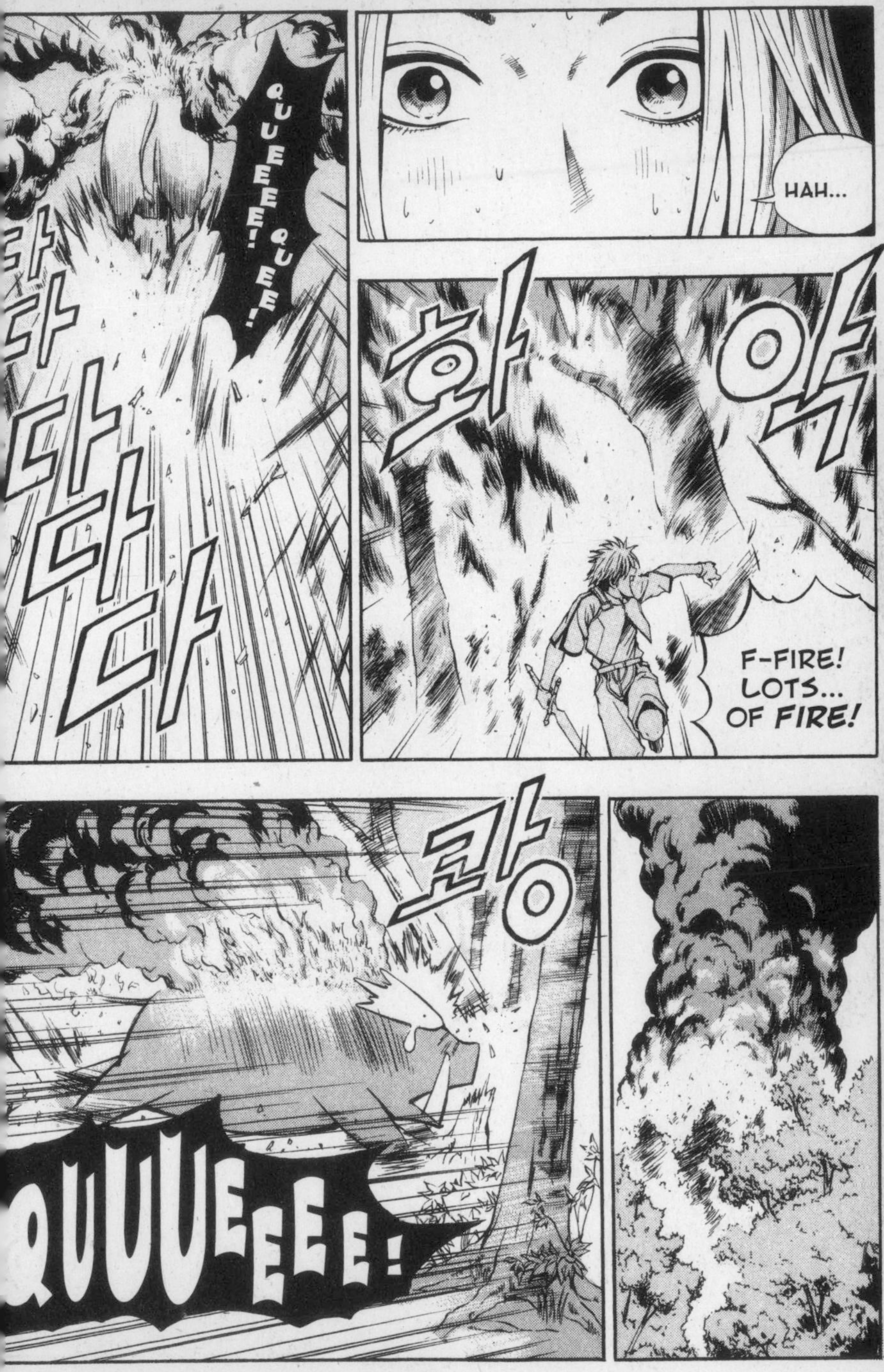
QUEEEE! QUEE!
HAH...
화악
F-FIRE! LOTS... OF FIRE!
콰앙
QUUUEEEE!

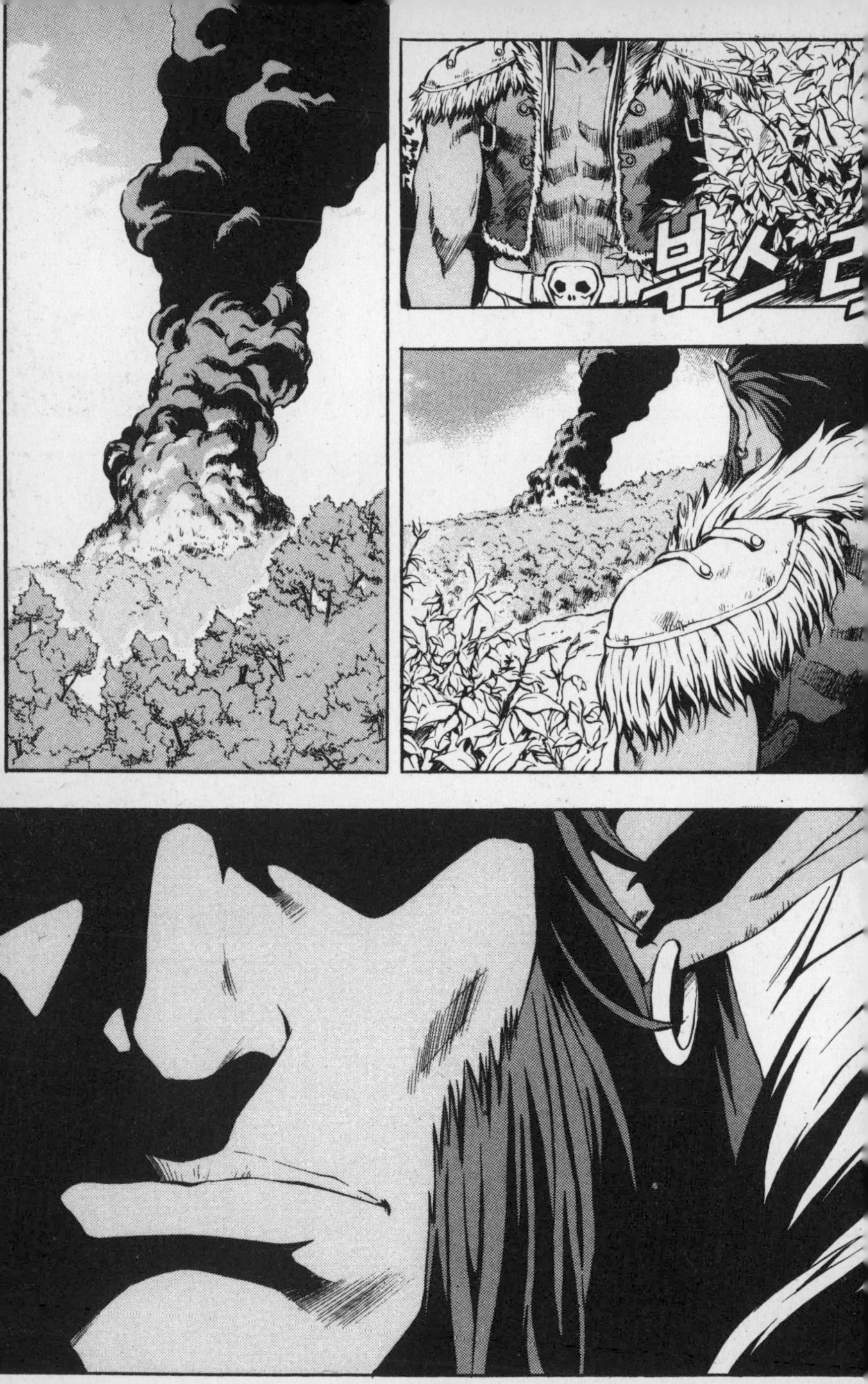
부스

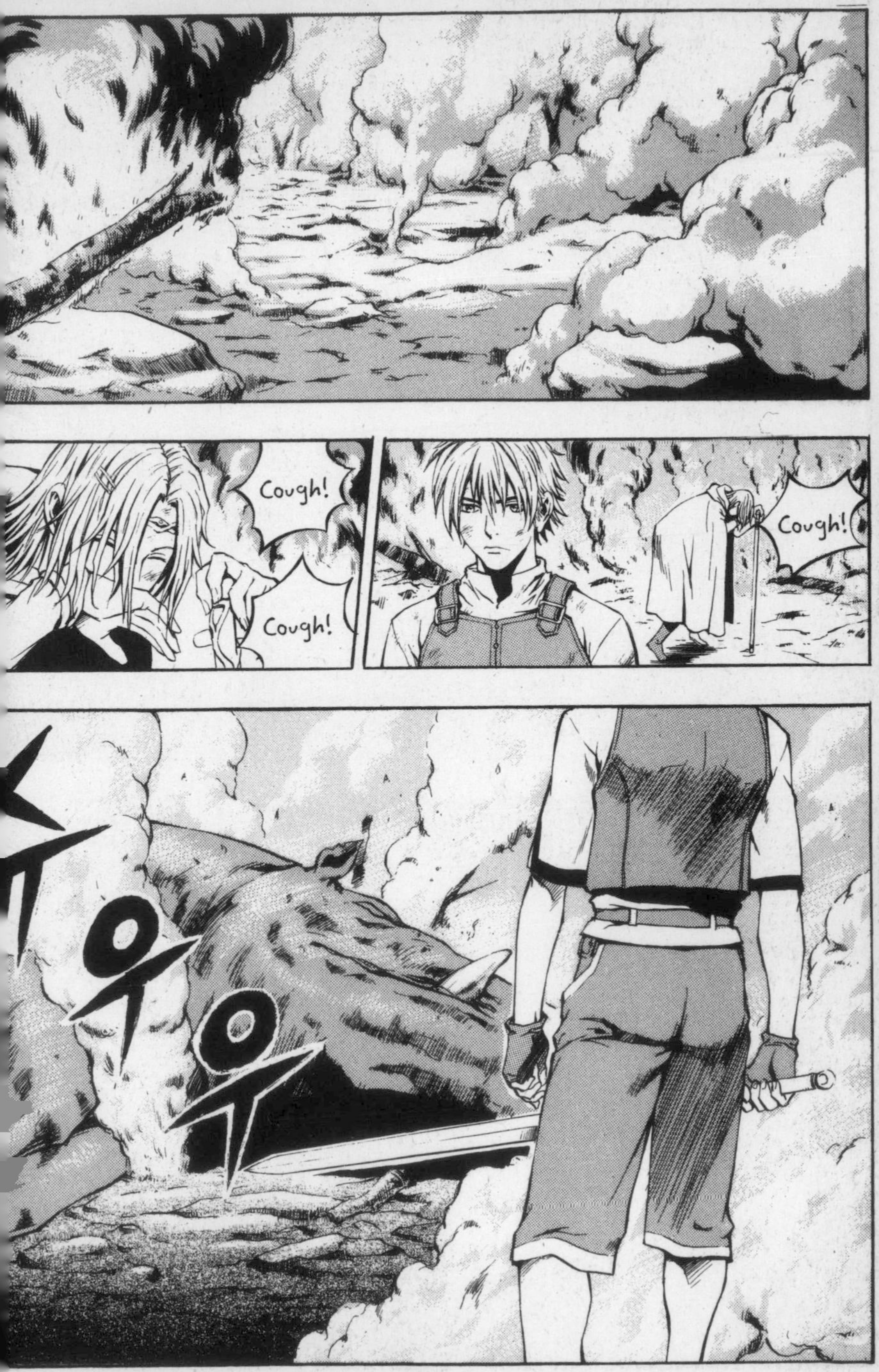
Cough!
Cough!
Cough!

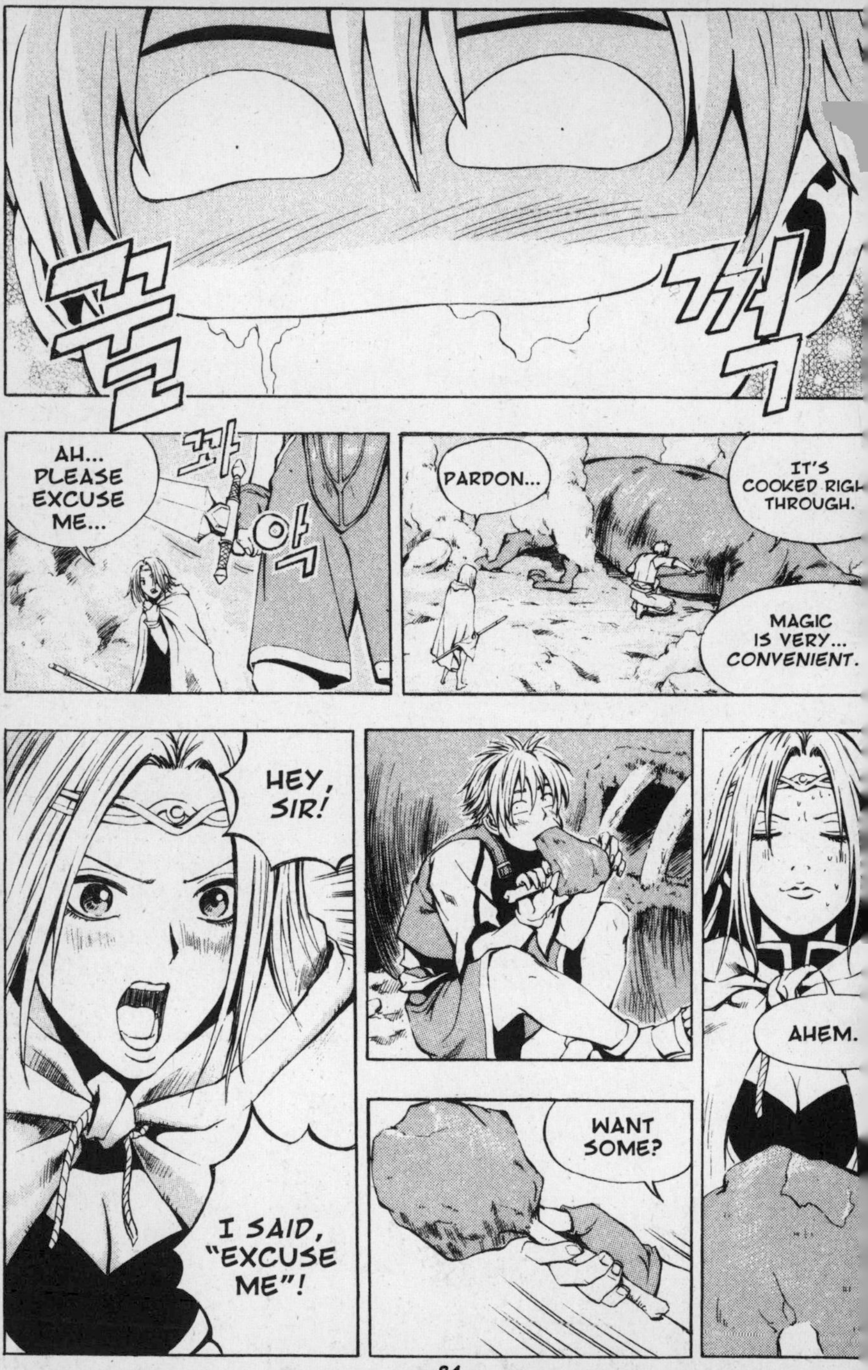
AH... PLEASE EXCUSE ME...
꽈악
PARDON...
IT'S COOKED RIGH THROUGH.
MAGIC IS VERY... CONVENIENT.
HEY, SIR!
I SAID, "EXCUSE ME"!
WANT SOME?
AHEM.

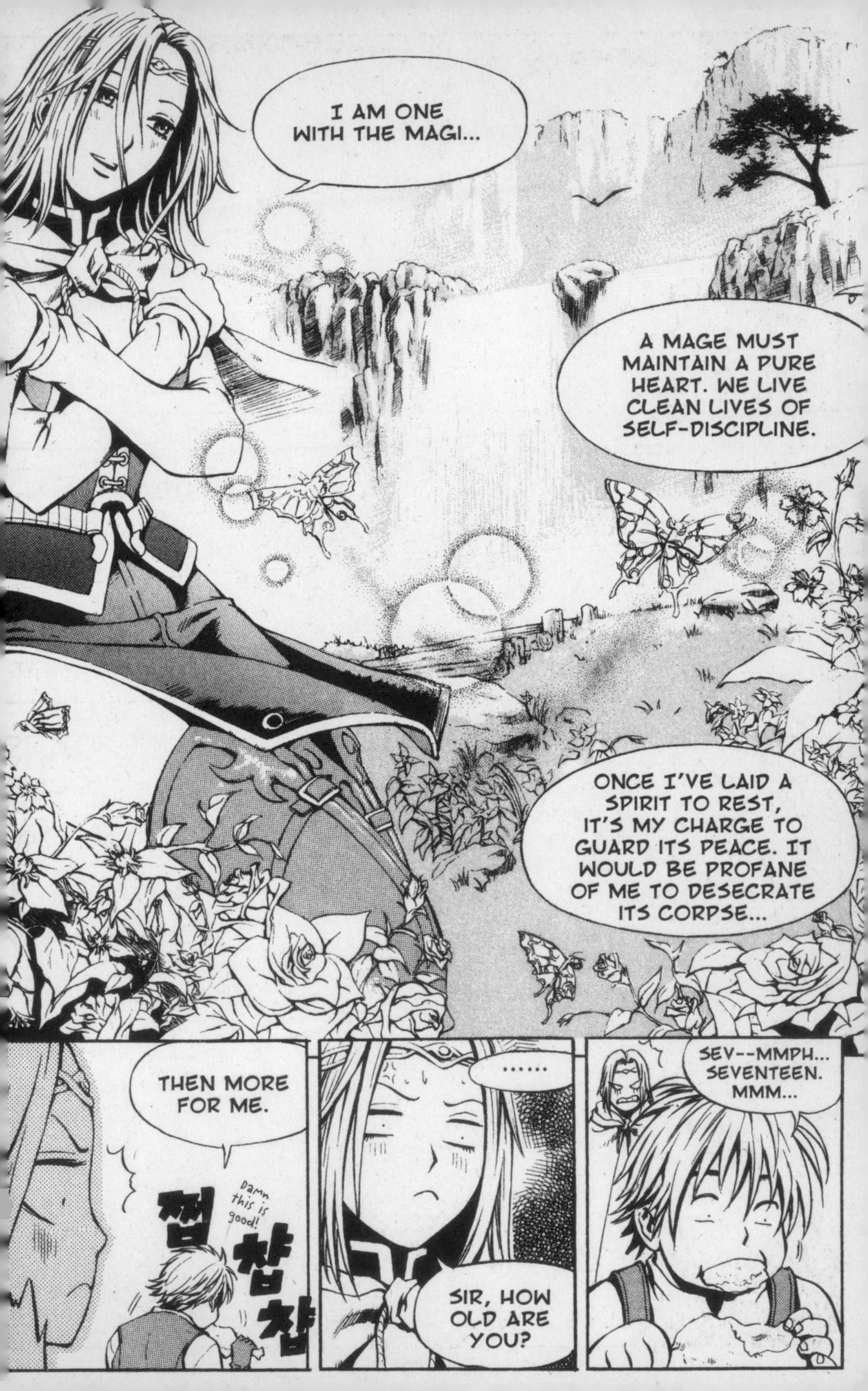
I AM ONE WITH THE MAGI...
A MAGE MUST MAINTAIN A PURE HEART. WE LIVE CLEAN LIVES OF SELF-DISCIPLINE.
ONCE I'VE LAID A SPIRIT TO REST, IT'S MY CHARGE TO GUARD ITS PEACE. IT WOULD BE PROFANE OF ME TO DESECRATE ITS CORPSE...
THEN MORE FOR ME.
Damn this is good!
쩝 찹 찹
......
SIR, HOW OLD ARE YOU?
SEV--MMPH... SEVENTEEN. MMM...

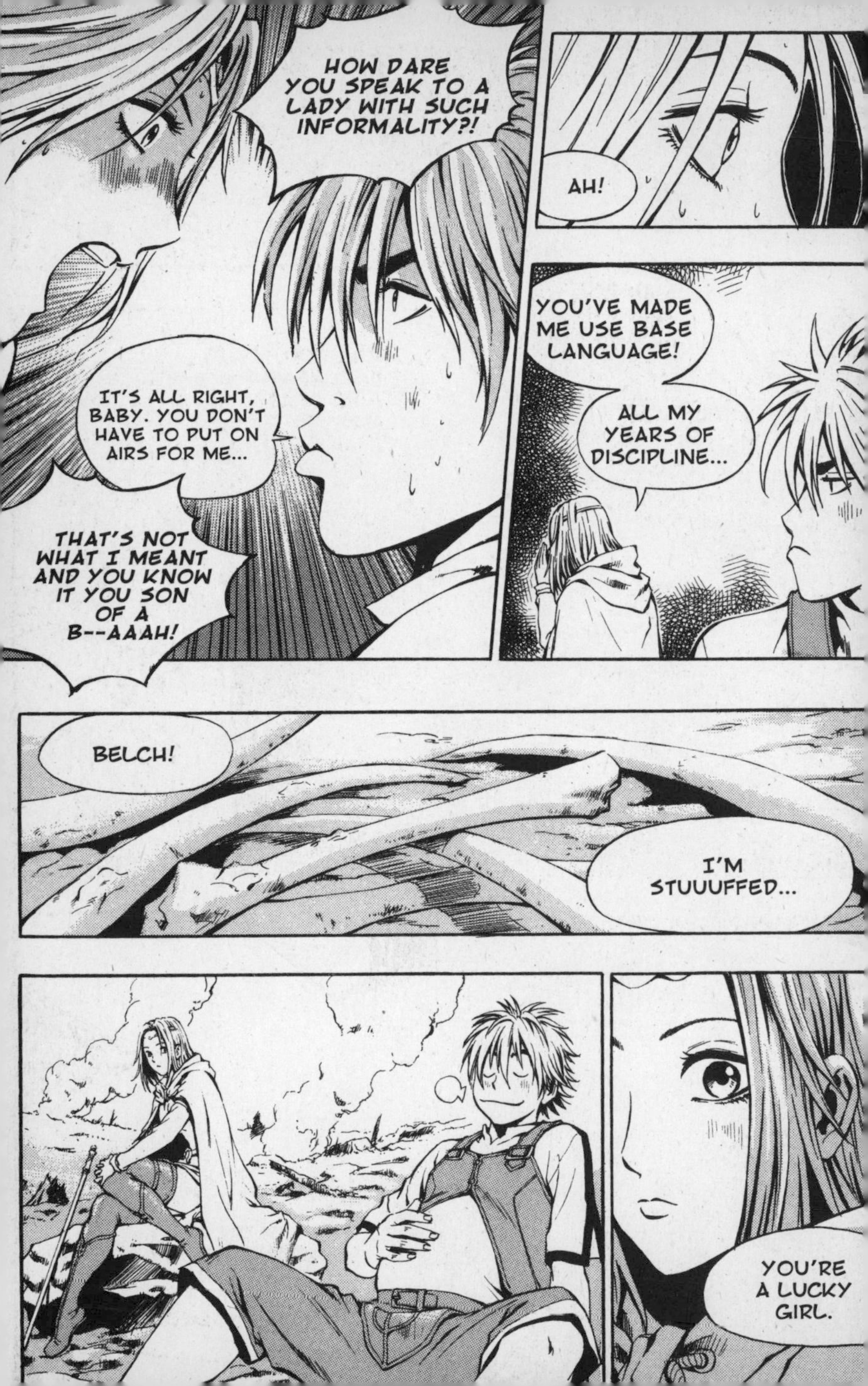
HOW DARE YOU SPEAK TO A LADY WITH SUCH INFORMALITY?!
IT'S ALL RIGHT, BABY. YOU DON'T HAVE TO PUT ON AIRS FOR ME...
THAT'S NOT WHAT I MEANT AND YOU KNOW IT YOU SON OF A B--AAAH!
AH!
YOU'VE MADE ME USE BASE LANGUAGE!
ALL MY YEARS OF DISCIPLINE...
BELCH!
I'M STUUUFFED...
YOU'RE A LUCKY GIRL.

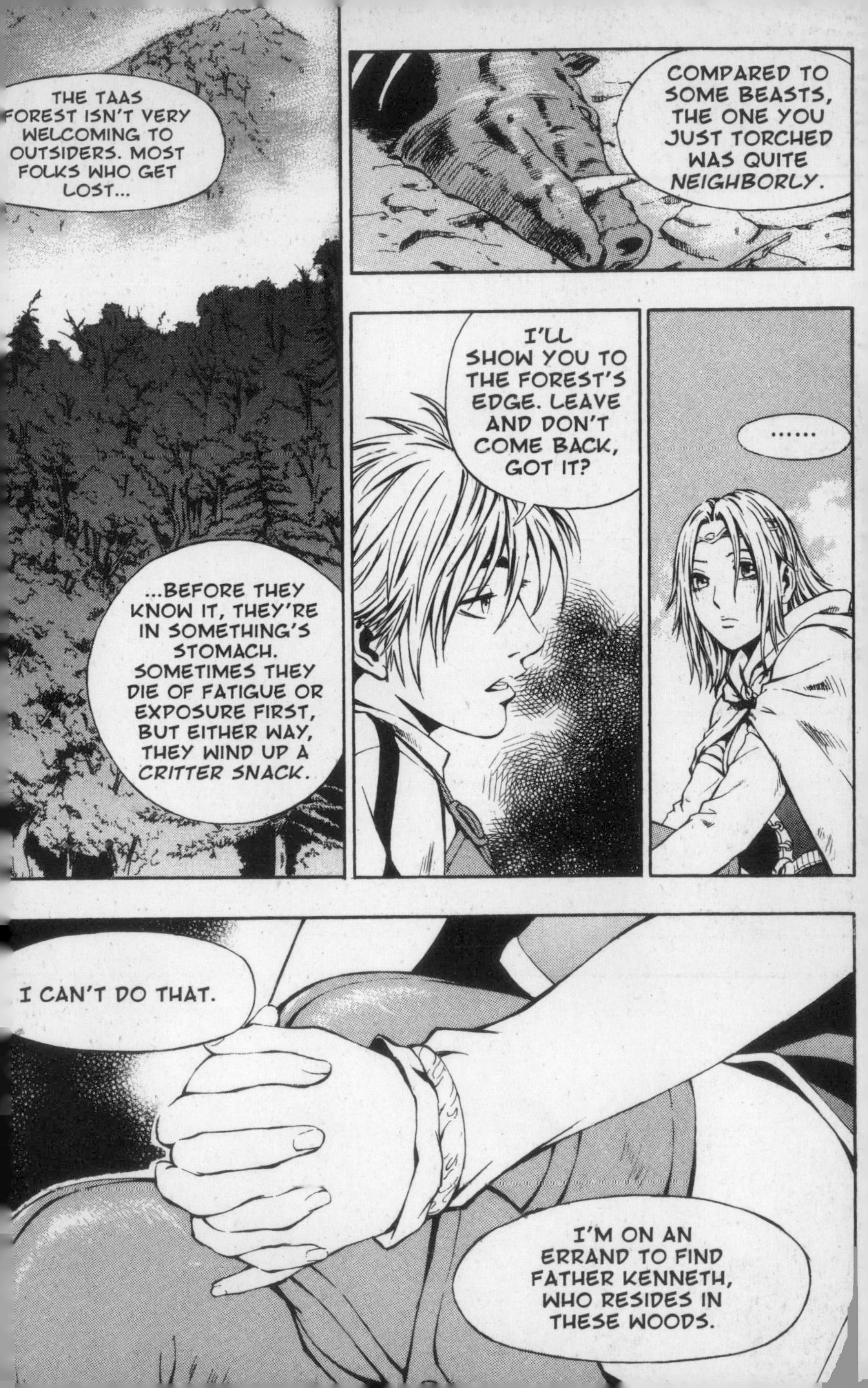
THE TAAS FOREST ISN'T VERY WELCOMING TO OUTSIDERS. MOST FOLKS WHO GET LOST...
...BEFORE THEY KNOW IT, THEY'RE IN SOMETHING'S STOMACH. SOMETIMES THEY DIE OF FATIGUE OR EXPOSURE FIRST, BUT EITHER WAY, THEY WIND UP A *CRITTER SNACK*.
COMPARED TO SOME BEASTS, THE ONE YOU JUST TORCHED WAS QUITE *NEIGHBORLY*.
I'LL SHOW YOU TO THE FOREST'S EDGE. LEAVE AND DON'T COME BACK, GOT IT?
......
I CAN'T DO THAT.
I'M ON AN ERRAND TO FIND FATHER KENNETH, WHO RESIDES IN THESE WOODS.

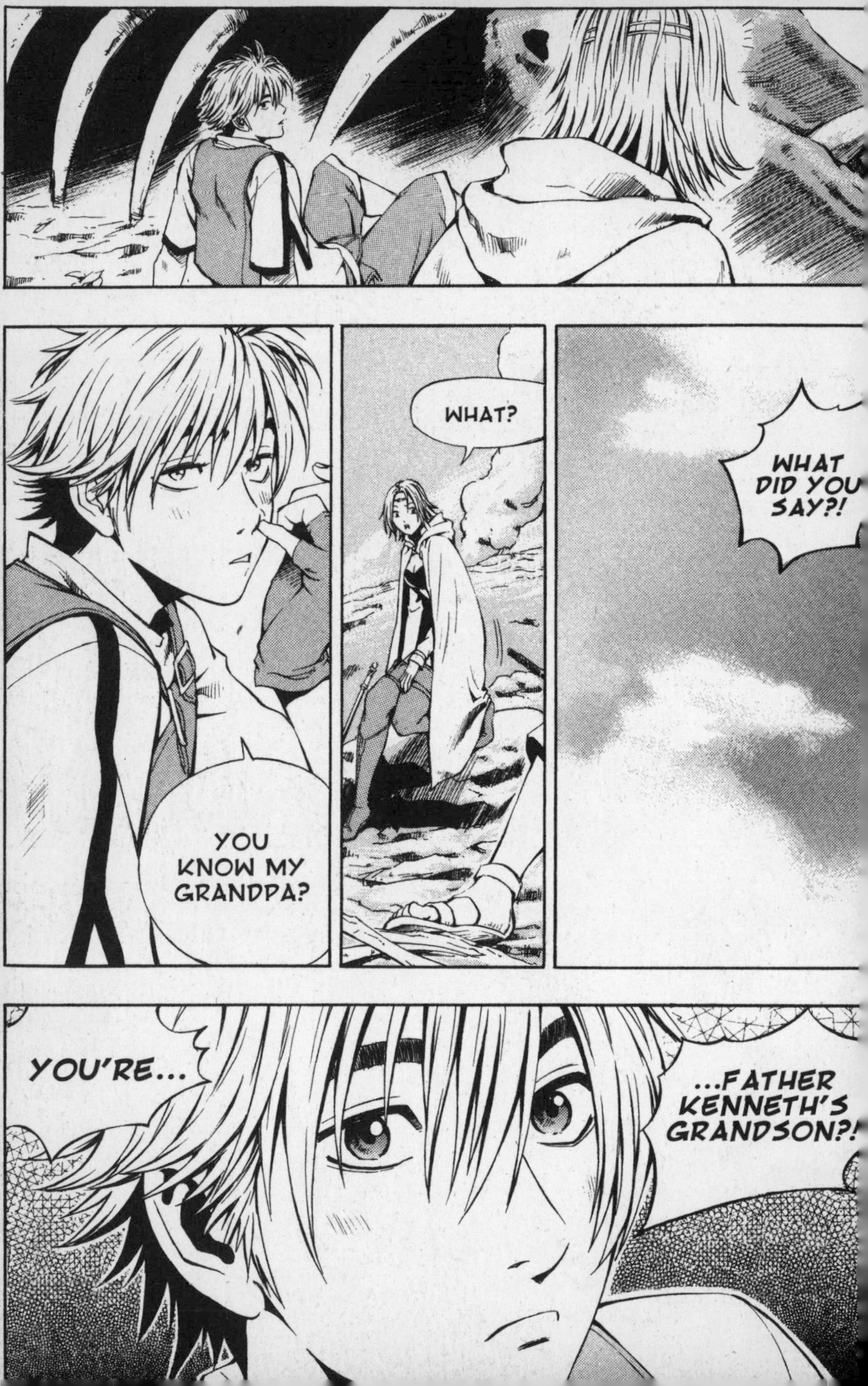
YOU KNOW MY GRANDPA?
WHAT?
WHAT DID YOU SAY?!
YOU'RE...
...FATHER KENNETH'S GRANDSON?!

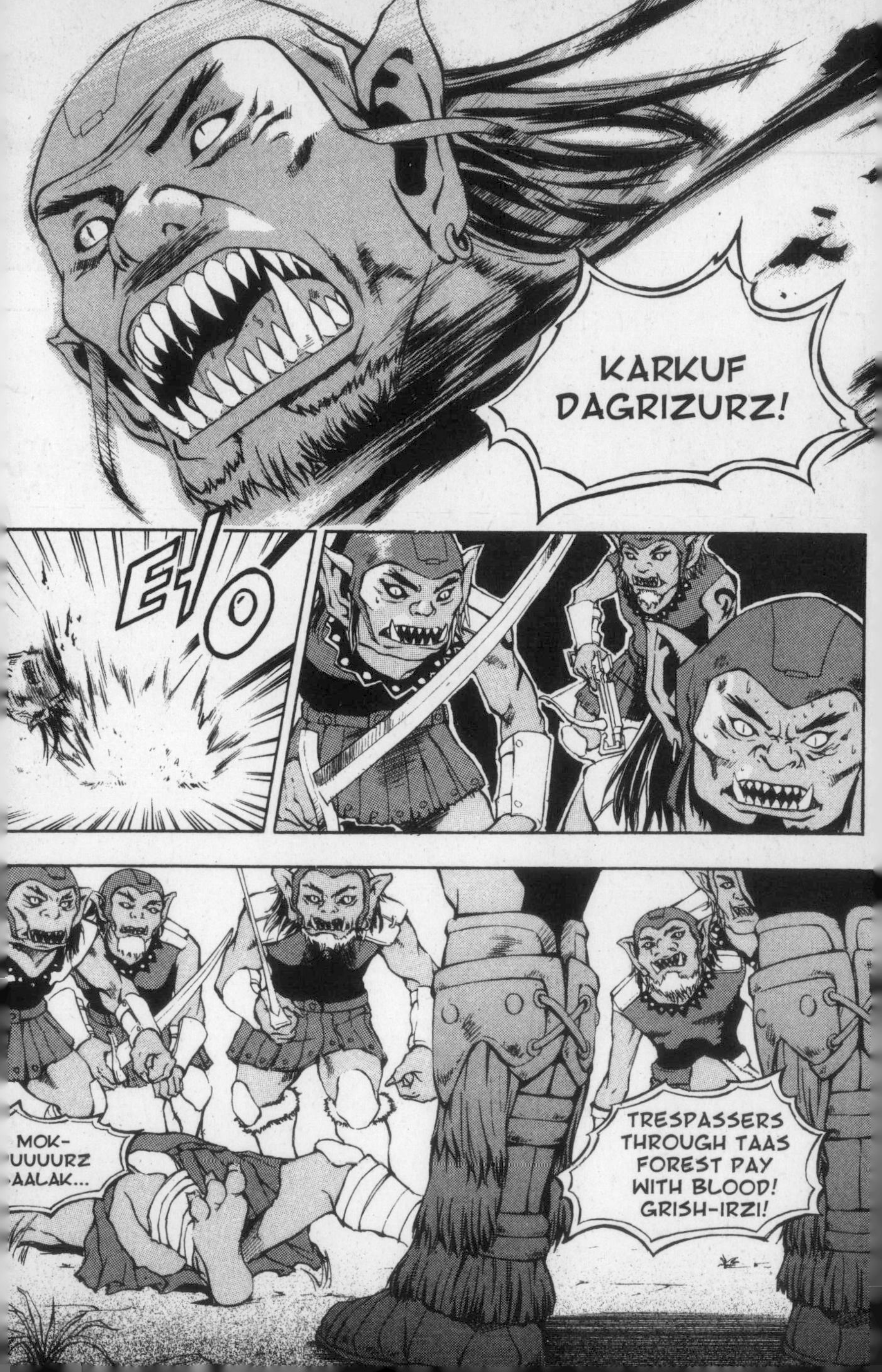
KARKUF DAGRIZURZ!
MOK-UUUURZ AALAK...
TRESPASSERS THROUGH TAAS FOREST PAY WITH BLOOD! GRISH-IRZI!

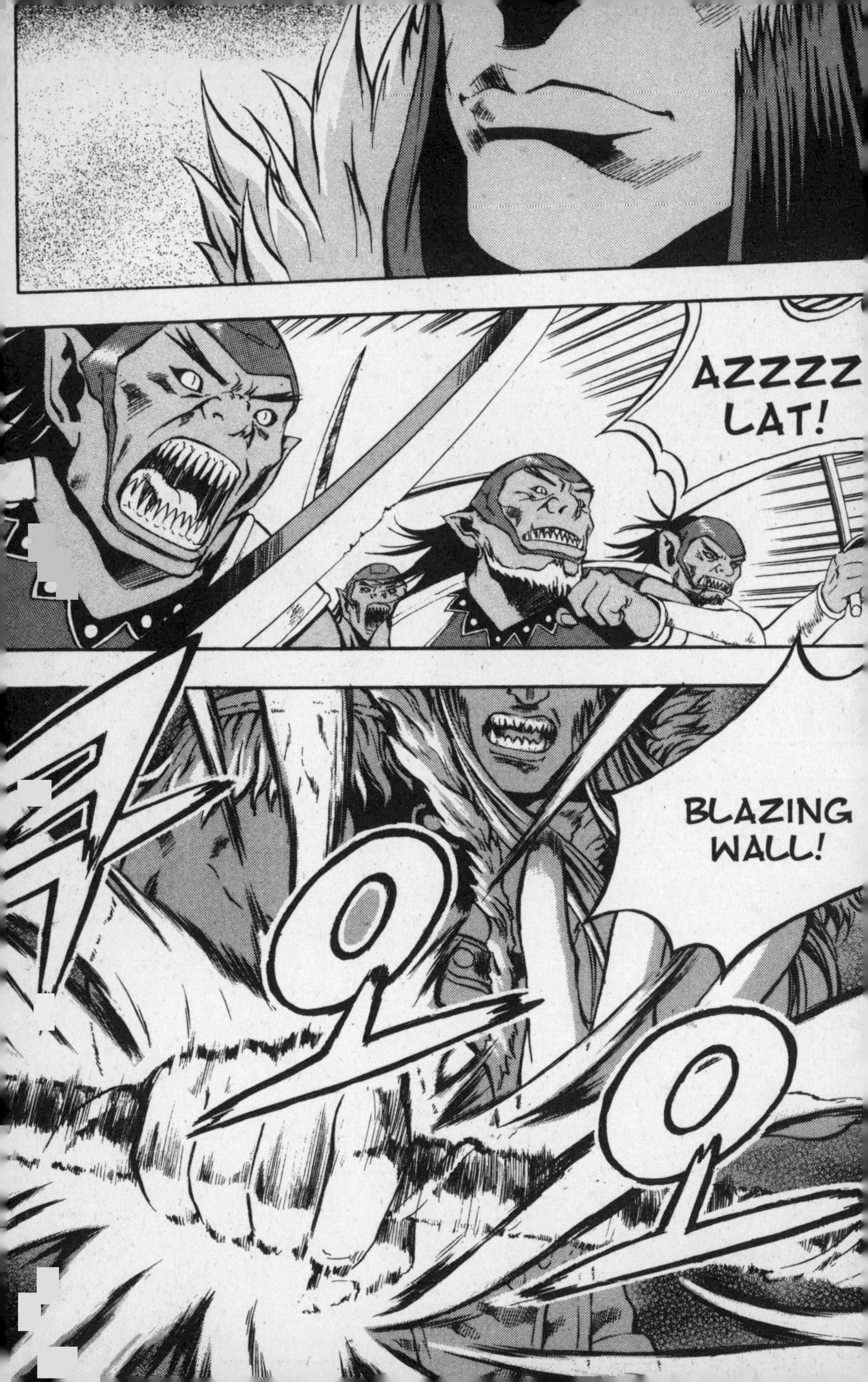
AZZZZ LAT!
BLAZING WALL!

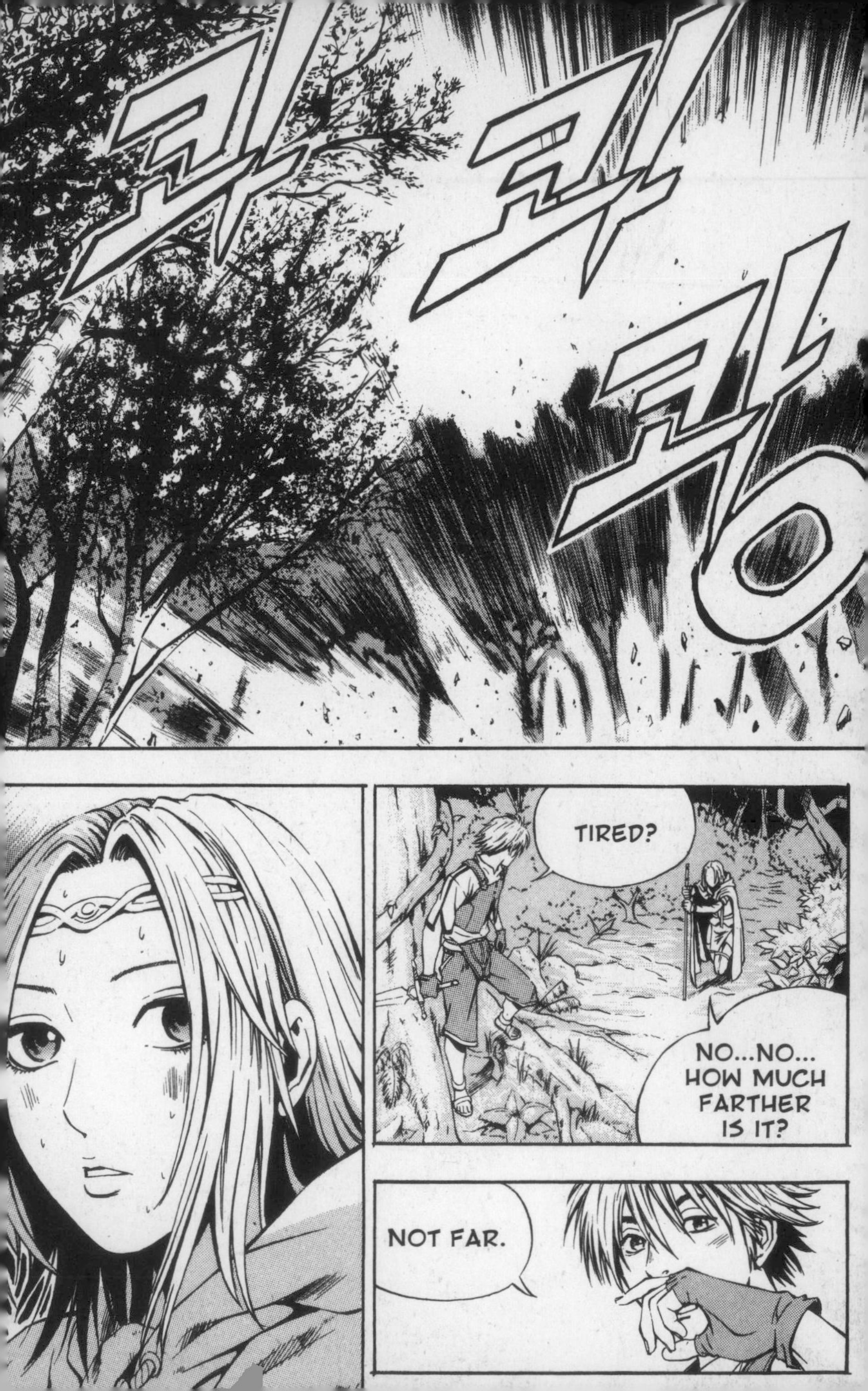
TIRED?
NO...NO... HOW MUCH FARTHER IS IT?
NOT FAR.

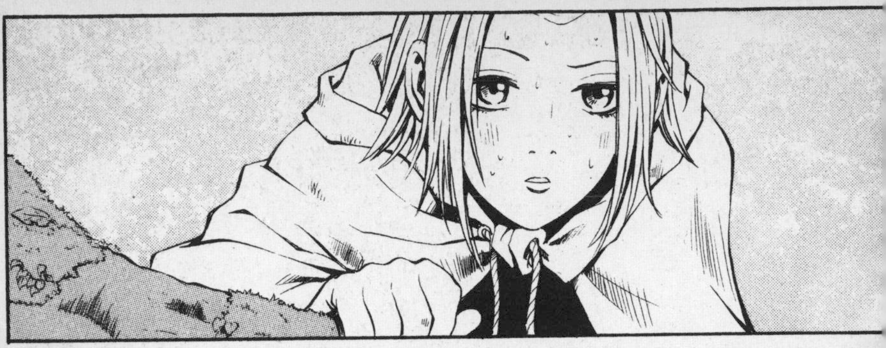

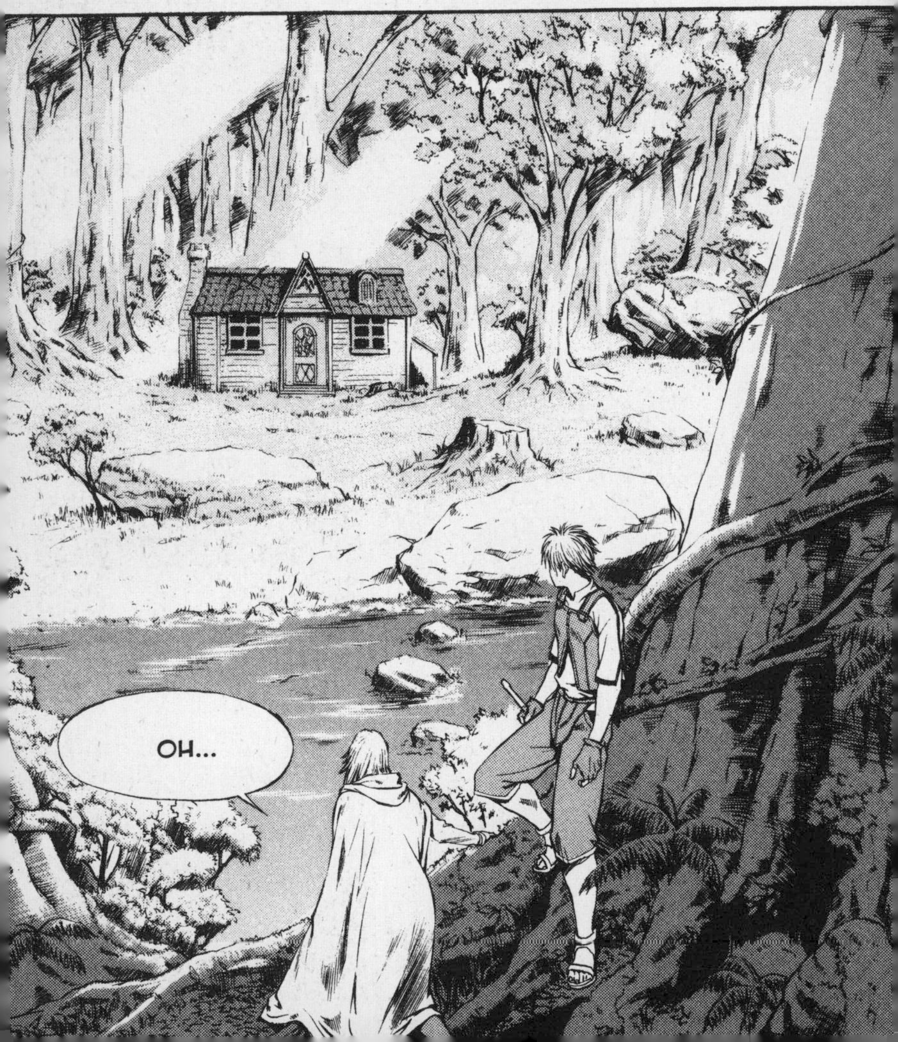
OH...

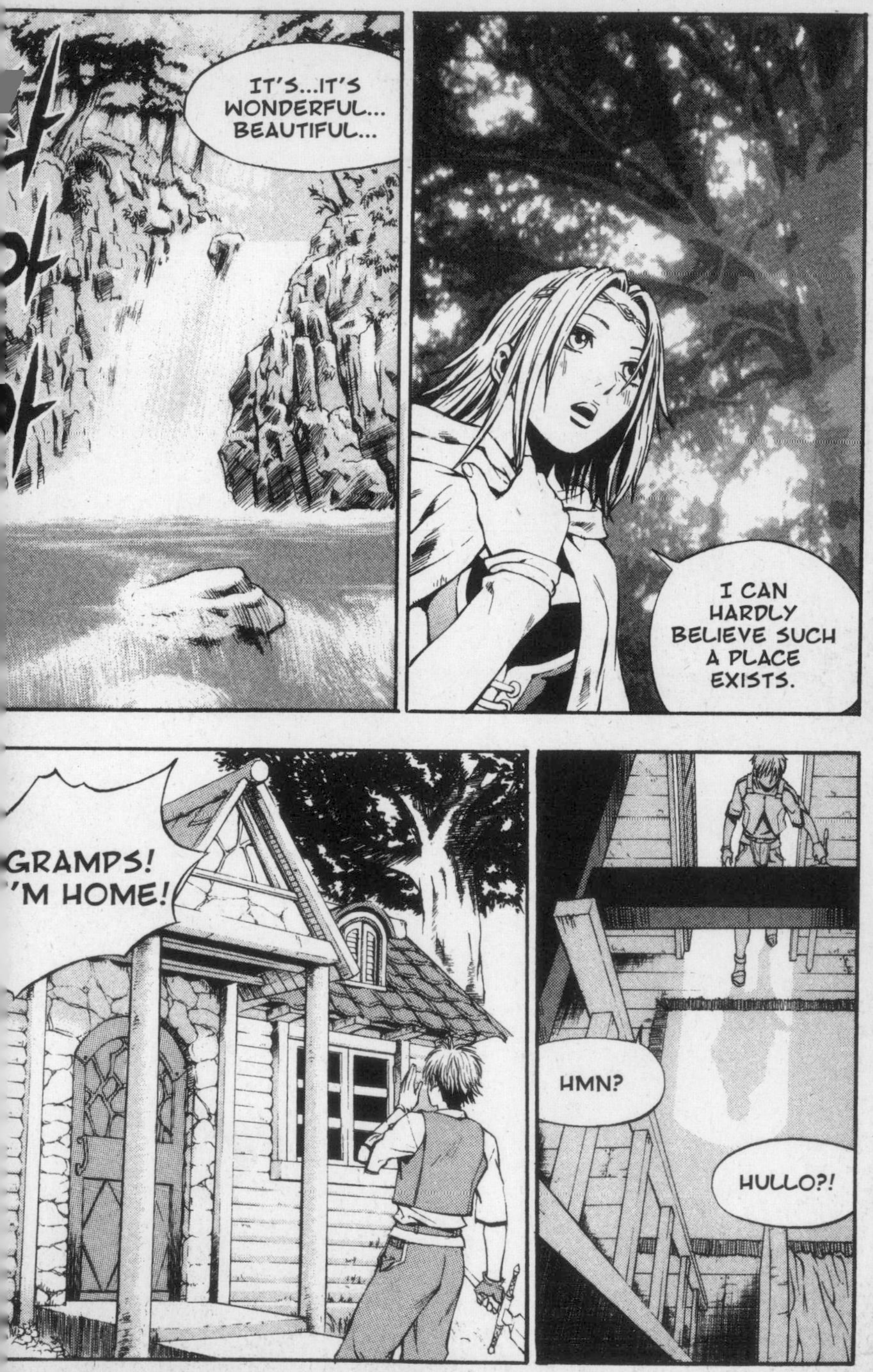
IT'S...IT'S WONDERFUL... BEAUTIFUL...
I CAN HARDLY BELIEVE SUCH A PLACE EXISTS.
GRAMPS! 'M HOME!
HMN?
HULLO?!

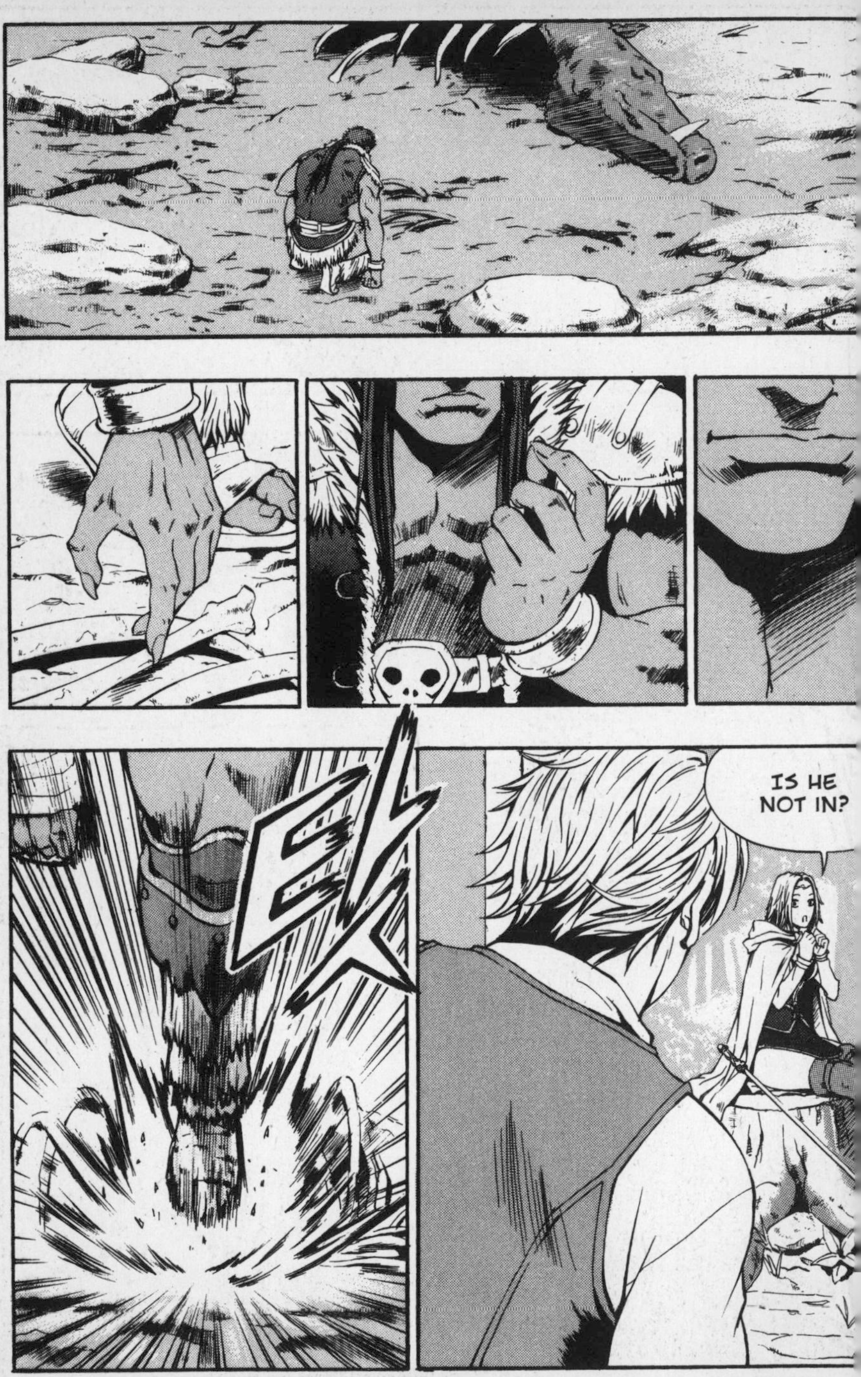
IS HE
NOT IN?

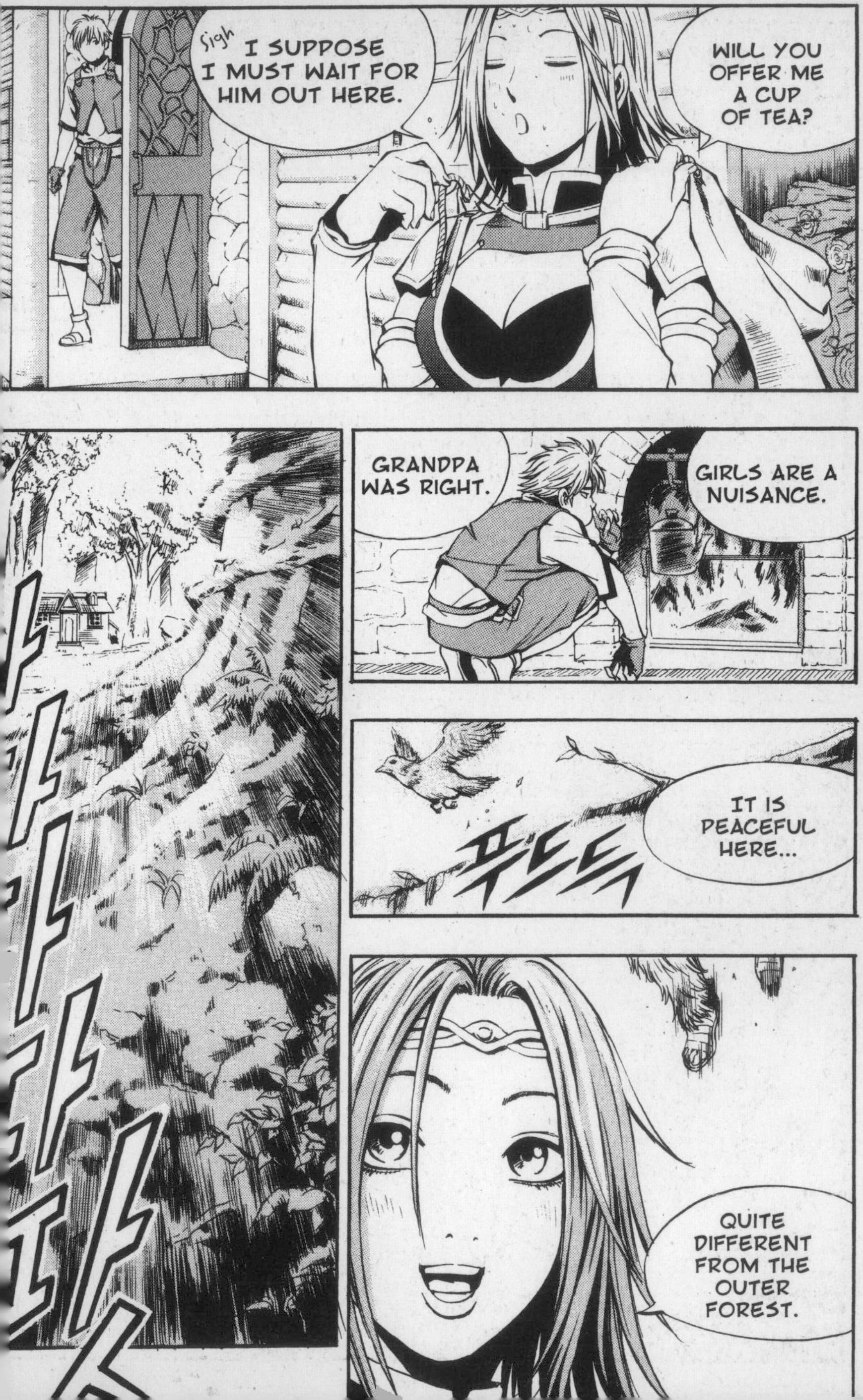
Sigh
I SUPPOSE I MUST WAIT FOR HIM OUT HERE.
WILL YOU OFFER ME A CUP OF TEA?
GRANDPA WAS RIGHT.
GIRLS ARE A NUISANCE.
IT IS PEACEFUL HERE...
QUITE DIFFERENT FROM THE OUTER FOREST.

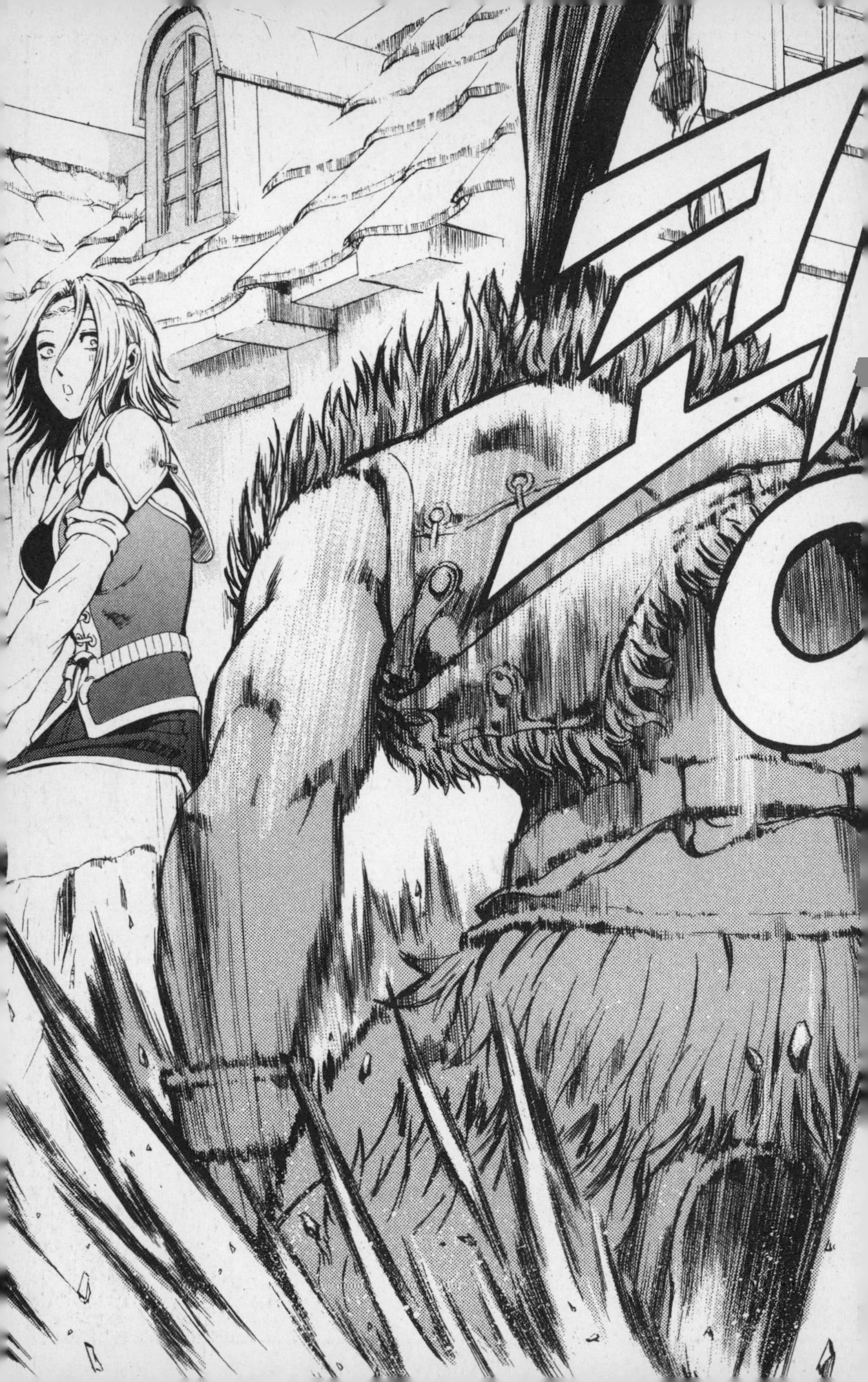

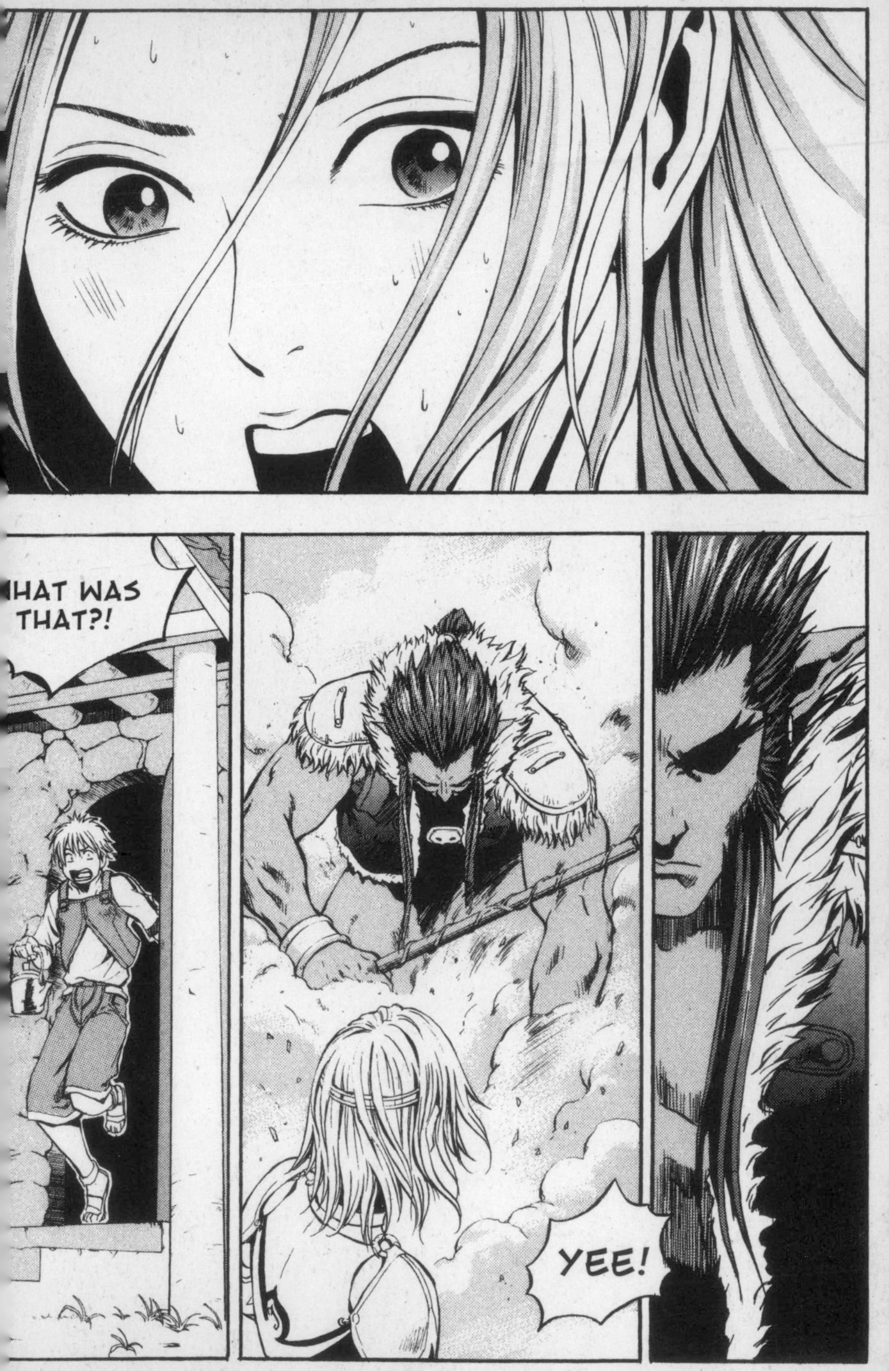

HAT WAS THAT?!
YEE!

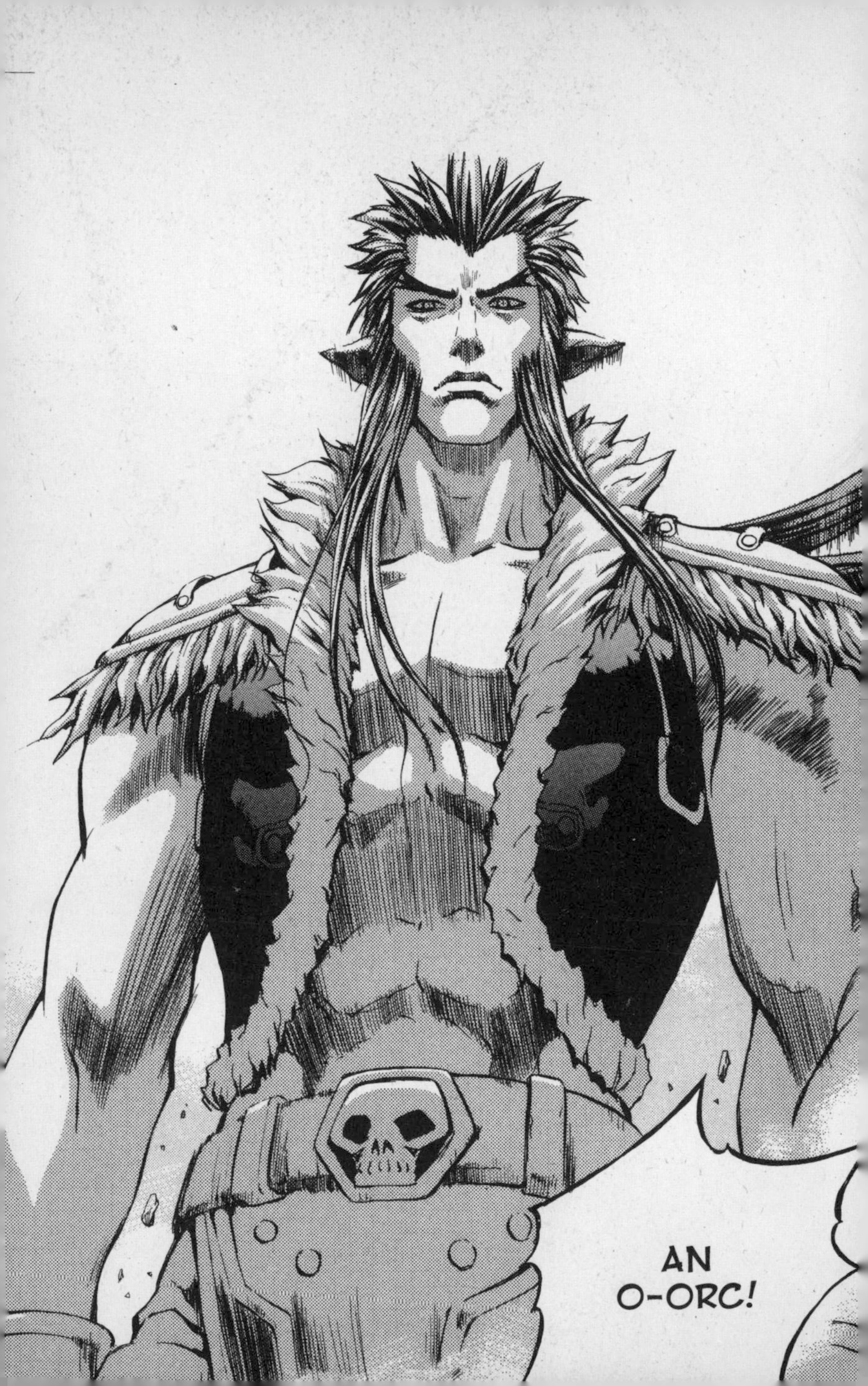
AN O-ORC!

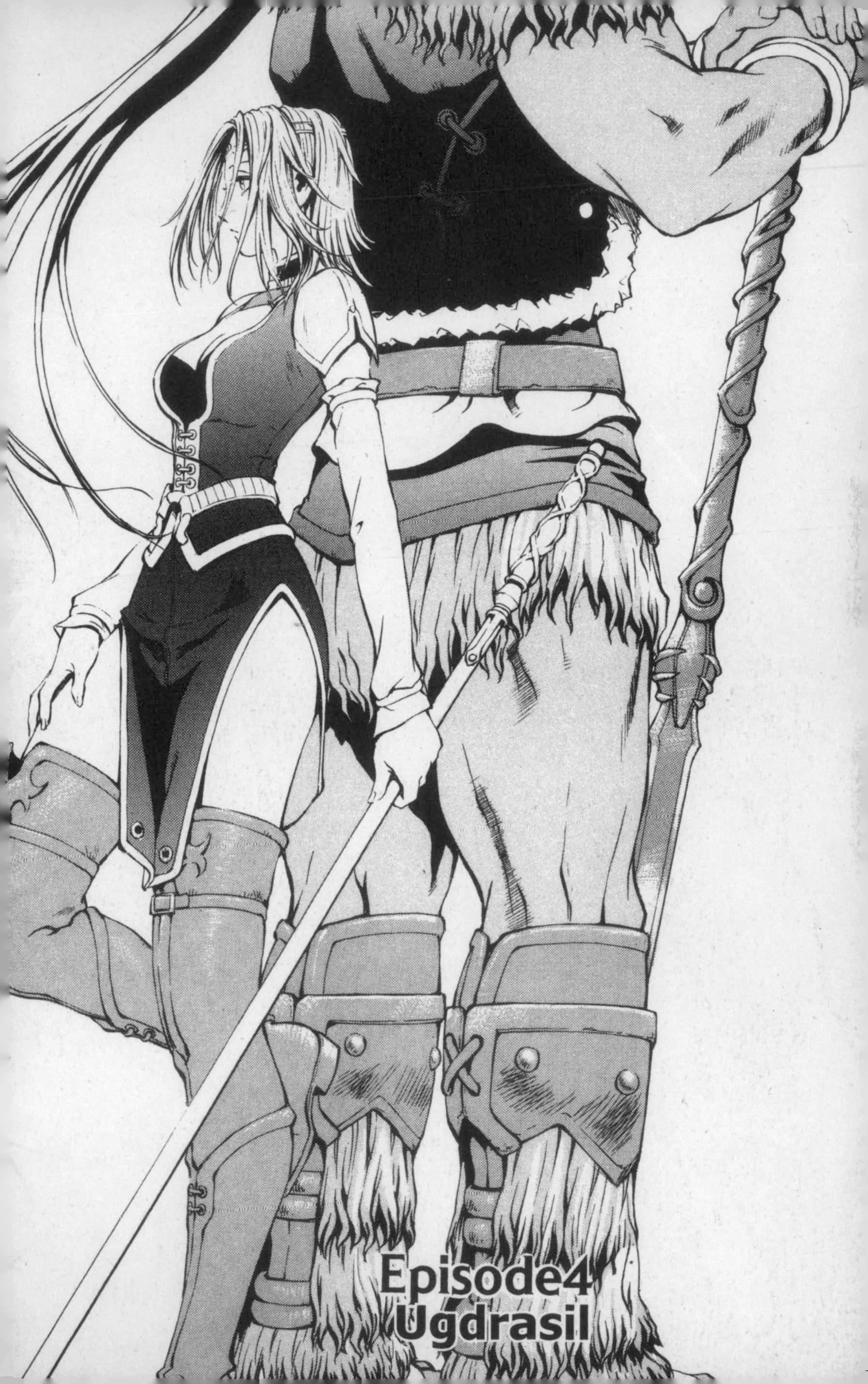
Episode4
Ugdrasil

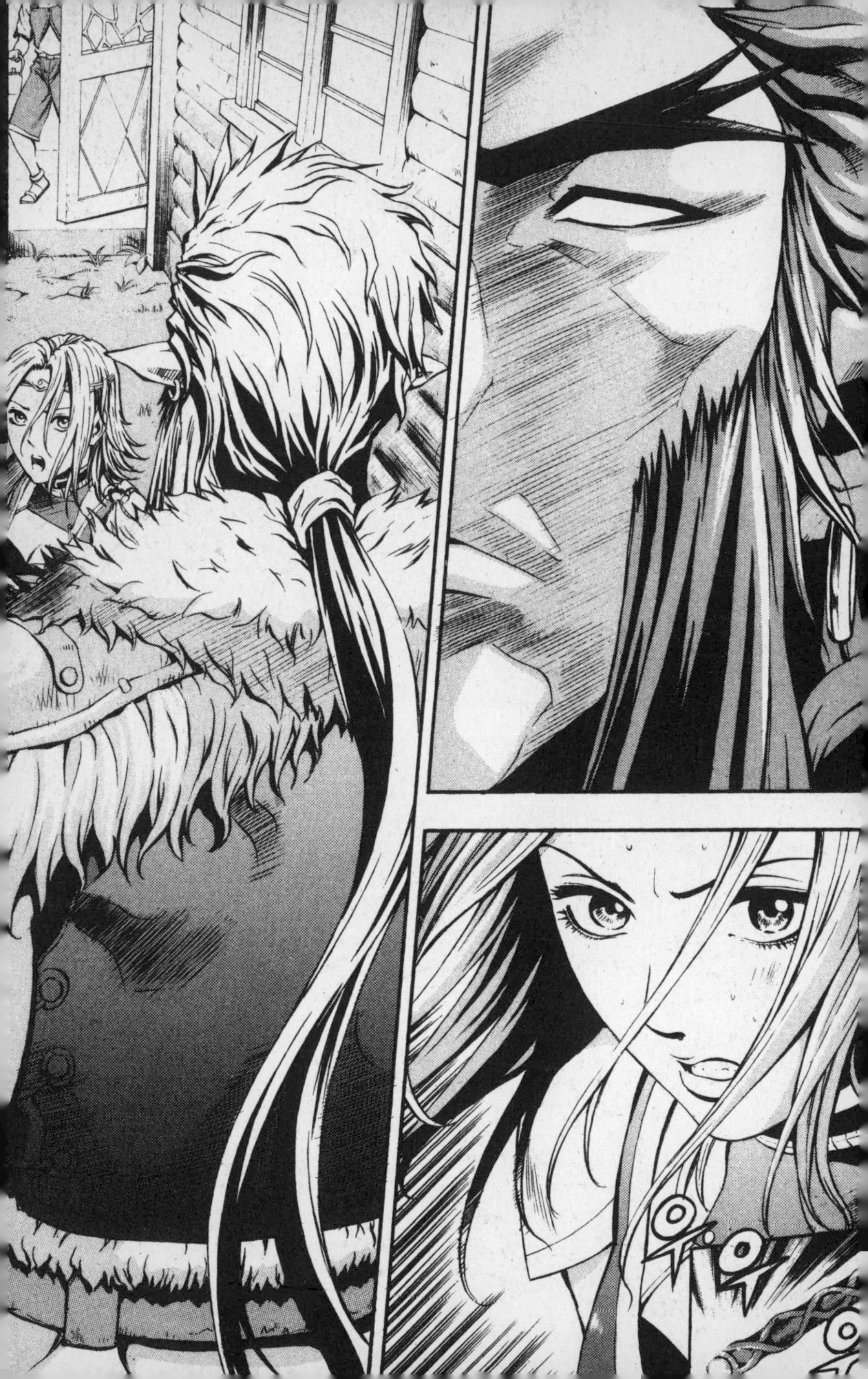

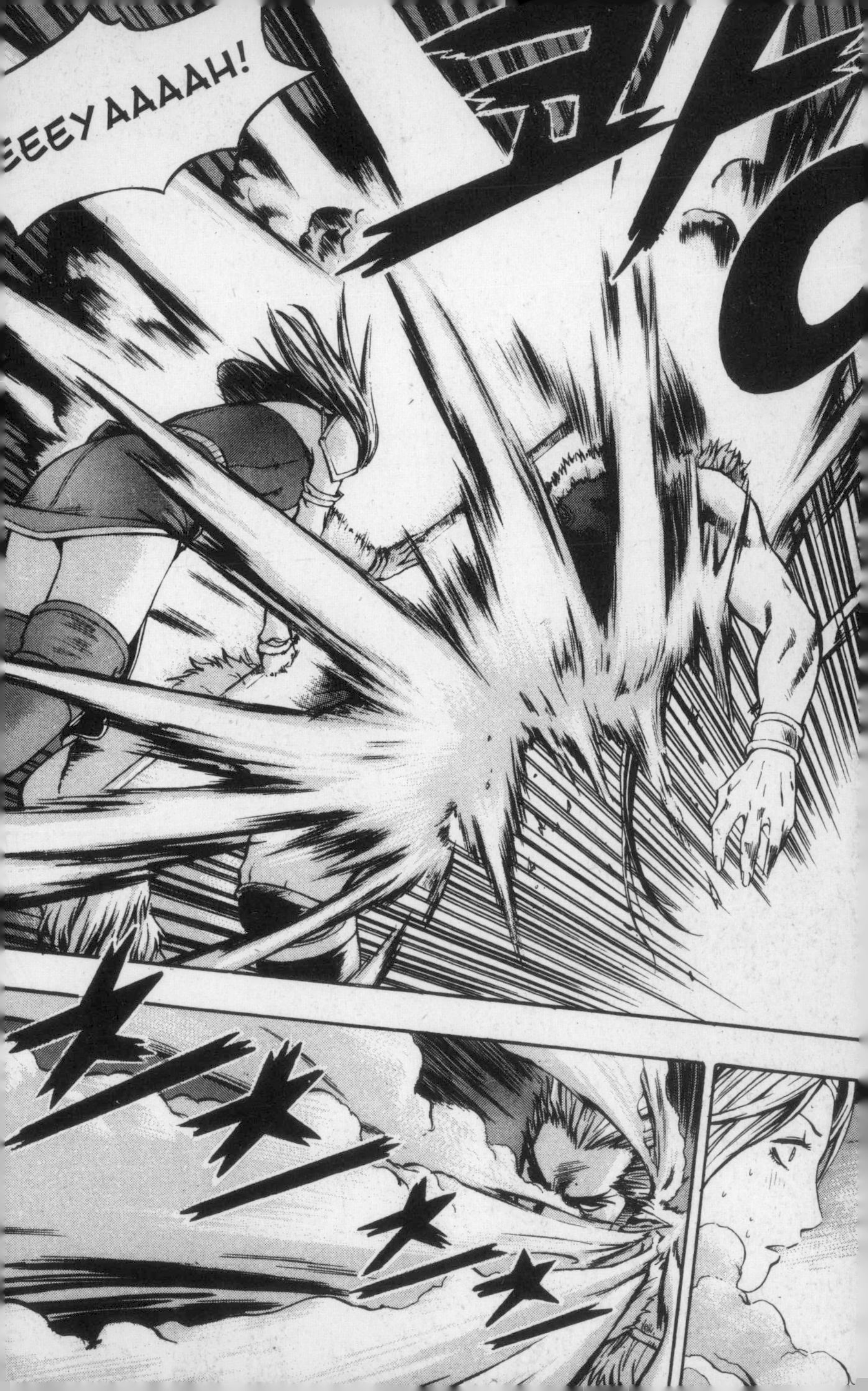
EEEYAAAAH!

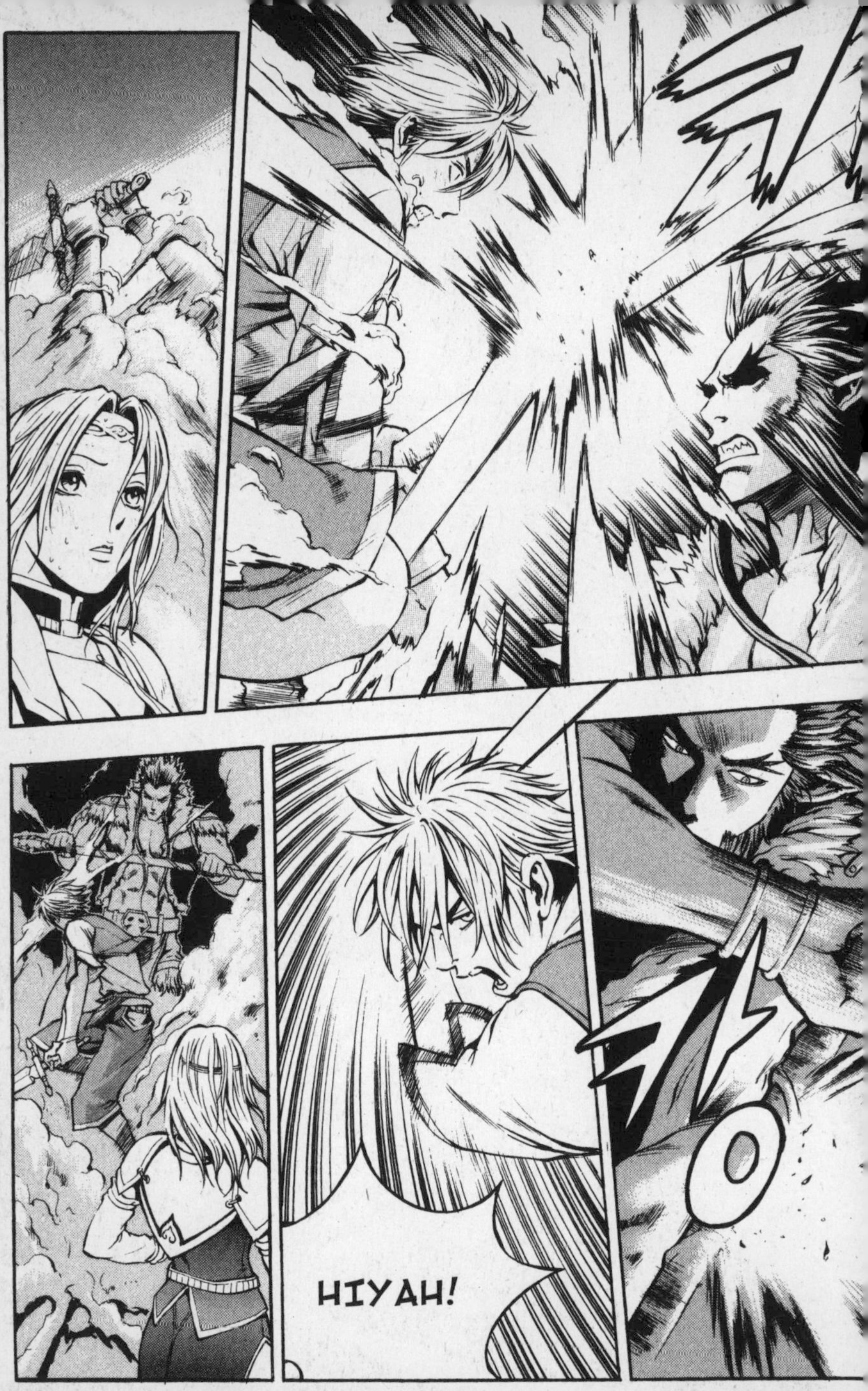
HIYAH!

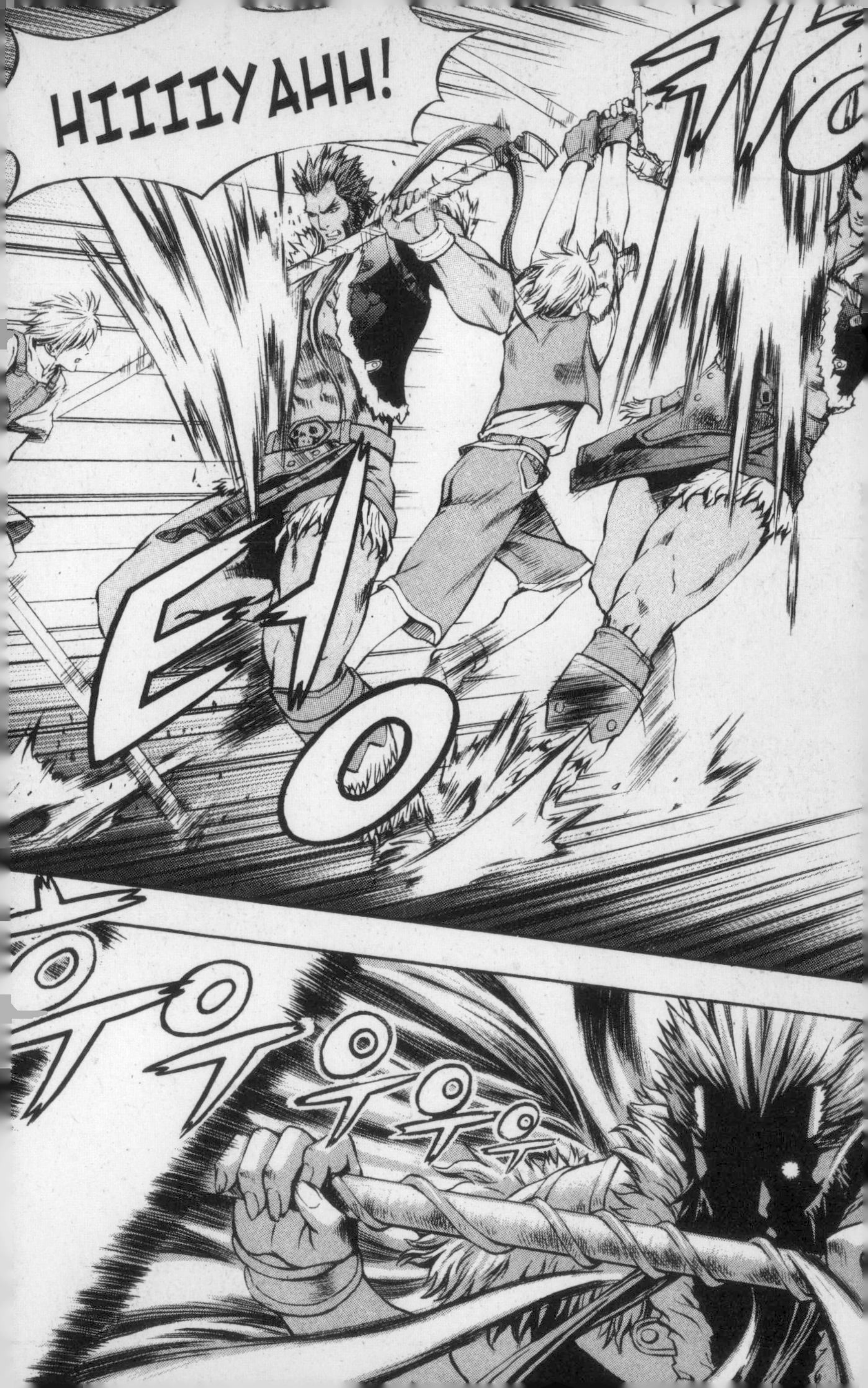
HIIIIYAHH!

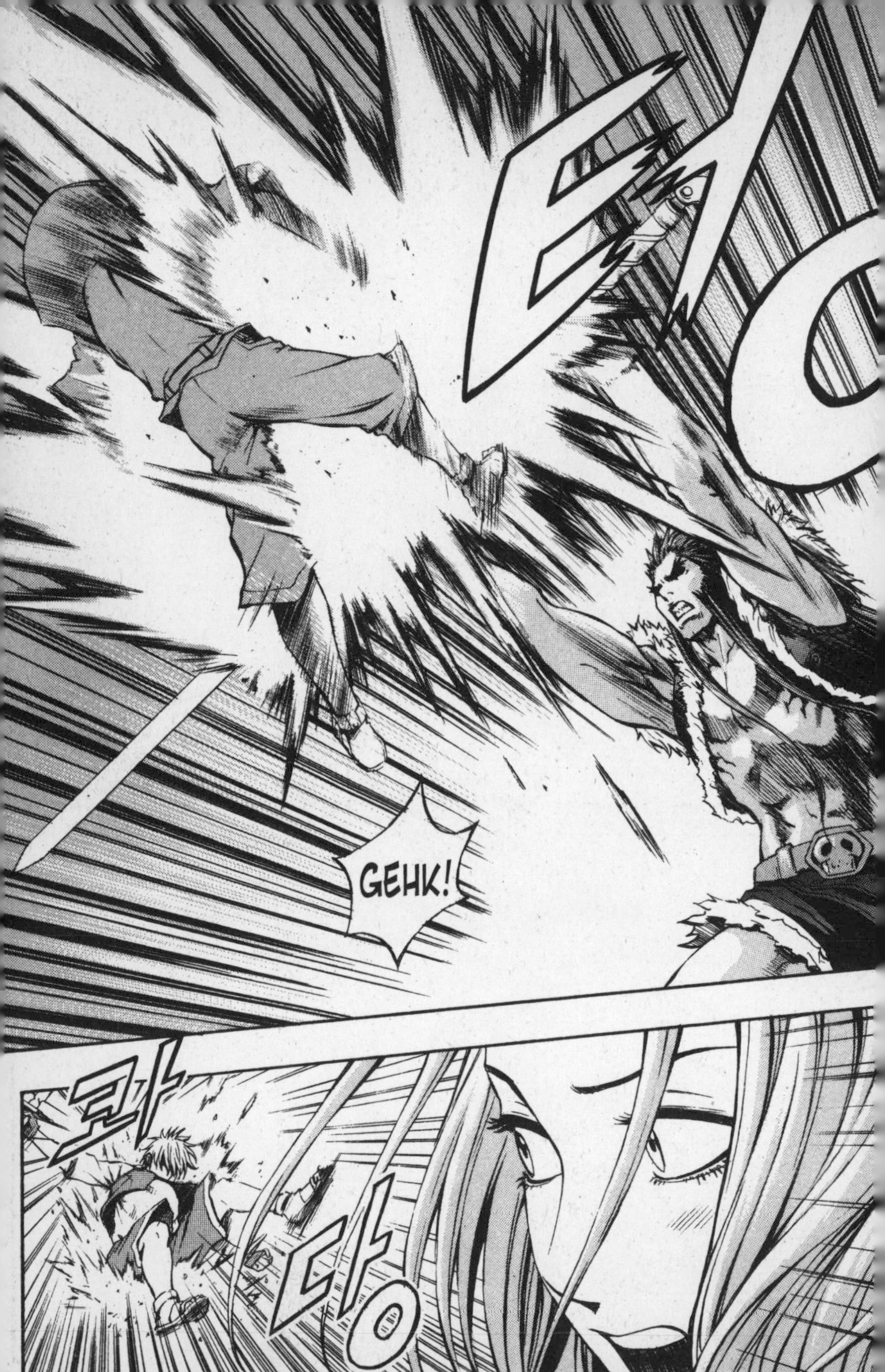
GEHK!

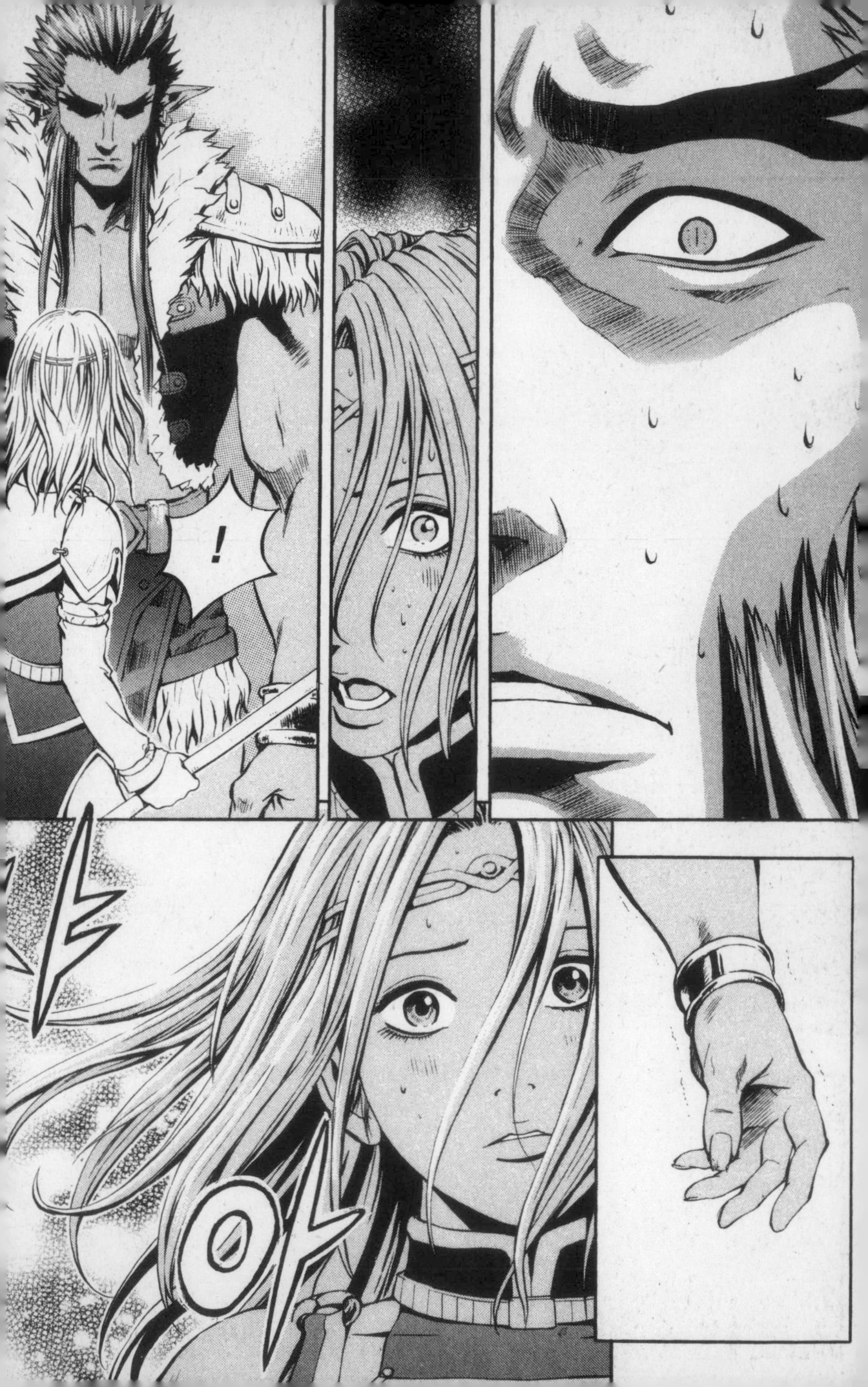
!

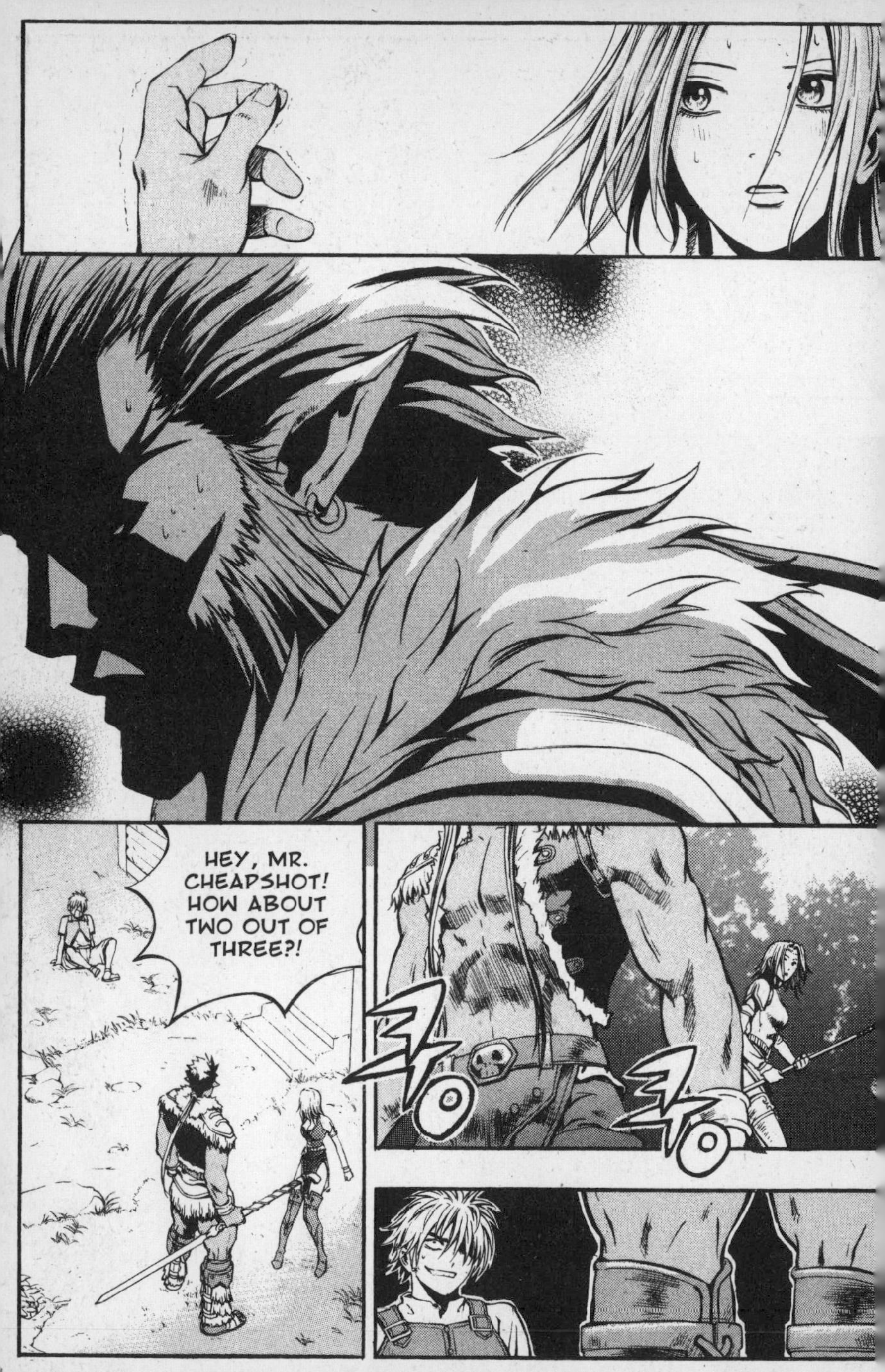
HEY, MR. CHEAPSHOT! HOW ABOUT TWO OUT OF THREE?!

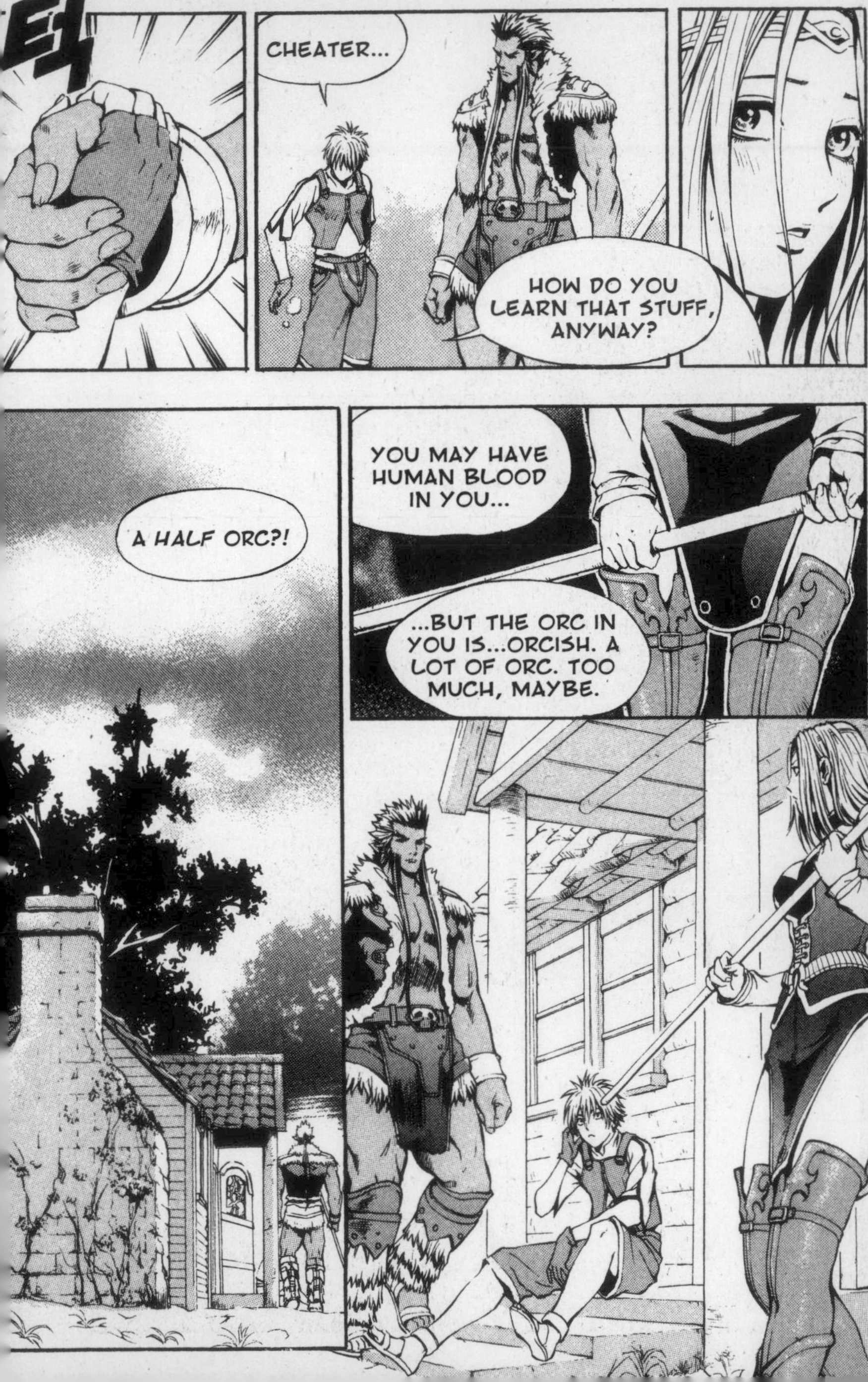
CHEATER...
HOW DO YOU LEARN THAT STUFF, ANYWAY?
A HALF ORC?!
YOU MAY HAVE HUMAN BLOOD IN YOU...
...BUT THE ORC IN YOU IS...ORCISH. A LOT OF ORC. TOO MUCH, MAYBE.

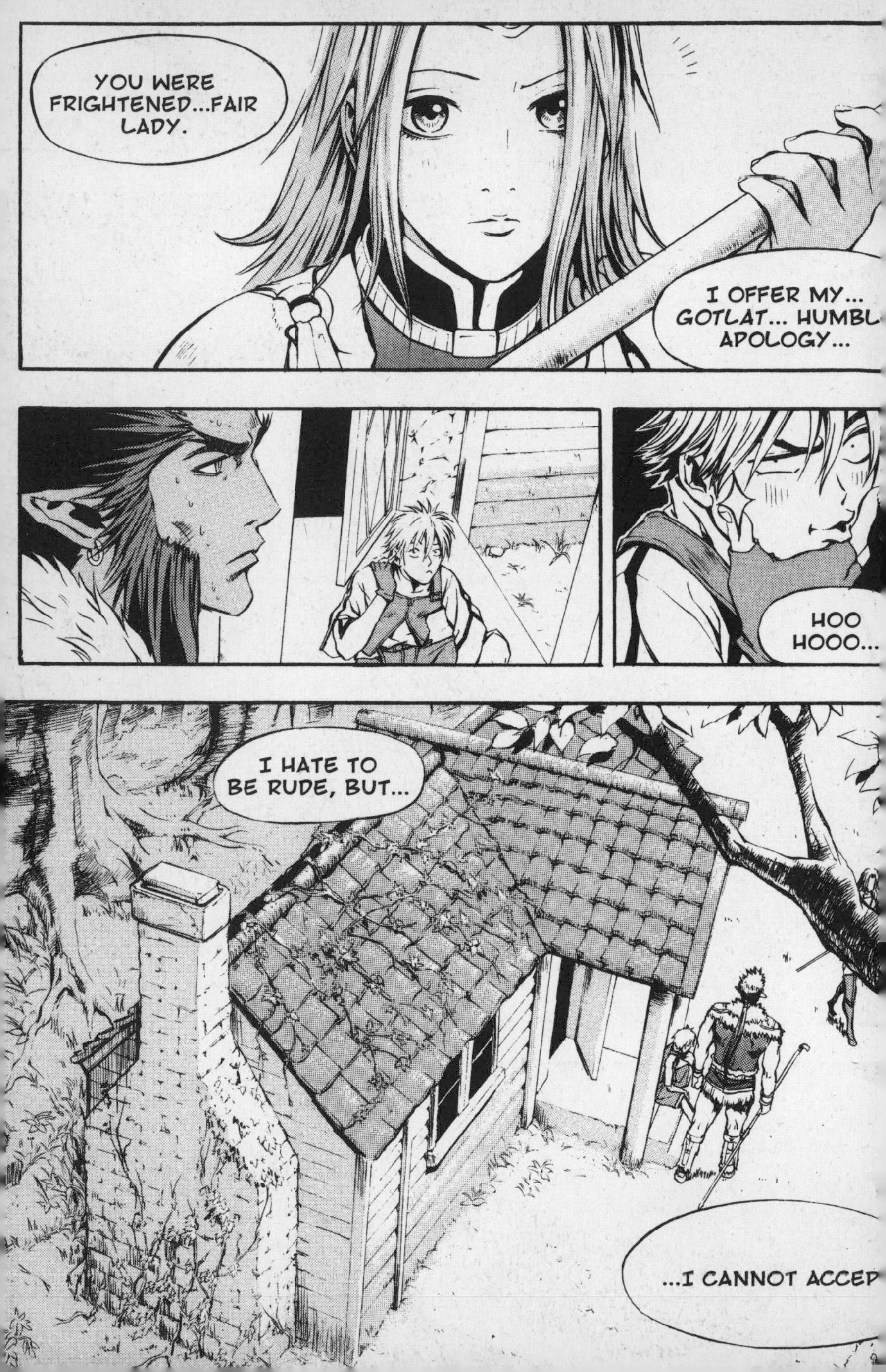
YOU WERE FRIGHTENED...FAIR LADY.
I OFFER MY... GOTLAT... HUMBL APOLOGY...
HOO HOOO...
I HATE TO BE RUDE, BUT...
...I CANNOT ACCEP

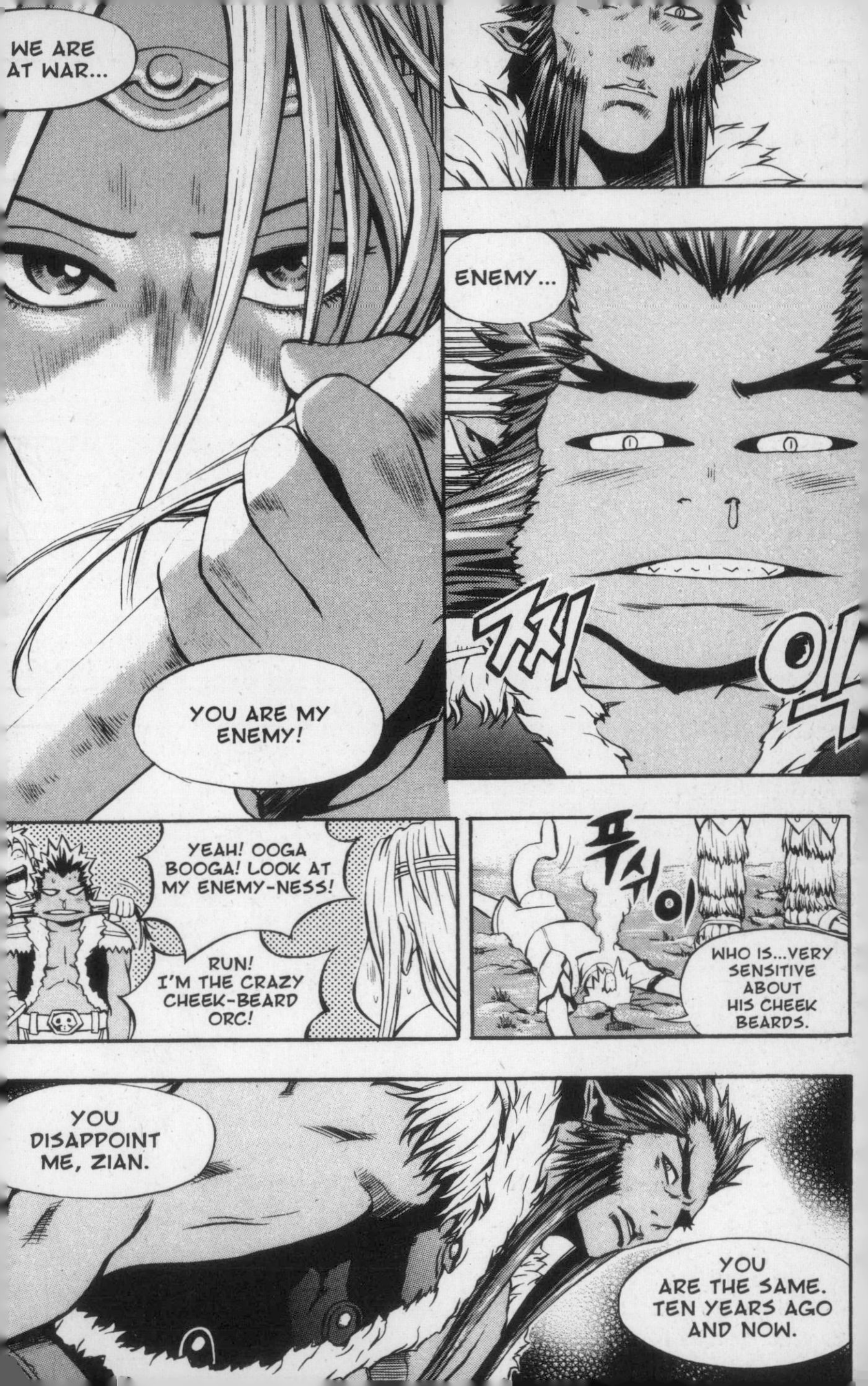
WE ARE AT WAR...
YOU ARE MY ENEMY!
ENEMY...
YEAH! OOGA BOOGA! LOOK AT MY ENEMY-NESS!
RUN! I'M THE CRAZY CHEEK-BEARD ORC!
WHO IS...VERY SENSITIVE ABOUT HIS CHEEK BEARDS.
YOU DISAPPOINT ME, ZIAN.
YOU ARE THE SAME. TEN YEARS AGO AND NOW.

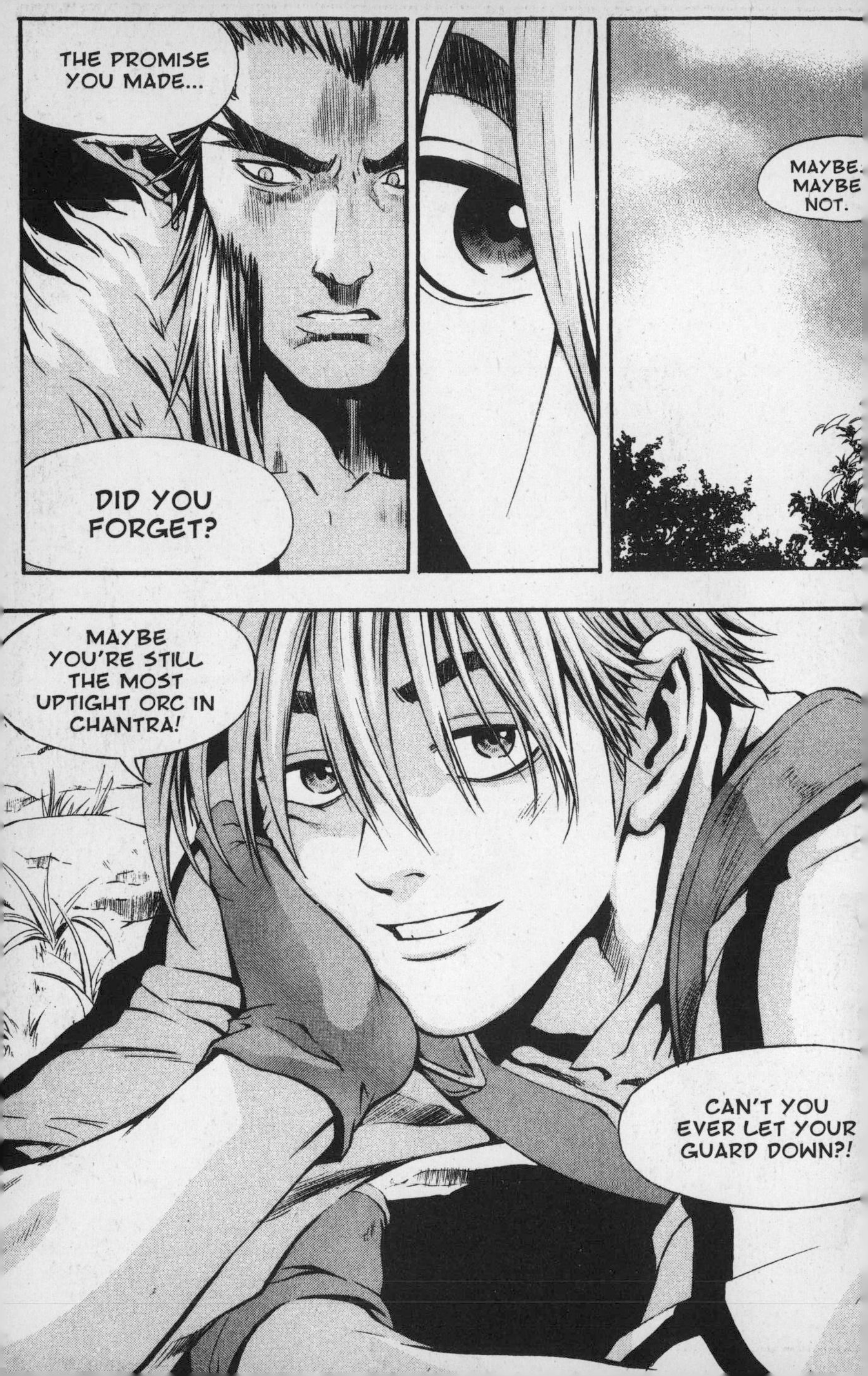
THE PROMISE YOU MADE...
DID YOU FORGET?
MAYBE. MAYBE NOT.
MAYBE YOU'RE STILL THE MOST UPTIGHT ORC IN CHANTRA!
CAN'T YOU EVER LET YOUR GUARD DOWN?!

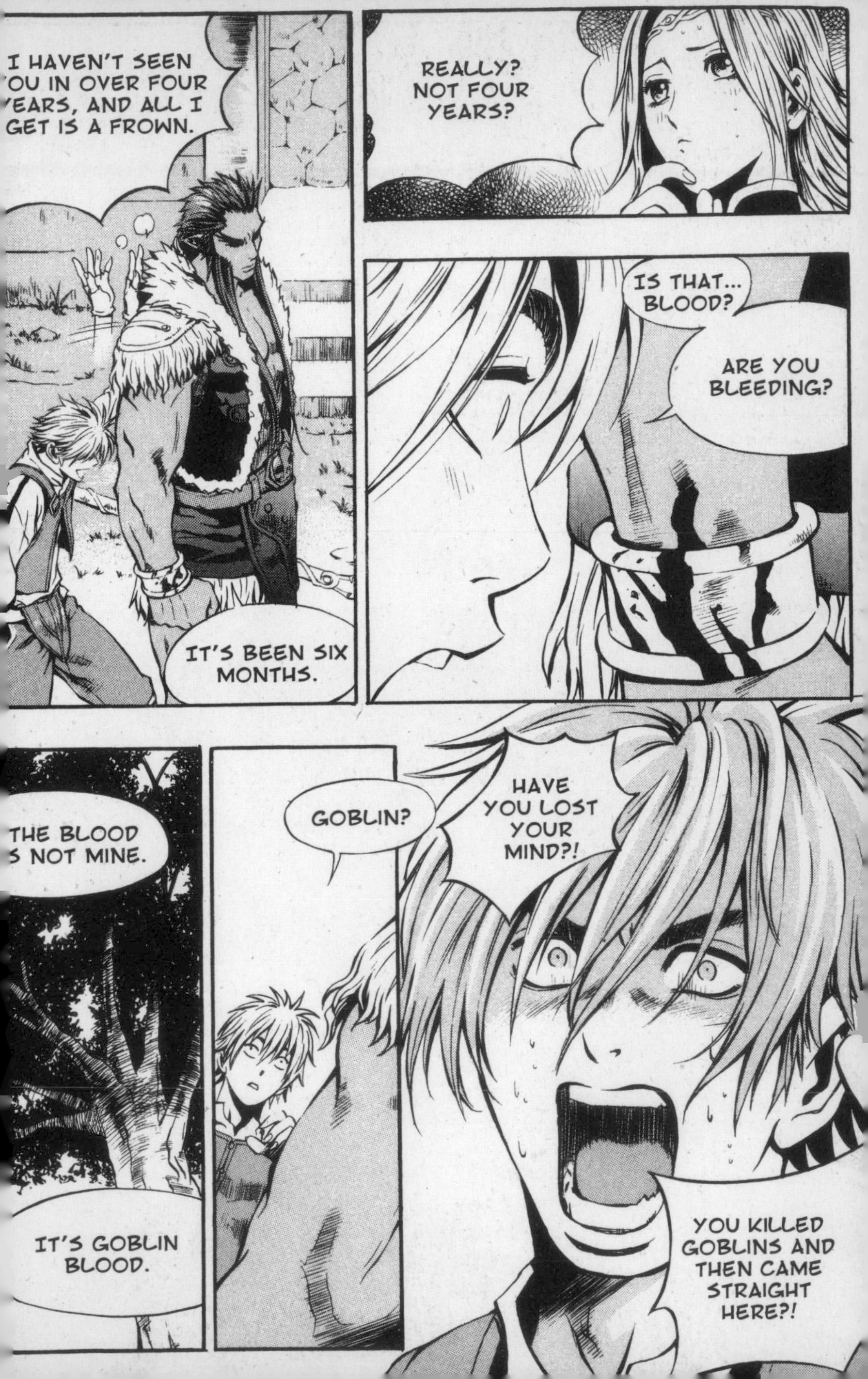
I HAVEN'T SEEN YOU IN OVER FOUR YEARS, AND ALL I GET IS A FROWN.
IT'S BEEN SIX MONTHS.
REALLY? NOT FOUR YEARS?
IS THAT... BLOOD?
ARE YOU BLEEDING?
THE BLOOD IS NOT MINE.
IT'S GOBLIN BLOOD.
GOBLIN?
HAVE YOU LOST YOUR MIND?!
YOU KILLED GOBLINS AND THEN CAME STRAIGHT HERE?!

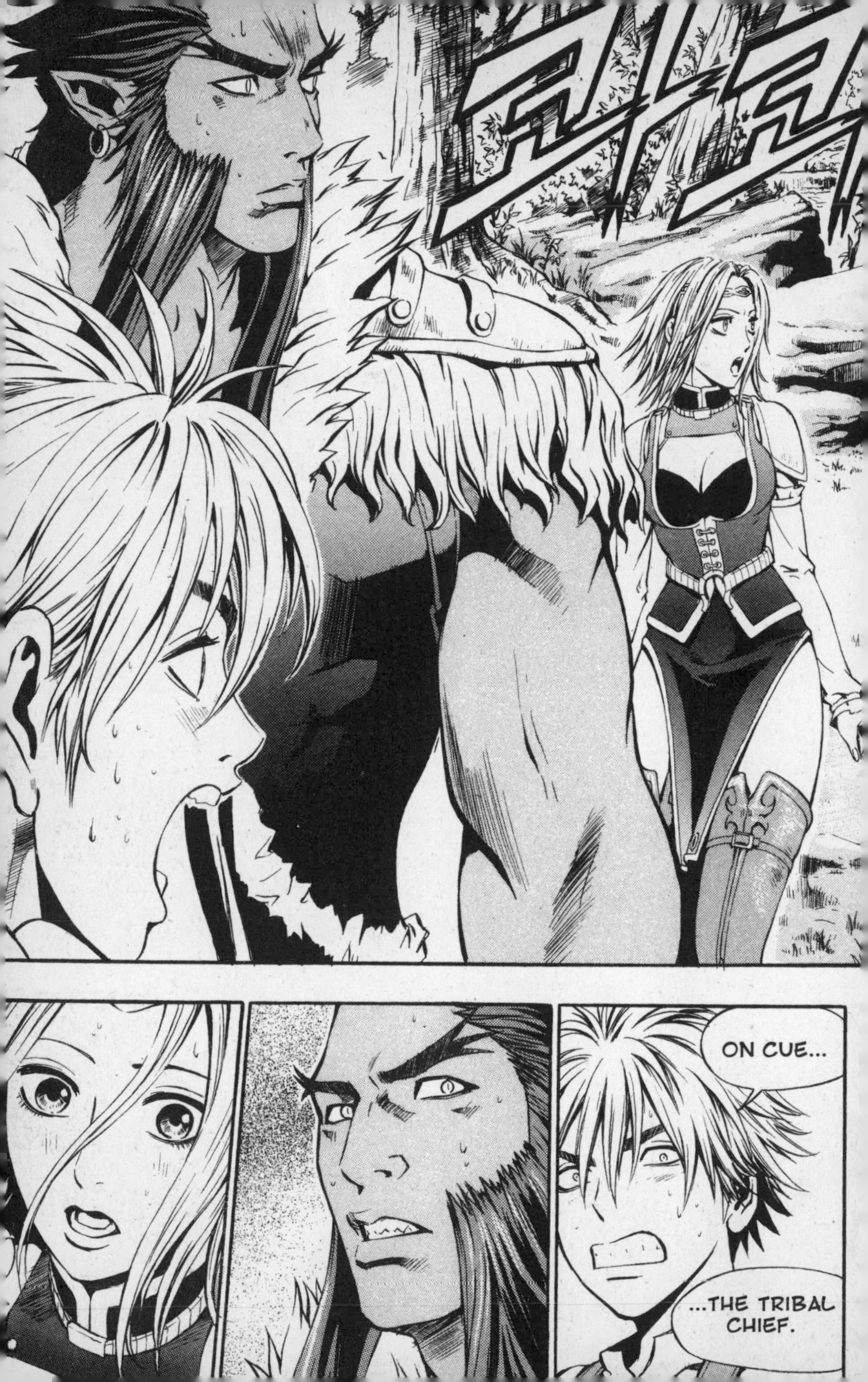
ON CUE...
...THE TRIBAL CHIEF.

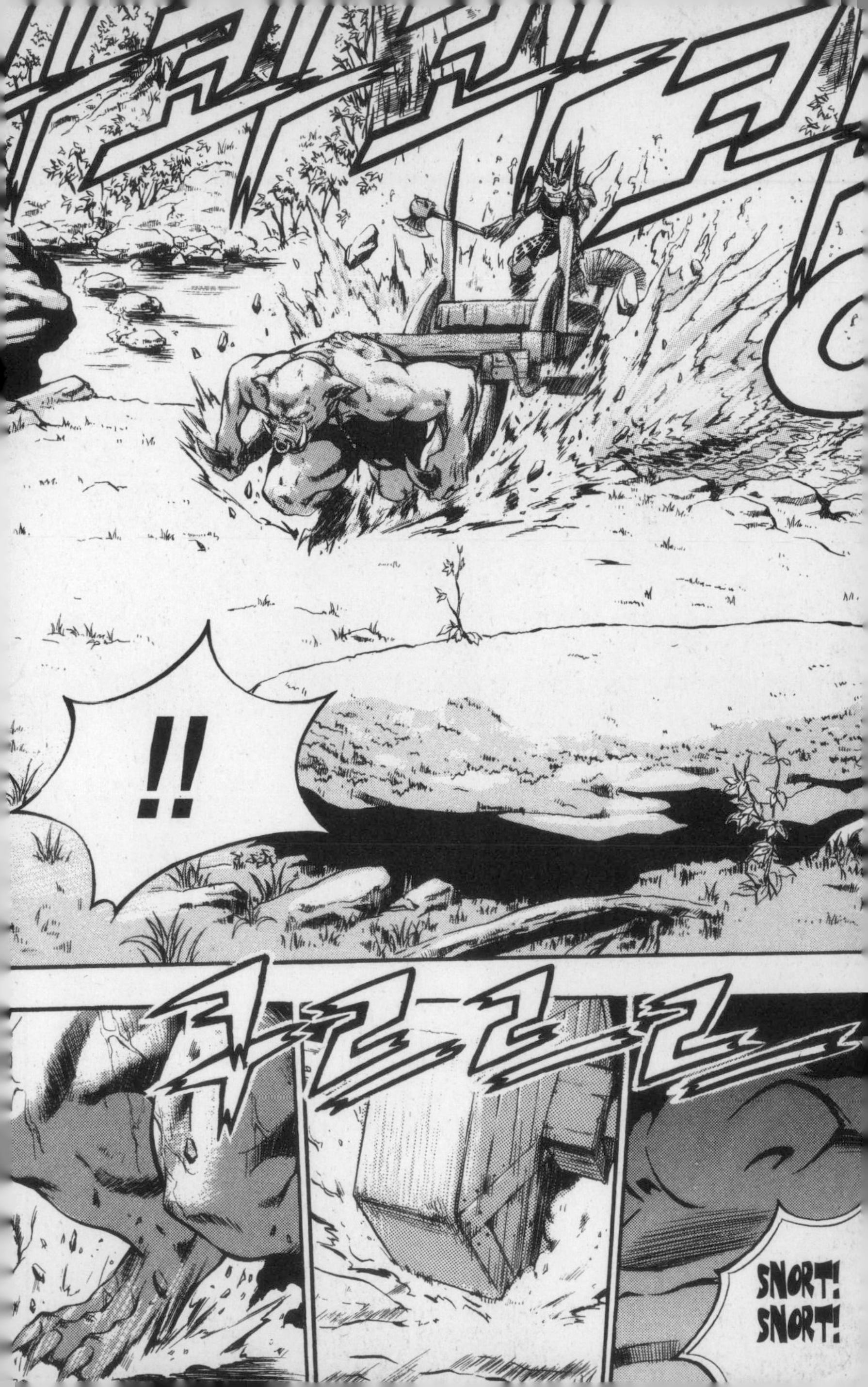
!!
SNORT! SNORT!

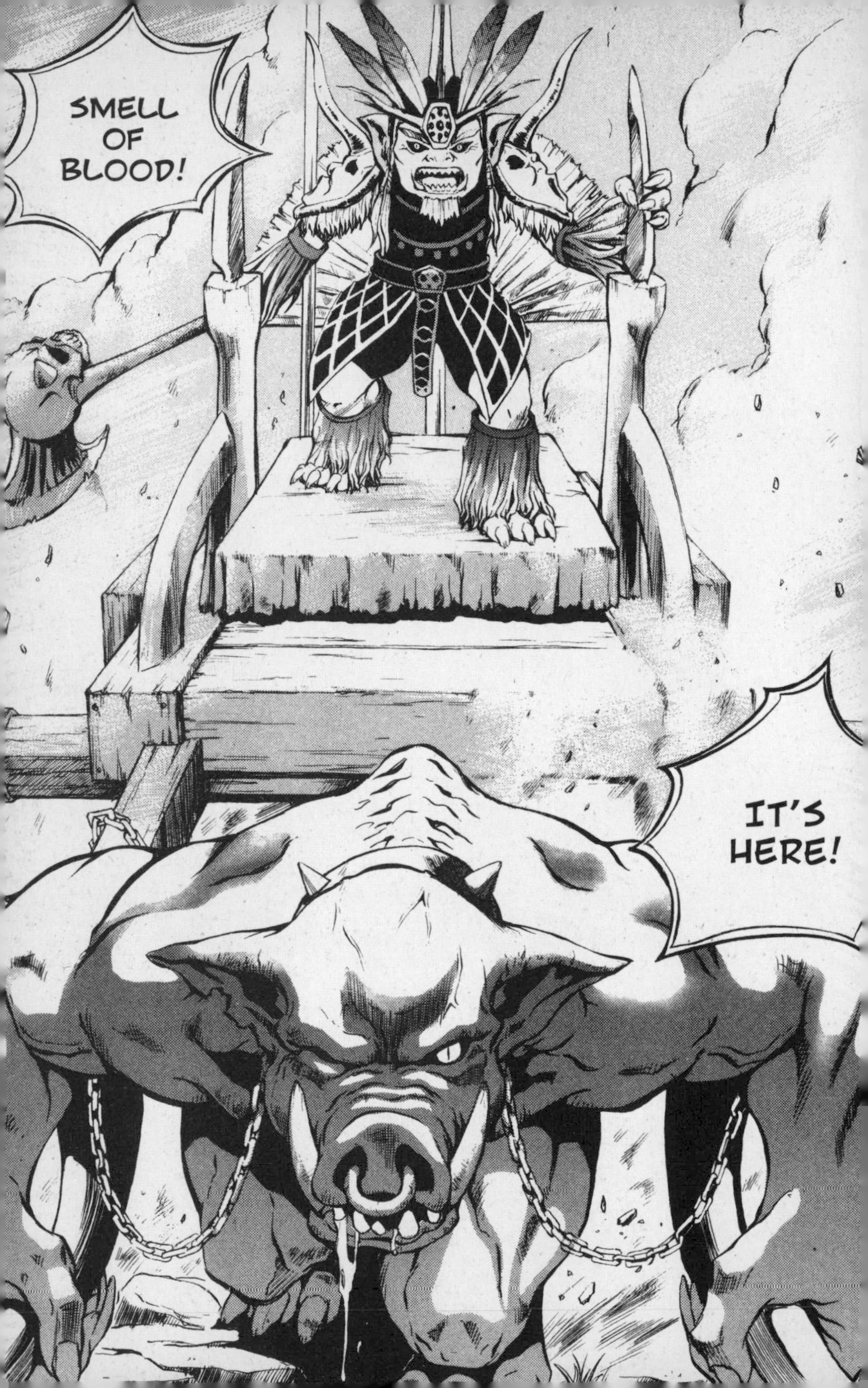
SMELL OF BLOOD!
IT'S HERE!

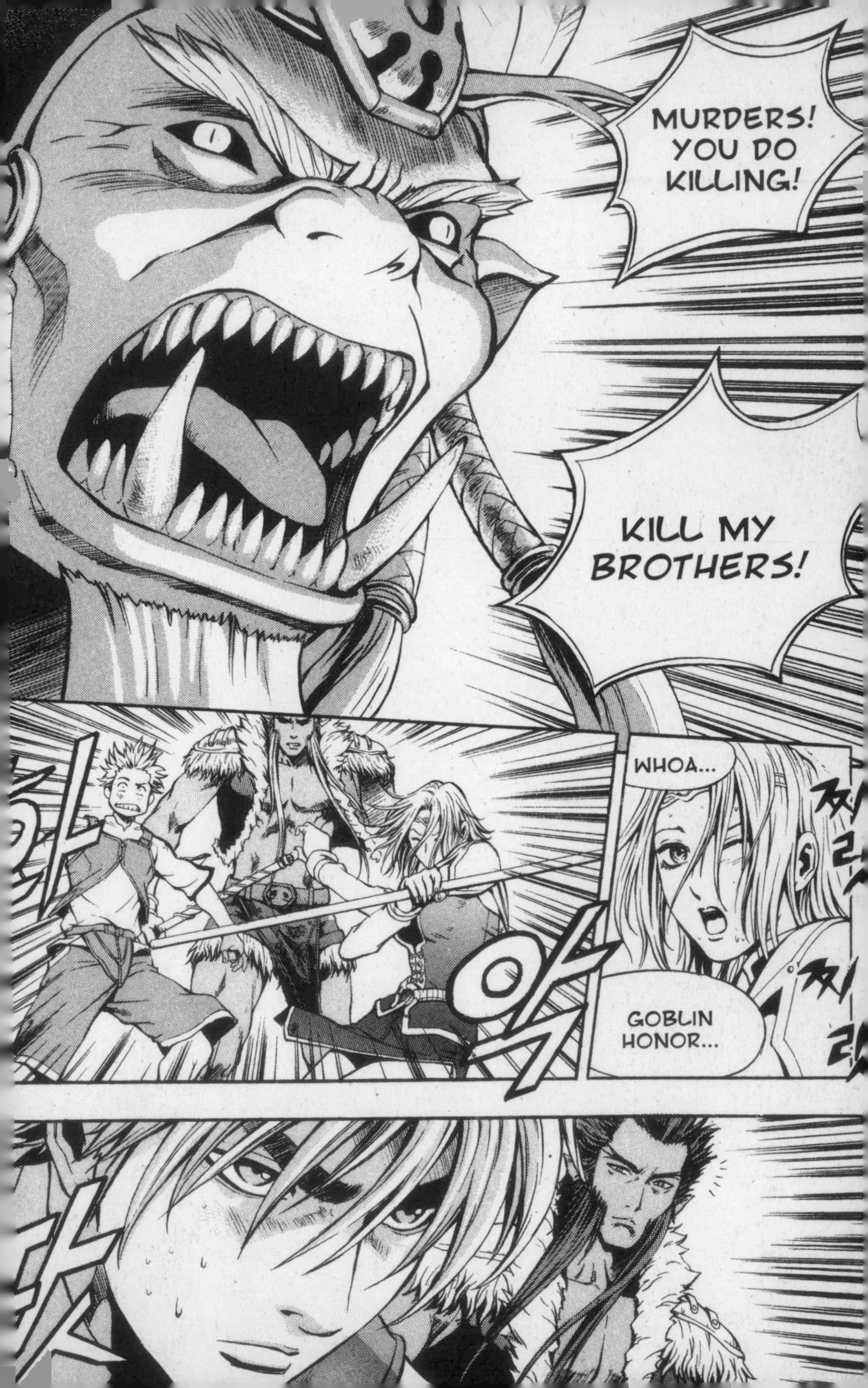
MURDERS! YOU DO KILLING!
KILL MY BROTHERS!
WHOA...
GOBLIN HONOR...

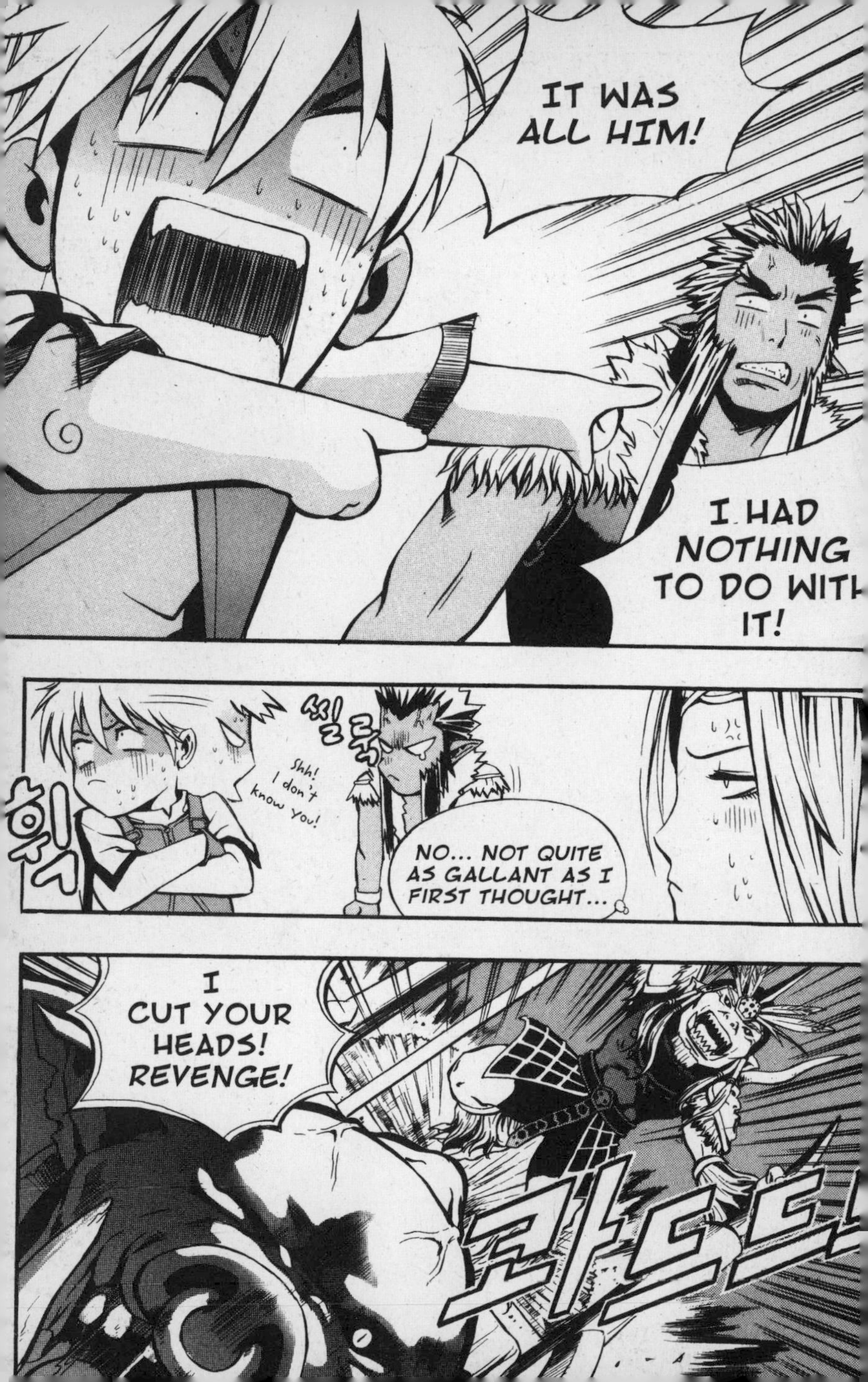
IT WAS ALL HIM!
I HAD NOTHING TO DO WITH IT!
Shh! I don't know you!
NO... NOT QUITE AS GALLANT AS I FIRST THOUGHT...
I CUT YOUR HEADS! REVENGE!

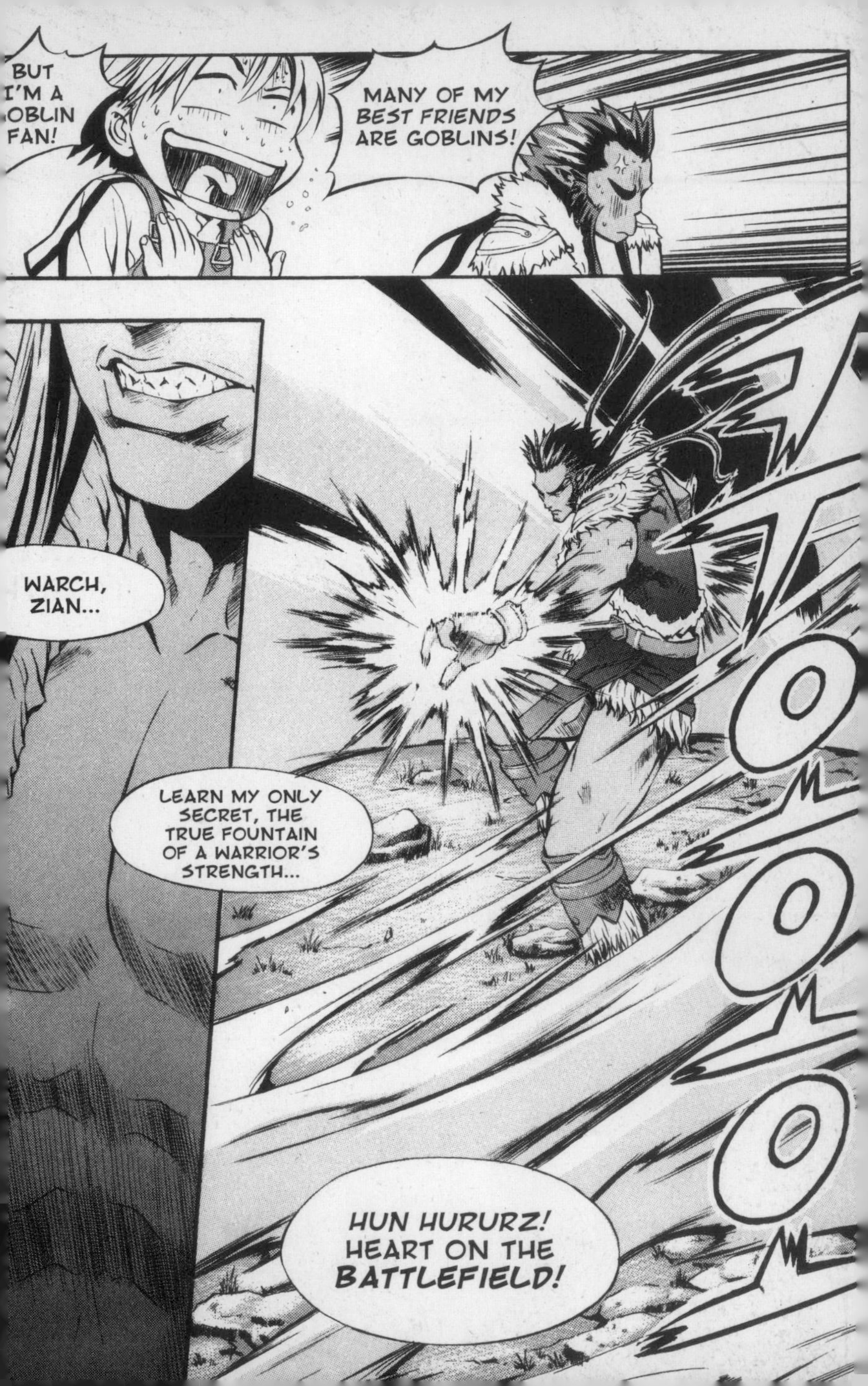
BUT I'M A GOBLIN FAN!
MANY OF MY BEST FRIENDS ARE GOBLINS!
WARCH, ZIAN...
LEARN MY ONLY SECRET, THE TRUE FOUNTAIN OF A WARRIOR'S STRENGTH...
HUN HURURZ! HEART ON THE BATTLEFIELD!

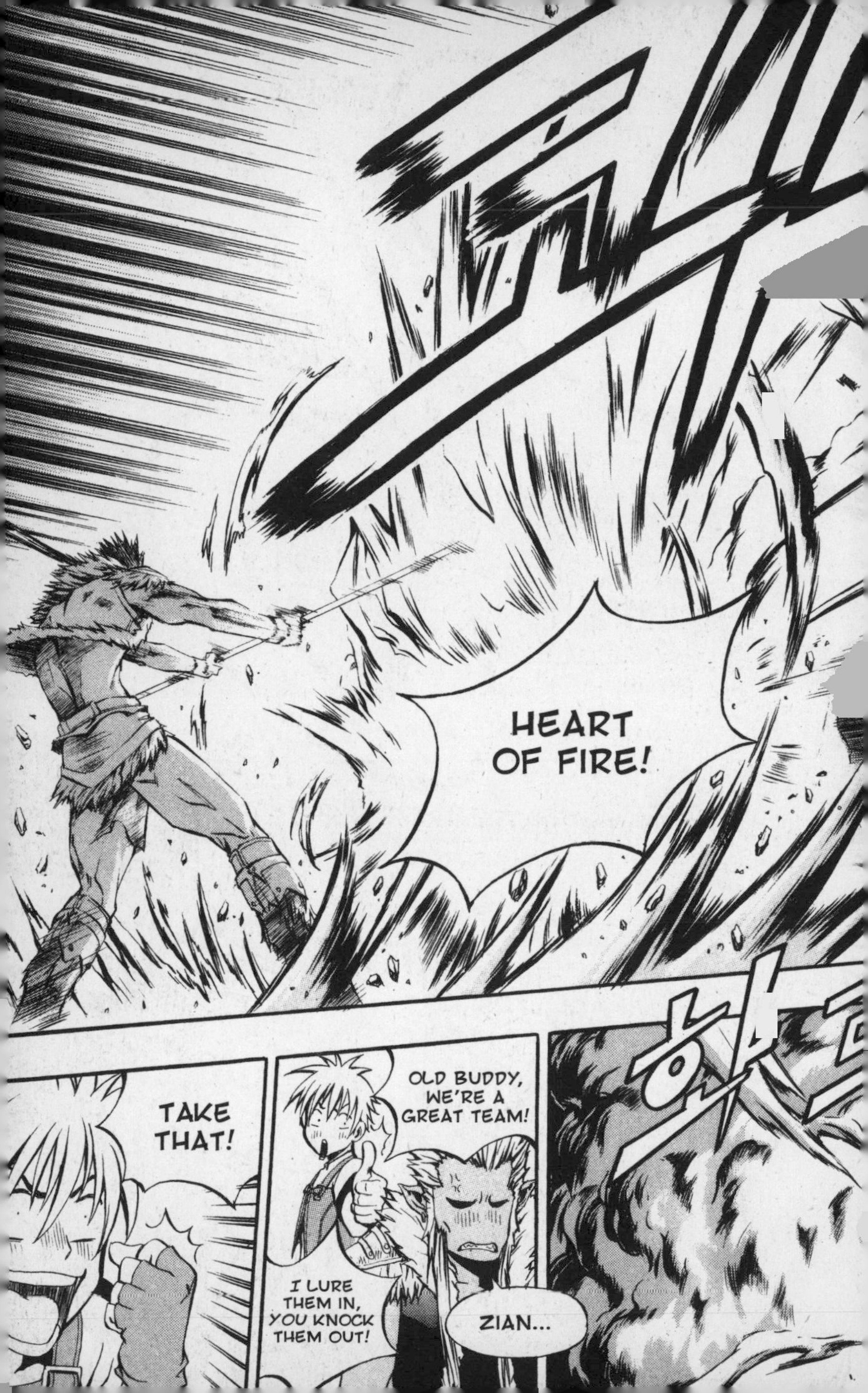
HEART OF FIRE!
TAKE THAT!
OLD BUDDY, WE'RE A GREAT TEAM!
I LURE THEM IN, YOU KNOCK THEM OUT!
ZIAN...

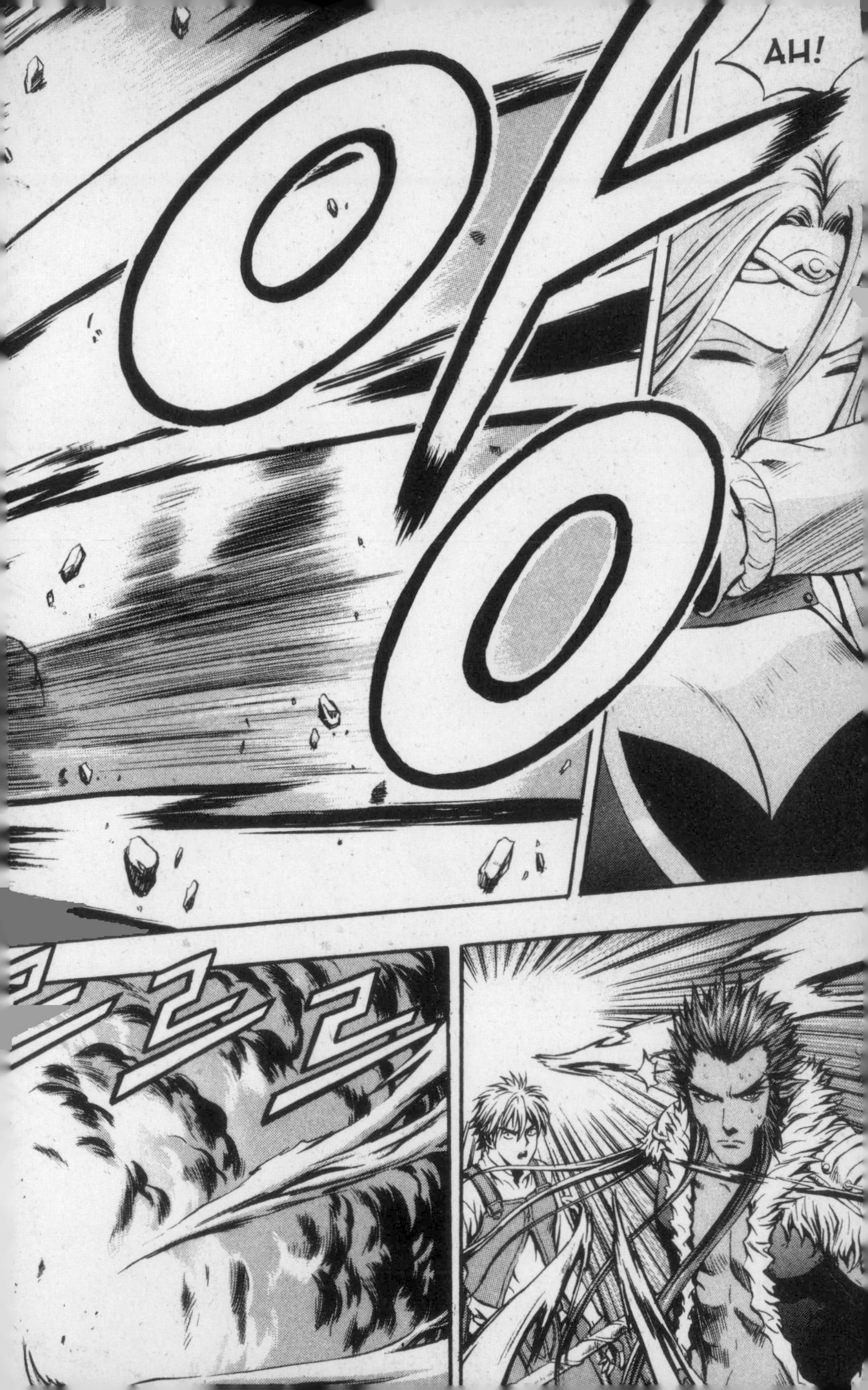
AH!

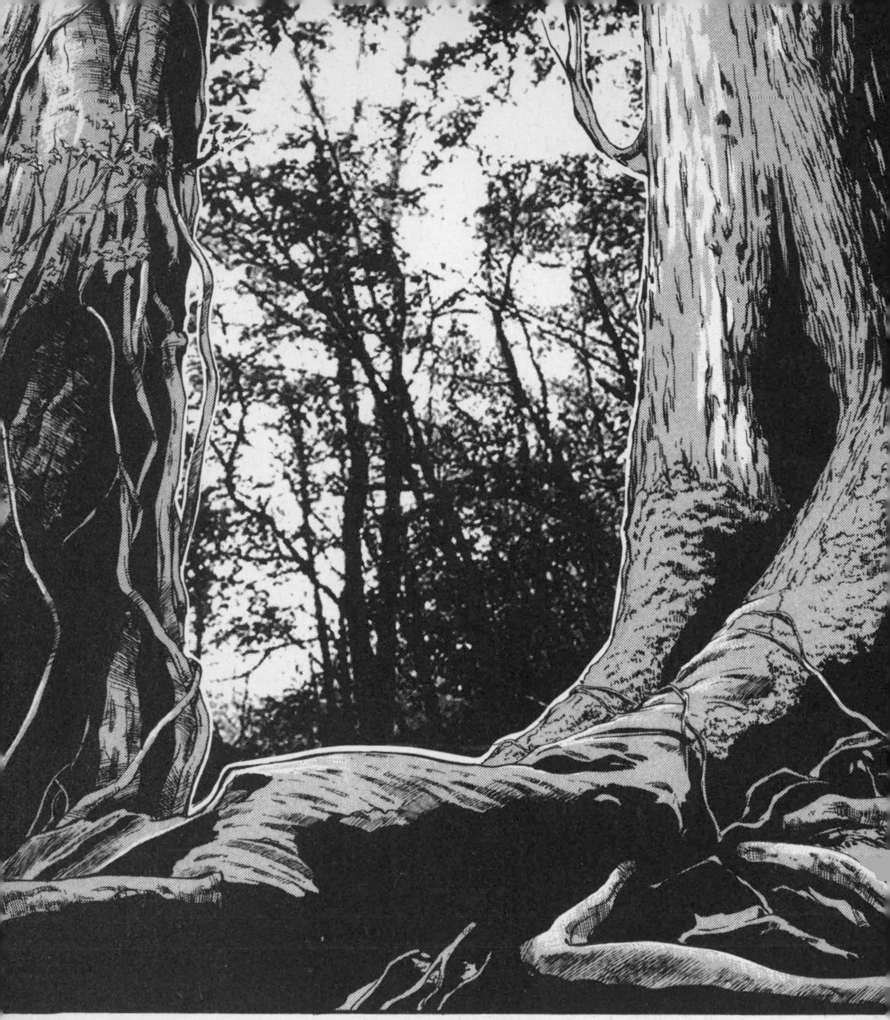

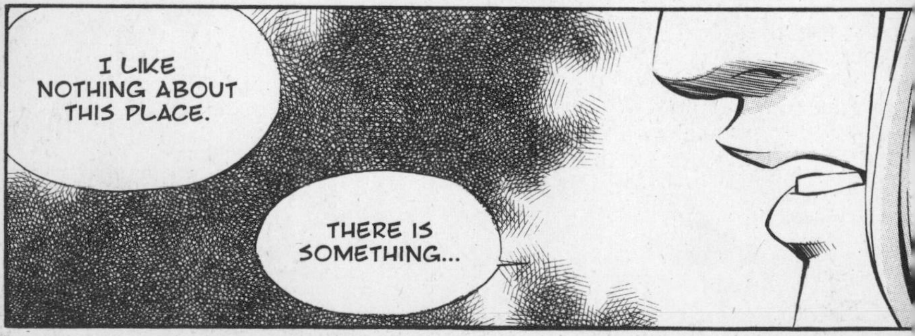
I LIKE NOTHING ABOUT THIS PLACE.
THERE IS SOMETHING...

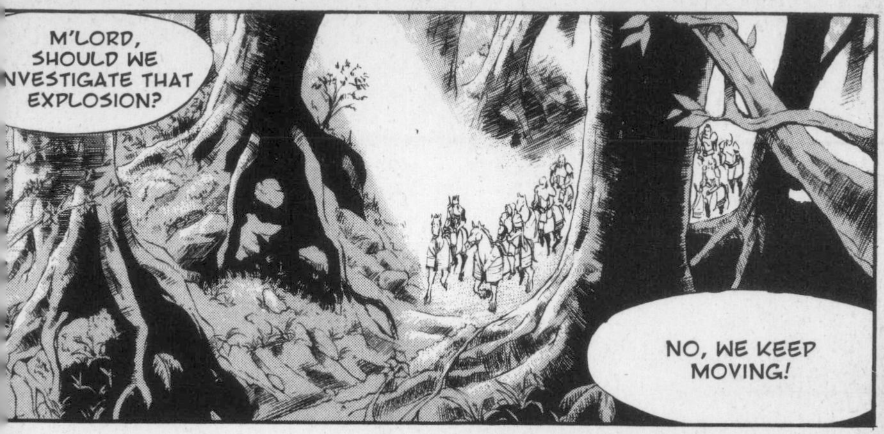
M'LORD, SHOULD WE INVESTIGATE THAT EXPLOSION?
NO, WE KEEP MOVING!
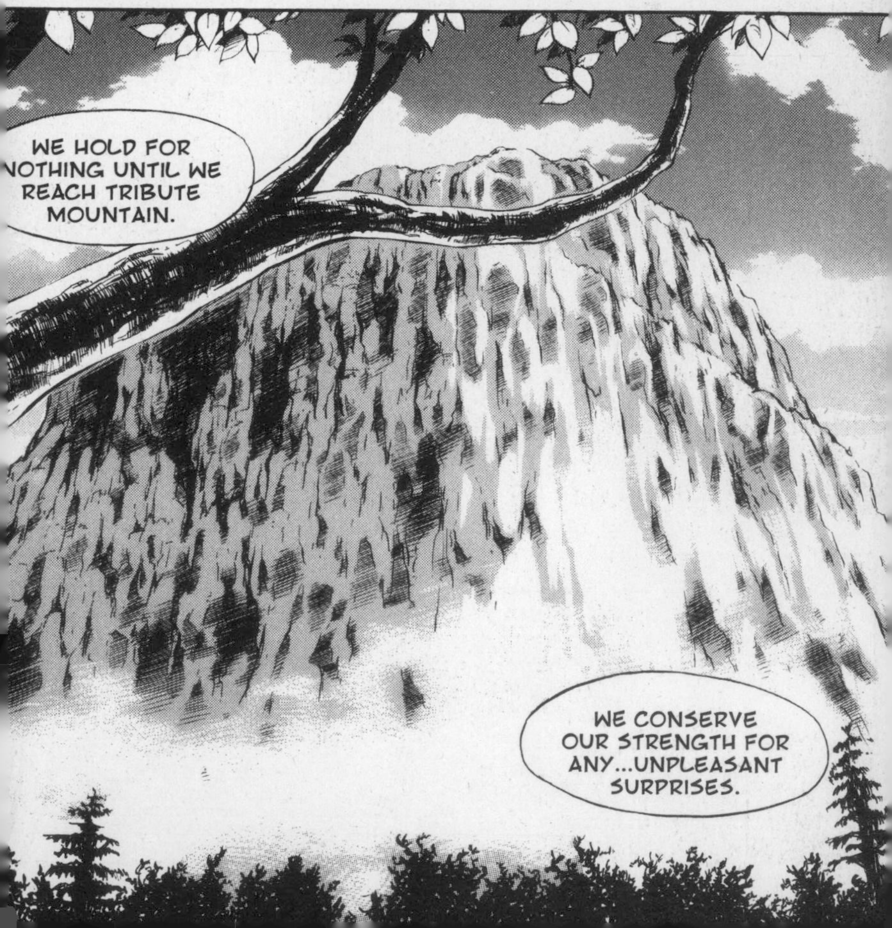
WE HOLD FOR NOTHING UNTIL WE REACH TRIBUTE MOUNTAIN.
WE CONSERVE OUR STRENGTH FOR ANY...UNPLEASANT SURPRISES.

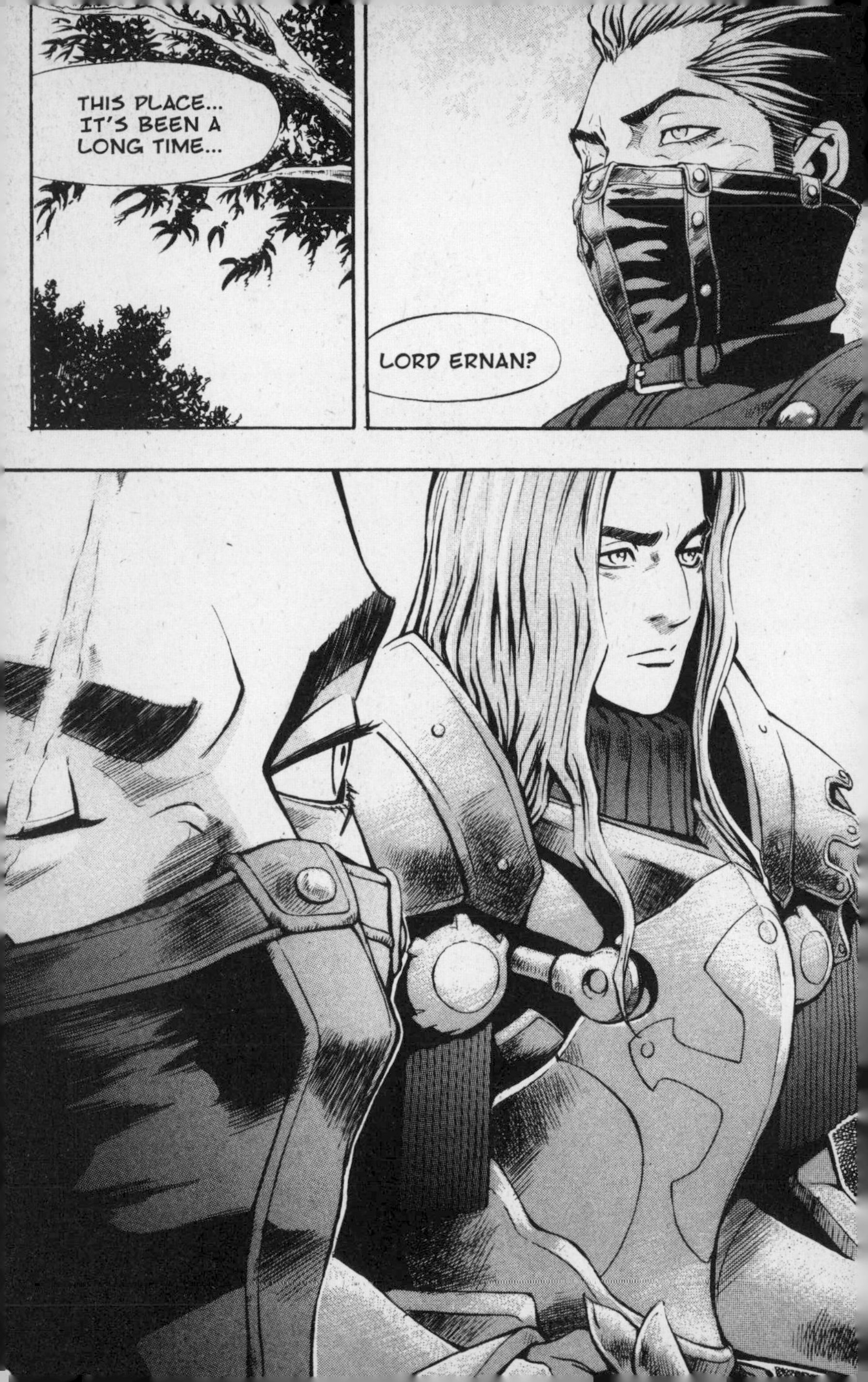
THIS PLACE... IT'S BEEN A LONG TIME...
LORD ERNAN?

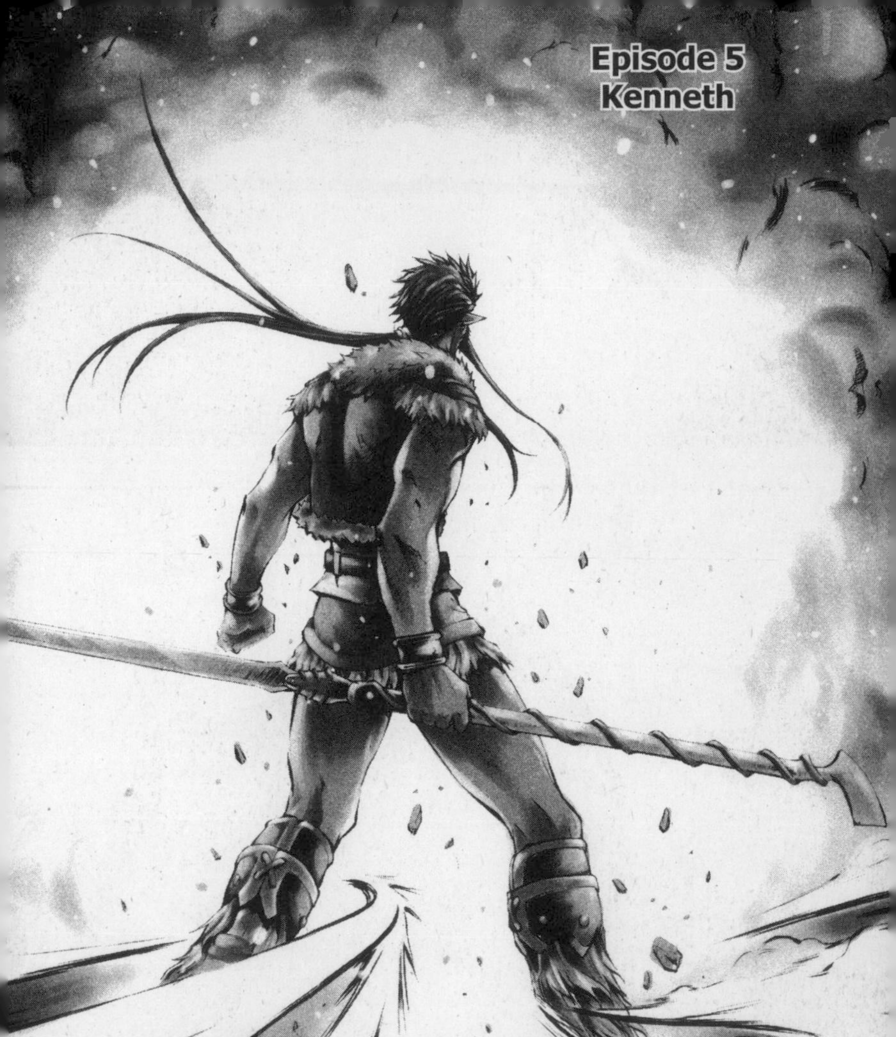
Episode 5
Kenneth
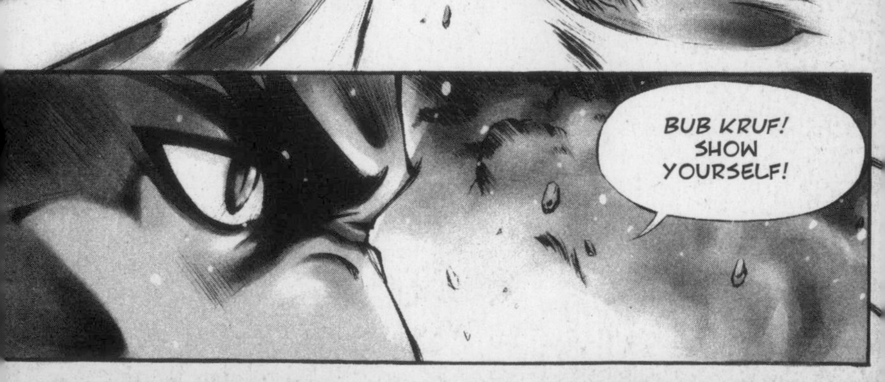
BUB KRUF! SHOW YOURSELF!

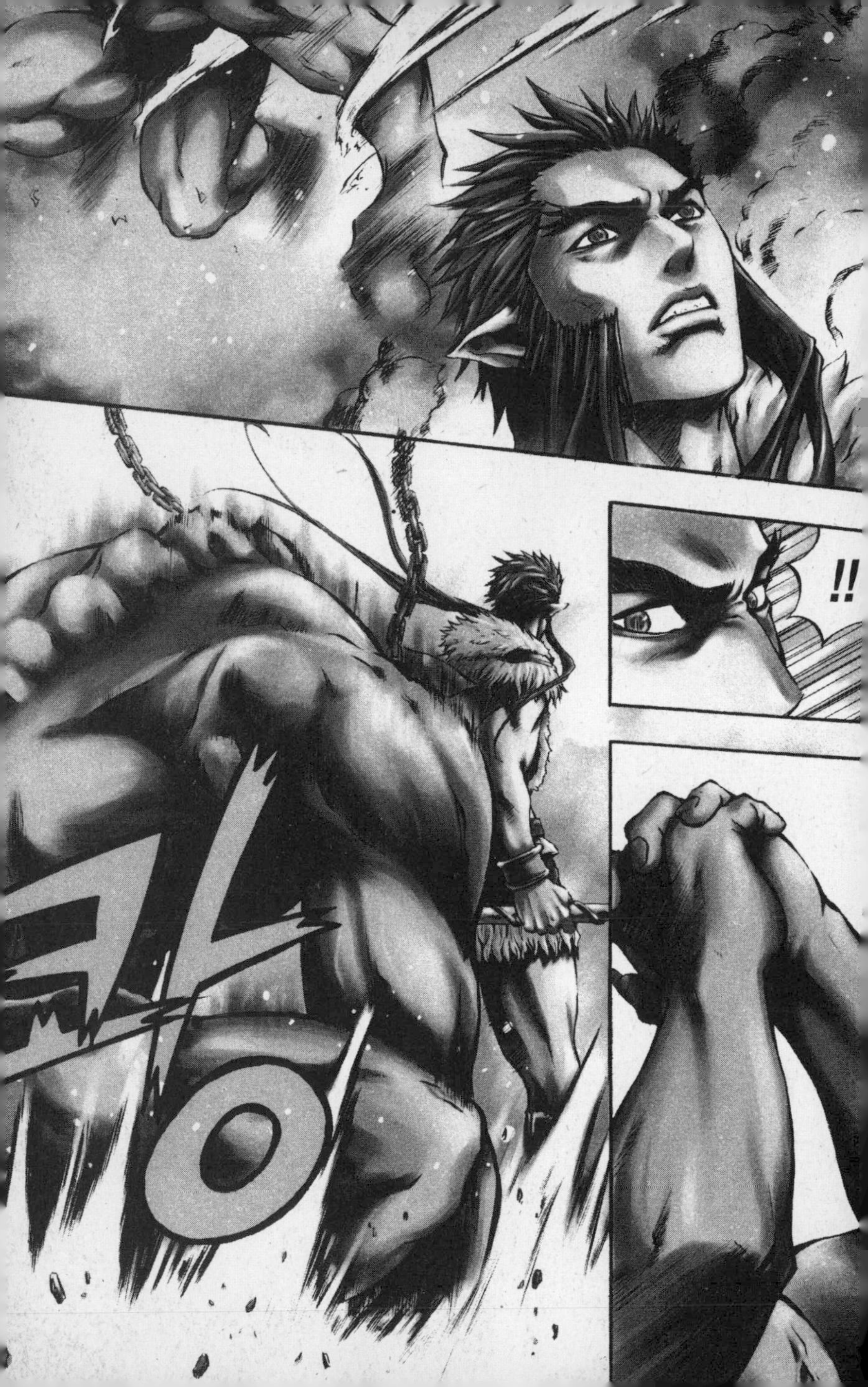
!!

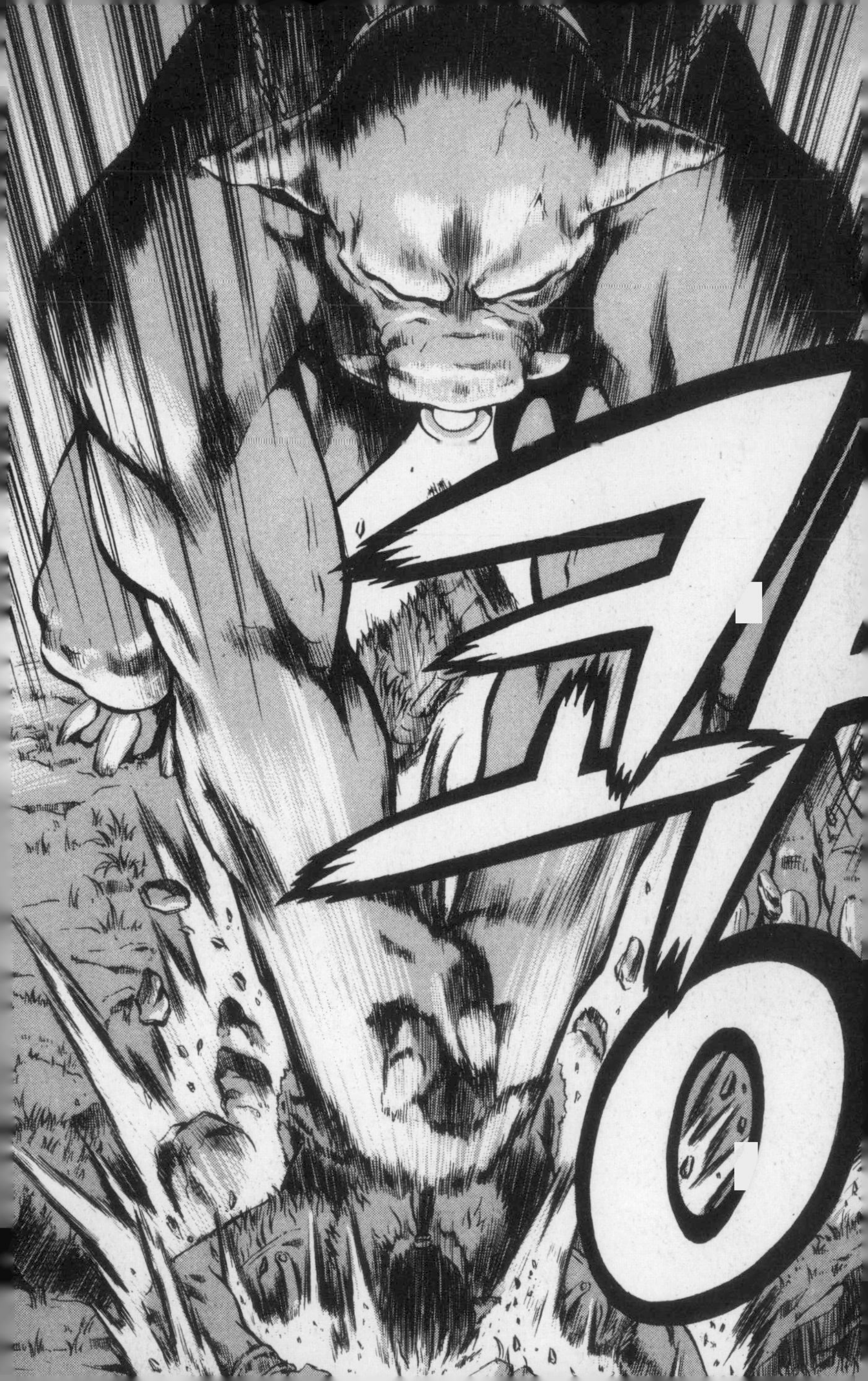

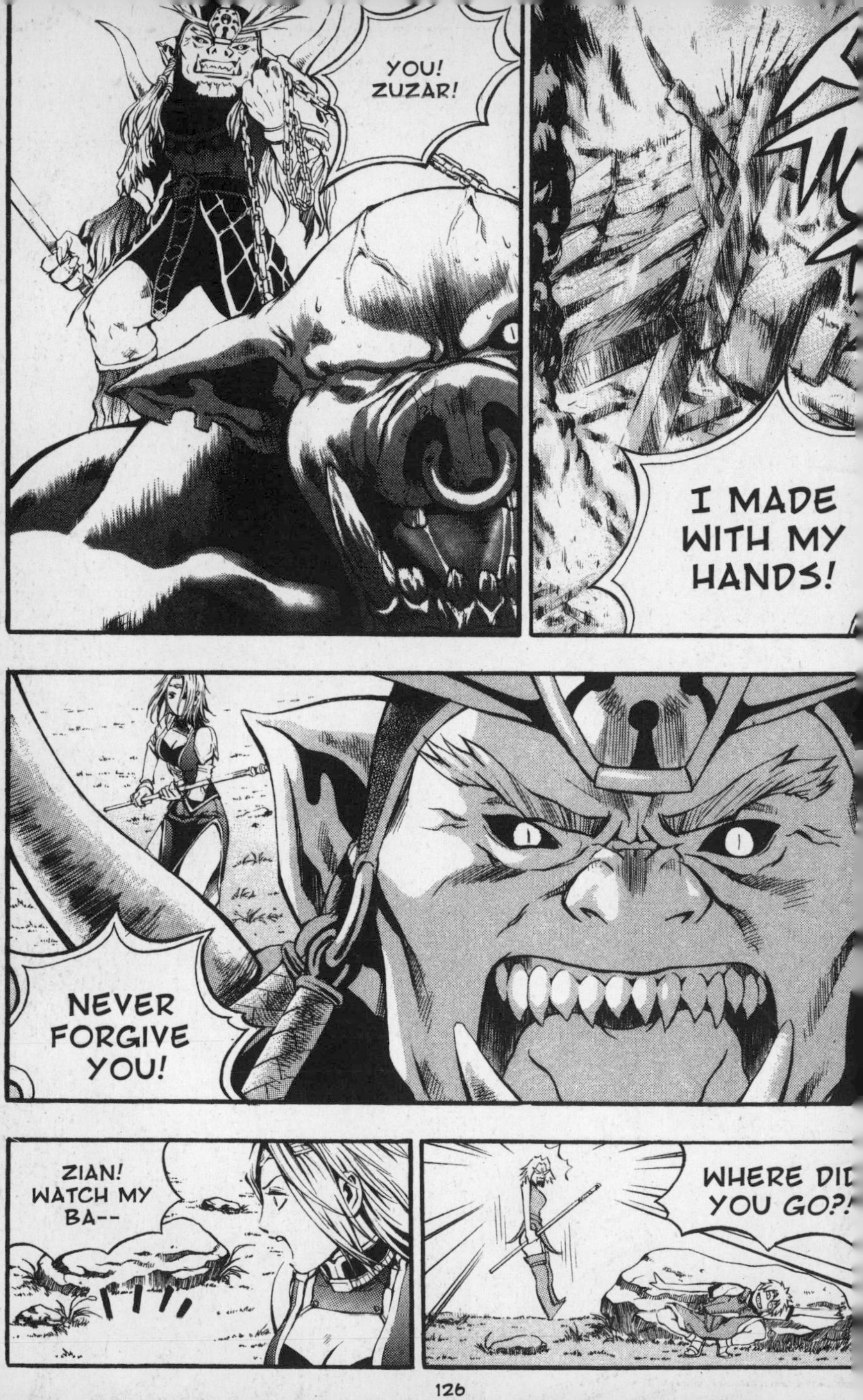

YOU! ZUZAR!
I MADE WITH MY HANDS!
NEVER FORGIVE YOU!
ZIAN! WATCH MY BA--
WHERE DID YOU GO?!

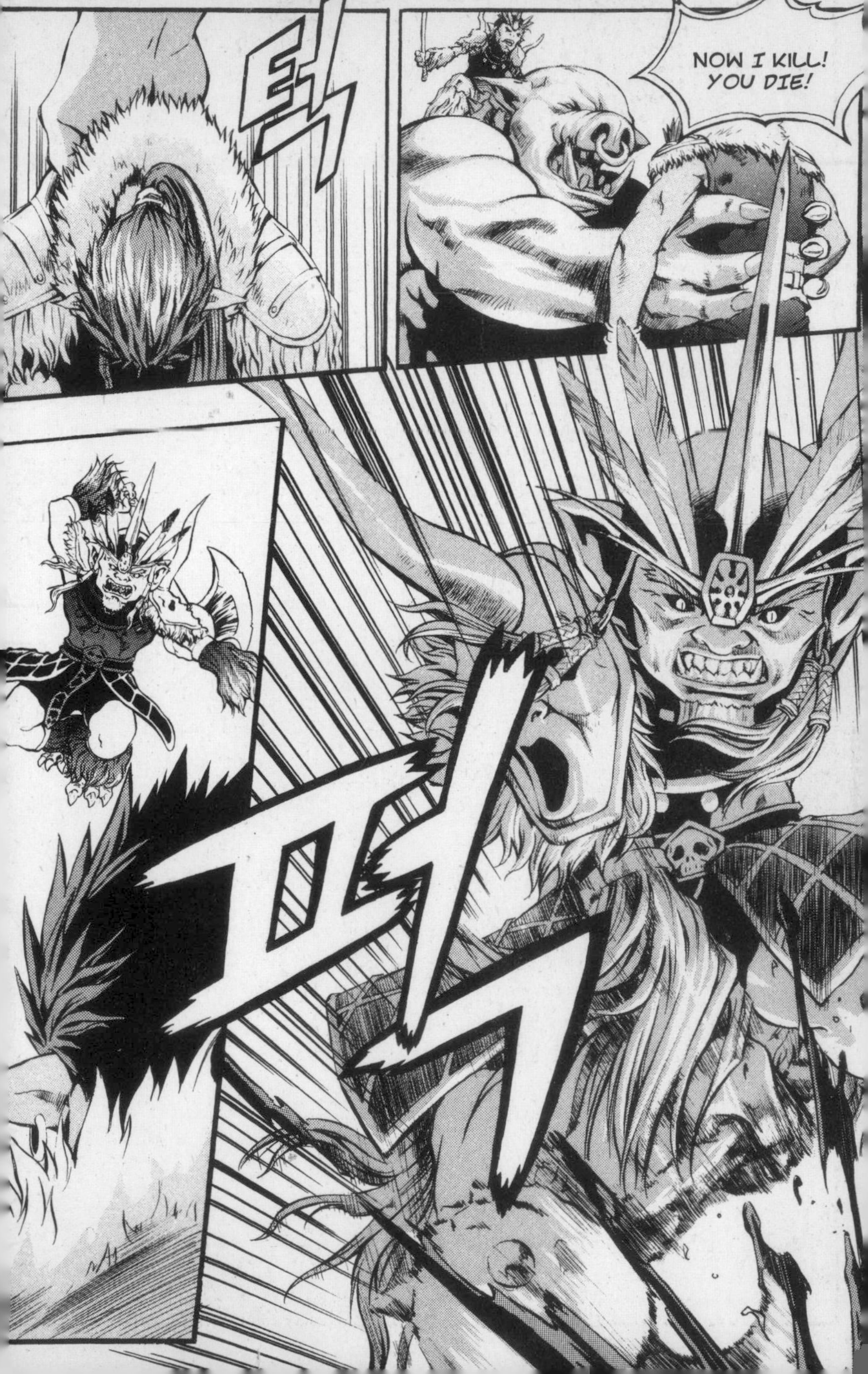
NOW I KILL! YOU DIE!

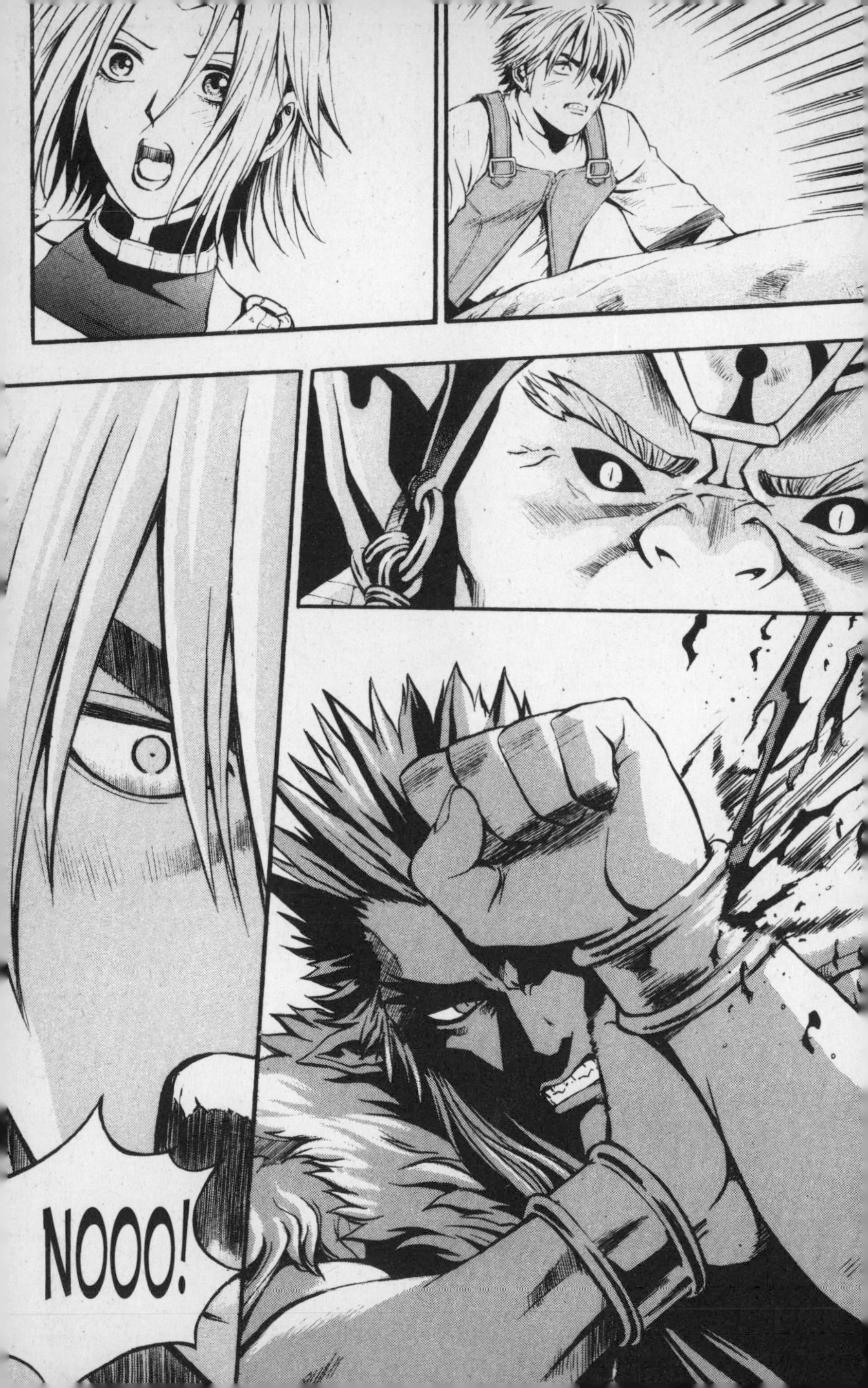
NOOO!

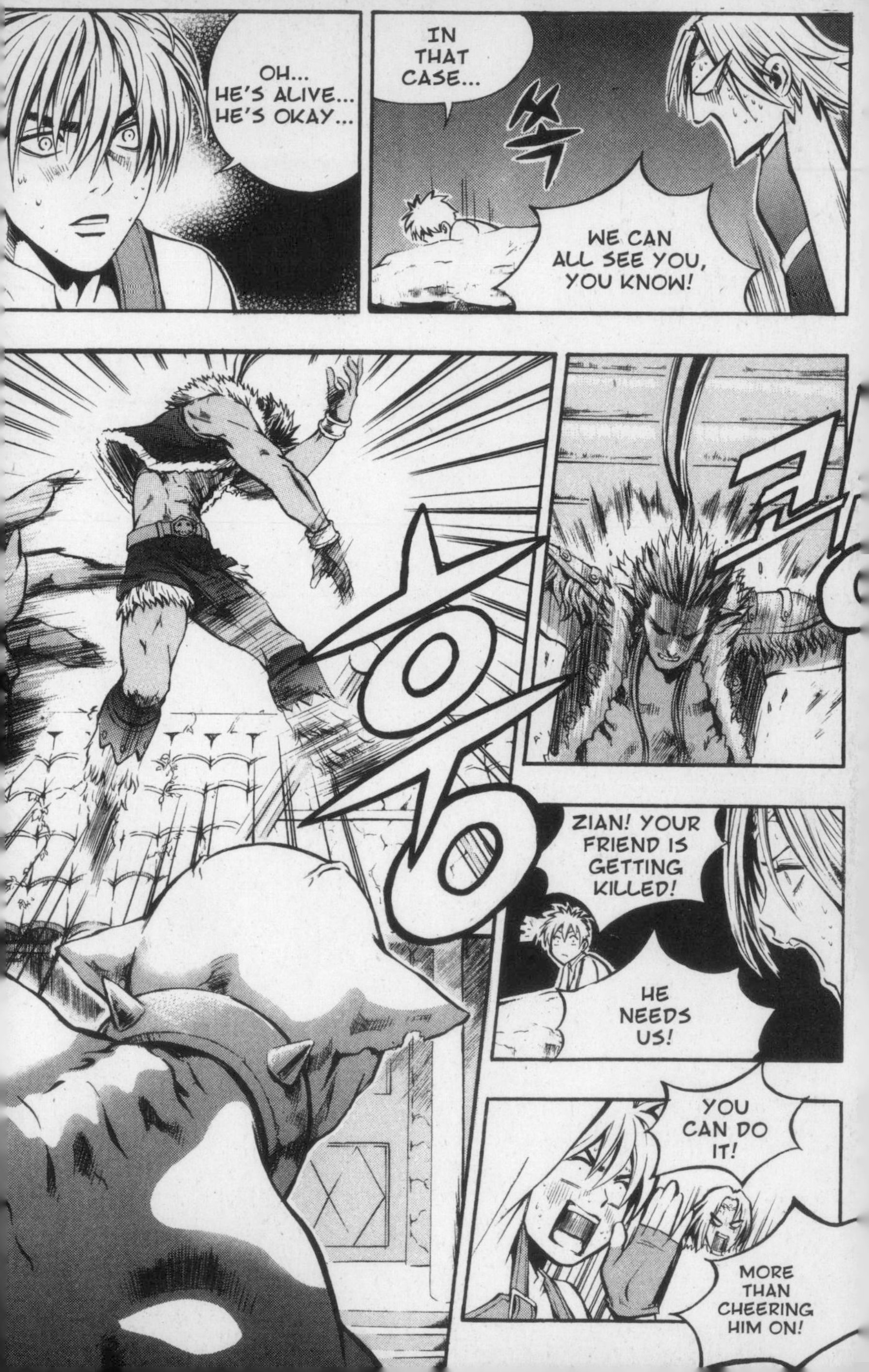
OH... HE'S ALIVE... HE'S OKAY...
IN THAT CASE...
WE CAN ALL SEE YOU, YOU KNOW!
ZIAN! YOUR FRIEND IS GETTING KILLED!
HE NEEDS US!
YOU CAN DO IT!
MORE THAN CHEERING HIM ON!

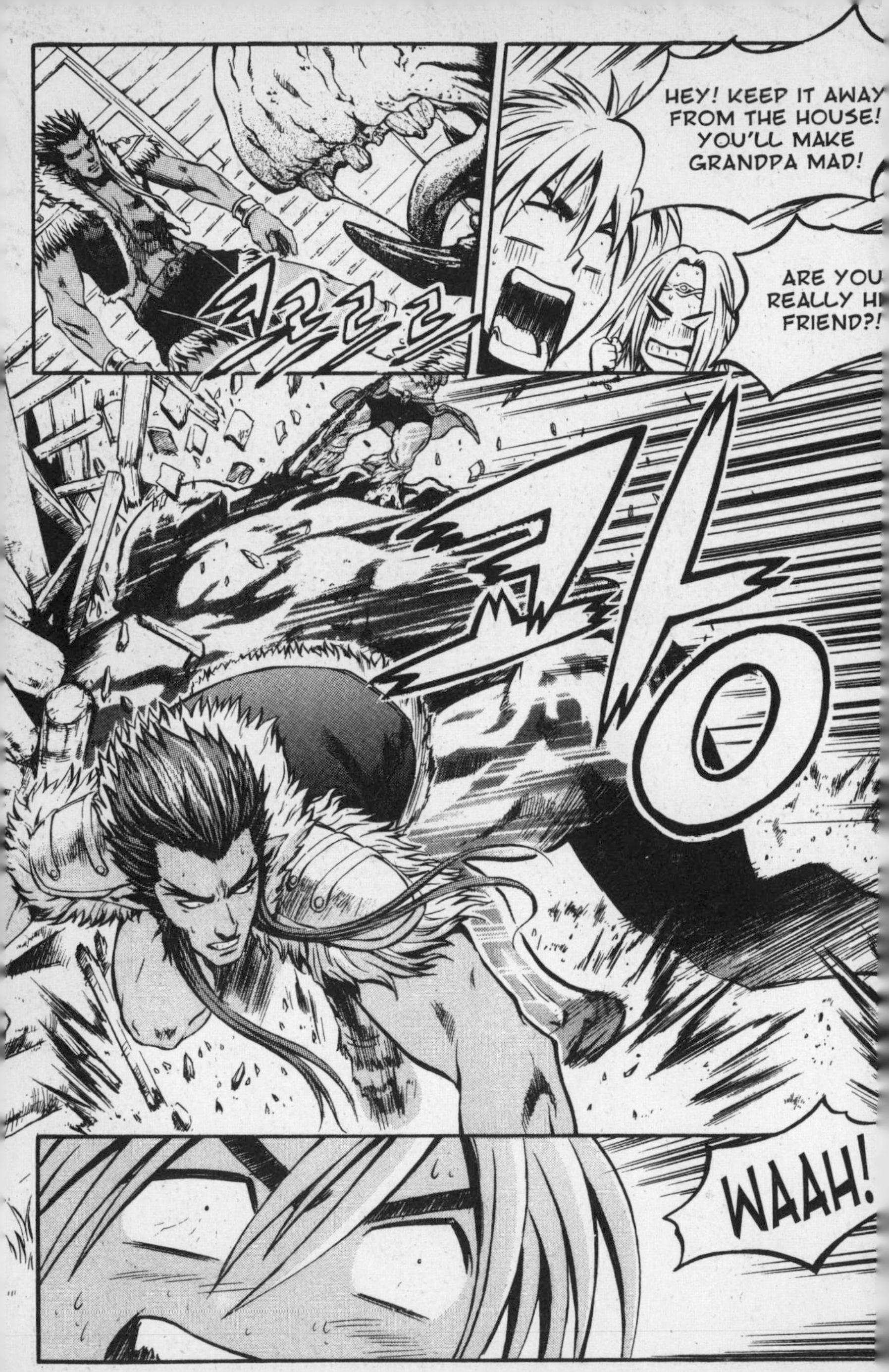

HEY! KEEP IT AWAY FROM THE HOUSE! YOU'LL MAKE GRANDPA MAD!
ARE YOU REALLY HI FRIEND?!
WAAH!

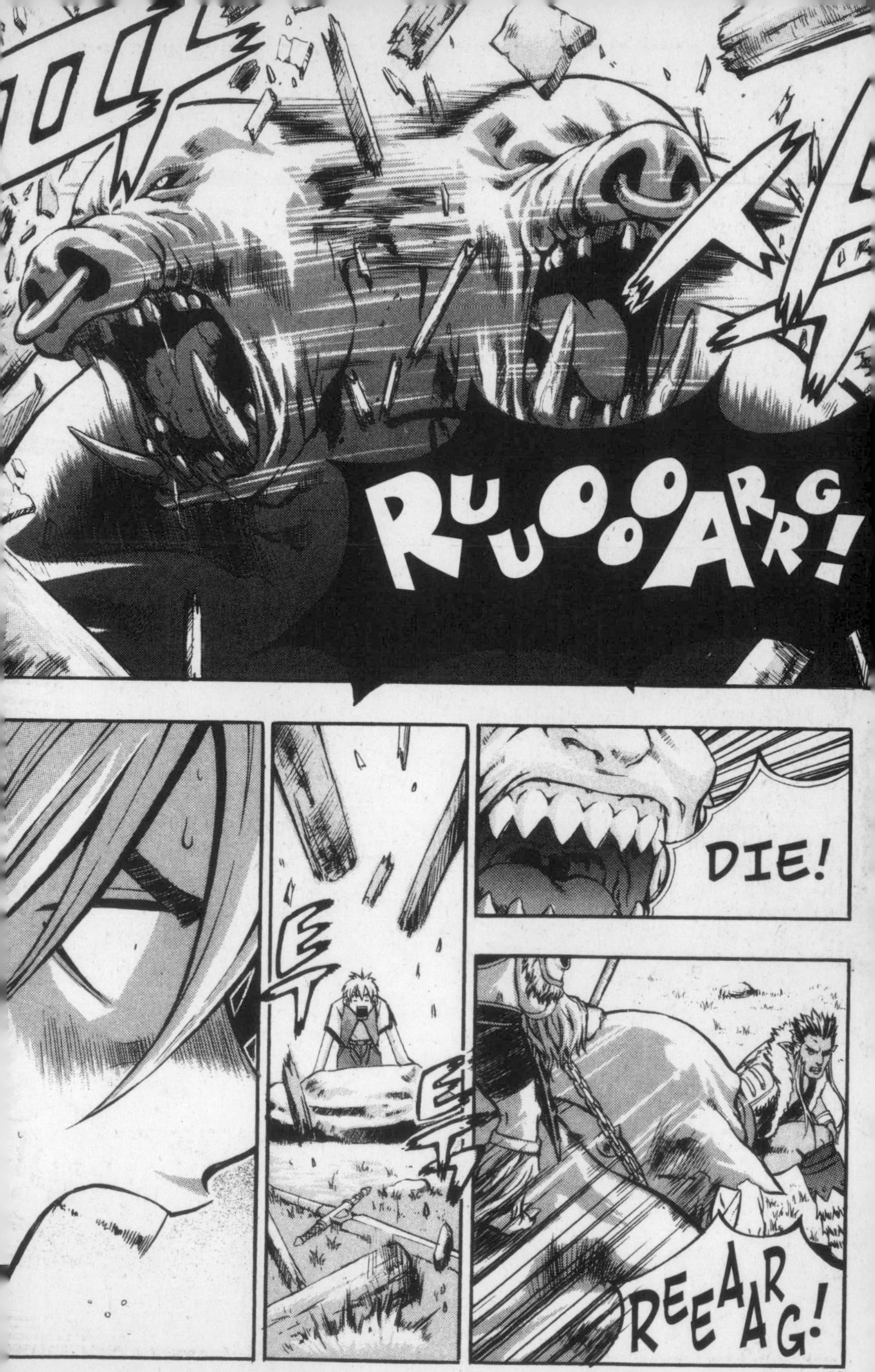
RUUOOOOARRG!
E
E
DIE!
REEEARAG!

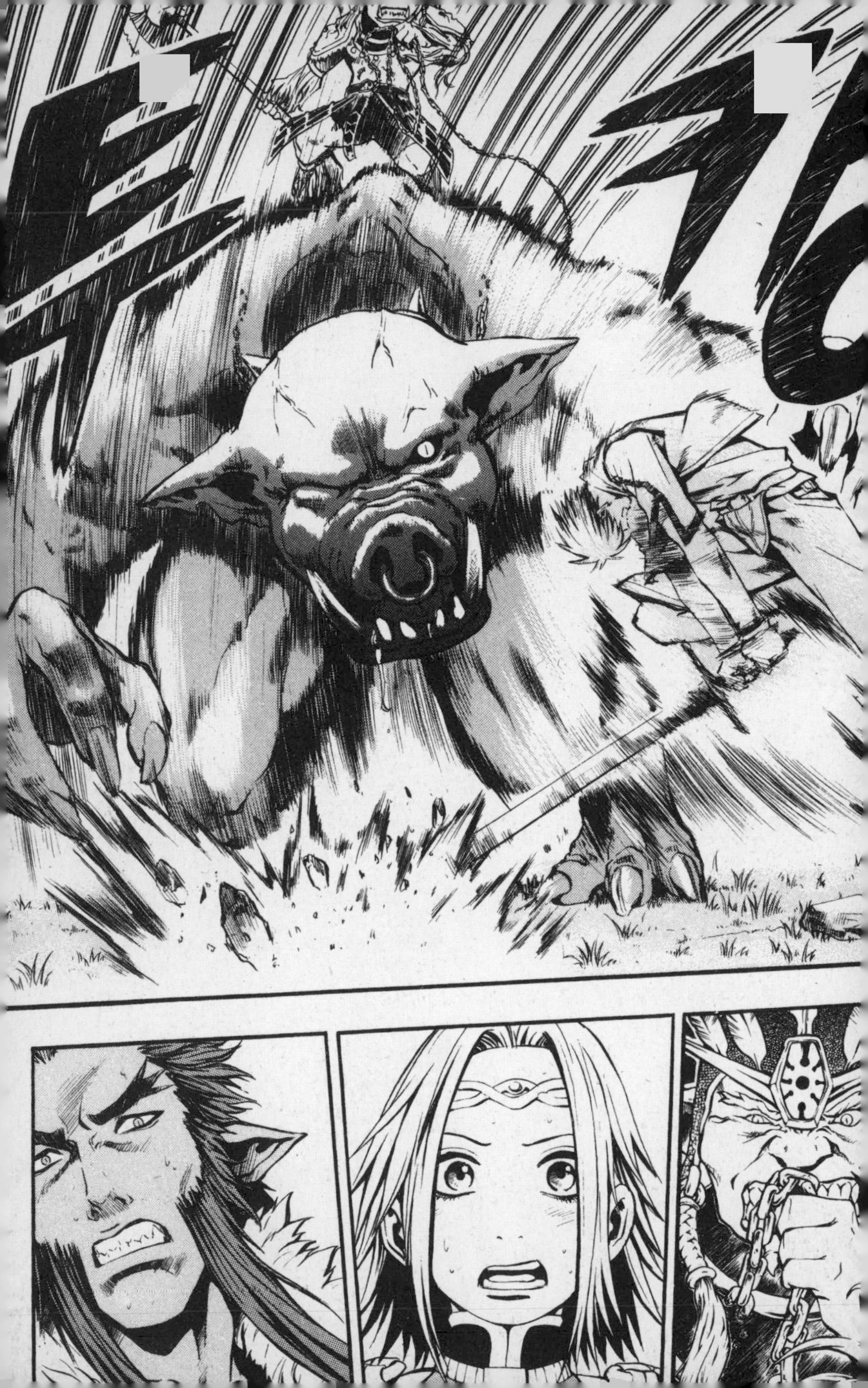

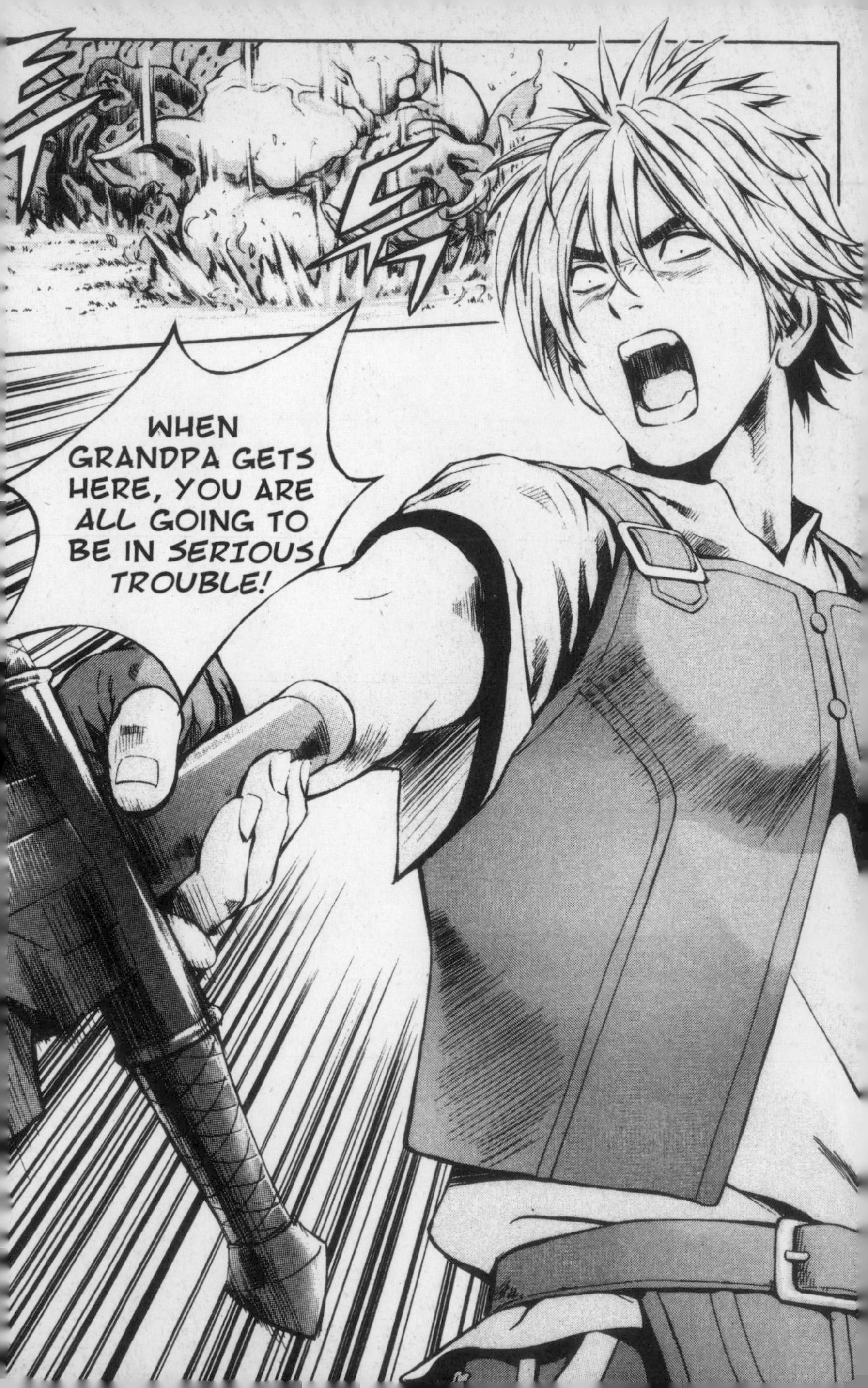
WHEN GRANDPA GETS HERE, YOU ARE ALL GOING TO BE IN SERIOUS TROUBLE!

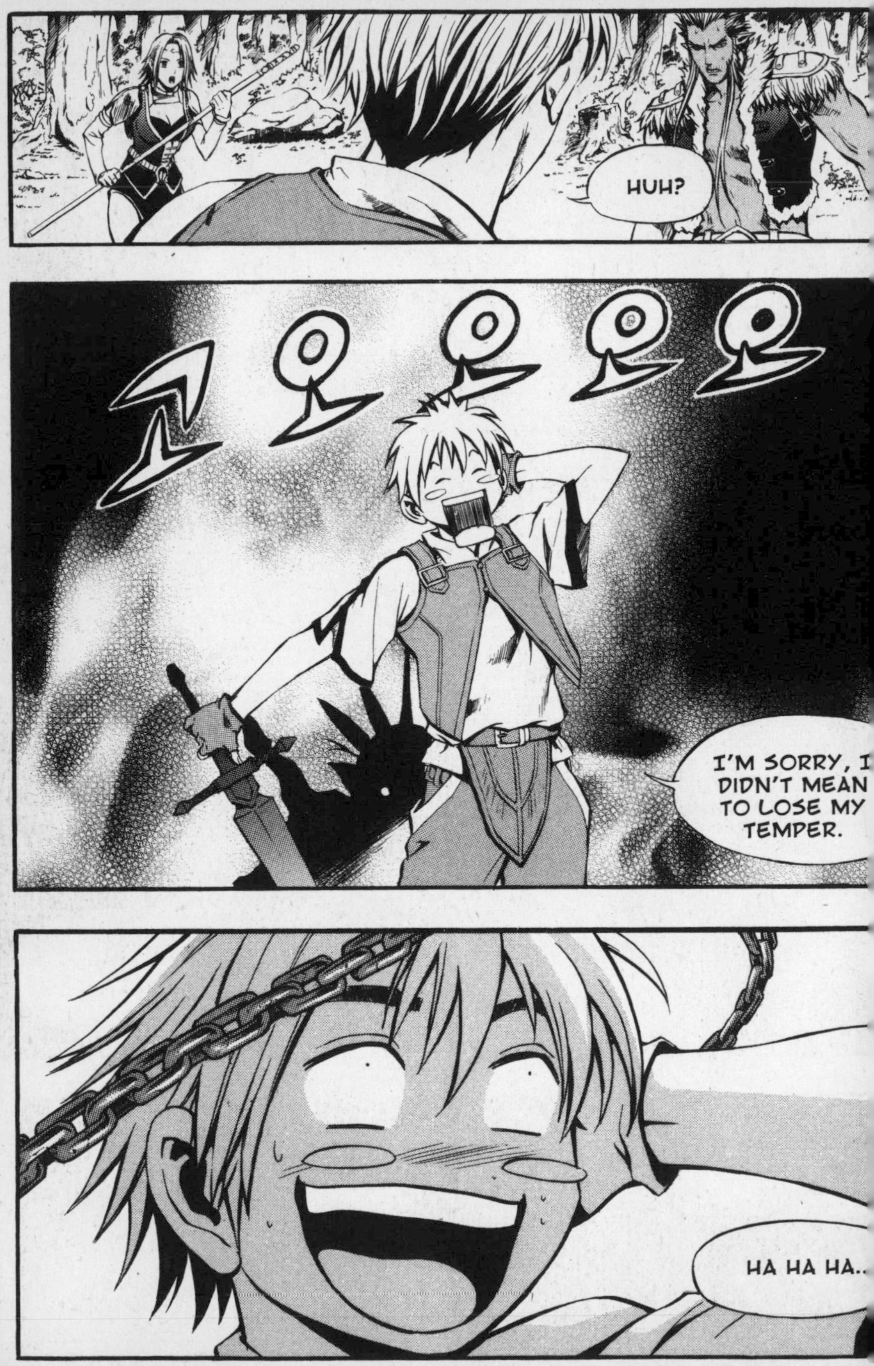
HUH?
I'M SORRY, I DIDN'T MEAN TO LOSE MY TEMPER.
HA HA HA...

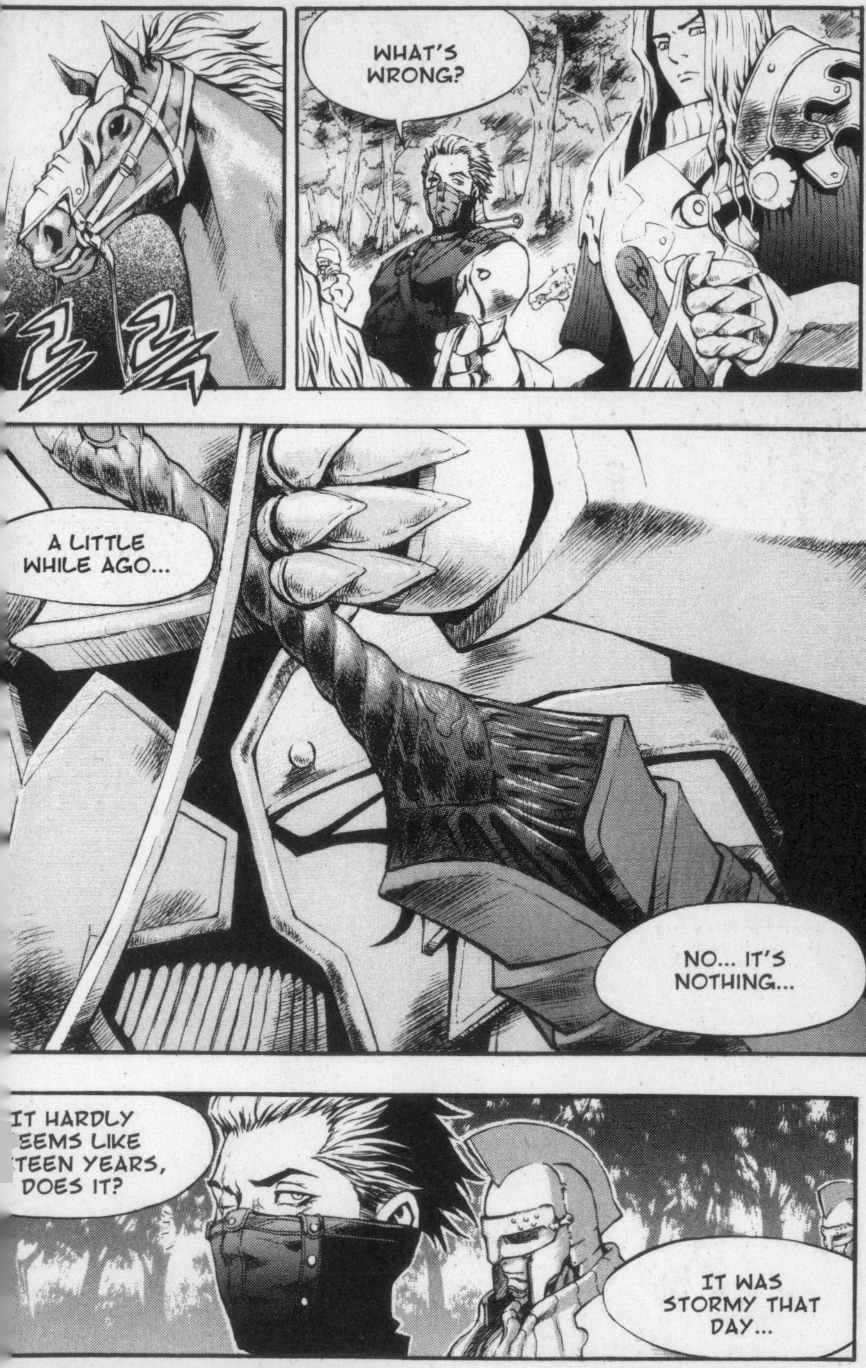
WHAT'S WRONG?
A LITTLE WHILE AGO...
NO... IT'S NOTHING...
IT HARDLY EEMS LIKE TEEN YEARS, DOES IT?
IT WAS STORMY THAT DAY...

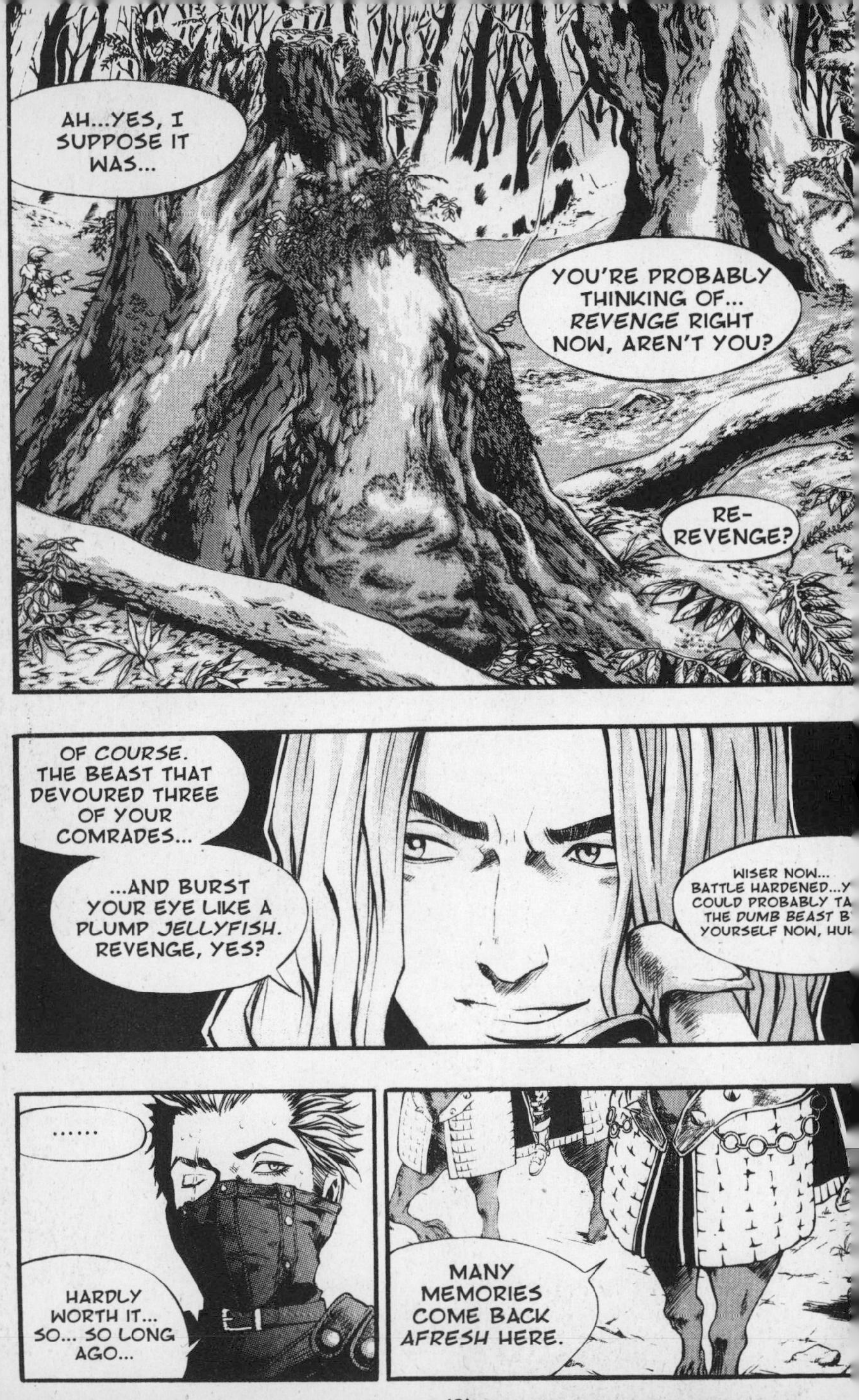
AH...YES, I SUPPOSE IT WAS...
YOU'RE PROBABLY THINKING OF... REVENGE RIGHT NOW, AREN'T YOU?
RE- REVENGE?
OF COURSE. THE BEAST THAT DEVOURED THREE OF YOUR COMRADES...
...AND BURST YOUR EYE LIKE A PLUMP JELLYFISH. REVENGE, YES?
WISER NOW... BATTLE HARDENED...Y COULD PROBABLY TA THE DUMB BEAST B YOURSELF NOW, HUH
......
HARDLY WORTH IT... SO... SO LONG AGO...
MANY MEMORIES COME BACK AFRESH HERE.

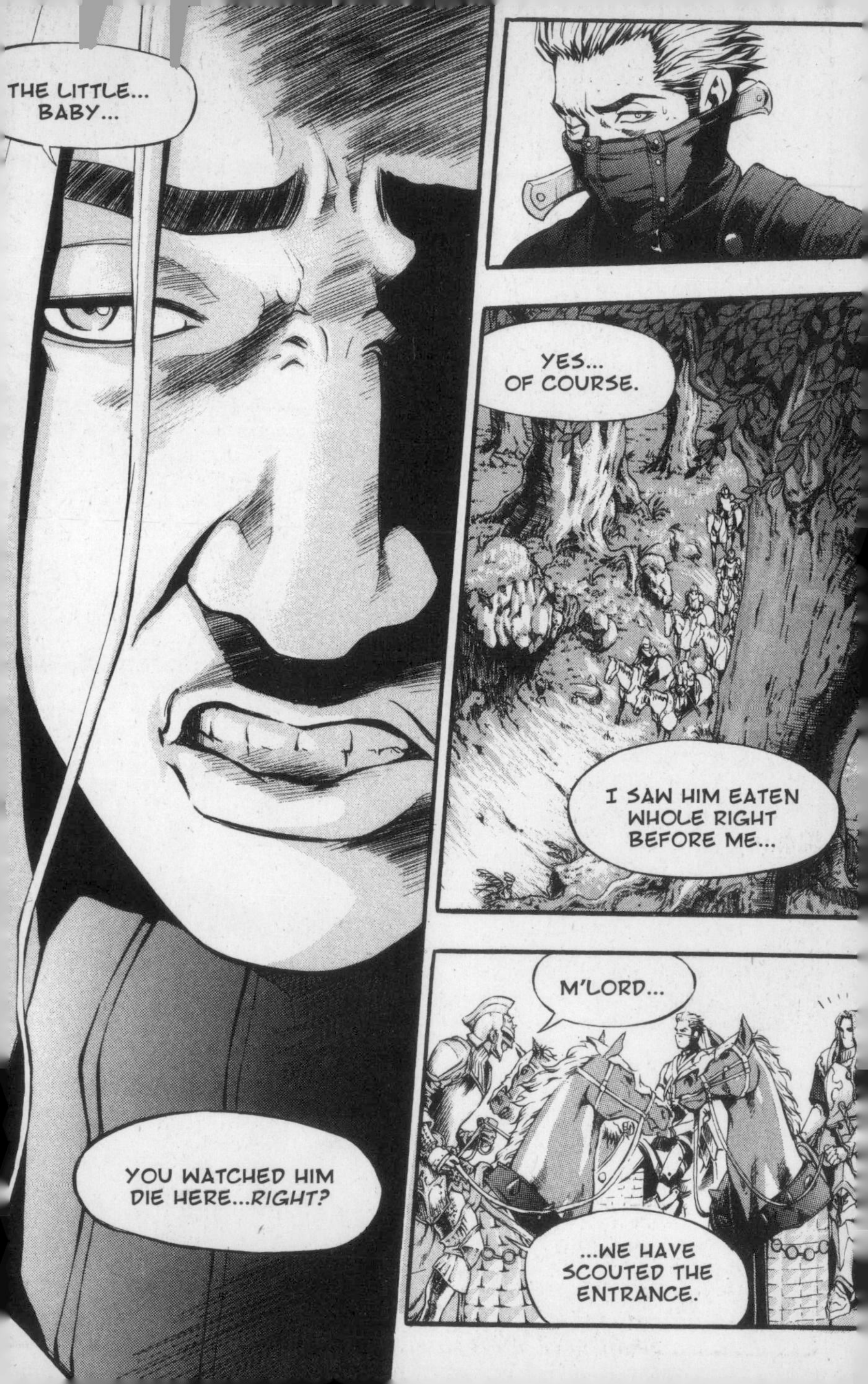
THE LITTLE... BABY...
YOU WATCHED HIM DIE HERE...*RIGHT?*
YES... OF COURSE.
I SAW HIM EATEN WHOLE RIGHT BEFORE ME...
M'LORD...
...WE HAVE SCOUTED THE ENTRANCE.

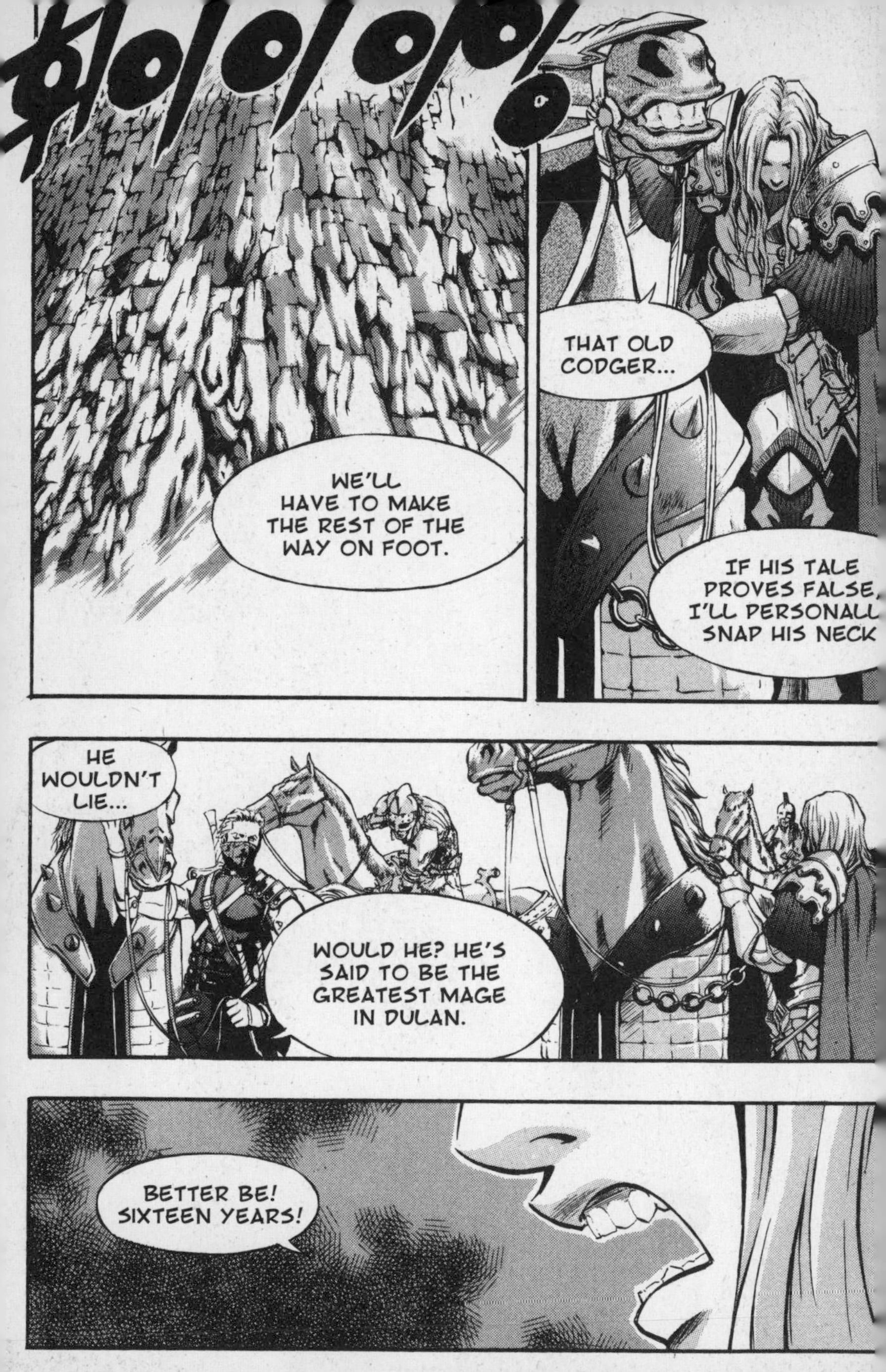
히이이이잉
WE'LL HAVE TO MAKE THE REST OF THE WAY ON FOOT.
THAT OLD CODGER...
IF HIS TALE PROVES FALSE, I'LL PERSONALL SNAP HIS NECK
HE WOULDN'T LIE...
WOULD HE? HE'S SAID TO BE THE GREATEST MAGE IN DULAN.
BETTER BE! SIXTEEN YEARS!

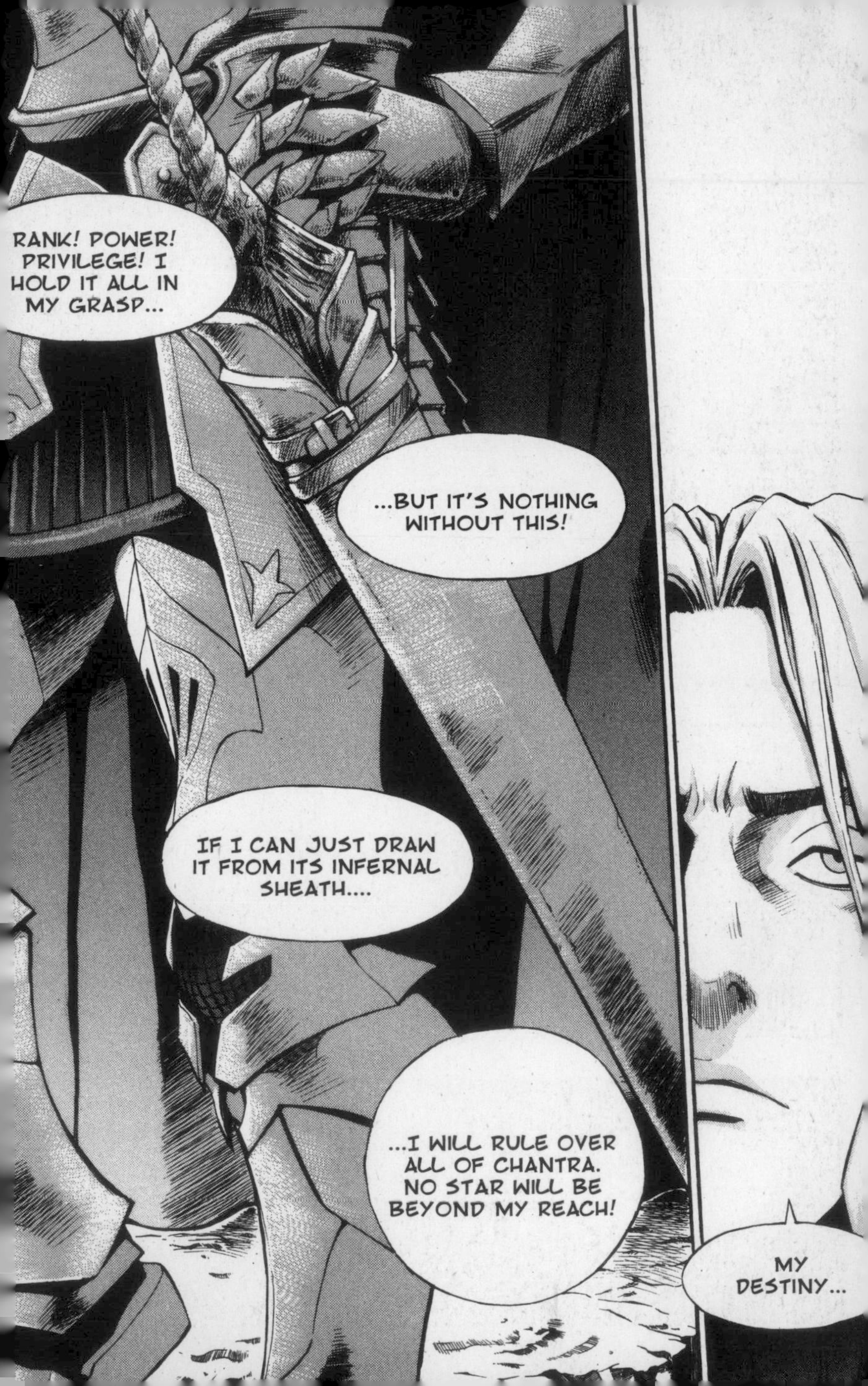
RANK! POWER! PRIVILEGE! I HOLD IT ALL IN MY GRASP...
...BUT IT'S NOTHING WITHOUT THIS!
IF I CAN JUST DRAW IT FROM ITS INFERNAL SHEATH....
...I WILL RULE OVER ALL OF CHANTRA. NO STAR WILL BE BEYOND MY REACH!
MY DESTINY...

...LIES ON TOP OF THAT MOUNTAIN.

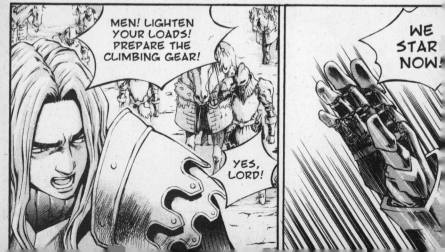

MEN! LIGHTEN YOUR LOADS! PREPARE THE CLIMBING GEAR!

YES, LORD!

WE STAR NOW!

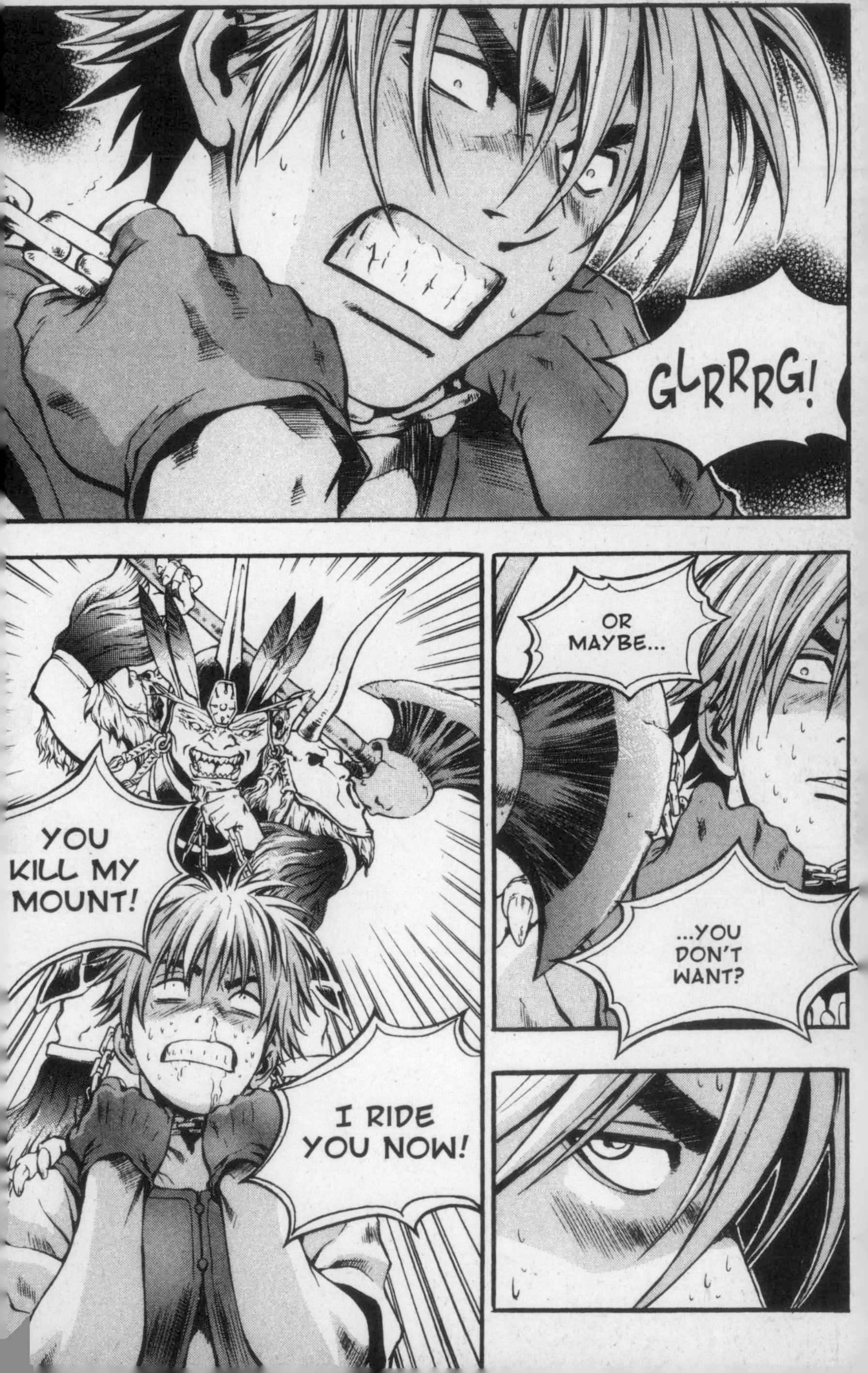
GLRRRG!
YOU KILL MY MOUNT!
I RIDE YOU NOW!
OR MAYBE...
...YOU DON'T WANT?

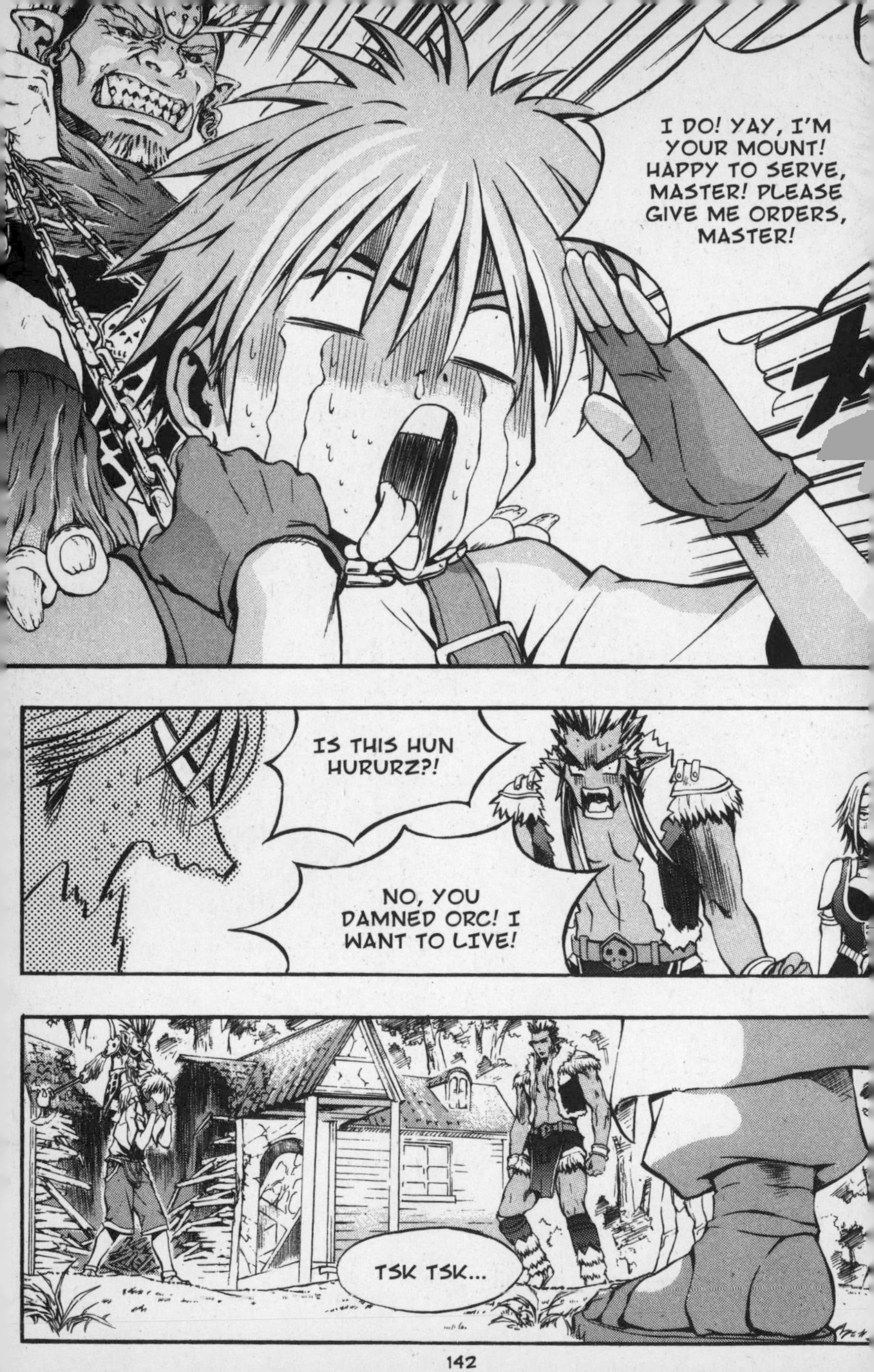
I DO! YAY, I'M YOUR MOUNT! HAPPY TO SERVE, MASTER! PLEASE GIVE ME ORDERS, MASTER!
IS THIS HUN HURURZ?!
NO, YOU DAMNED ORC! I WANT TO LIVE!
TSK TSK...

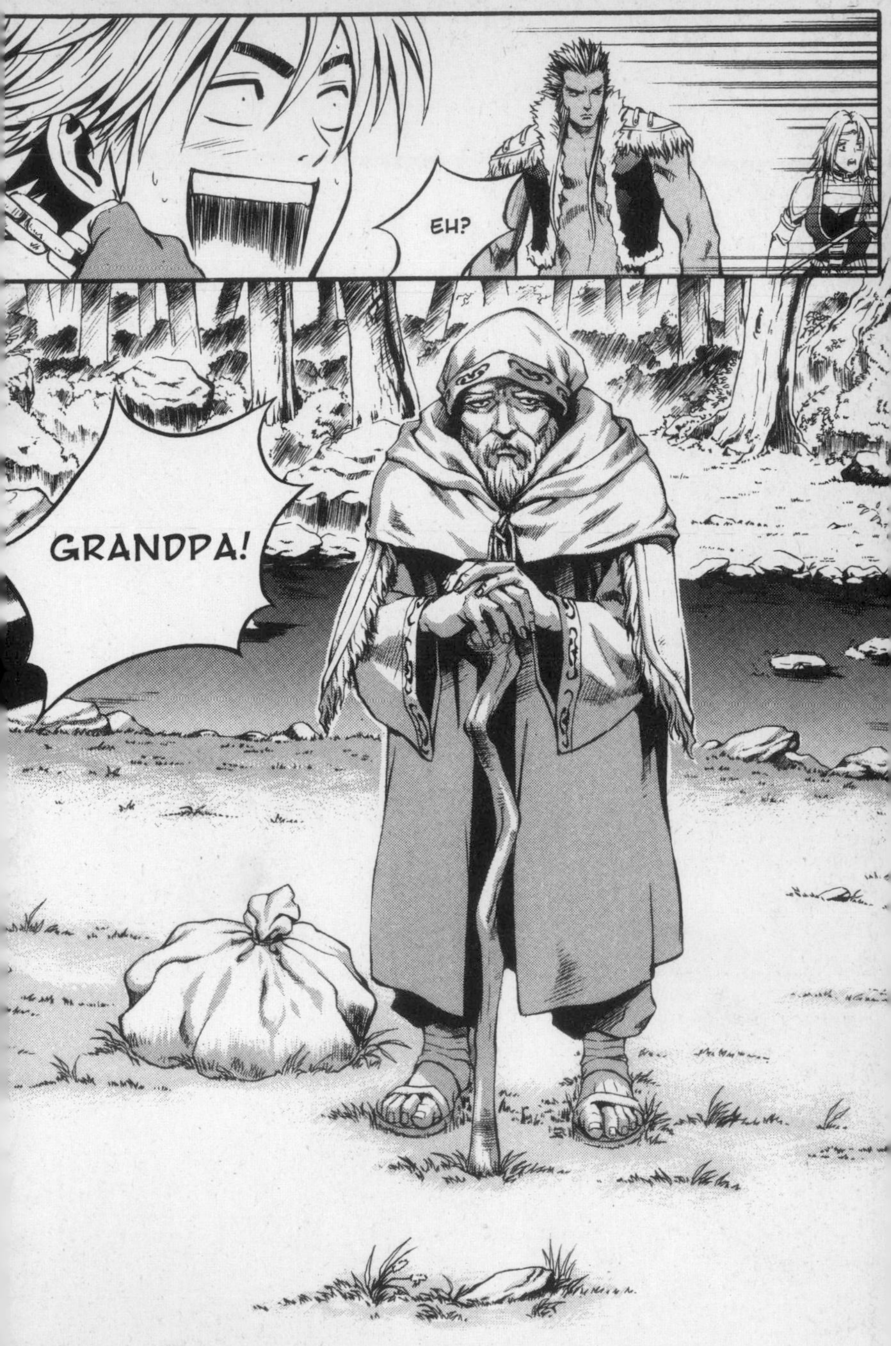
EH?
GRANDPA!

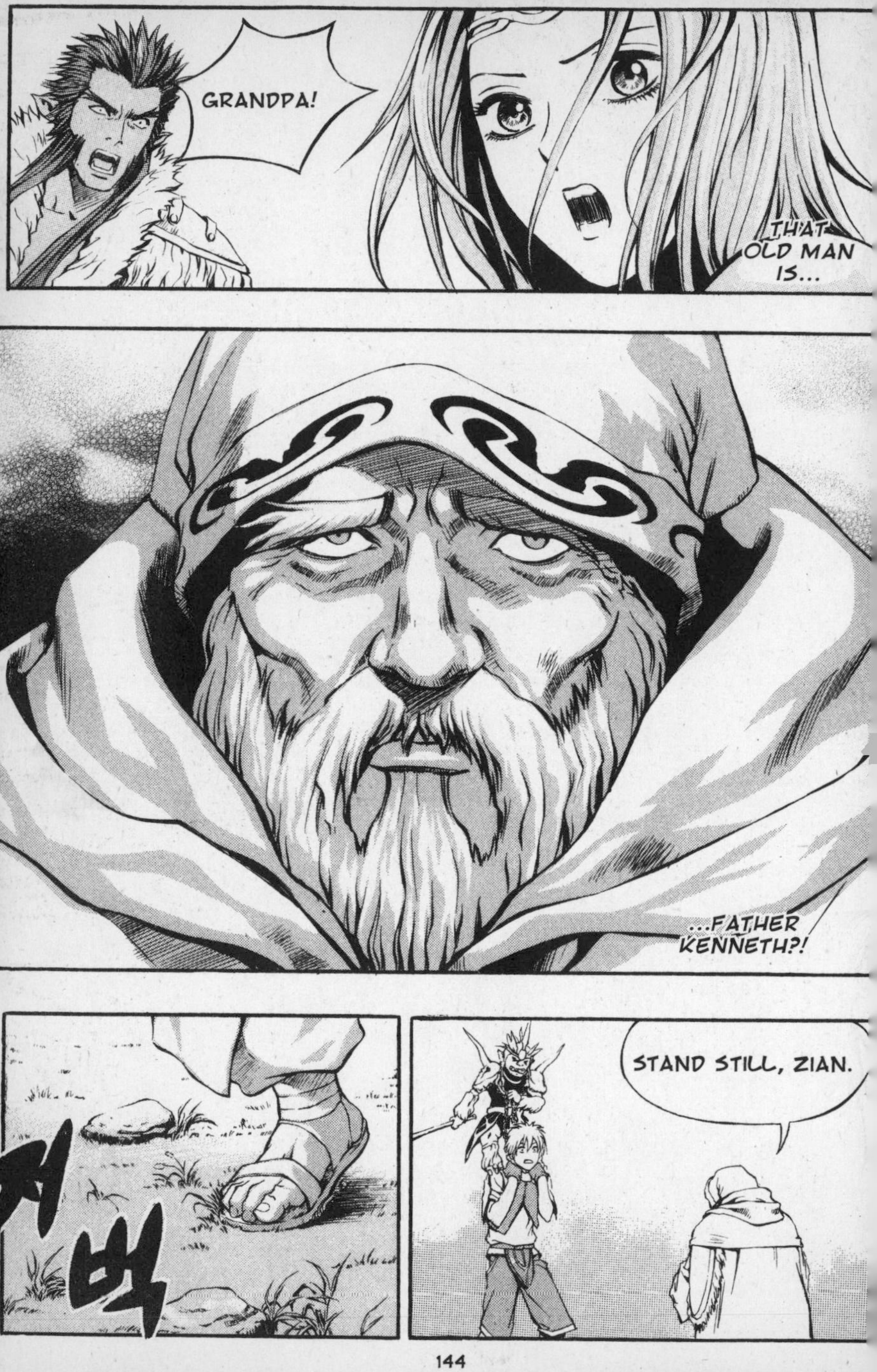
GRANDPA!
THAT OLD MAN IS...
...FATHER KENNETH?!
저벅
STAND STILL, ZIAN.

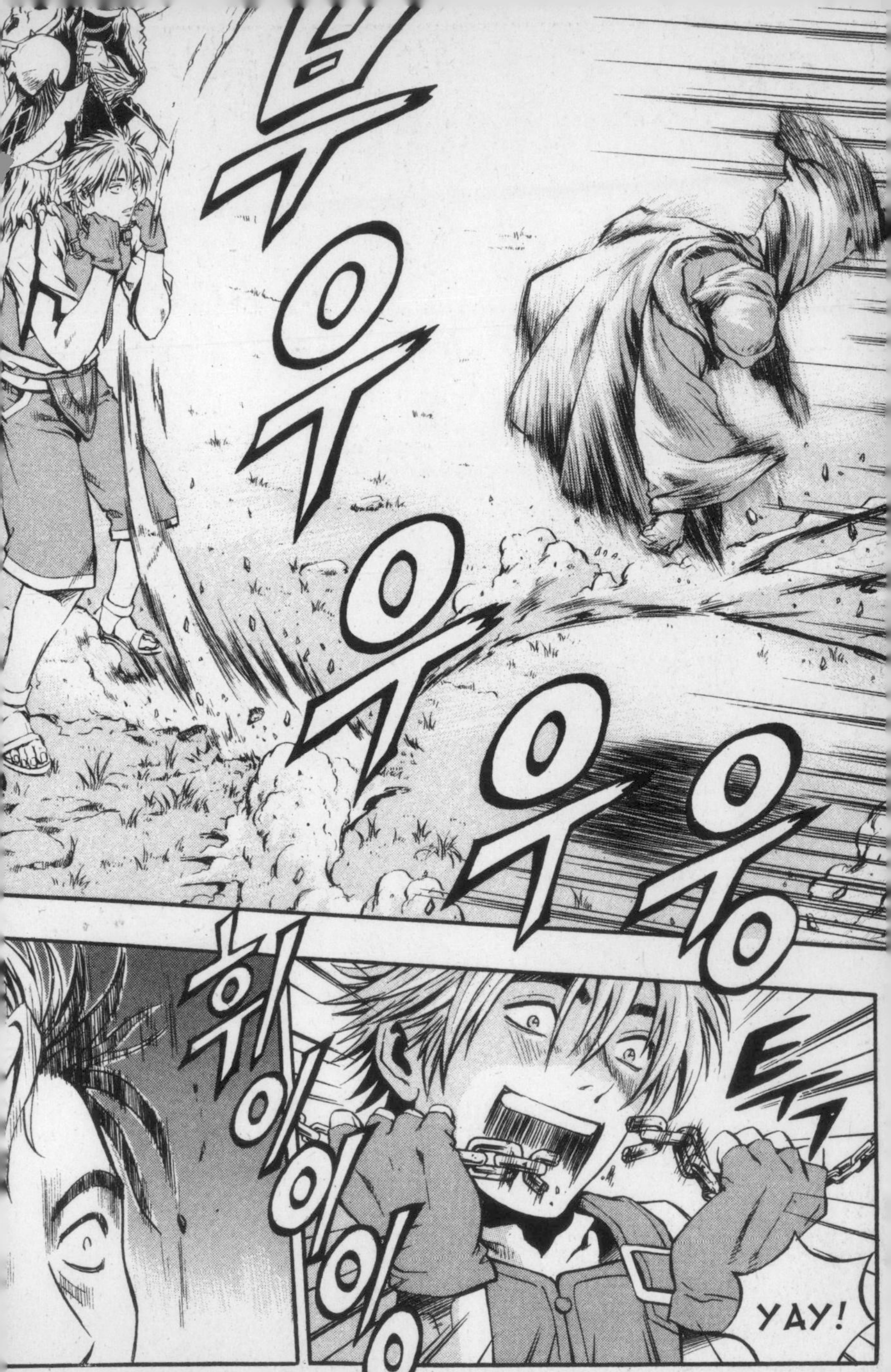
YAY!

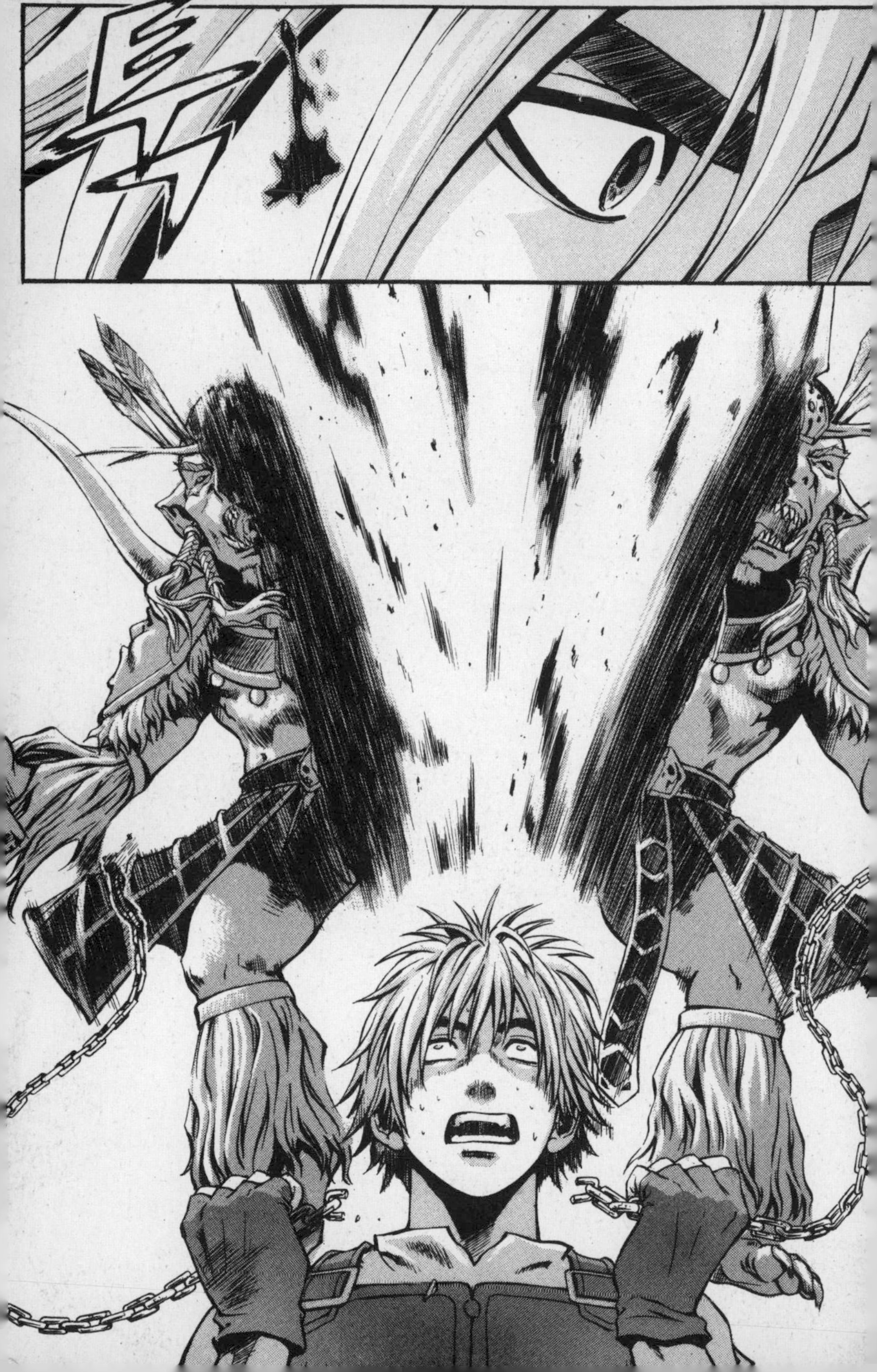

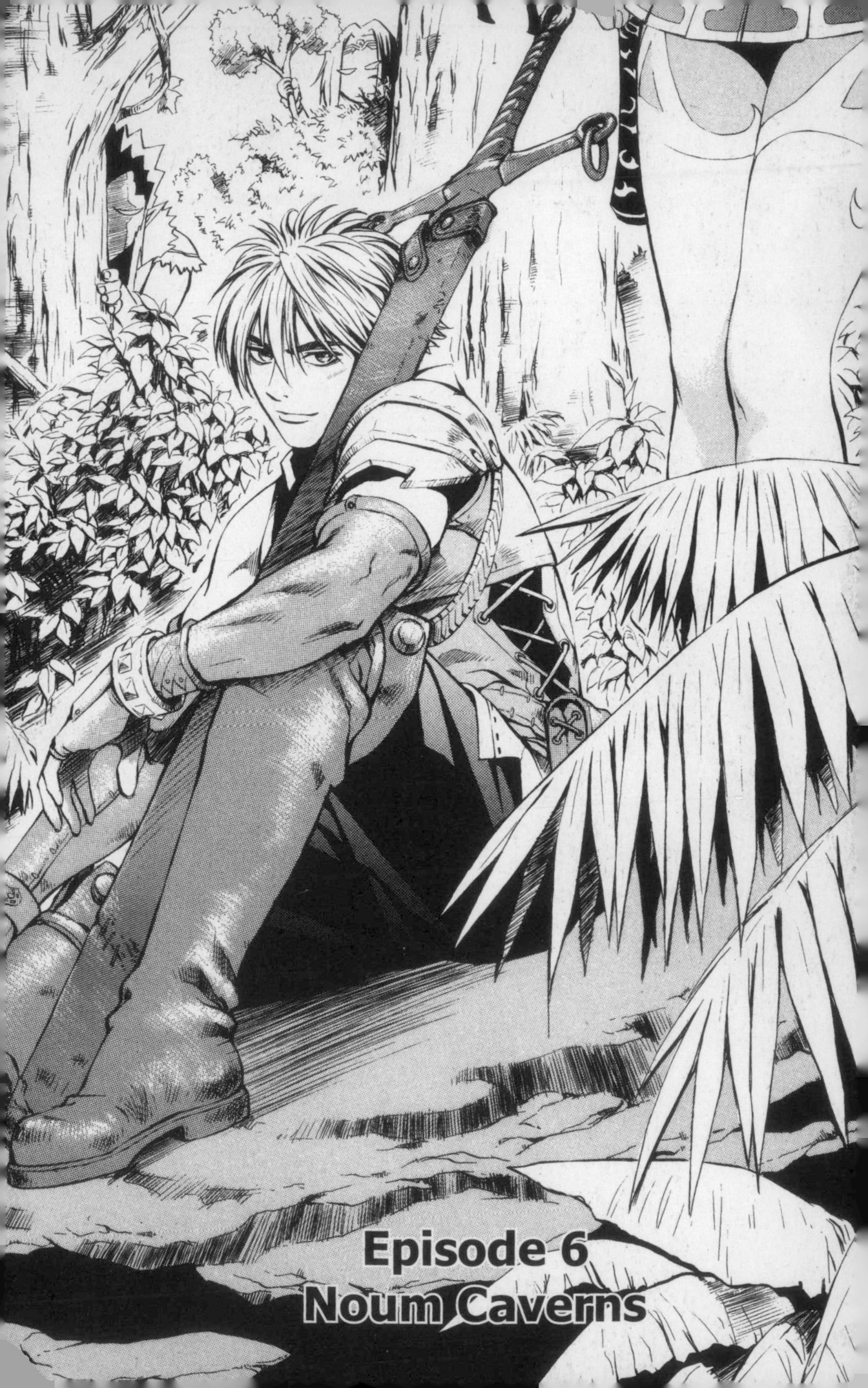
Episode 6
Noum Caverns

HURGH...

HUH-HA...

BIRDS...?

CAN'T BE FAR FROM THE SUMMIT...

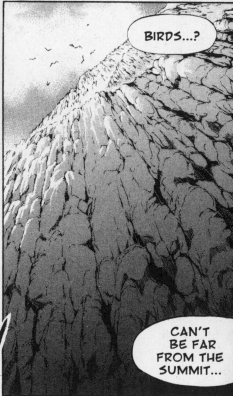

M'LORD...

THOSE AREN'T BIRDS.

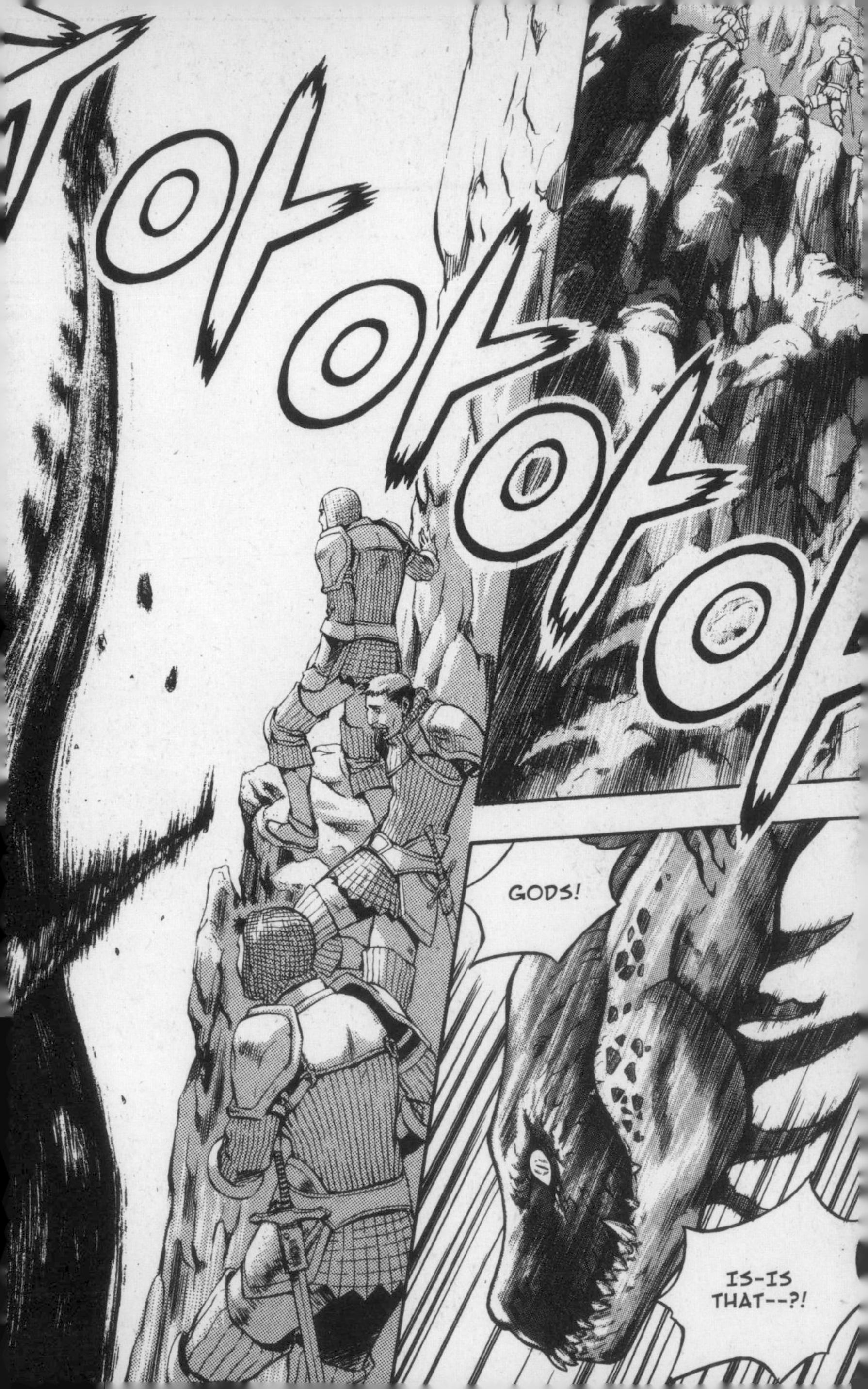
GODS!
IS-IS THAT--?!

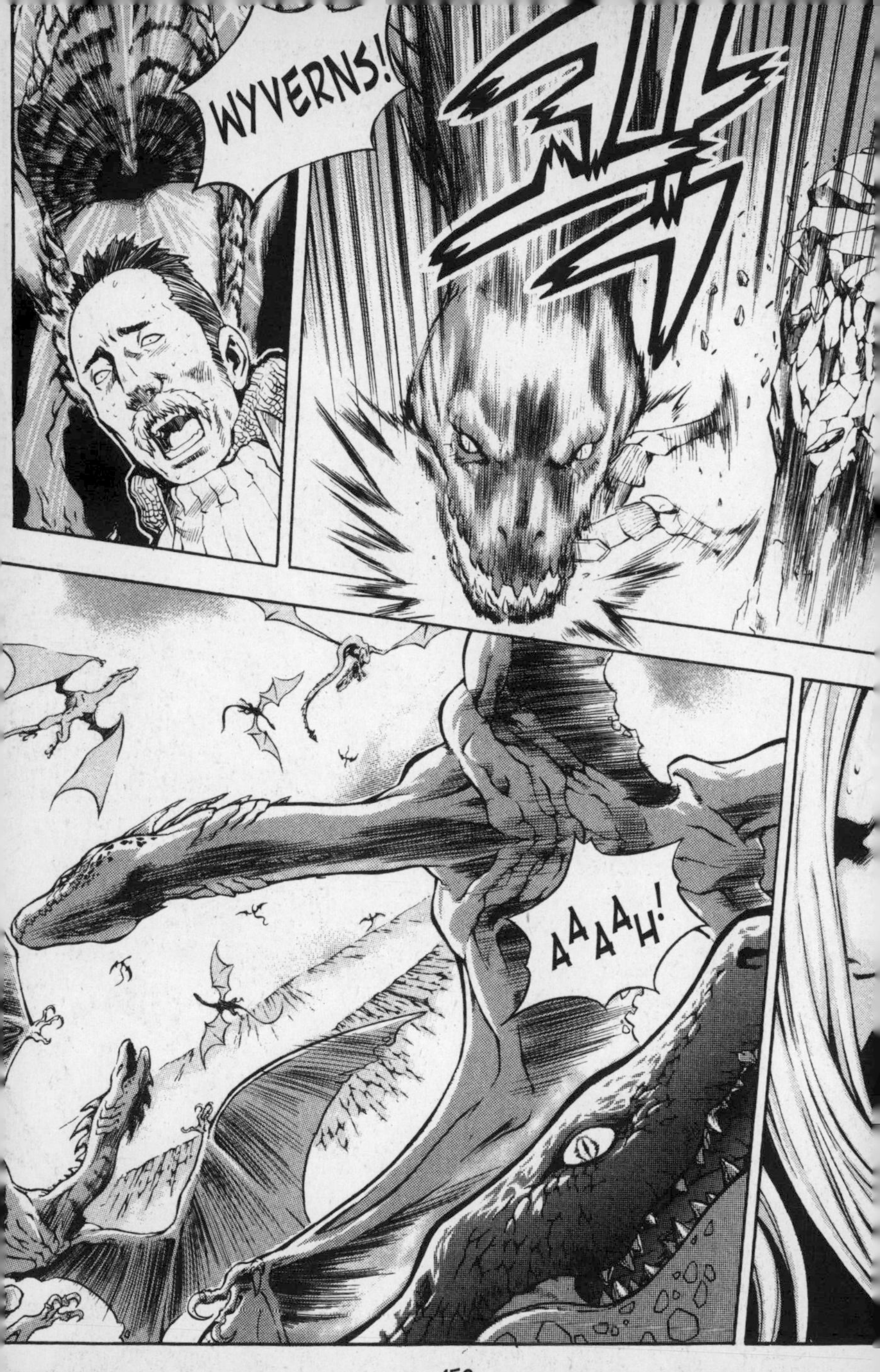
WYVERNS!
AAAAH!

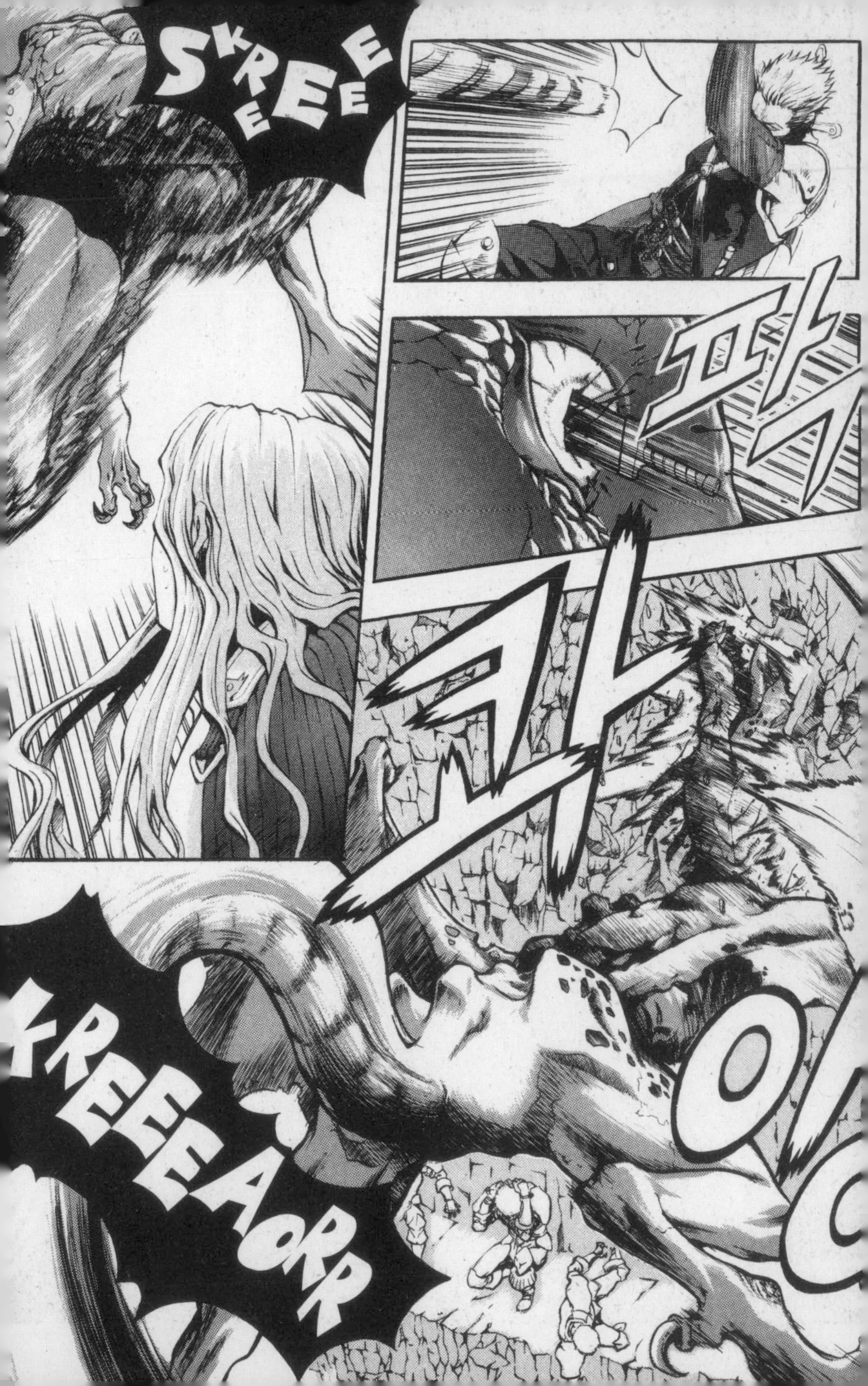
SKREEEE
콰
KREEEAORR

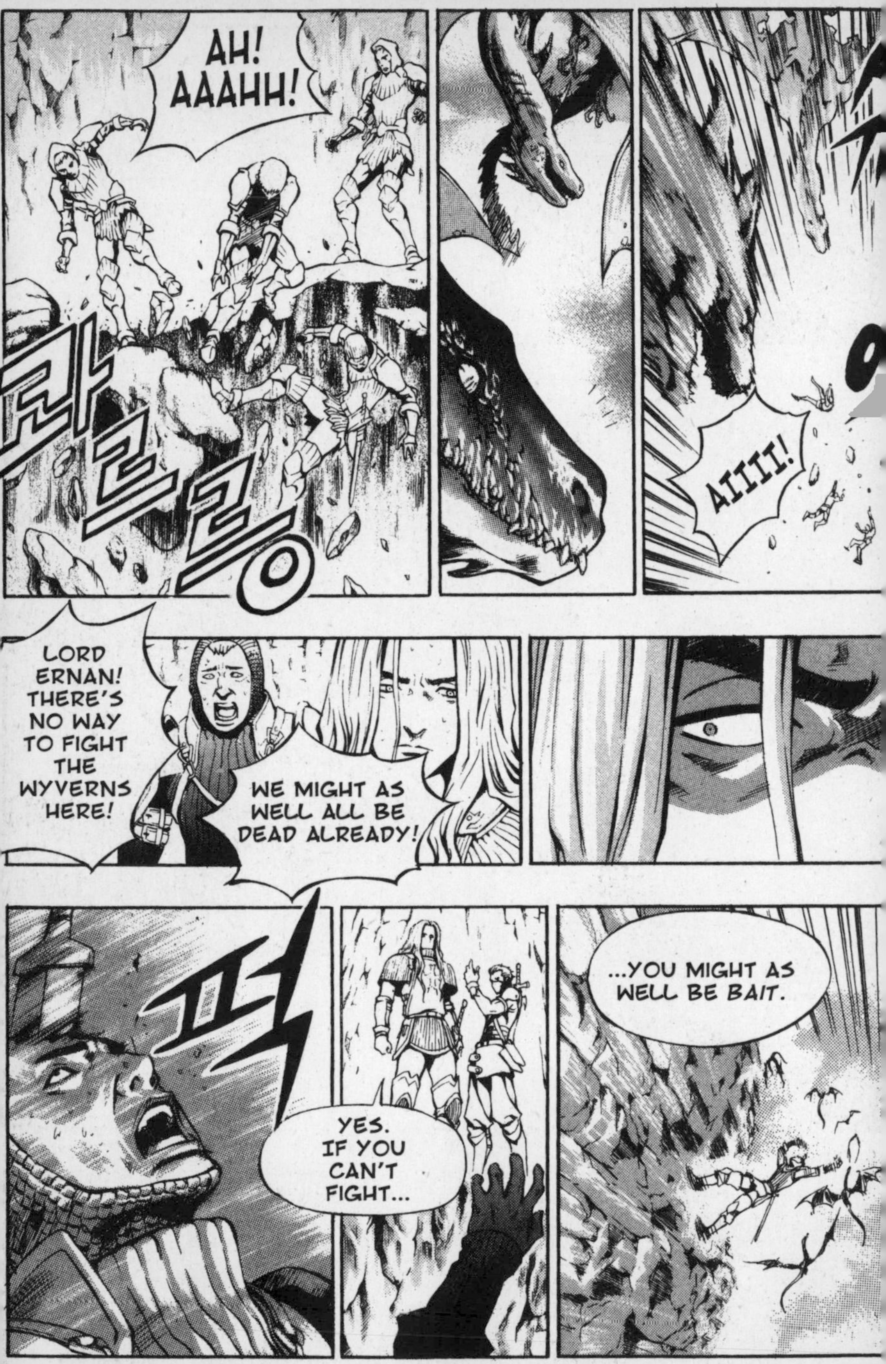
AH! AAAHH!
콰르르릉
AIIII!
LORD ERNAN! THERE'S NO WAY TO FIGHT THE WYVERNS HERE!
WE MIGHT AS WELL ALL BE DEAD ALREADY!
파
YES. IF YOU CAN'T FIGHT...
...YOU MIGHT AS WELL BE BAIT.

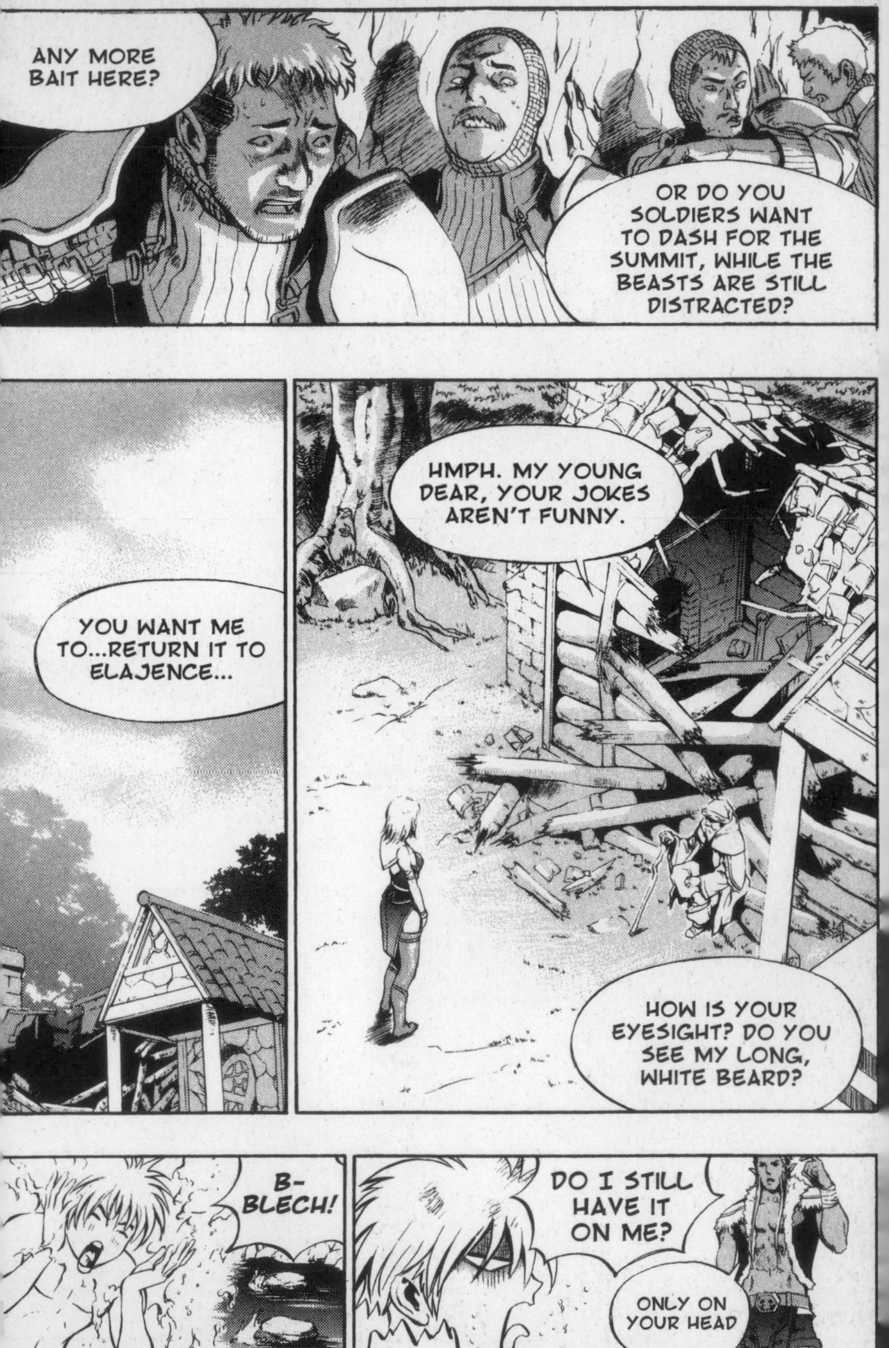
ANY MORE BAIT HERE?
OR DO YOU SOLDIERS WANT TO DASH FOR THE SUMMIT, WHILE THE BEASTS ARE STILL DISTRACTED?
YOU WANT ME TO...RETURN IT TO ELAJENCE...
HMPH. MY YOUNG DEAR, YOUR JOKES AREN'T FUNNY.
HOW IS YOUR EYESIGHT? DO YOU SEE MY LONG, WHITE BEARD?
B-BLECH!
DO I STILL HAVE IT ON ME?
ONLY ON YOUR HEAD

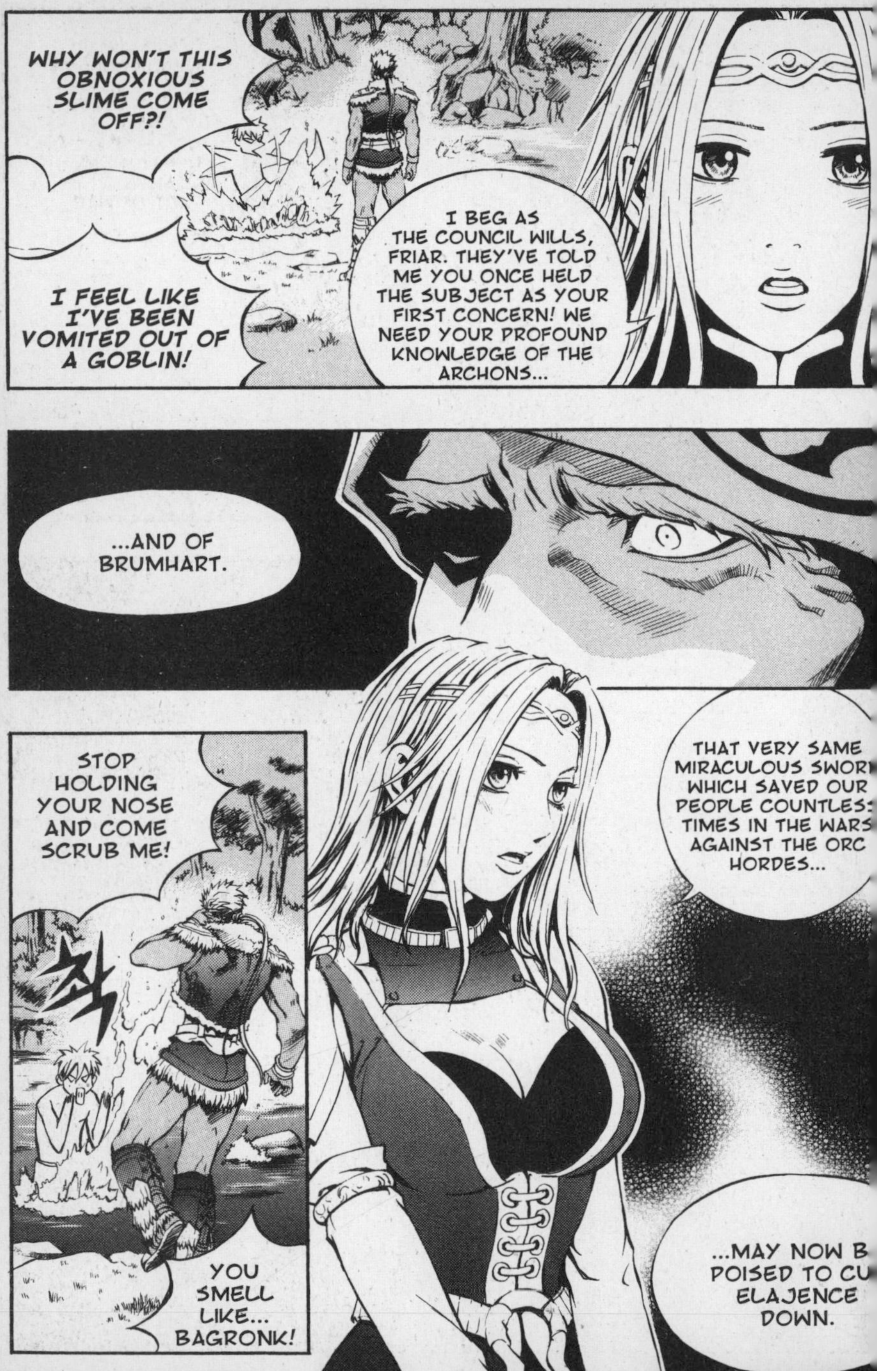
WHY WON'T THIS OBNOXIOUS SLIME COME OFF?!
I FEEL LIKE I'VE BEEN VOMITED OUT OF A GOBLIN!
I BEG AS THE COUNCIL WILLS, FRIAR. THEY'VE TOLD ME YOU ONCE HELD THE SUBJECT AS YOUR FIRST CONCERN! WE NEED YOUR PROFOUND KNOWLEDGE OF THE ARCHONS...
...AND OF BRUMHART.
STOP HOLDING YOUR NOSE AND COME SCRUB ME!
YOU SMELL LIKE... BAGRONK!
THAT VERY SAME MIRACULOUS SWOR WHICH SAVED OUR PEOPLE COUNTLES TIMES IN THE WARS AGAINST THE ORC HORDES...
...MAY NOW B POISED TO CU ELAJENCE DOWN.

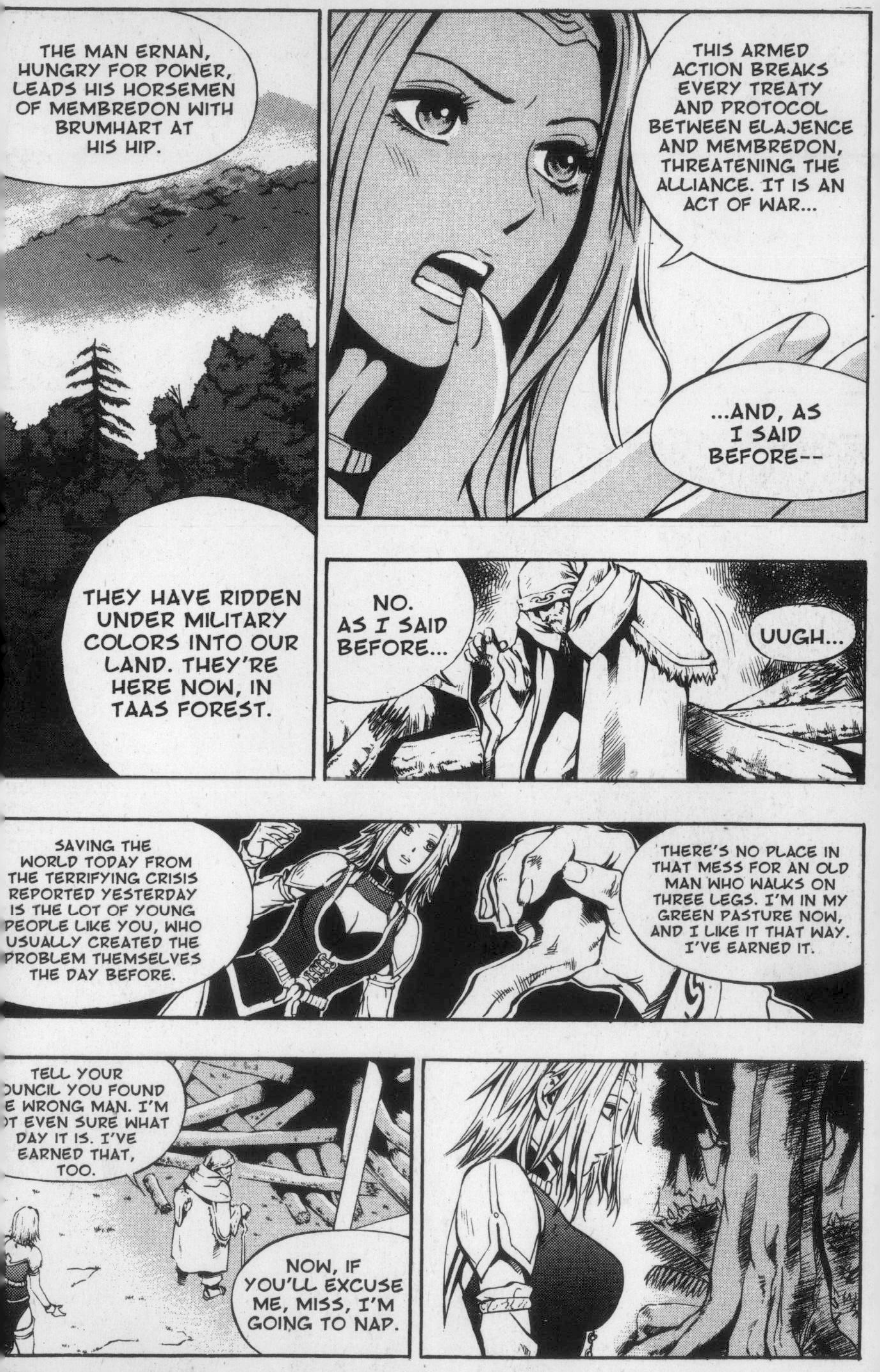
THE MAN ERNAN, HUNGRY FOR POWER, LEADS HIS HORSEMEN OF MEMBREDON WITH BRUMHART AT HIS HIP.
THIS ARMED ACTION BREAKS EVERY TREATY AND PROTOCOL BETWEEN ELAJENCE AND MEMBREDON, THREATENING THE ALLIANCE. IT IS AN ACT OF WAR...
...AND, AS I SAID BEFORE--
THEY HAVE RIDDEN UNDER MILITARY COLORS INTO OUR LAND. THEY'RE HERE NOW, IN TAAS FOREST.
NO. AS I SAID BEFORE...
UUGH...
SAVING THE WORLD TODAY FROM THE TERRIFYING CRISIS REPORTED YESTERDAY IS THE LOT OF YOUNG PEOPLE LIKE YOU, WHO USUALLY CREATED THE PROBLEM THEMSELVES THE DAY BEFORE.
THERE'S NO PLACE IN THAT MESS FOR AN OLD MAN WHO WALKS ON THREE LEGS. I'M IN MY GREEN PASTURE NOW, AND I LIKE IT THAT WAY. I'VE EARNED IT.
TELL YOUR OUNCIL YOU FOUND E WRONG MAN. I'M OT EVEN SURE WHAT DAY IT IS. I'VE EARNED THAT, TOO.
NOW, IF YOU'LL EXCUSE ME, MISS, I'M GOING TO NAP.

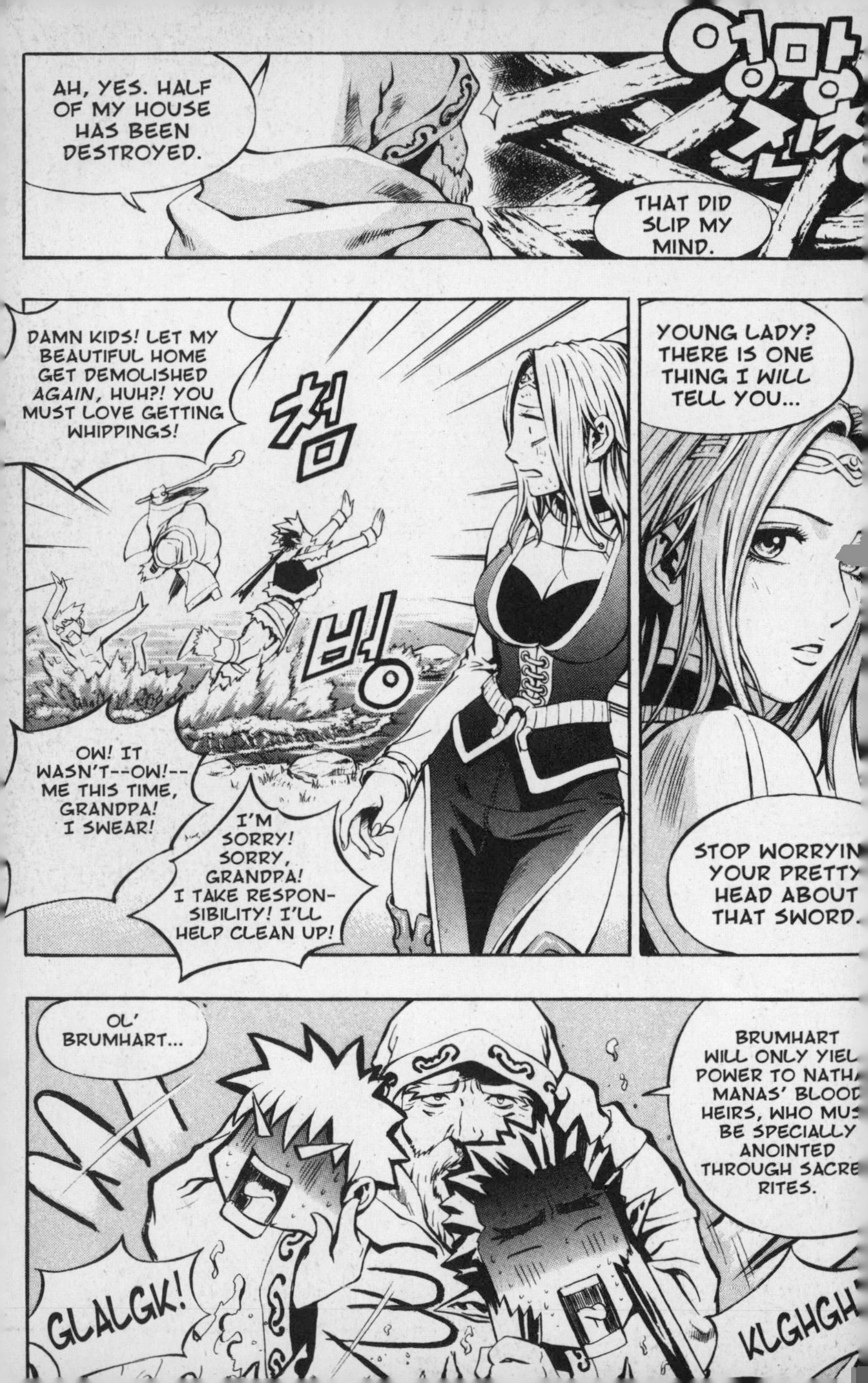
AH, YES. HALF OF MY HOUSE HAS BEEN DESTROYED.
엉망
THAT DID SLIP MY MIND.
DAMN KIDS! LET MY BEAUTIFUL HOME GET DEMOLISHED *AGAIN*, HUH?! YOU MUST LOVE GETTING WHIPPINGS!
첨벙
OW! IT WASN'T--OW!--ME THIS TIME, GRANDPA! I SWEAR!
I'M SORRY! SORRY, GRANDPA! I TAKE RESPONSIBILITY! I'LL HELP CLEAN UP!
YOUNG LADY? THERE IS ONE THING I *WILL* TELL YOU...
STOP WORRYIN YOUR PRETTY HEAD ABOUT THAT SWORD.
OL' BRUMHART...
BRUMHART WILL ONLY YIEL POWER TO NATH MANAS' BLOOD HEIRS, WHO MUS BE SPECIALLY ANOINTED THROUGH SACRE RITES.
GLALGK!
KLGHGH

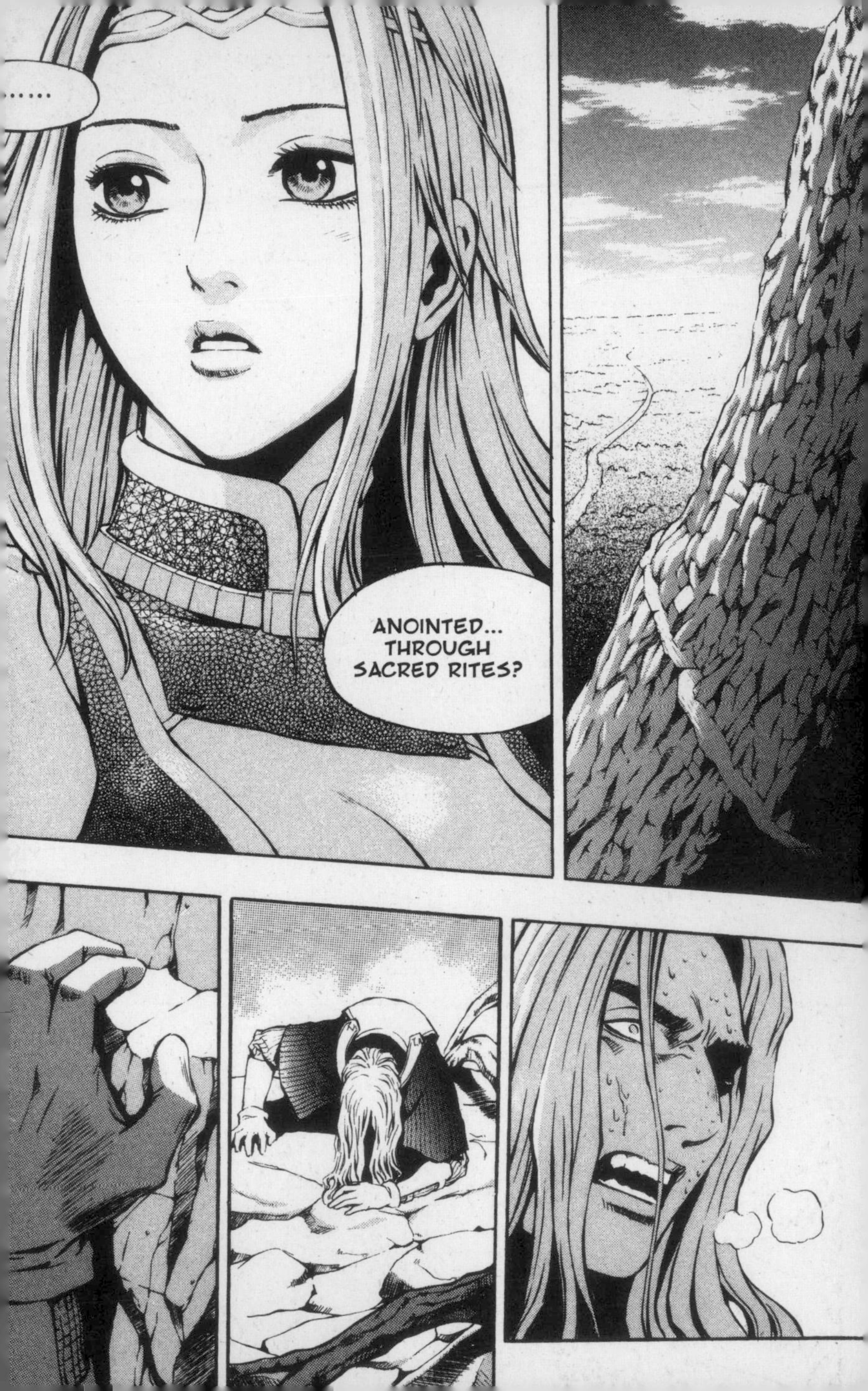
......
ANOINTED... THROUGH SACRED RITES?

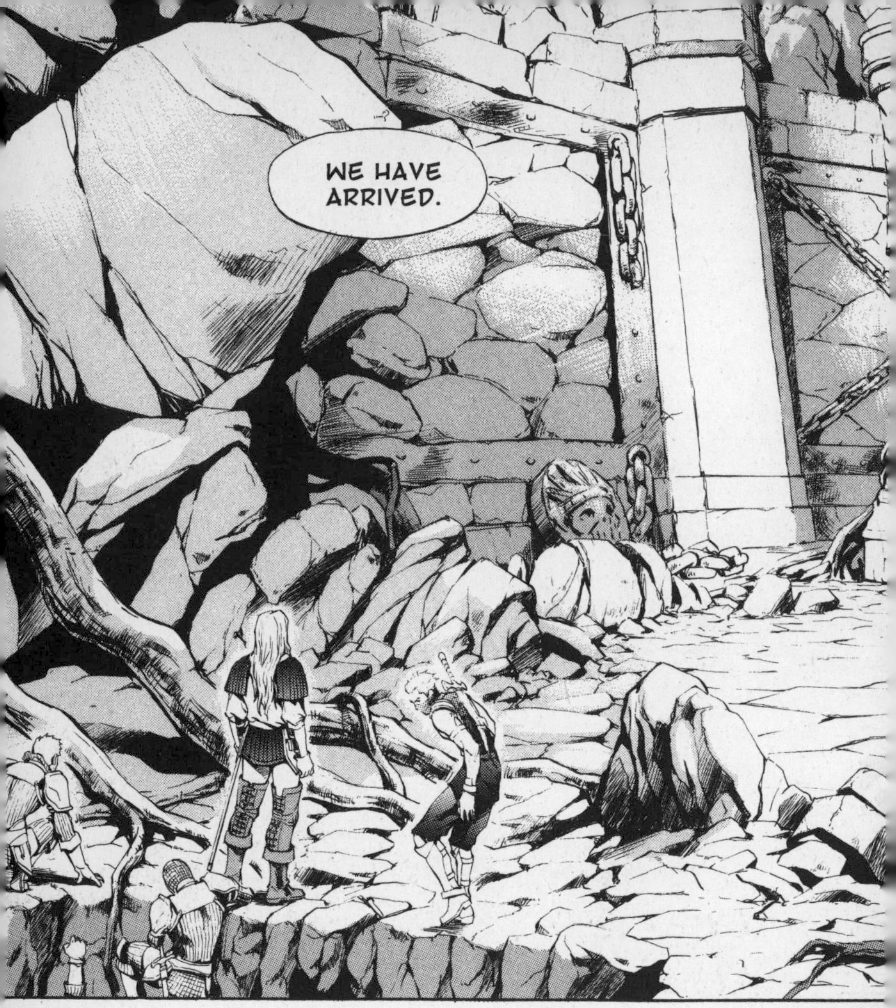
WE HAVE ARRIVED.

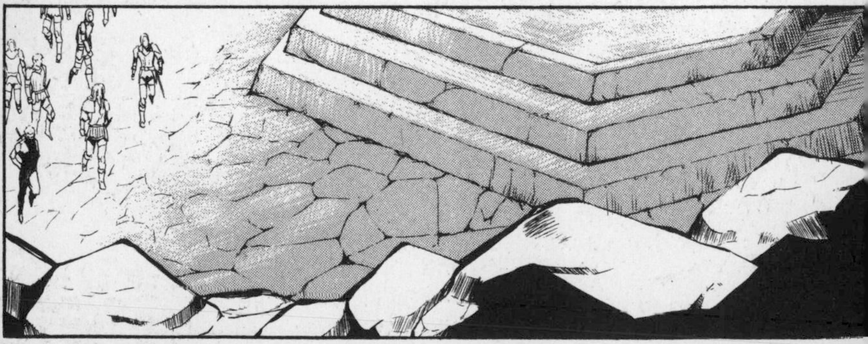

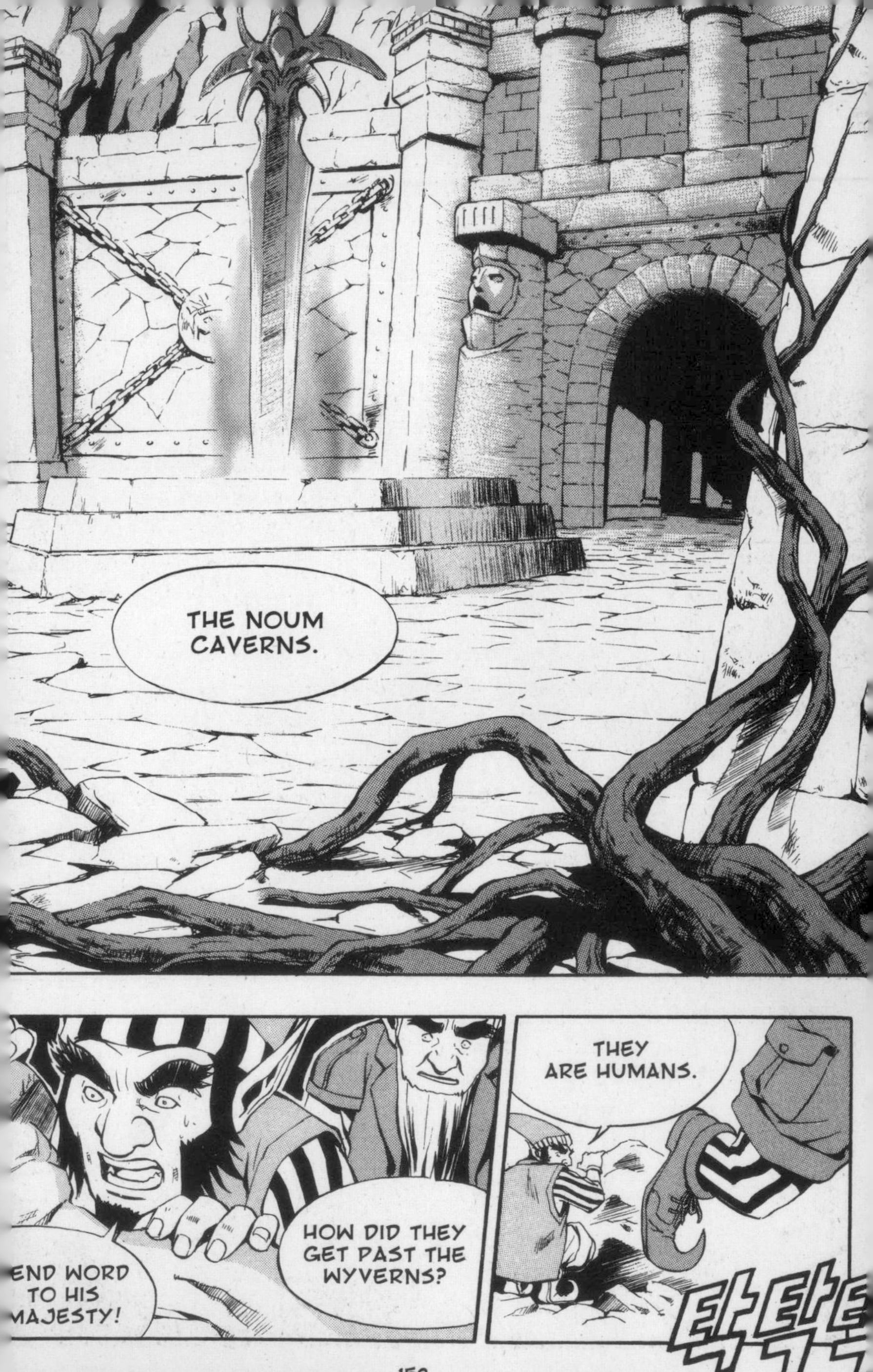
THE NOUM CAVERNS.
END WORD TO HIS MAJESTY!
HOW DID THEY GET PAST THE WYVERNS?
THEY ARE HUMANS.

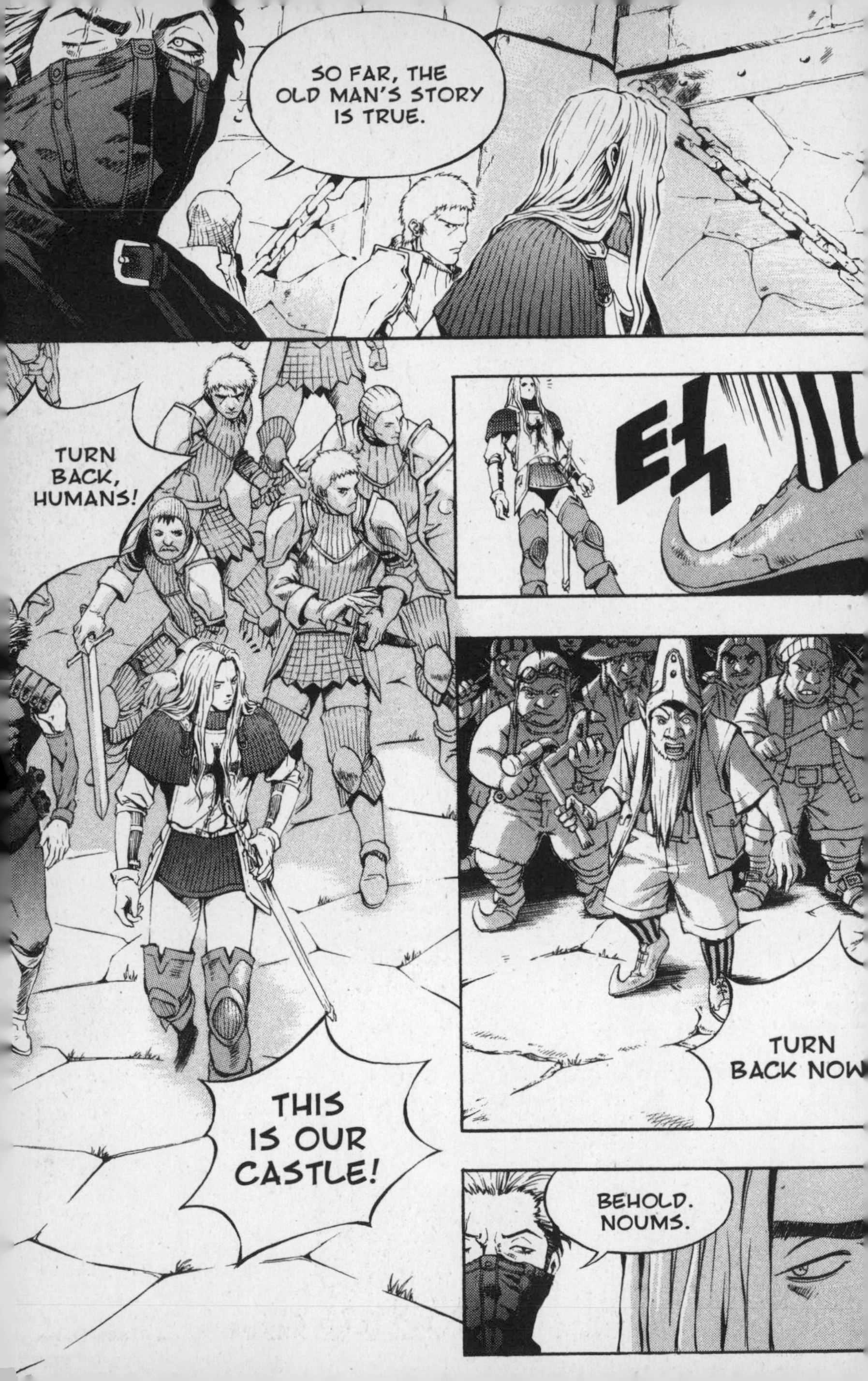

SO FAR, THE OLD MAN'S STORY IS TRUE.
TURN BACK, HUMANS!
THIS IS OUR CASTLE!
TURN BACK NOW
BEHOLD. NOUMS.

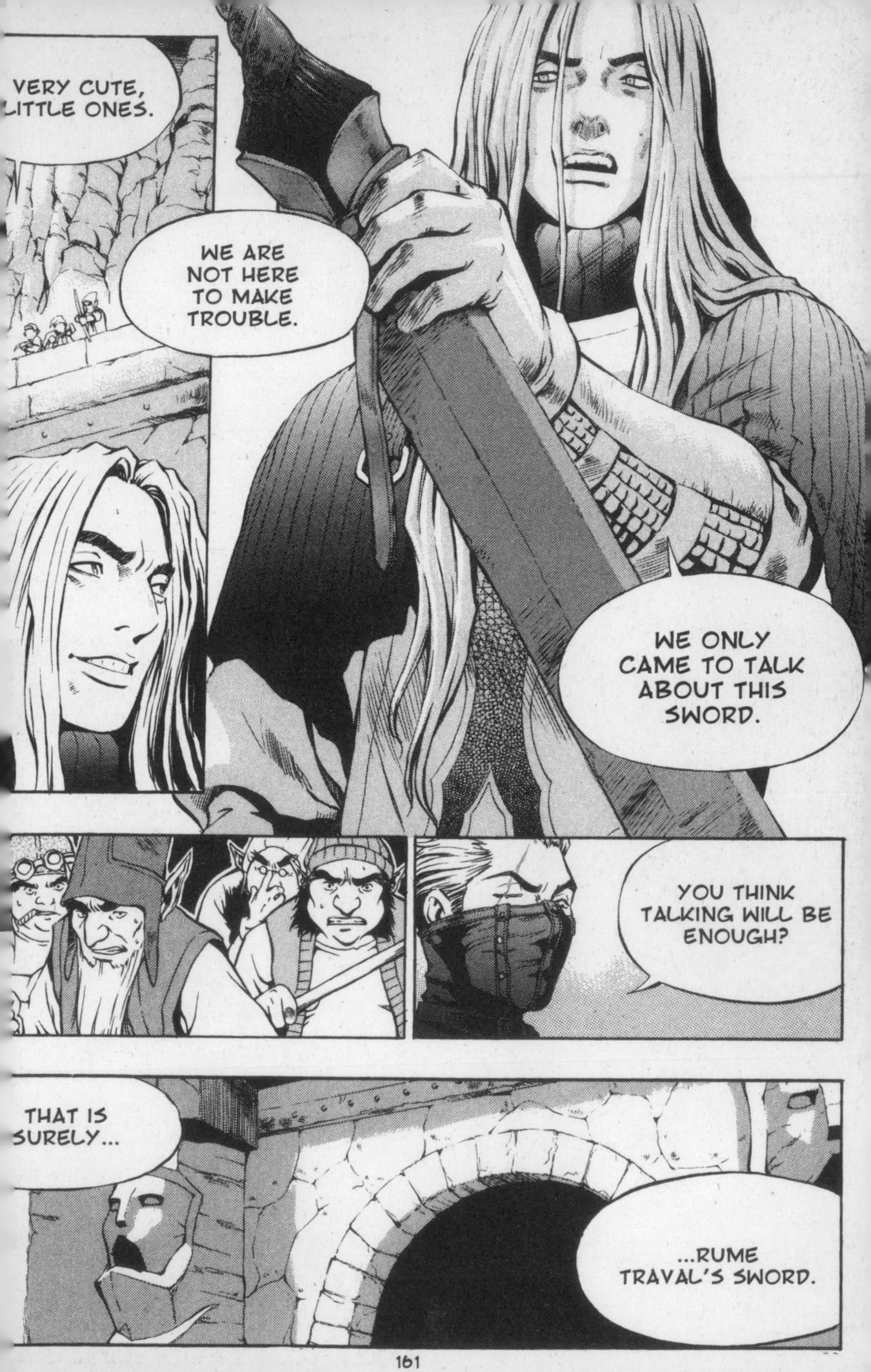
VERY CUTE, LITTLE ONES.
WE ARE NOT HERE TO MAKE TROUBLE.
WE ONLY CAME TO TALK ABOUT THIS SWORD.
YOU THINK TALKING WILL BE ENOUGH?
THAT IS SURELY...
...RUME TRAVAL'S SWORD.

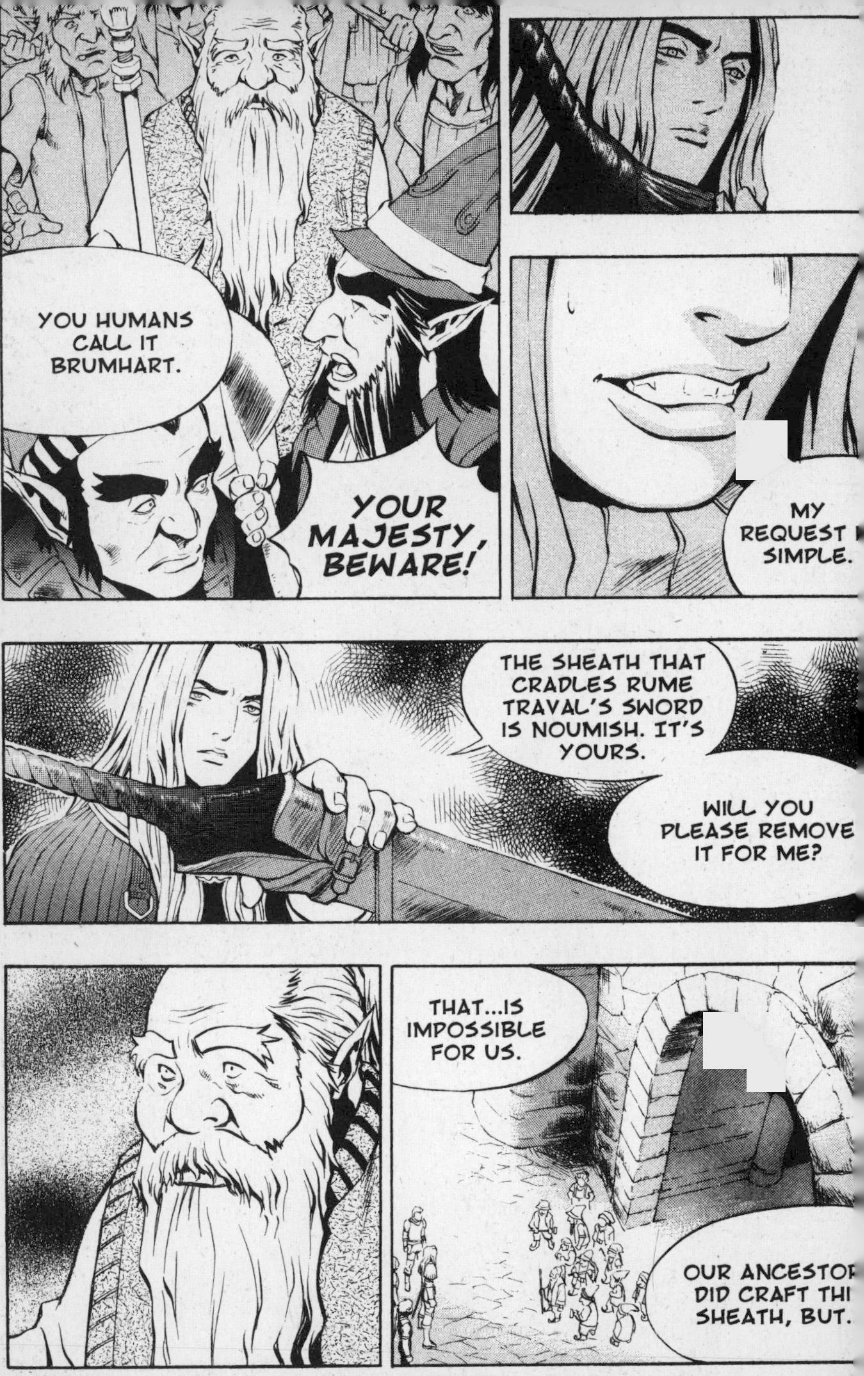
YOU HUMANS CALL IT BRUMHART.
YOUR MAJESTY, BEWARE!
MY REQUEST I SIMPLE.
THE SHEATH THAT CRADLES RUME TRAVAL'S SWORD IS NOUMISH. IT'S YOURS.
WILL YOU PLEASE REMOVE IT FOR ME?
THAT...IS IMPOSSIBLE FOR US.
OUR ANCESTOR DID CRAFT THI SHEATH, BUT.

...A GREAT BLOOD SIGIL HAS SEALED IT. MOST POWERFUL RUNES.

ONLY ONE OF MANAS' LINE CAN--

THE MANAS LINE HAS ENDED, EXCELLENT KING. FOR THE GOOD OF ALL...

...IT IS TIME FOR BRUMHART TO SERVE A NEW MASTER.

...THE SIGIL MUST BE MELTED...THE RUNES REWRITTEN. YOU MUST KNOW A WAY.

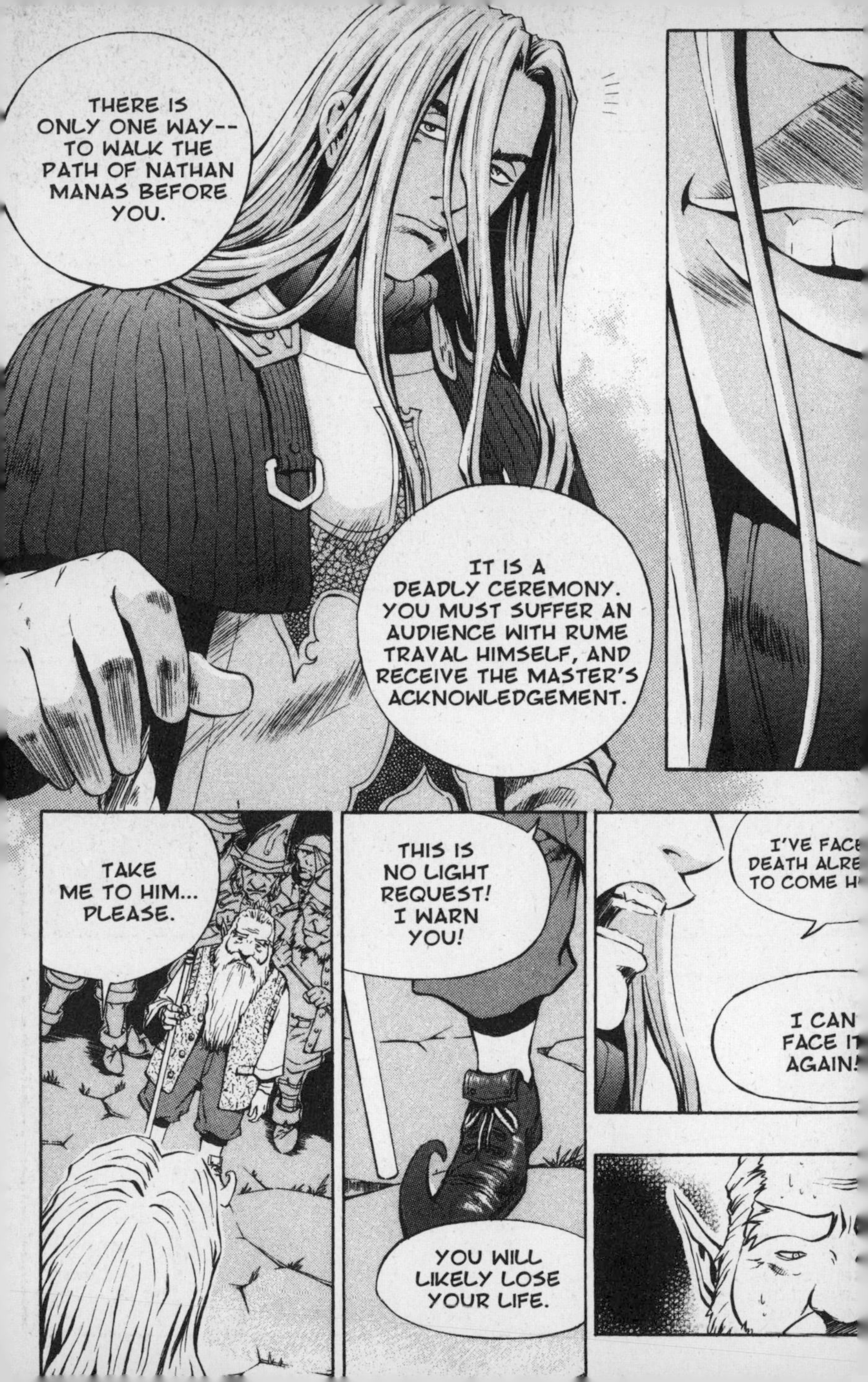
THERE IS ONLY ONE WAY-- TO WALK THE PATH OF NATHAN MANAS BEFORE YOU.
IT IS A DEADLY CEREMONY. YOU MUST SUFFER AN AUDIENCE WITH RUME TRAVAL HIMSELF, AND RECEIVE THE MASTER'S ACKNOWLEDGEMENT.
TAKE ME TO HIM... PLEASE.
THIS IS NO LIGHT REQUEST! I WARN YOU!
YOU WILL LIKELY LOSE YOUR LIFE.
I'VE FACE DEATH ALRE TO COME H
I CAN FACE IT AGAIN!

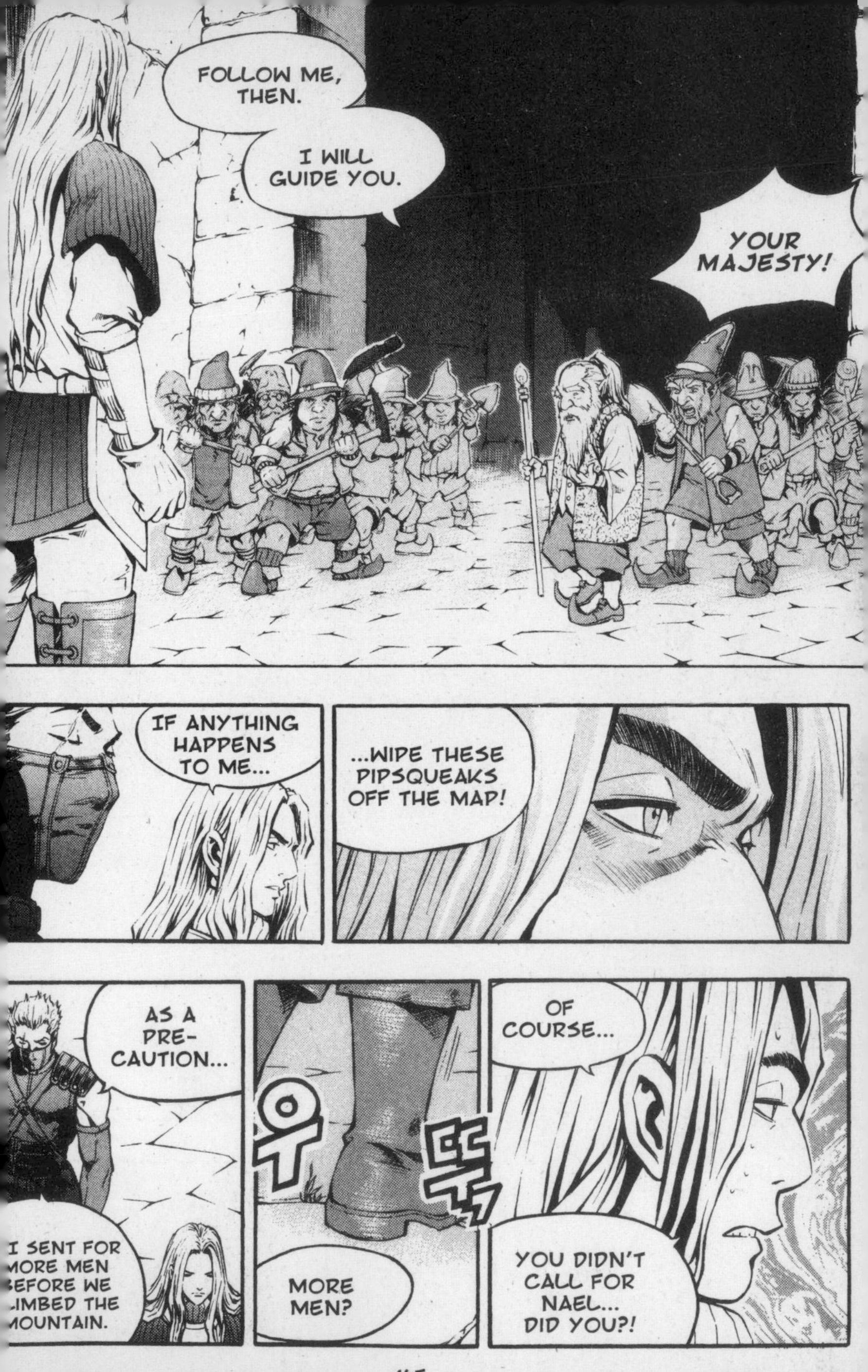
FOLLOW ME, THEN.
I WILL GUIDE YOU.
YOUR MAJESTY!
IF ANYTHING HAPPENS TO ME...
...WIPE THESE PIPSQUEAKS OFF THE MAP!
AS A PRE-CAUTION...
I SENT FOR MORE MEN BEFORE WE CLIMBED THE MOUNTAIN.
MORE MEN?
OF COURSE...
YOU DIDN'T CALL FOR NAEL... DID YOU?!

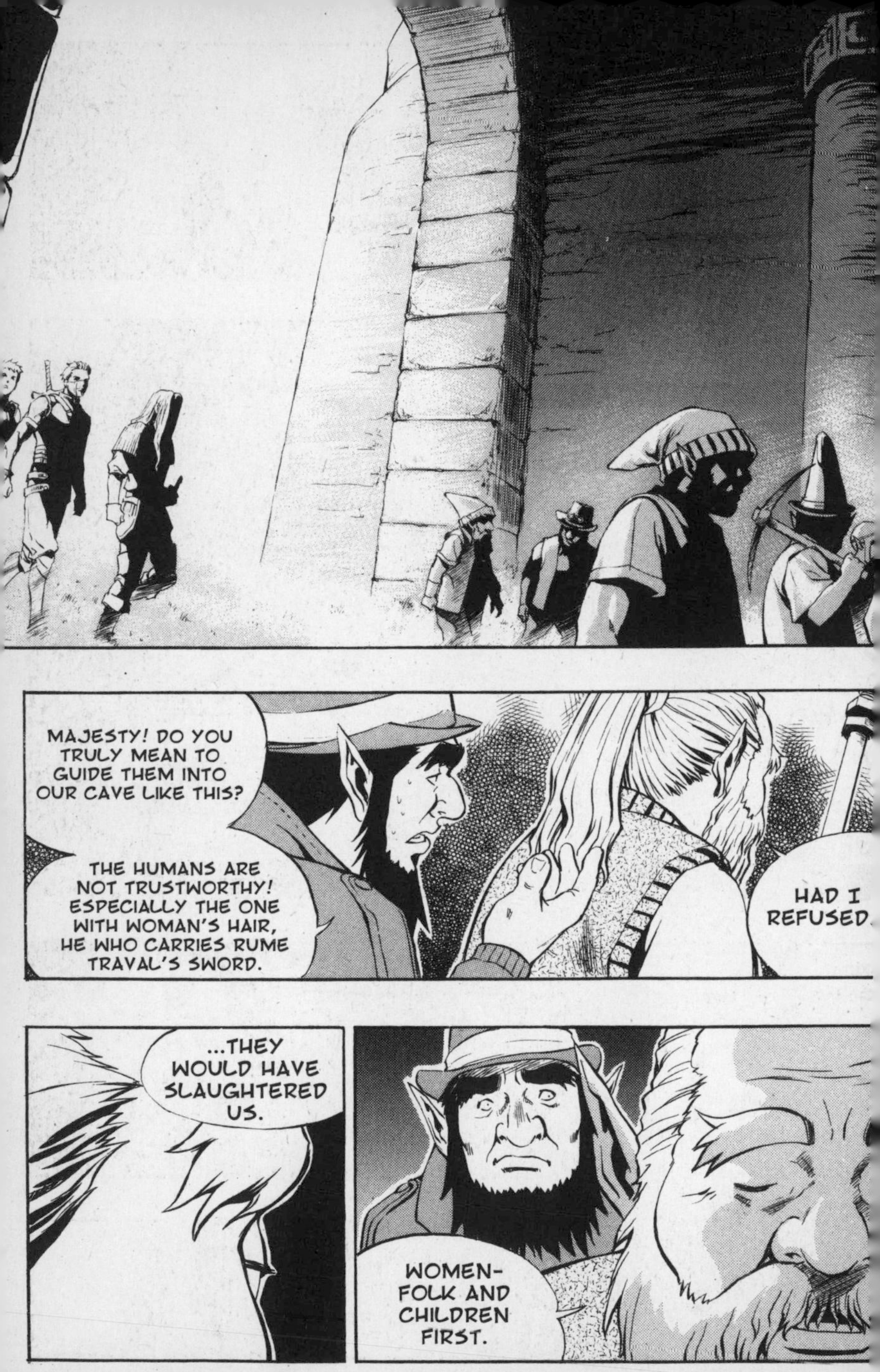
MAJESTY! DO YOU TRULY MEAN TO GUIDE THEM INTO OUR CAVE LIKE THIS?
THE HUMANS ARE NOT TRUSTWORTHY! ESPECIALLY THE ONE WITH WOMAN'S HAIR, HE WHO CARRIES RUME TRAVAL'S SWORD.
HAD I REFUSED.
...THEY WOULD HAVE SLAUGHTERED US.
WOMEN-FOLK AND CHILDREN FIRST.

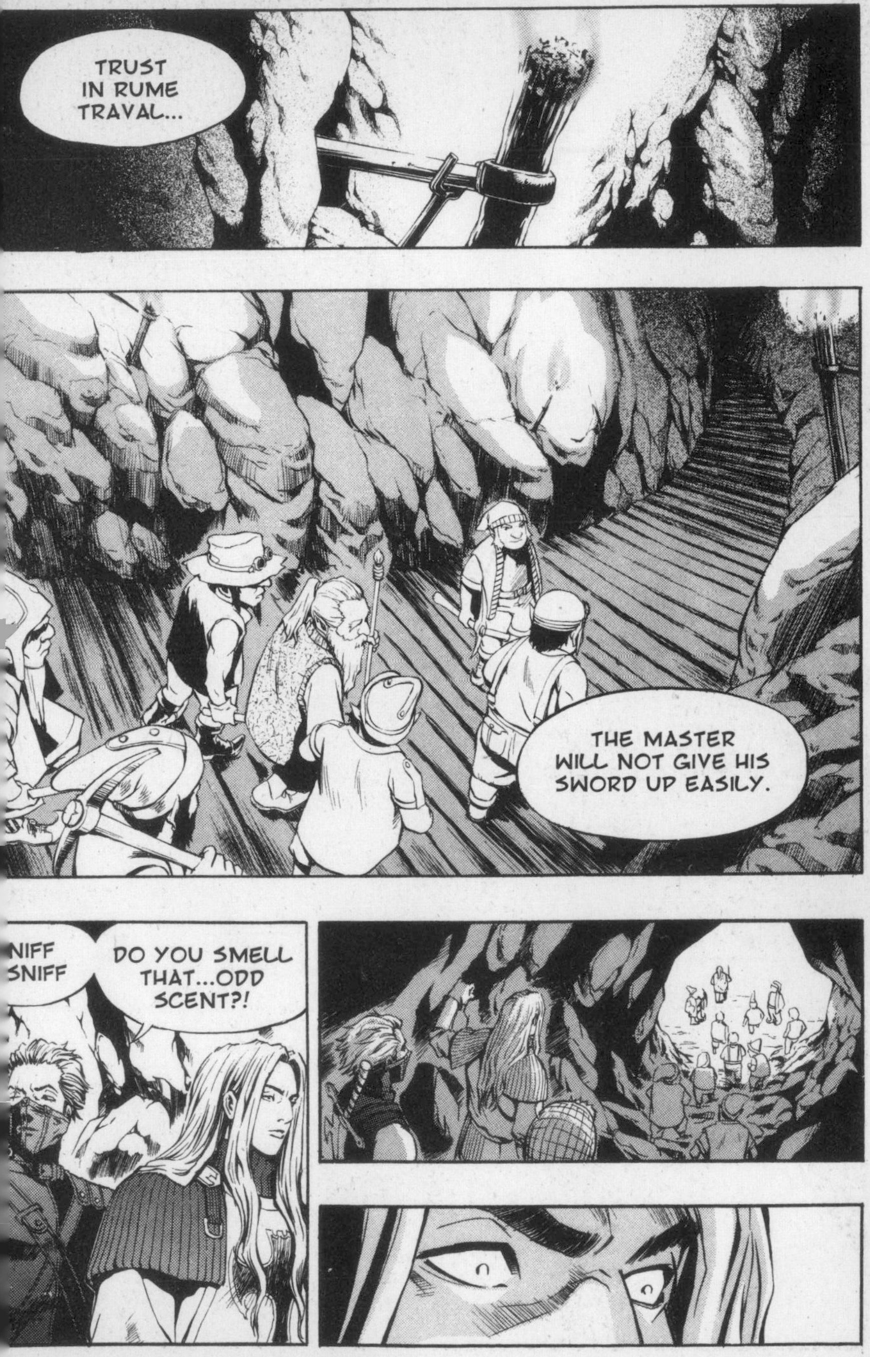
TRUST IN RUME TRAVAL...
THE MASTER WILL NOT GIVE HIS SWORD UP EASILY.
NIFF SNIFF
DO YOU SMELL THAT...ODD SCENT?!

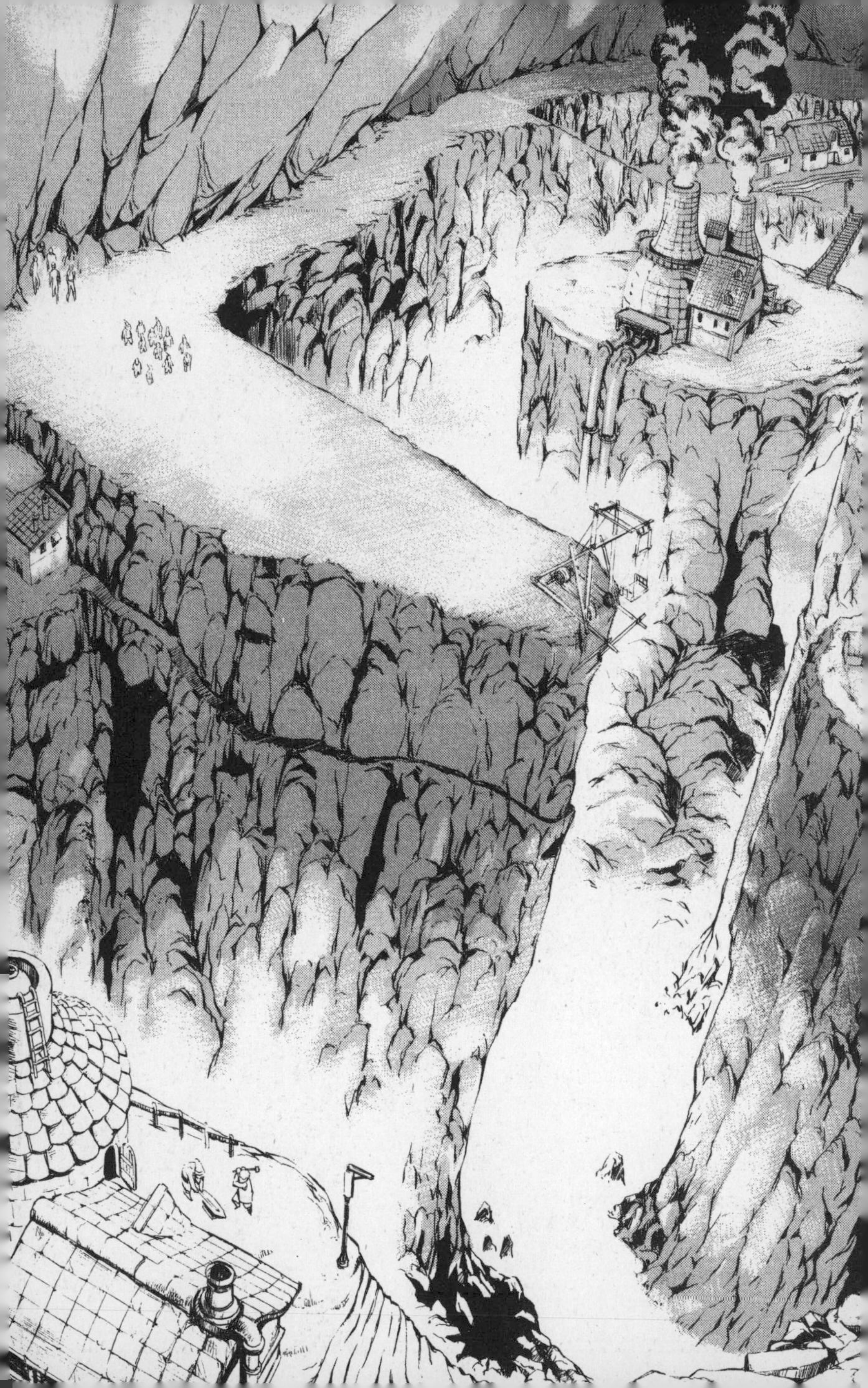

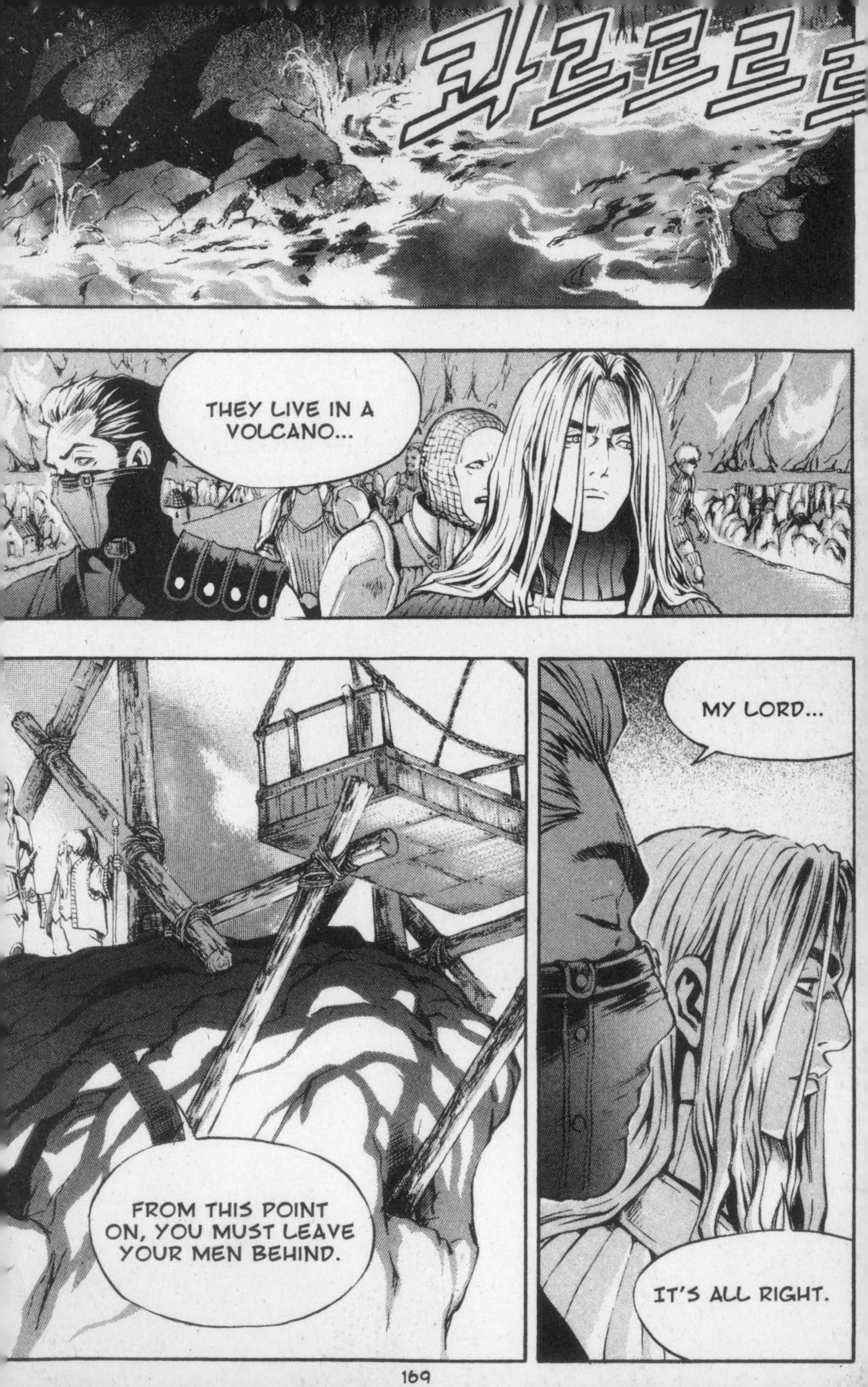
THEY LIVE IN A VOLCANO...
FROM THIS POINT ON, YOU MUST LEAVE YOUR MEN BEHIND.
MY LORD...
IT'S ALL RIGHT.

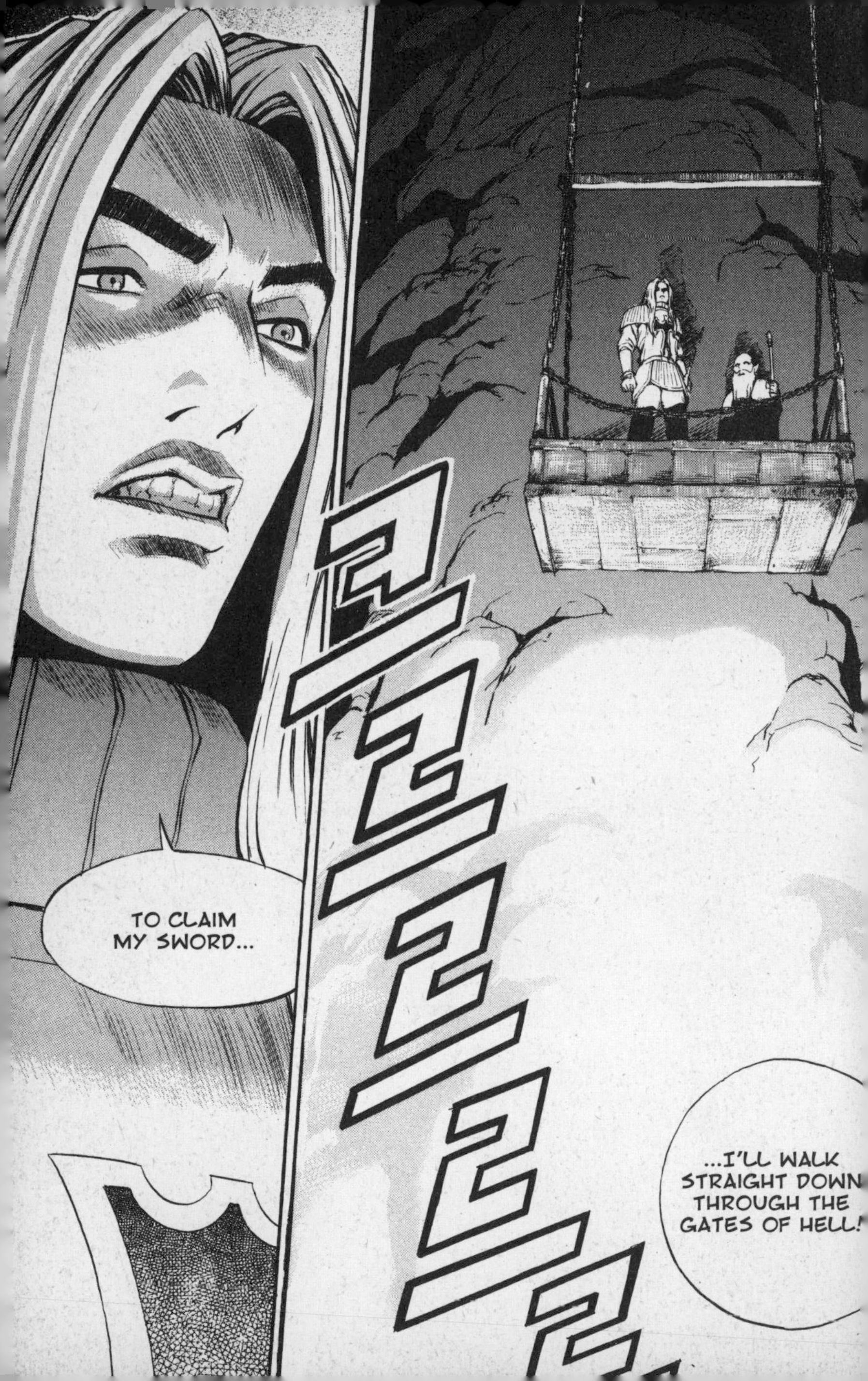
TO CLAIM MY SWORD...
...I'LL WALK STRAIGHT DOWN THROUGH THE GATES OF HELL!

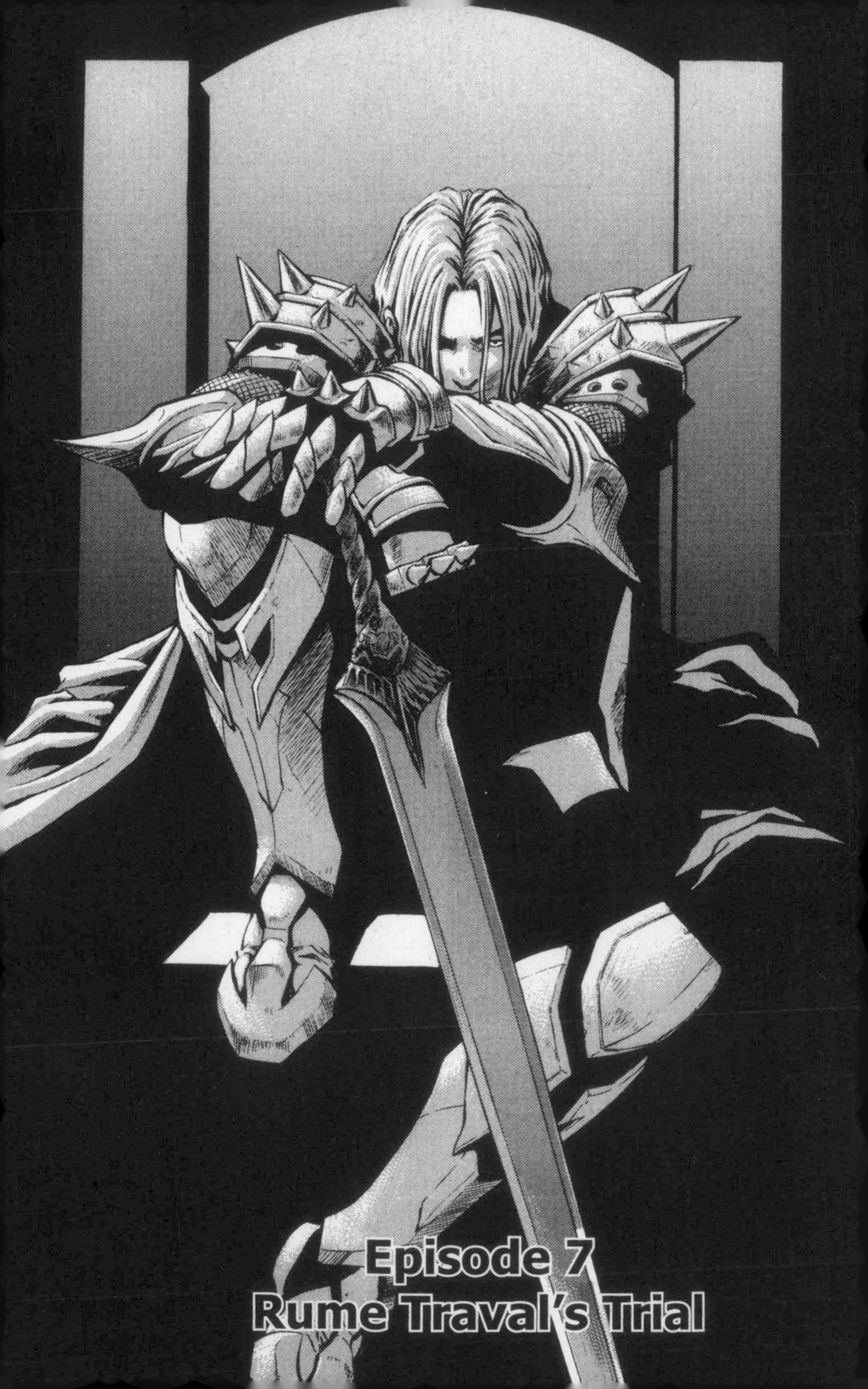
Episode 7
Rume Traval's Trial

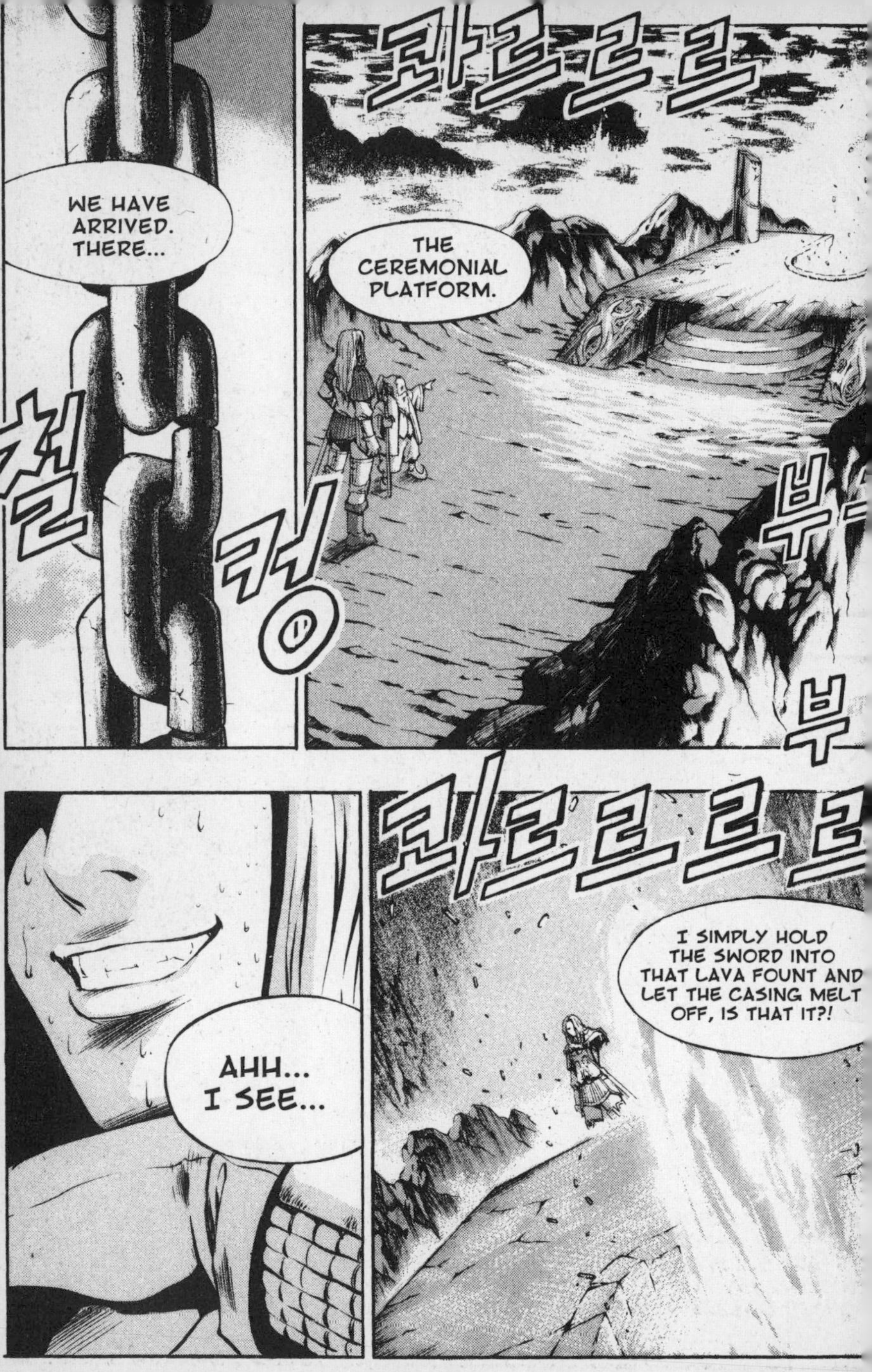
WE HAVE ARRIVED. THERE...
철컹
콰르르르
THE CEREMONIAL PLATFORM.
AHH... I SEE...
콰르르르르
I SIMPLY HOLD THE SWORD INTO THAT LAVA FOUNT AND LET THE CASING MELT OFF, IS THAT IT?!

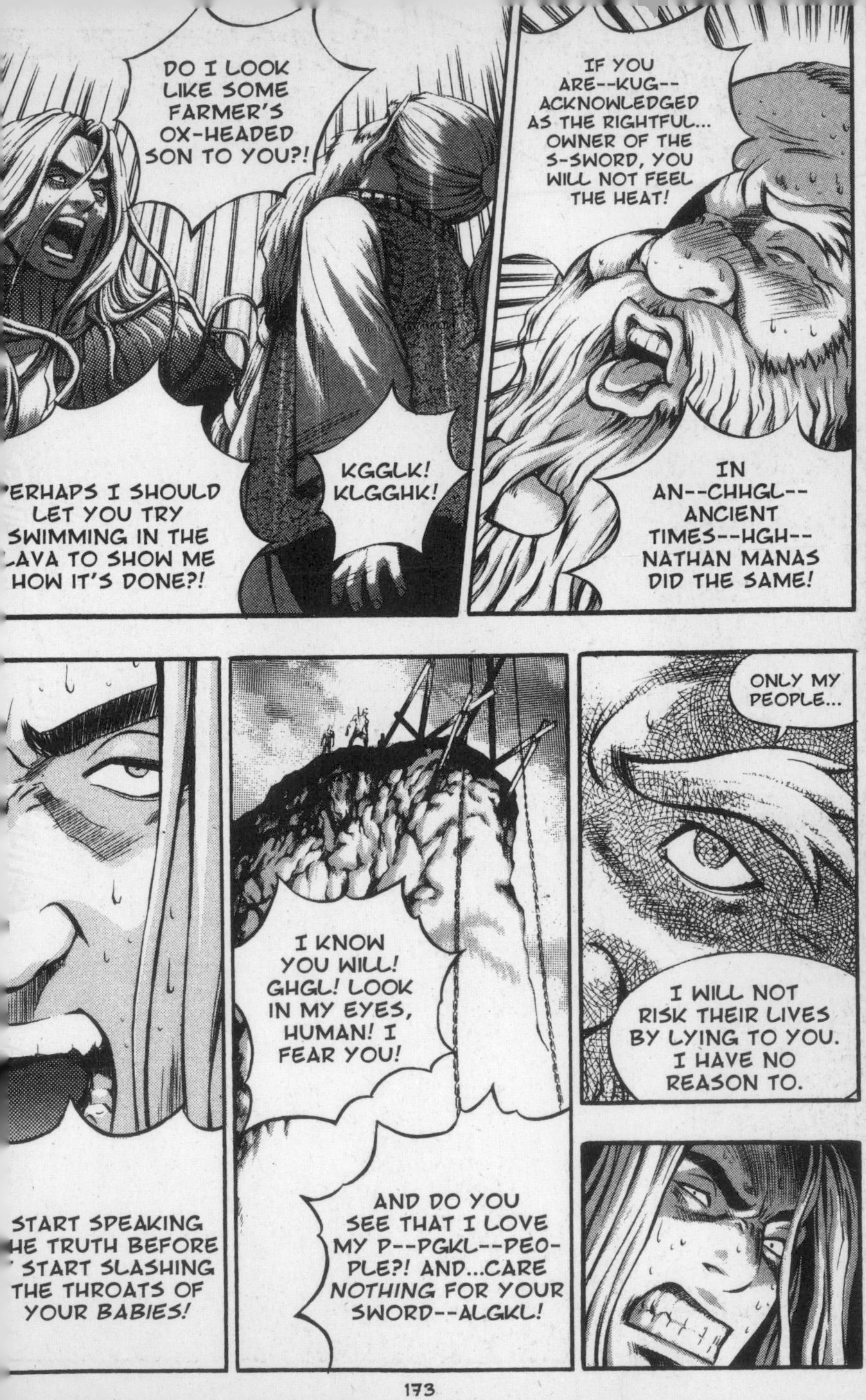
DO I LOOK LIKE SOME FARMER'S OX-HEADED SON TO YOU?!
ERHAPS I SHOULD LET YOU TRY SWIMMING IN THE AVA TO SHOW ME HOW IT'S DONE?!
KGGLK! KLGGHK!
IF YOU ARE--KUG--ACKNOWLEDGED AS THE RIGHTFUL... OWNER OF THE S-SWORD, YOU WILL NOT FEEL THE HEAT!
IN AN--CHHGL--ANCIENT TIMES--HGH--NATHAN MANAS DID THE SAME!
START SPEAKING HE TRUTH BEFORE START SLASHING THE THROATS OF YOUR BABIES!
I KNOW YOU WILL! GHGL! LOOK IN MY EYES, HUMAN! I FEAR YOU!
AND DO YOU SEE THAT I LOVE MY P--PGKL--PEOPLE?! AND...CARE NOTHING FOR YOUR SWORD--ALGKL!
ONLY MY PEOPLE...
I WILL NOT RISK THEIR LIVES BY LYING TO YOU. I HAVE NO REASON TO.

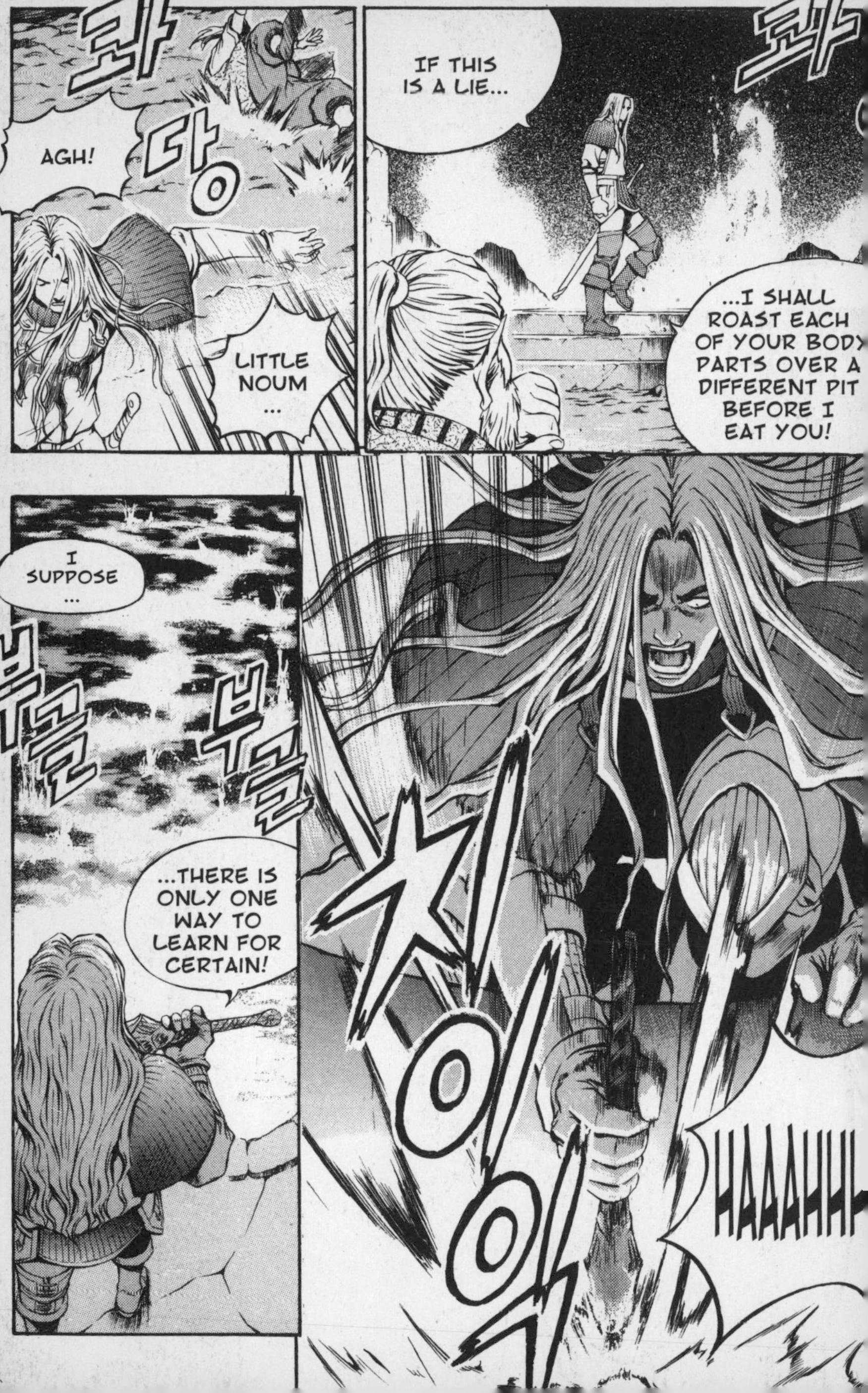

콰당
AGH!
LITTLE NOUM ...
IF THIS IS A LIE...
콰
...I SHALL ROAST EACH OF YOUR BODY PARTS OVER A DIFFERENT PIT BEFORE I EAT YOU!
I SUPPOSE ...
부글 부글
...THERE IS ONLY ONE WAY TO LEARN FOR CERTAIN!
HAAAHH

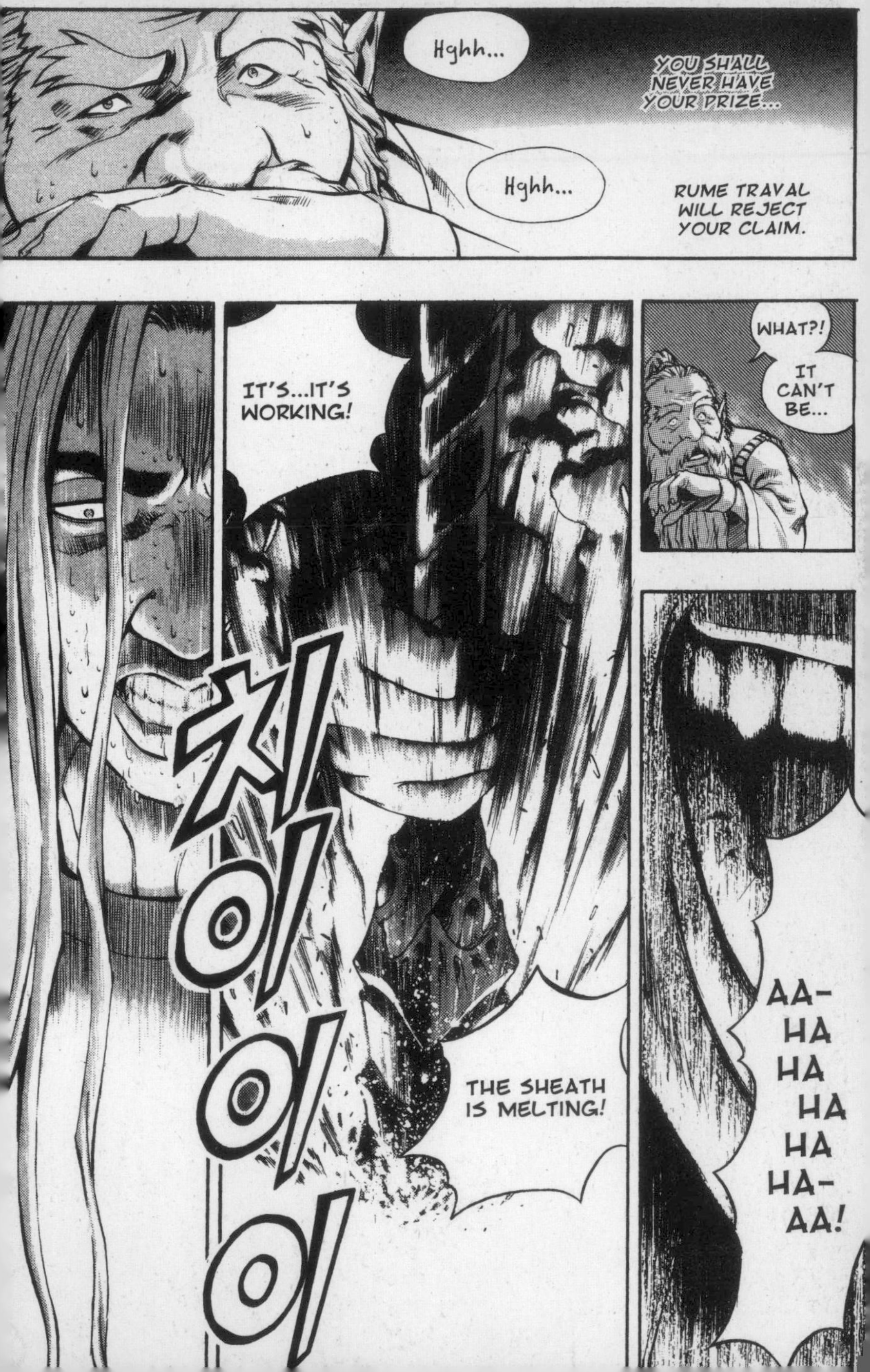
Hghh...
YOU SHALL NEVER HAVE YOUR PRIZE...
Hghh...
RUME TRAVAL WILL REJECT YOUR CLAIM.
치이이이
IT'S...IT'S WORKING!
THE SHEATH IS MELTING!
WHAT?!
IT CAN'T BE...
AA-HA HA HA HA HA-AA!

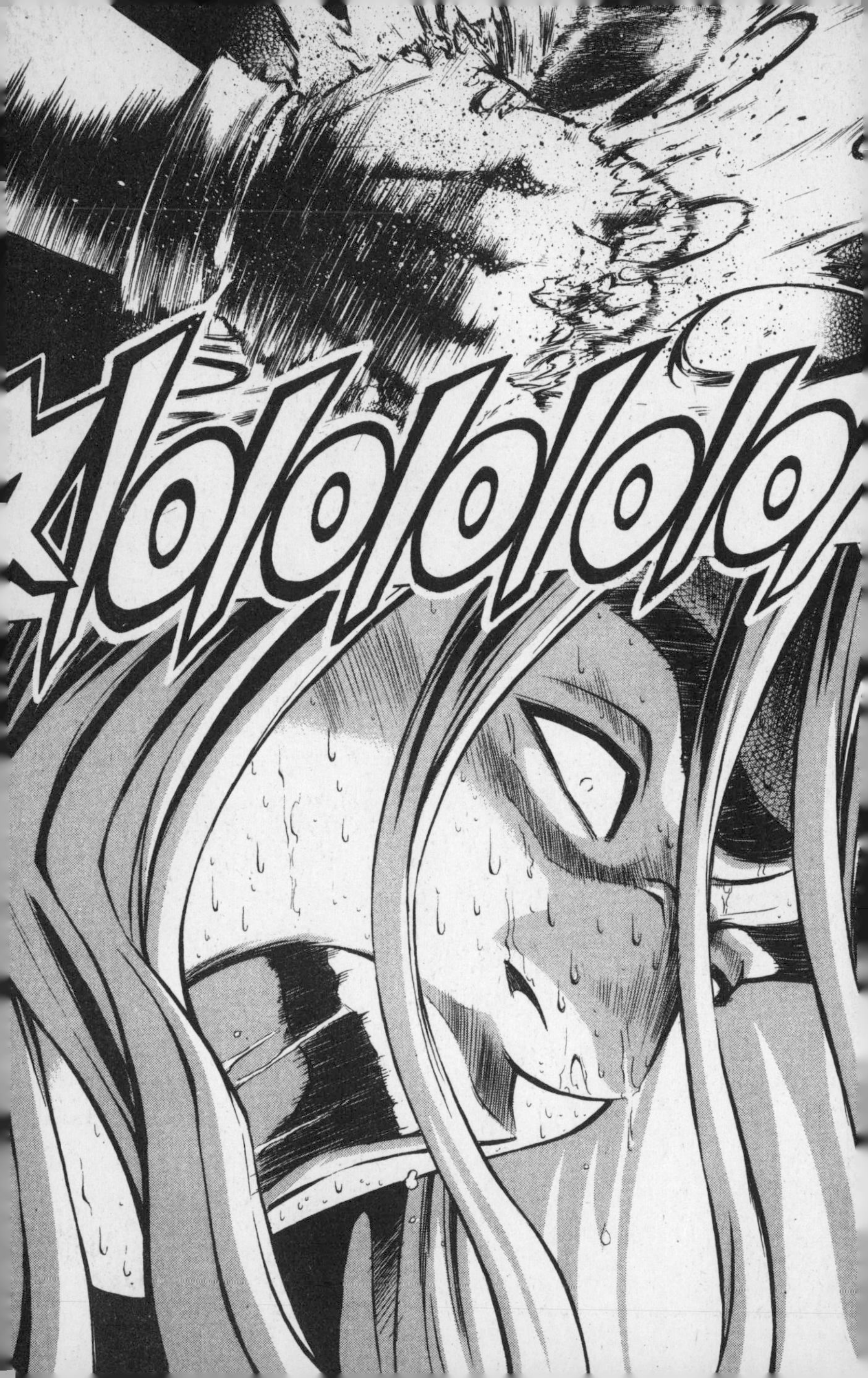

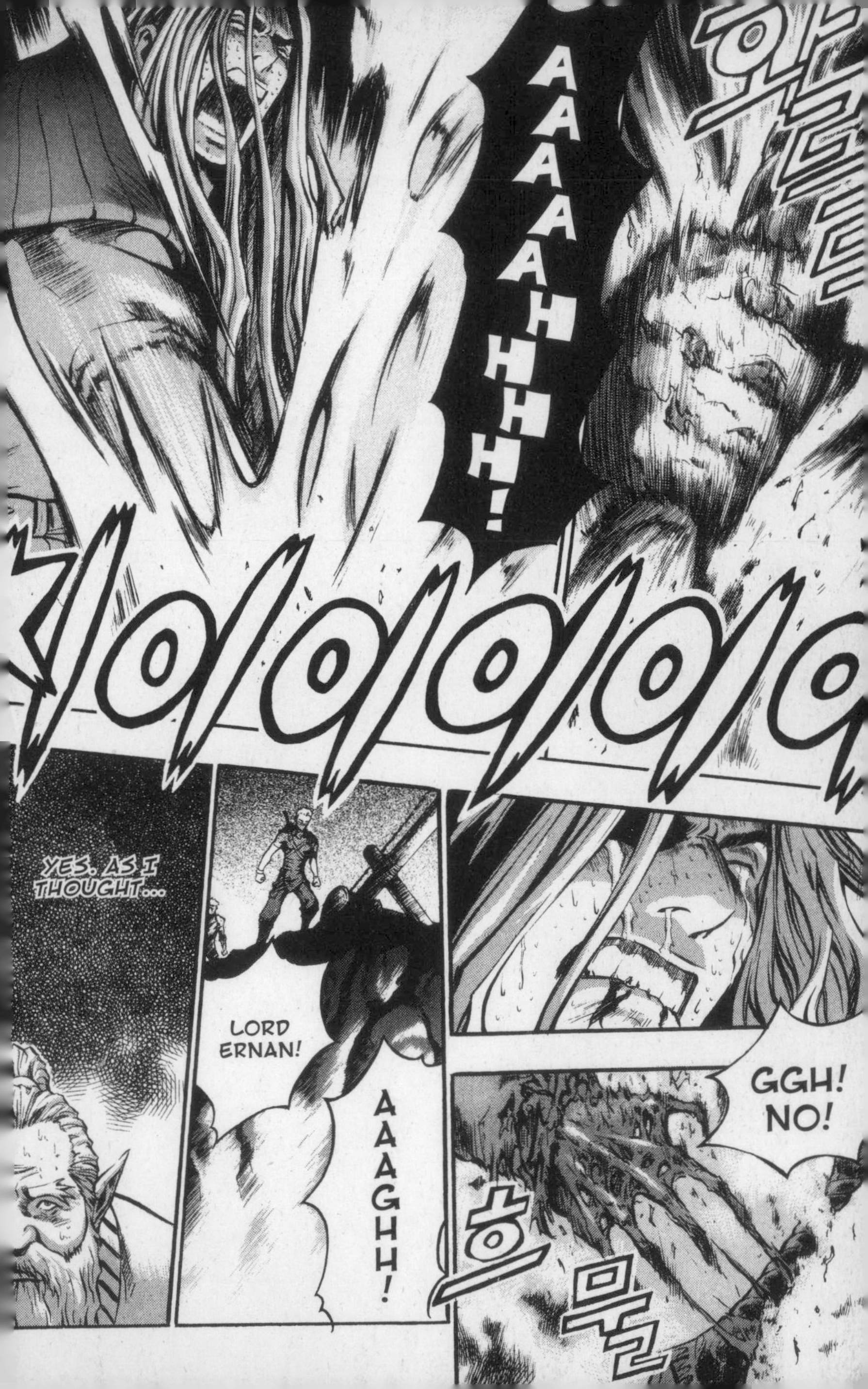
AAAAAHHHHH!
YES. AS I THOUGHT...
LORD ERNAN!
AAAGHH!
GGH! NO!

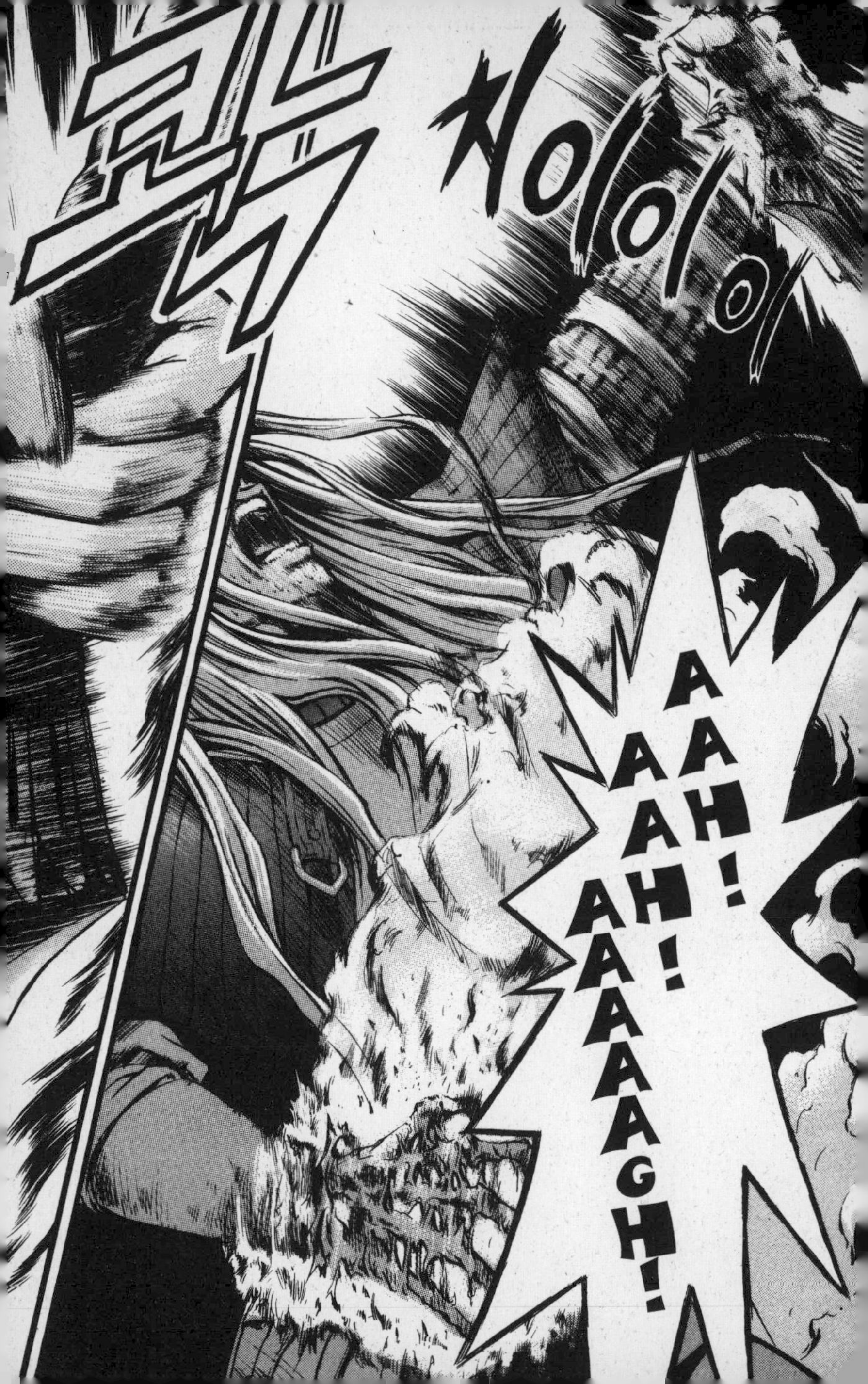
AAH!
AAH!
AAAAAGH!!

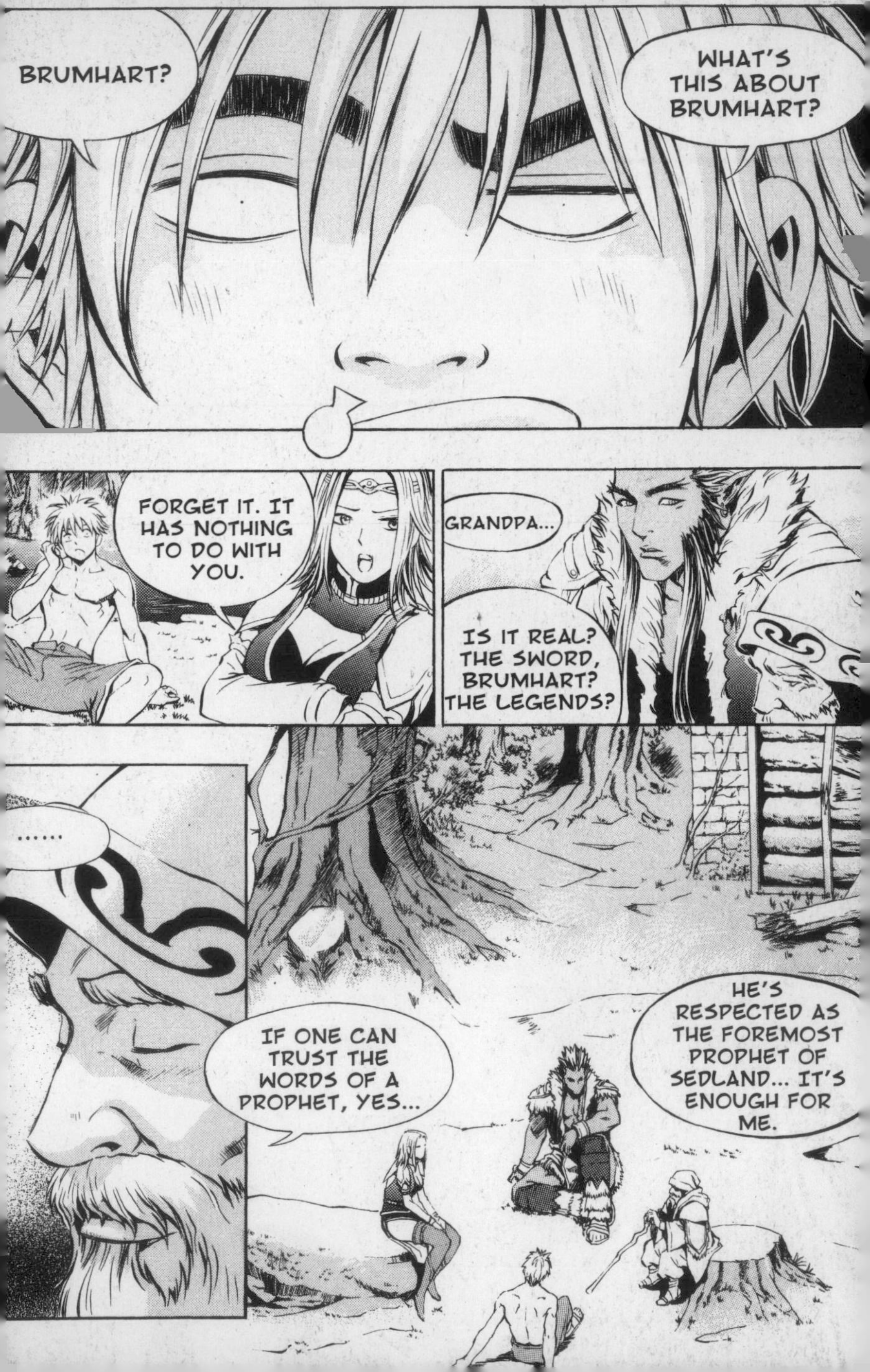
BRUMHART?
WHAT'S THIS ABOUT BRUMHART?
FORGET IT. IT HAS NOTHING TO DO WITH YOU.
GRANDPA...
IS IT REAL? THE SWORD, BRUMHART? THE LEGENDS?
......
IF ONE CAN TRUST THE WORDS OF A PROPHET, YES...
HE'S RESPECTED AS THE FOREMOST PROPHET OF SEDLAND... IT'S ENOUGH FOR ME.

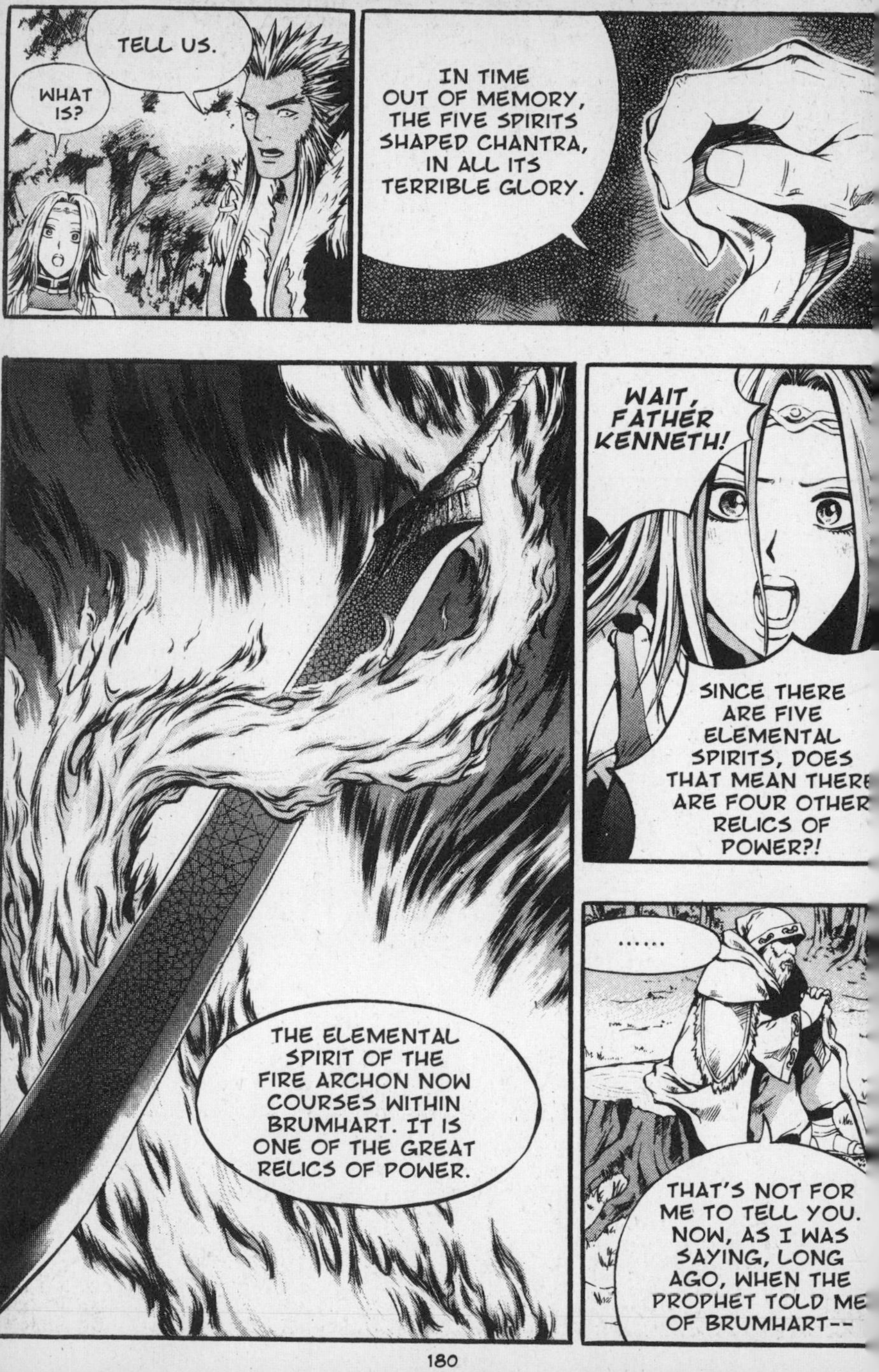
WHAT IS?
TELL US.
IN TIME OUT OF MEMORY, THE FIVE SPIRITS SHAPED CHANTRA, IN ALL ITS TERRIBLE GLORY.
THE ELEMENTAL SPIRIT OF THE FIRE ARCHON NOW COURSES WITHIN BRUMHART. IT IS ONE OF THE GREAT RELICS OF POWER.
WAIT, FATHER KENNETH!
SINCE THERE ARE FIVE ELEMENTAL SPIRITS, DOES THAT MEAN THERE ARE FOUR OTHER RELICS OF POWER?!
......
THAT'S NOT FOR ME TO TELL YOU. NOW, AS I WAS SAYING, LONG AGO, WHEN THE PROPHET TOLD ME OF BRUMHART--

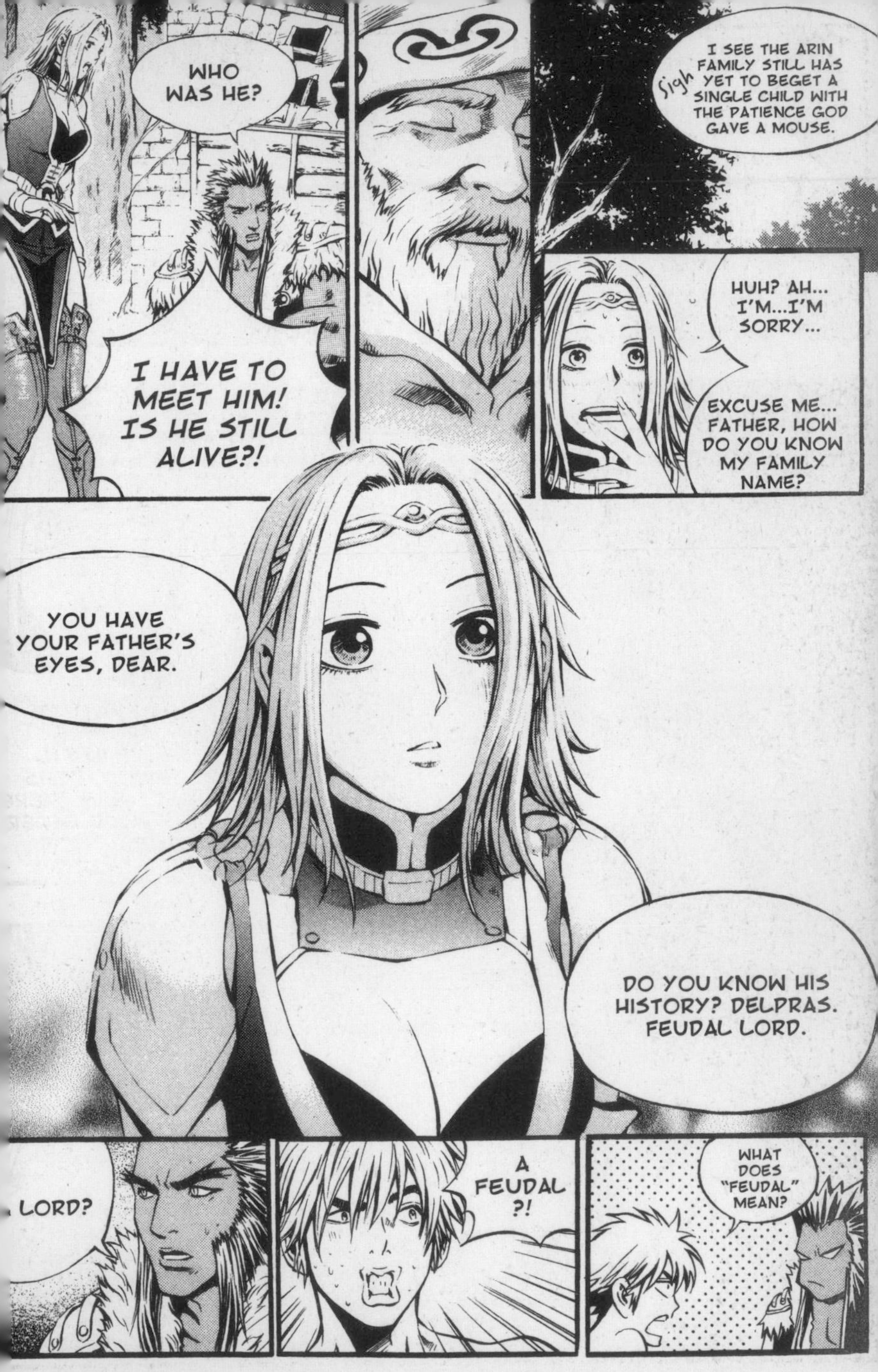
WHO WAS HE?
I HAVE TO MEET HIM! IS HE STILL ALIVE?!
Sigh
I SEE THE ARIN FAMILY STILL HAS YET TO BEGET A SINGLE CHILD WITH THE PATIENCE GOD GAVE A MOUSE.
HUH? AH... I'M...I'M SORRY...
EXCUSE ME... FATHER, HOW DO YOU KNOW MY FAMILY NAME?
YOU HAVE YOUR FATHER'S EYES, DEAR.
DO YOU KNOW HIS HISTORY? DELPRAS. FEUDAL LORD.
LORD?
A FEUDAL ?!
WHAT DOES "FEUDAL" MEAN?

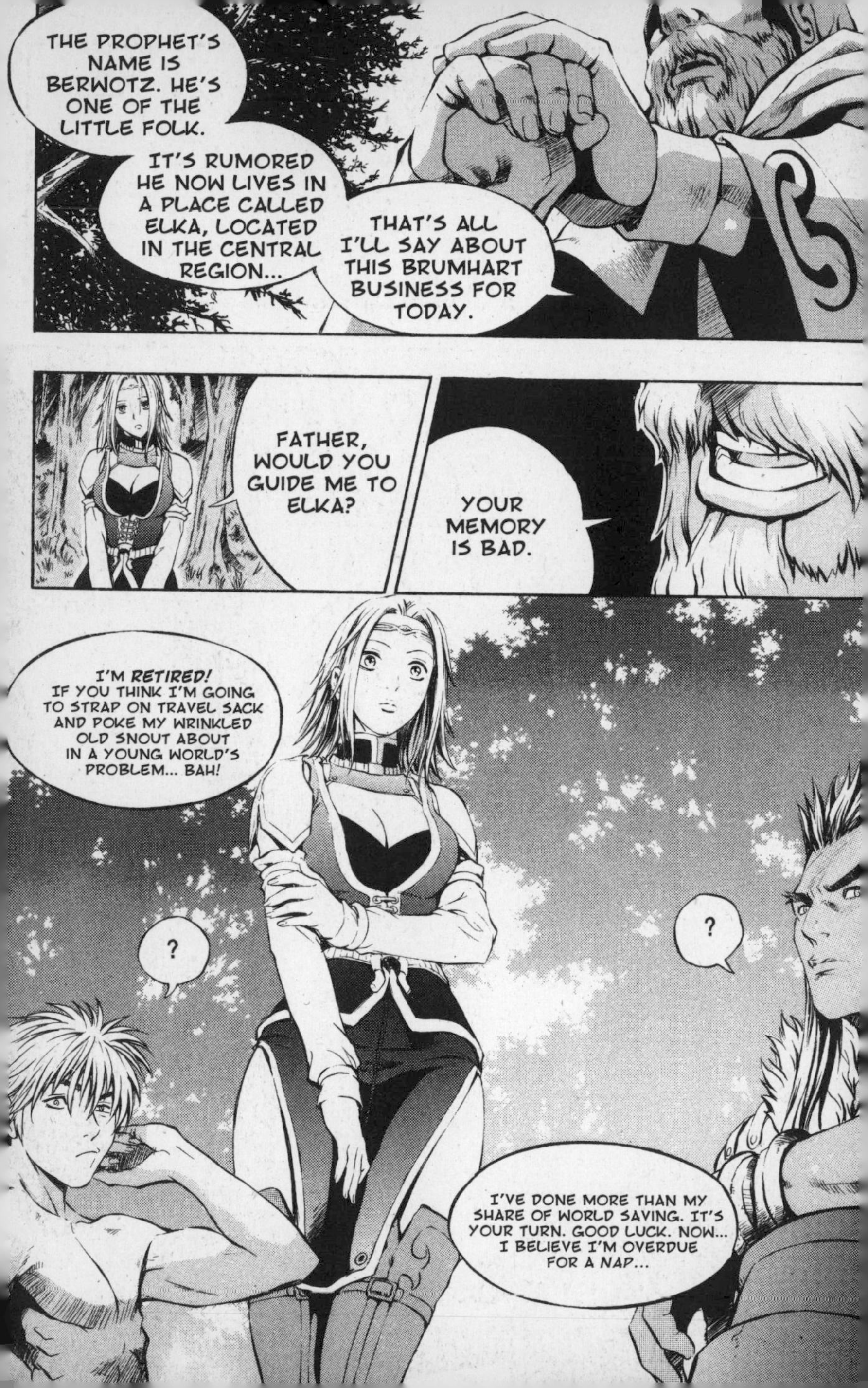
THE PROPHET'S NAME IS BERWOTZ. HE'S ONE OF THE LITTLE FOLK.
IT'S RUMORED HE NOW LIVES IN A PLACE CALLED ELKA, LOCATED IN THE CENTRAL REGION...
THAT'S ALL I'LL SAY ABOUT THIS BRUMHART BUSINESS FOR TODAY.
FATHER, WOULD YOU GUIDE ME TO ELKA?
YOUR MEMORY IS BAD.
I'M *RETIRED!* IF YOU THINK I'M GOING TO STRAP ON TRAVEL SACK AND POKE MY WRINKLED OLD SNOUT ABOUT IN A YOUNG WORLD'S PROBLEM... BAH!
?
?
I'VE DONE MORE THAN MY SHARE OF WORLD SAVING. IT'S YOUR TURN. GOOD LUCK. NOW... I BELIEVE I'M OVERDUE FOR A NAP...

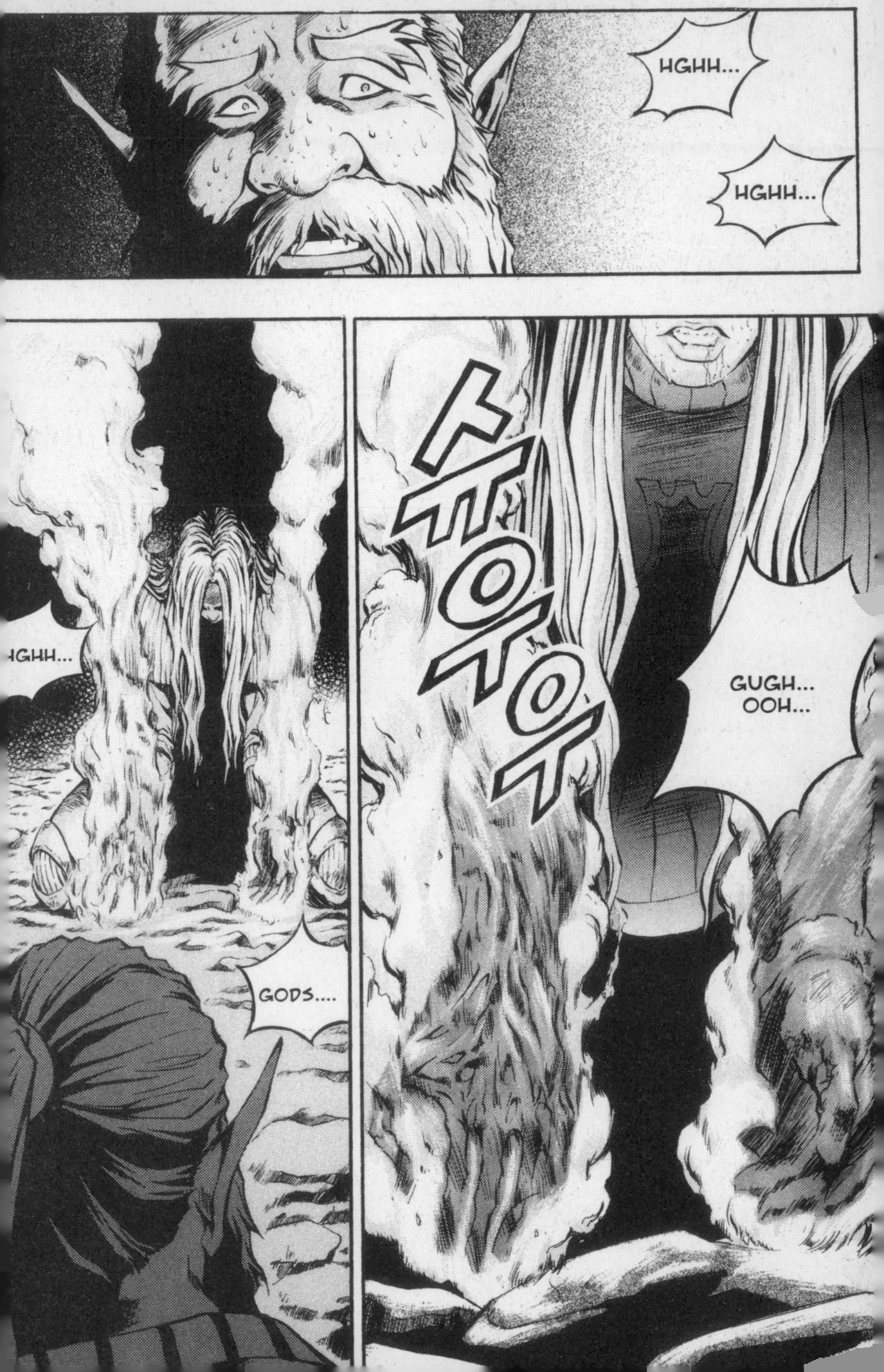
HGHH...
HGHH...
HGHH...
GODS....
TOKTOKTOK
GUGH... OOH...

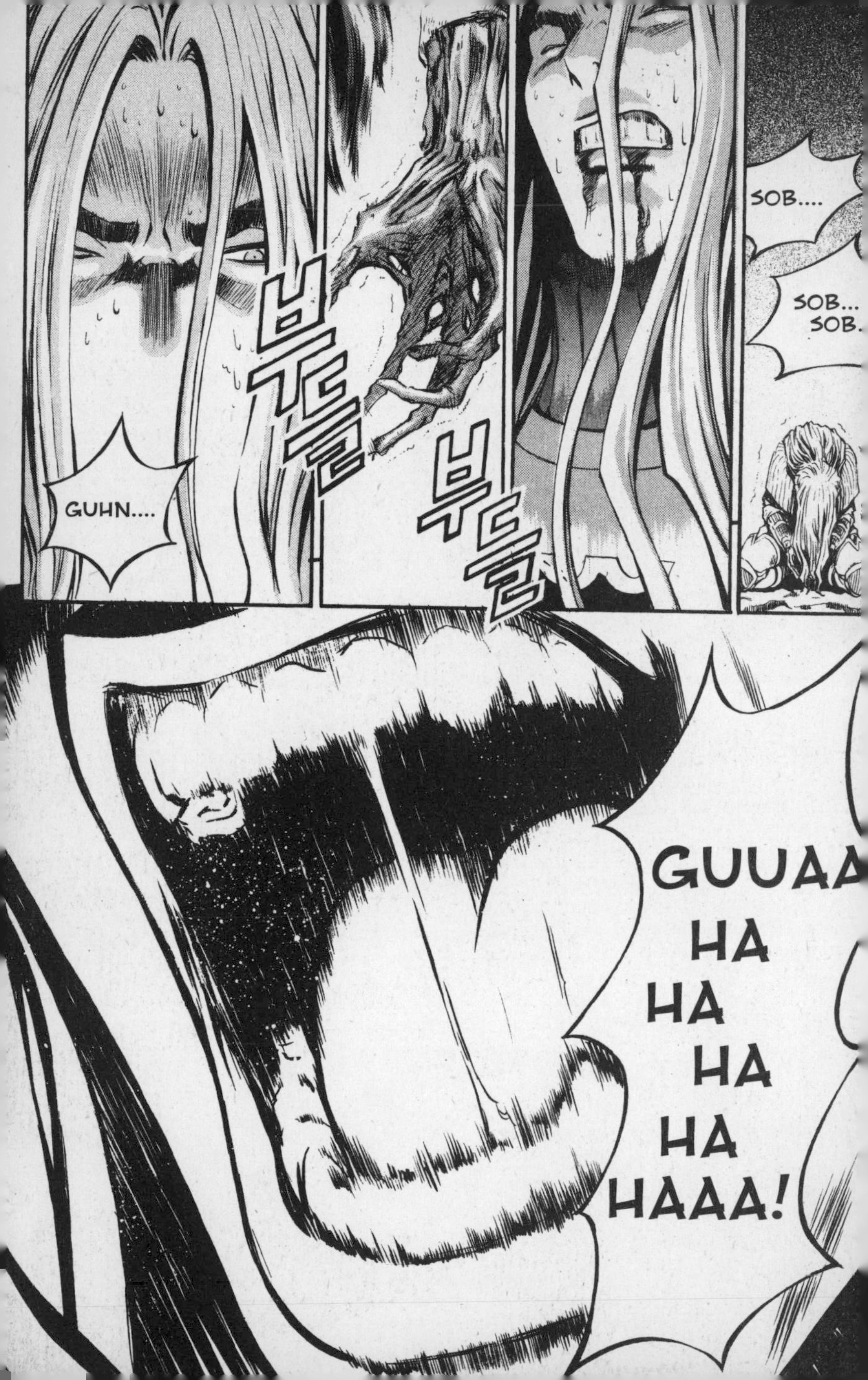
GUHN....
부들
부들
SOB....
SOB... SOB...
GUUAA HA HA HA HA HAAA!

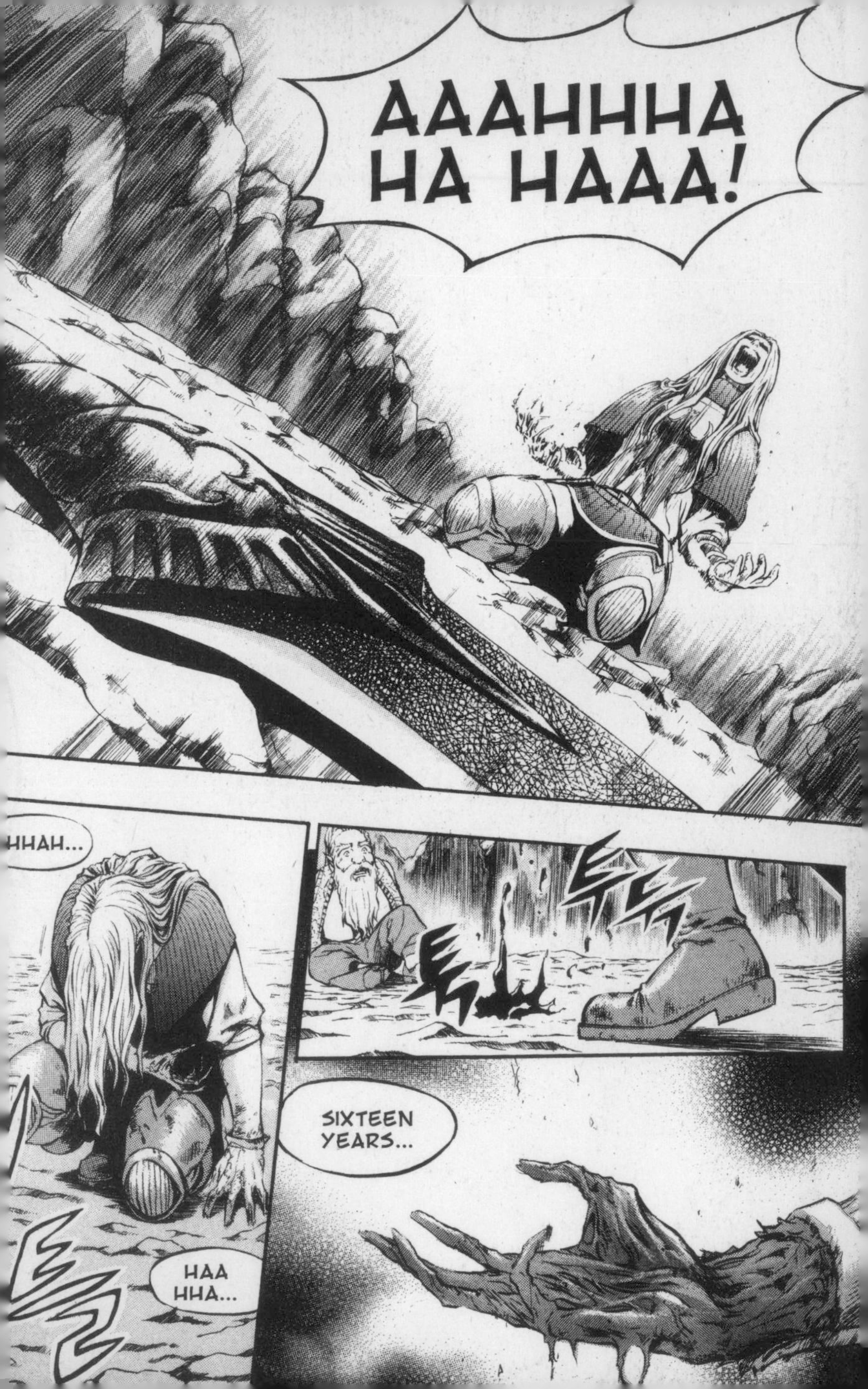
AAAHHHA HA HAAA!
HHAH...
HAA HHA...
SIXTEEN YEARS...

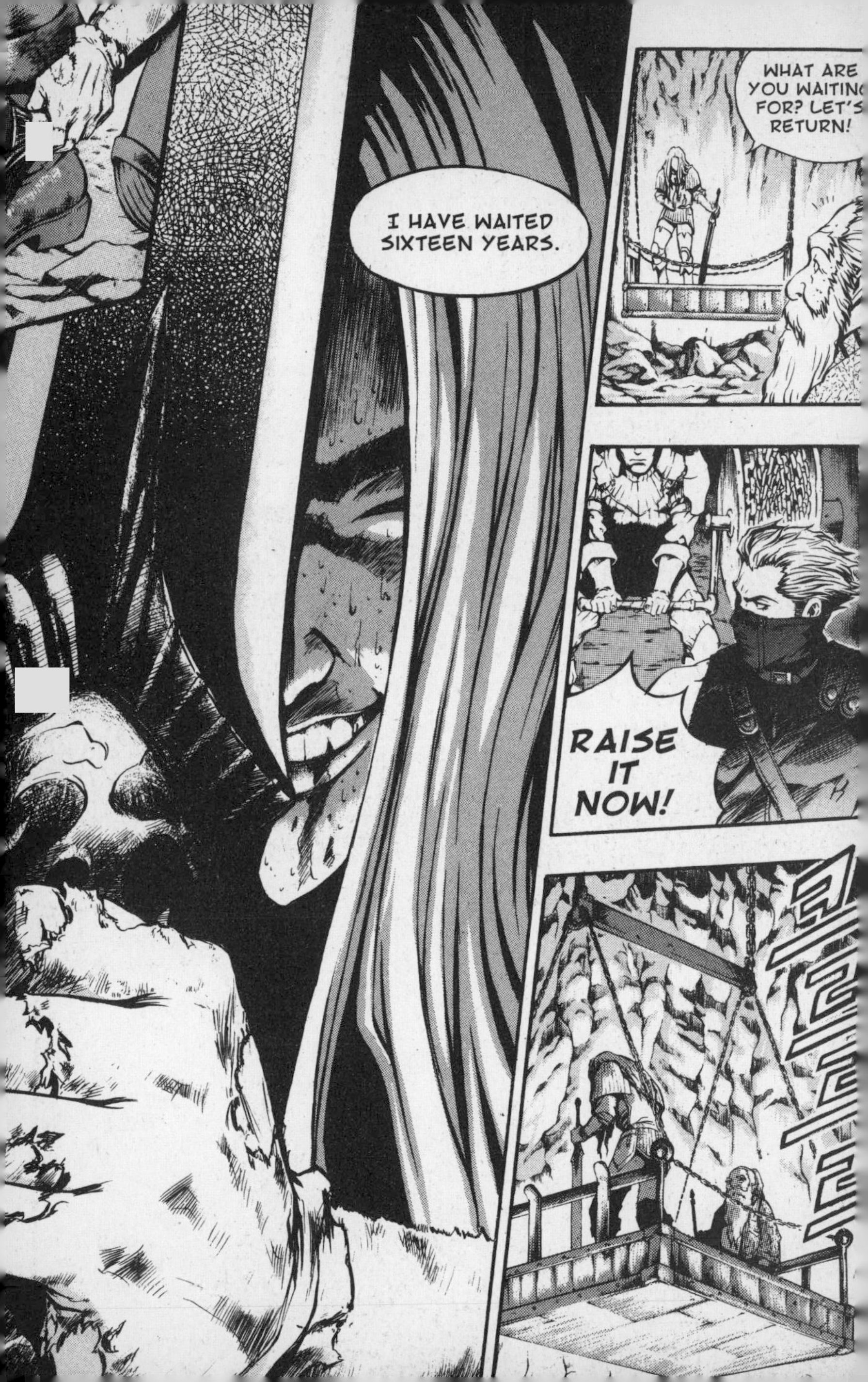
I HAVE WAITED SIXTEEN YEARS.
WHAT ARE YOU WAITIN FOR? LET'S RETURN!
RAISE IT NOW!

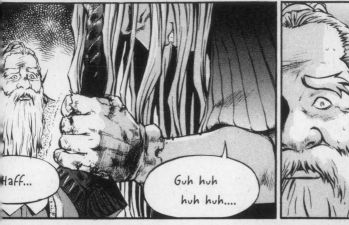

HOW...

Haff...

Guh huh
huh huh....

Human, my
sword is not
for you.

WHO...
WHO SAID
THAT?

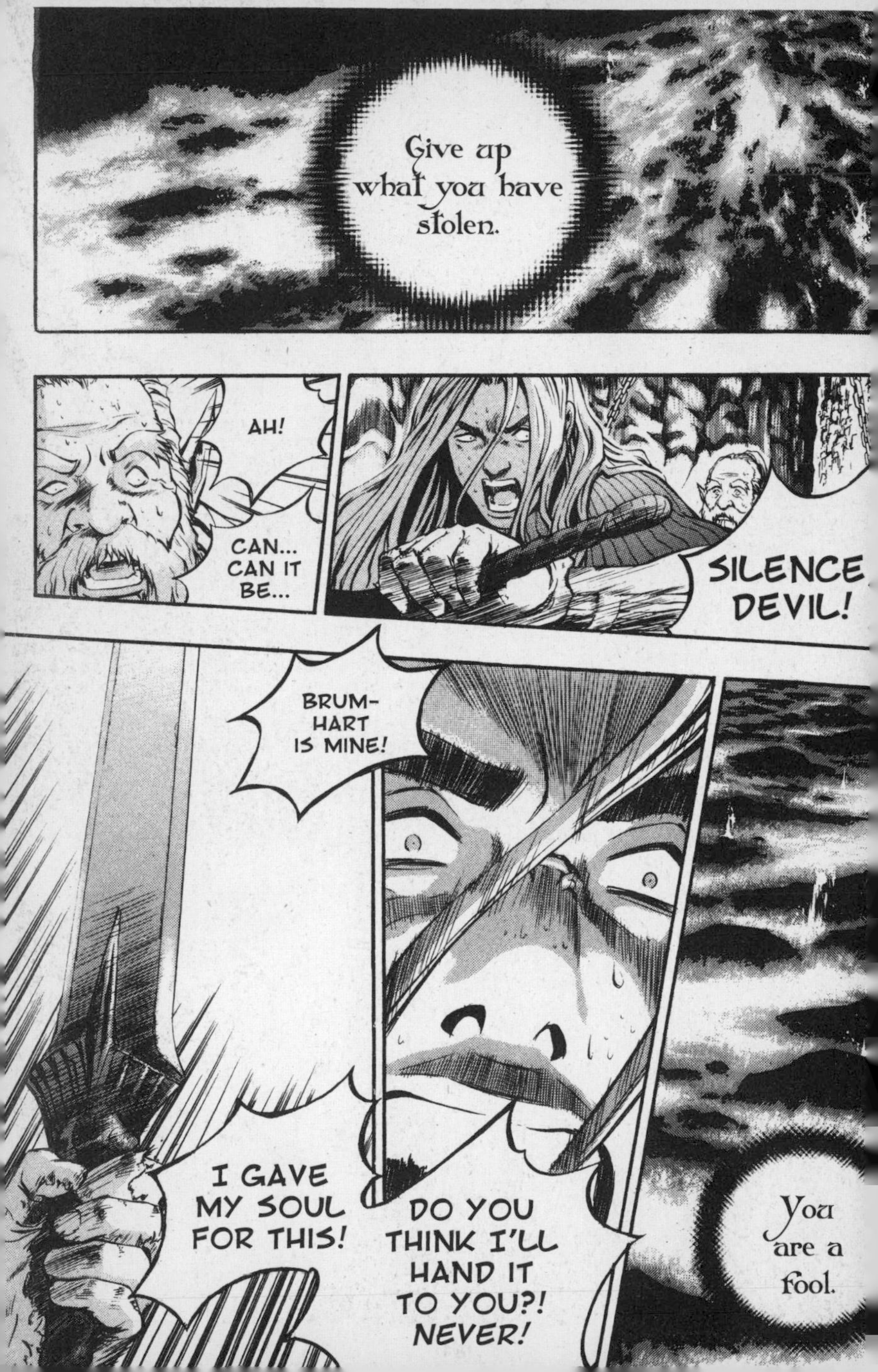
Give up what you have stolen.
AH!
CAN... CAN IT BE...
SILENCE DEVIL!
BRUM-HART IS MINE!
I GAVE MY SOUL FOR THIS!
DO YOU THINK I'LL HAND IT TO YOU?! NEVER!
You are a fool.

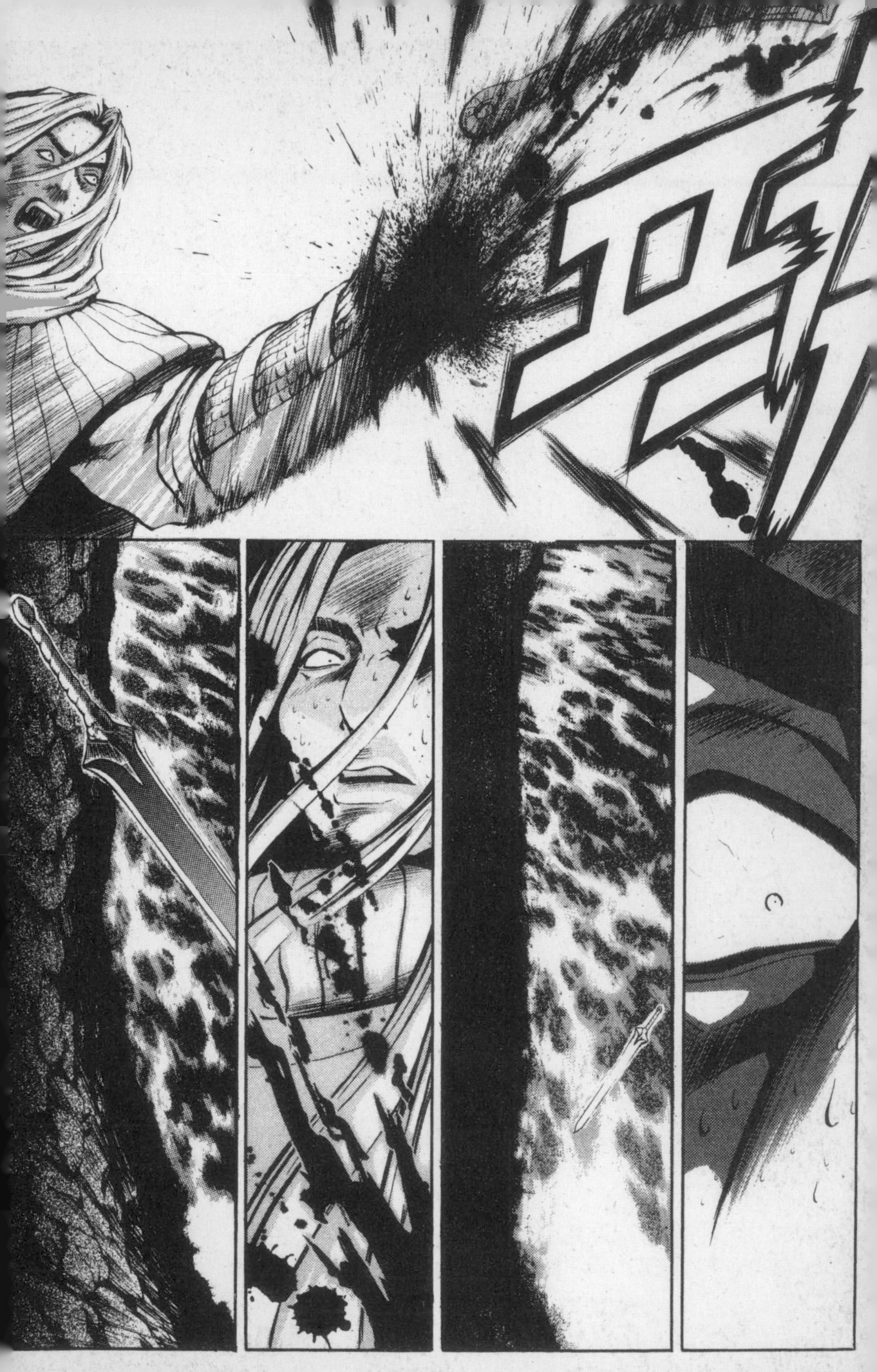

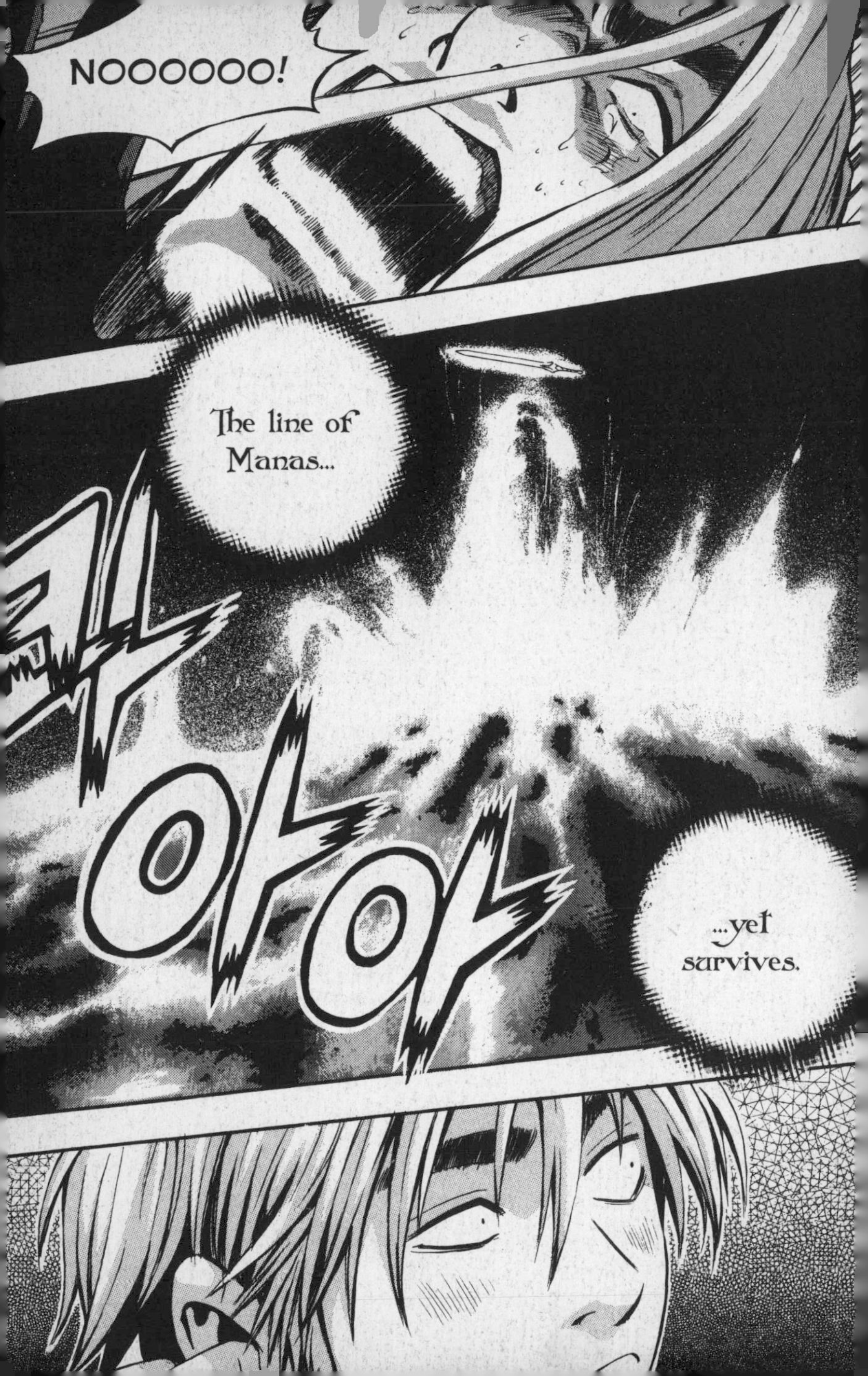
NOOOOOO!
The line of Manas...
...yet survives.

To *be continued* ⋯

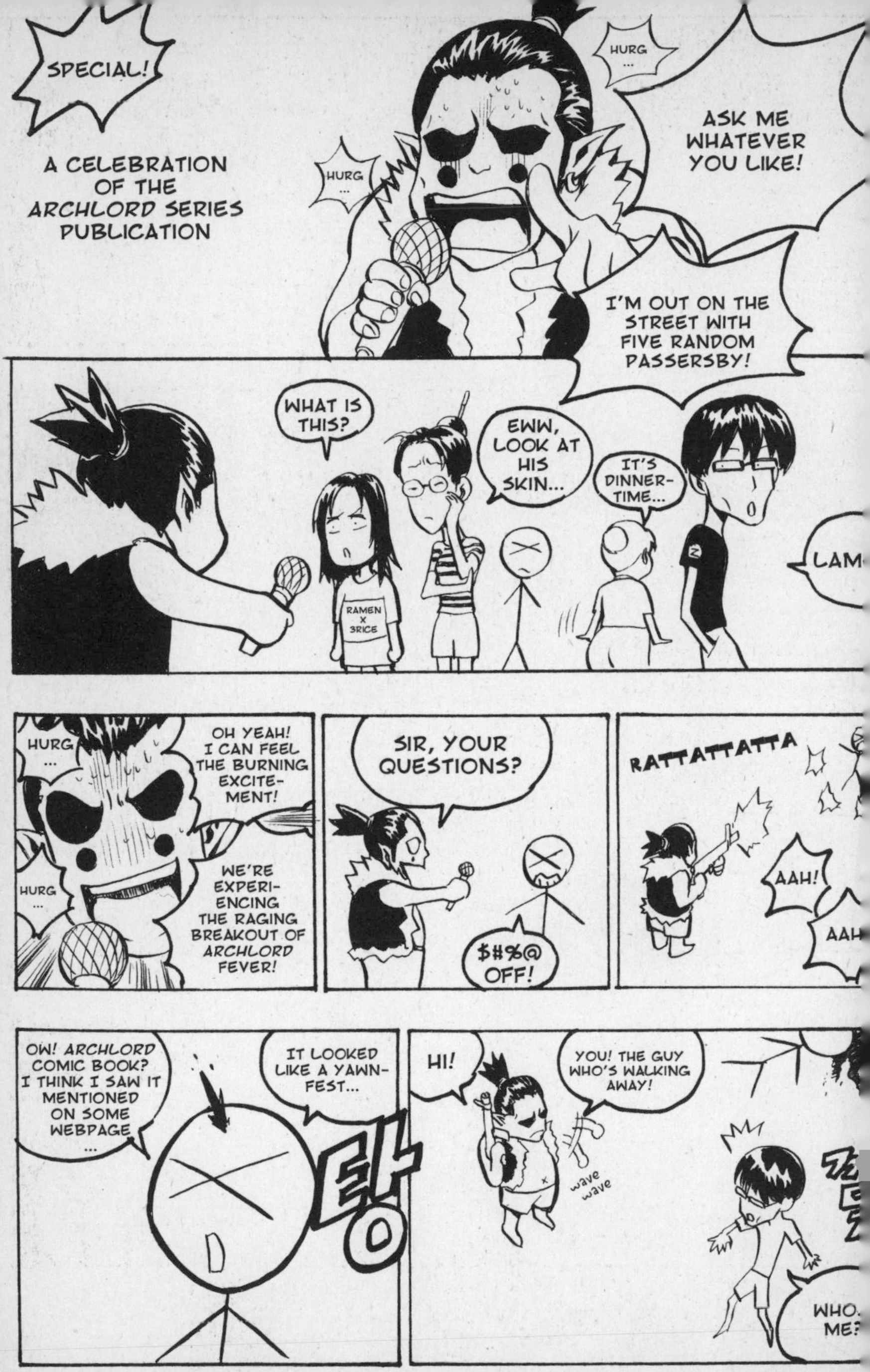
SPECIAL!
A CELEBRATION OF THE ARCHLORD SERIES PUBLICATION
HURG ...
HURG ...
ASK ME WHATEVER YOU LIKE!
I'M OUT ON THE STREET WITH FIVE RANDOM PASSERSBY!
WHAT IS THIS?
RAMEN X 3RICE
EWW, LOOK AT HIS SKIN...
IT'S DINNER-TIME...
HURG ...
OH YEAH! I CAN FEEL THE BURNING EXCITE-MENT!
HURG ...
WE'RE EXPERI-ENCING THE RAGING BREAKOUT OF ARCHLORD FEVER!
SIR, YOUR QUESTIONS?
$#%@ OFF!
RATTATTATTA
AAH!
OW! ARCHLORD COMIC BOOK? I THINK I SAW IT MENTIONED ON SOME WEBPAGE ...
IT LOOKED LIKE A YAWN-FEST...
HI!
YOU! THE GUY WHO'S WALKING AWAY!
wave wave

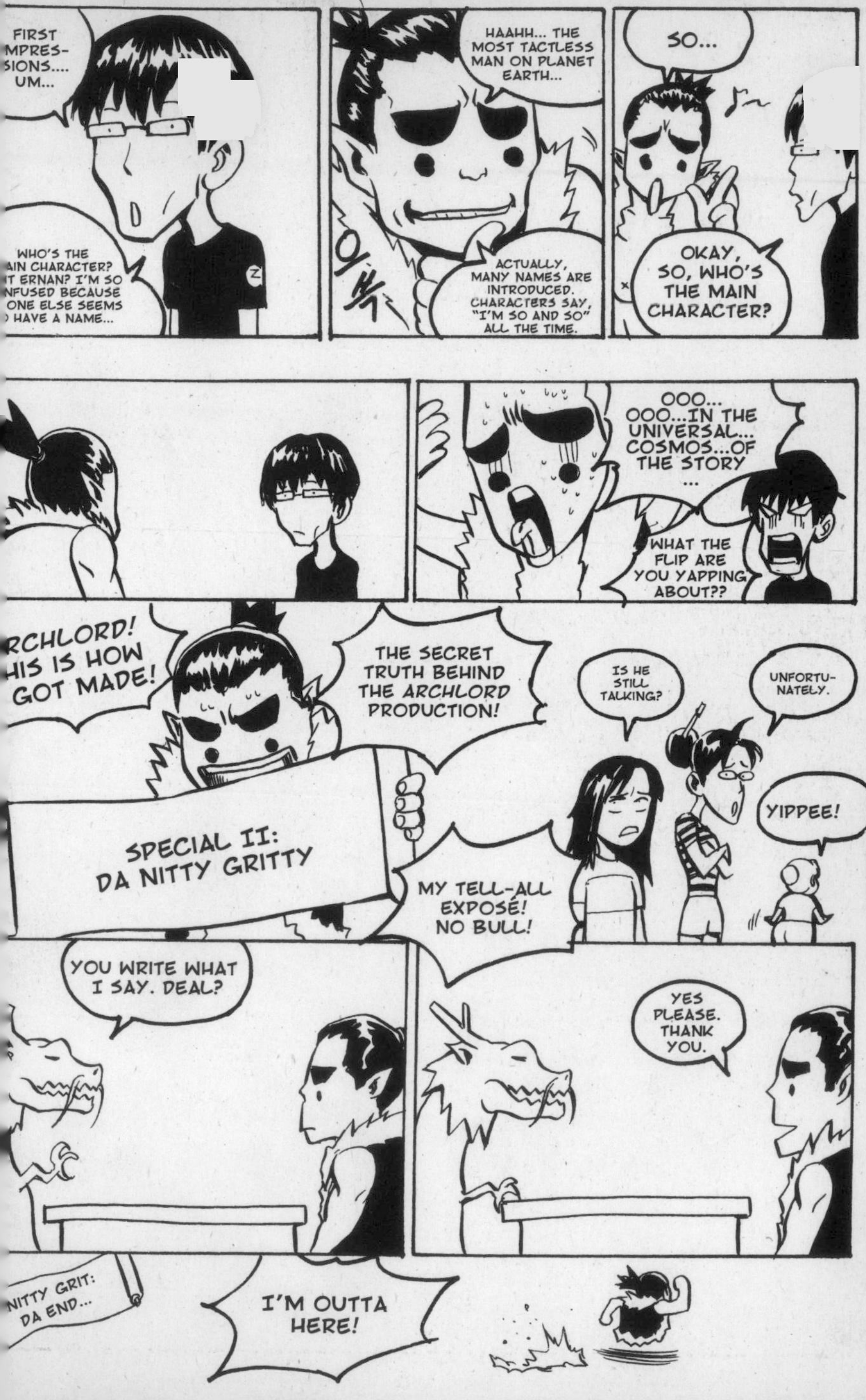
FIRST MPRES-SIONS.... UM...
WHO'S THE AIN CHARACTER? T ERNAN? I'M SO NFUSED BECAUSE ONE ELSE SEEMS HAVE A NAME...
HAAHH... THE MOST TACTLESS MAN ON PLANET EARTH...
으쓱
ACTUALLY, MANY NAMES ARE INTRODUCED. CHARACTERS SAY, "I'M SO AND SO" ALL THE TIME.
SO...
OKAY, SO, WHO'S THE MAIN CHARACTER?
OOO... OOO...IN THE UNIVERSAL... COSMOS...OF THE STORY ...
WHAT THE FLIP ARE YOU YAPPING ABOUT??
RCHLORD! HIS IS HOW GOT MADE!
THE SECRET TRUTH BEHIND THE ARCHLORD PRODUCTION!
SPECIAL II: DA NITTY GRITTY
MY TELL-ALL EXPOSÉ! NO BULL!
IS HE STILL TALKING?
UNFORTU-NATELY.
YIPPEE!
YOU WRITE WHAT I SAY. DEAL?
YES PLEASE. THANK YOU.
NITTY GRIT: DA END...
I'M OUTTA HERE!

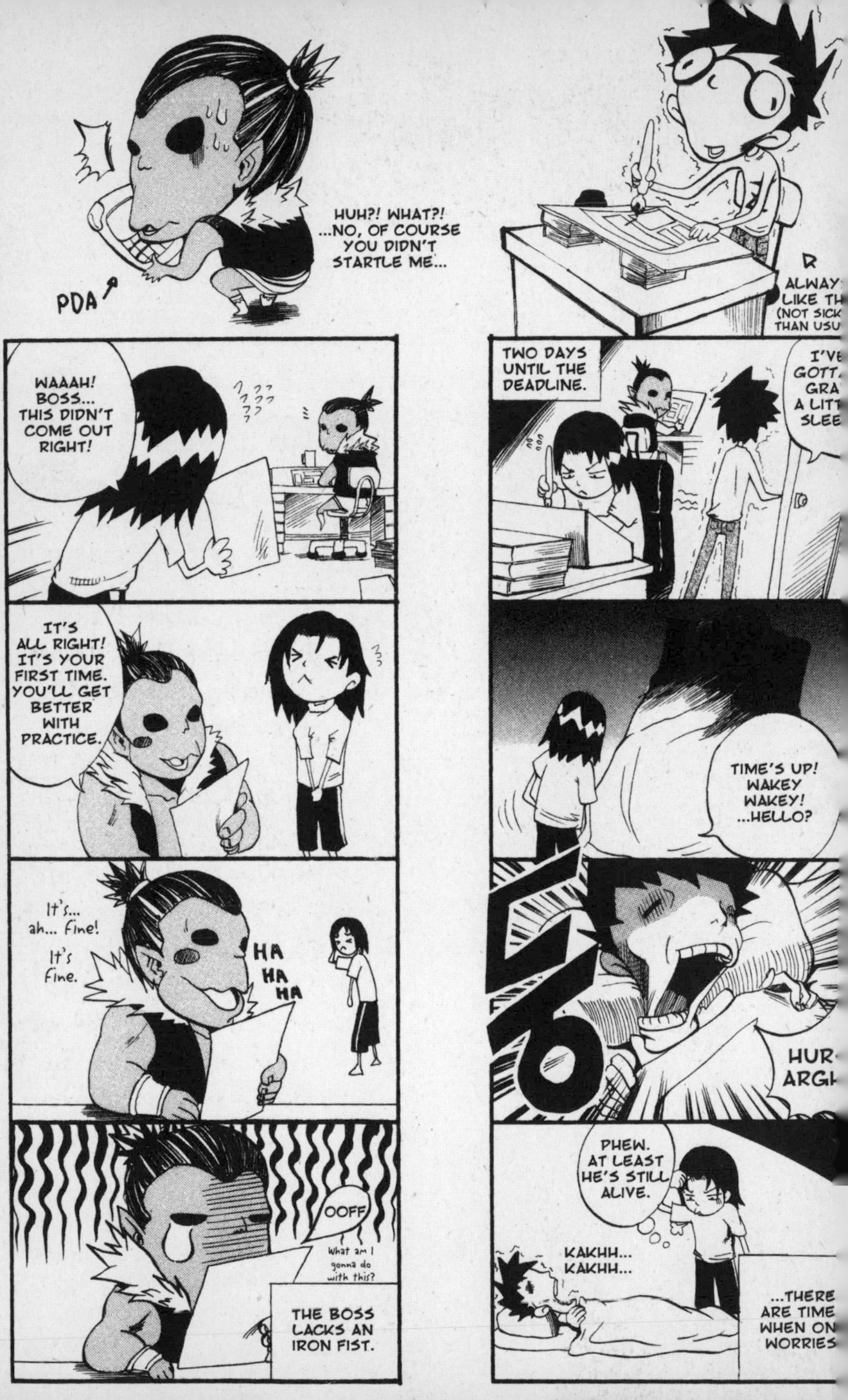
HUH?! WHAT?! ...NO, OF COURSE YOU DIDN'T STARTLE ME...
PDA
WAAAH! BOSS... THIS DIDN'T COME OUT RIGHT!
IT'S ALL RIGHT! IT'S YOUR FIRST TIME. YOU'LL GET BETTER WITH PRACTICE.
It's... ah... fine!
It's fine.
HA HA HA
OOFF
What am I gonna do with this?
THE BOSS LACKS AN IRON FIST.
ALWAYS LIKE TH
(NOT SICK
THAN USU
TWO DAYS UNTIL THE DEADLINE.
I'VE GOTT. GRA A LITT SLEE
TIME'S UP! WAKEY WAKEY! ...HELLO?
HUR- ARGH
PHEW. AT LEAST HE'S STILL ALIVE.
KAKHH... KAKHH...
...THERE ARE TIME WHEN ON WORRIES

In the Next Volume of

ARCHLORD

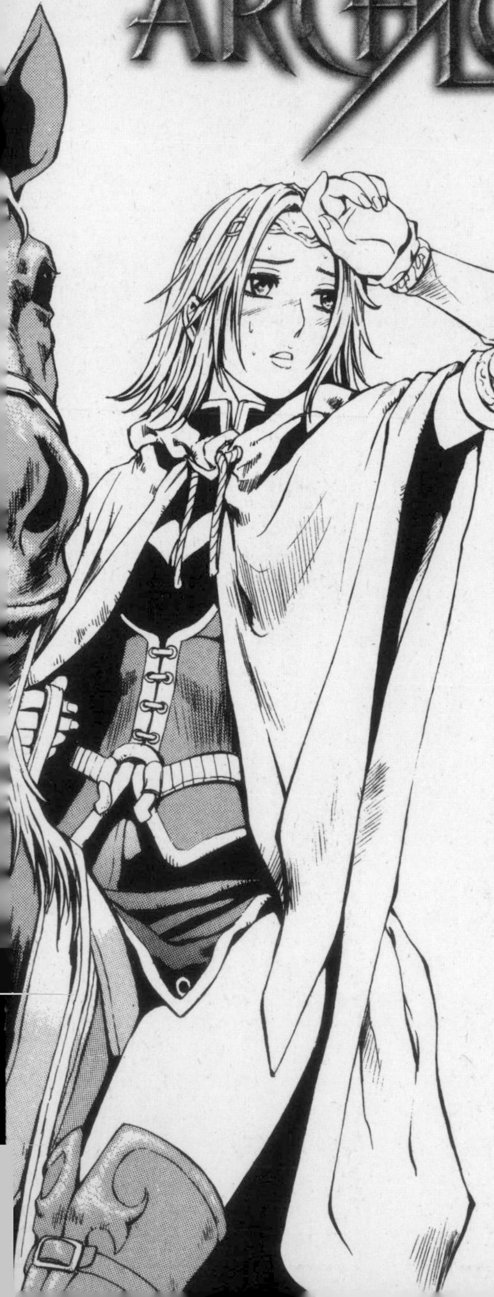

Ernan, horrified that the descendent of Nathan Manas he believed dispatched long ago is indeed alive, sends out two of his best men to find and kill Zian. Meanwhile, Arin decides to journeys with Zian and Ugdrasil to Elka to meet the prophet Berouze. And when the meet two more travelers, Scar and Talon, in the Taas Forest, suspicions mount on both sides.

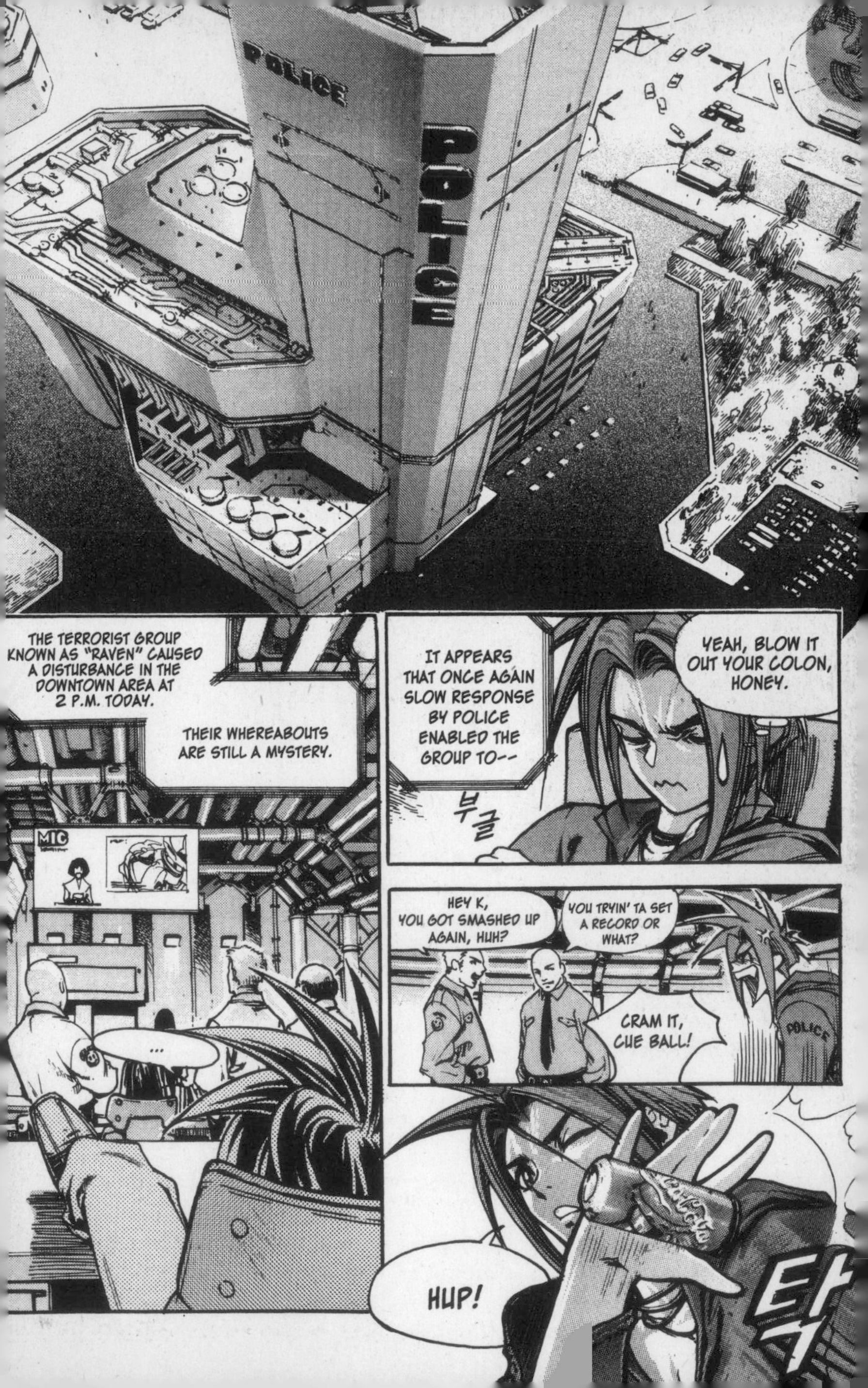
POLICE
POLICE
THE TERRORIST GROUP KNOWN AS "RAVEN" CAUSED A DISTURBANCE IN THE DOWNTOWN AREA AT 2 P.M. TODAY.
THEIR WHEREABOUTS ARE STILL A MYSTERY.
MIC
...
IT APPEARS THAT ONCE AGAIN SLOW RESPONSE BY POLICE ENABLED THE GROUP TO--
YEAH, BLOW IT OUT YOUR COLON, HONEY.
부글
HEY K, YOU GOT SMASHED UP AGAIN, HUH?
YOU TRYIN' TA SET A RECORD OR WHAT?
CRAM IT, CUE BALL!
POLICE
HUP!
탁

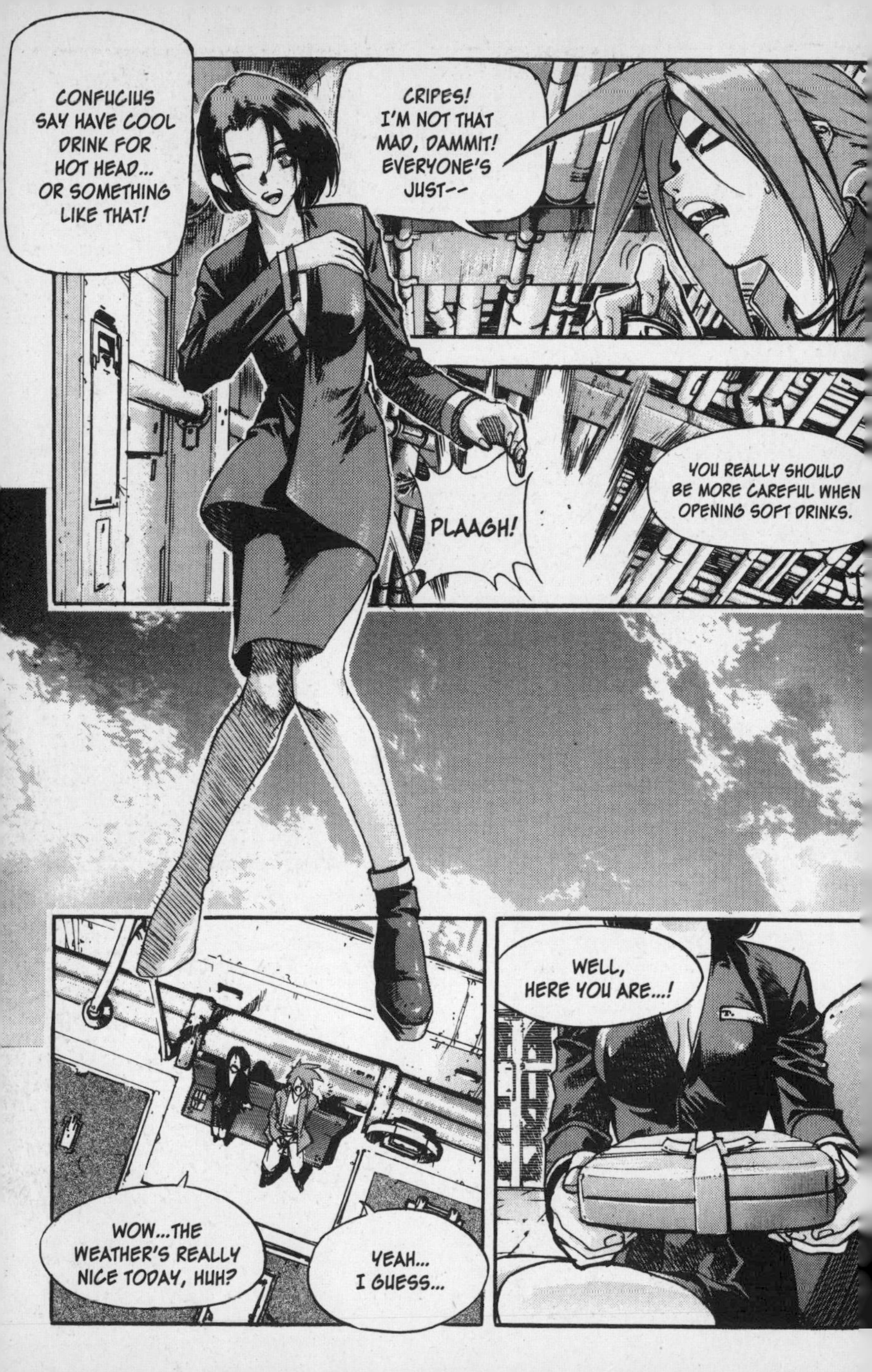
CONFUCIUS SAY HAVE COOL DRINK FOR HOT HEAD... OR SOMETHING LIKE THAT!
CRIPES! I'M NOT THAT MAD, DAMMIT! EVERYONE'S JUST--
PLAAGH!
YOU REALLY SHOULD BE MORE CAREFUL WHEN OPENING SOFT DRINKS.
WOW...THE WEATHER'S REALLY NICE TODAY, HUH?
YEAH... I GUESS...
WELL, HERE YOU ARE...!

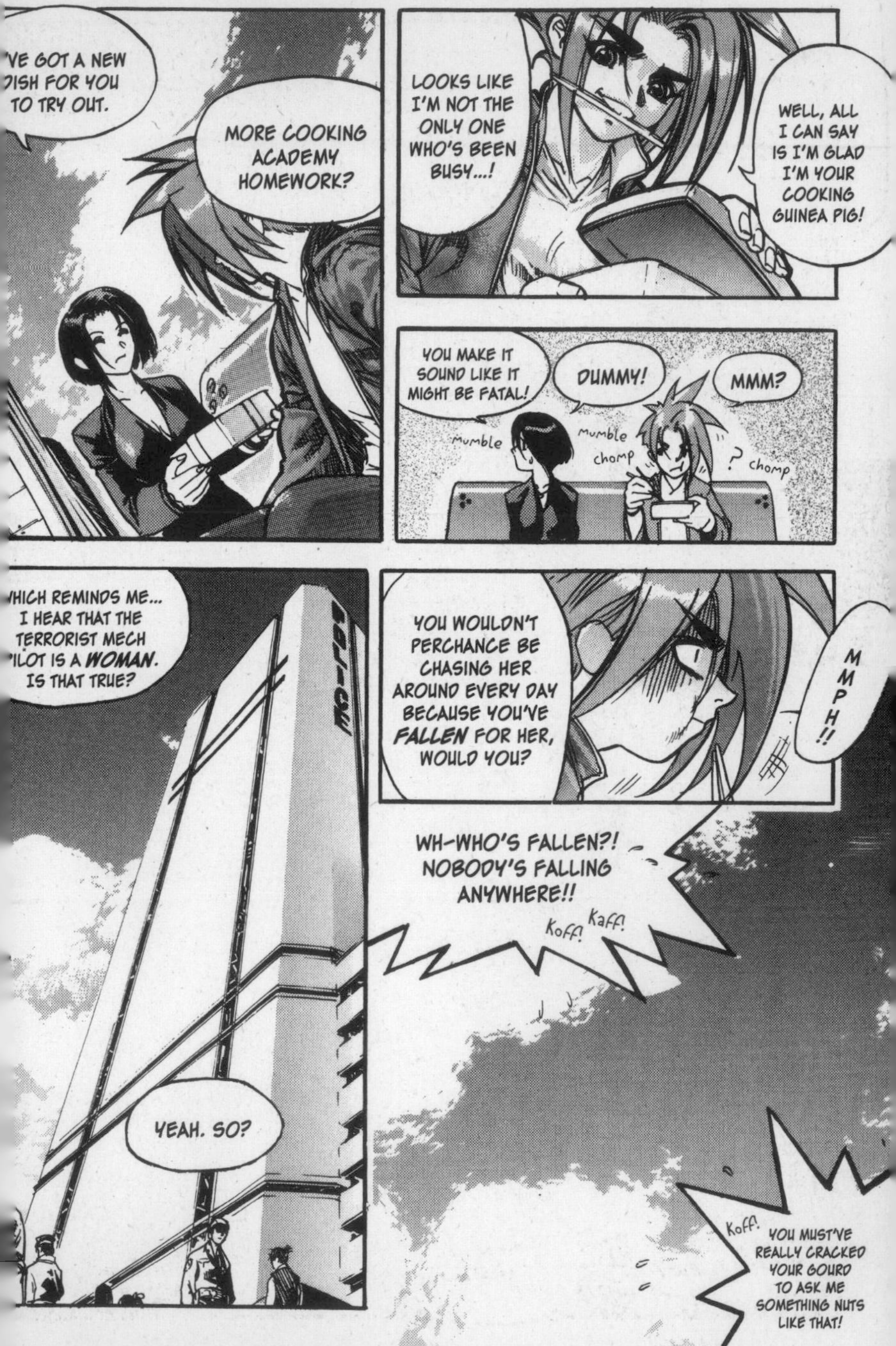
'VE GOT A NEW DISH FOR YOU TO TRY OUT.
MORE COOKING ACADEMY HOMEWORK?
LOOKS LIKE I'M NOT THE ONLY ONE WHO'S BEEN BUSY...!
WELL, ALL I CAN SAY IS I'M GLAD I'M YOUR COOKING GUINEA PIG!
YOU MAKE IT SOUND LIKE IT MIGHT BE FATAL!
DUMMY!
MMM?
mumble
mumble
chomp
?
chomp
WHICH REMINDS ME... I HEAR THAT THE TERRORIST MECH PILOT IS A *WOMAN*. IS THAT TRUE?
YEAH. SO?
YOU WOULDN'T PERCHANCE BE CHASING HER AROUND EVERY DAY BECAUSE YOU'VE *FALLEN* FOR HER, WOULD YOU?
MMPH!!
WH-WHO'S FALLEN?! NOBODY'S FALLING ANYWHERE!!
Koff!
Kaff!
Koff!
YOU MUST'VE REALLY CRACKED YOUR GOURD TO ASK ME SOMETHING NUTS LIKE THAT!

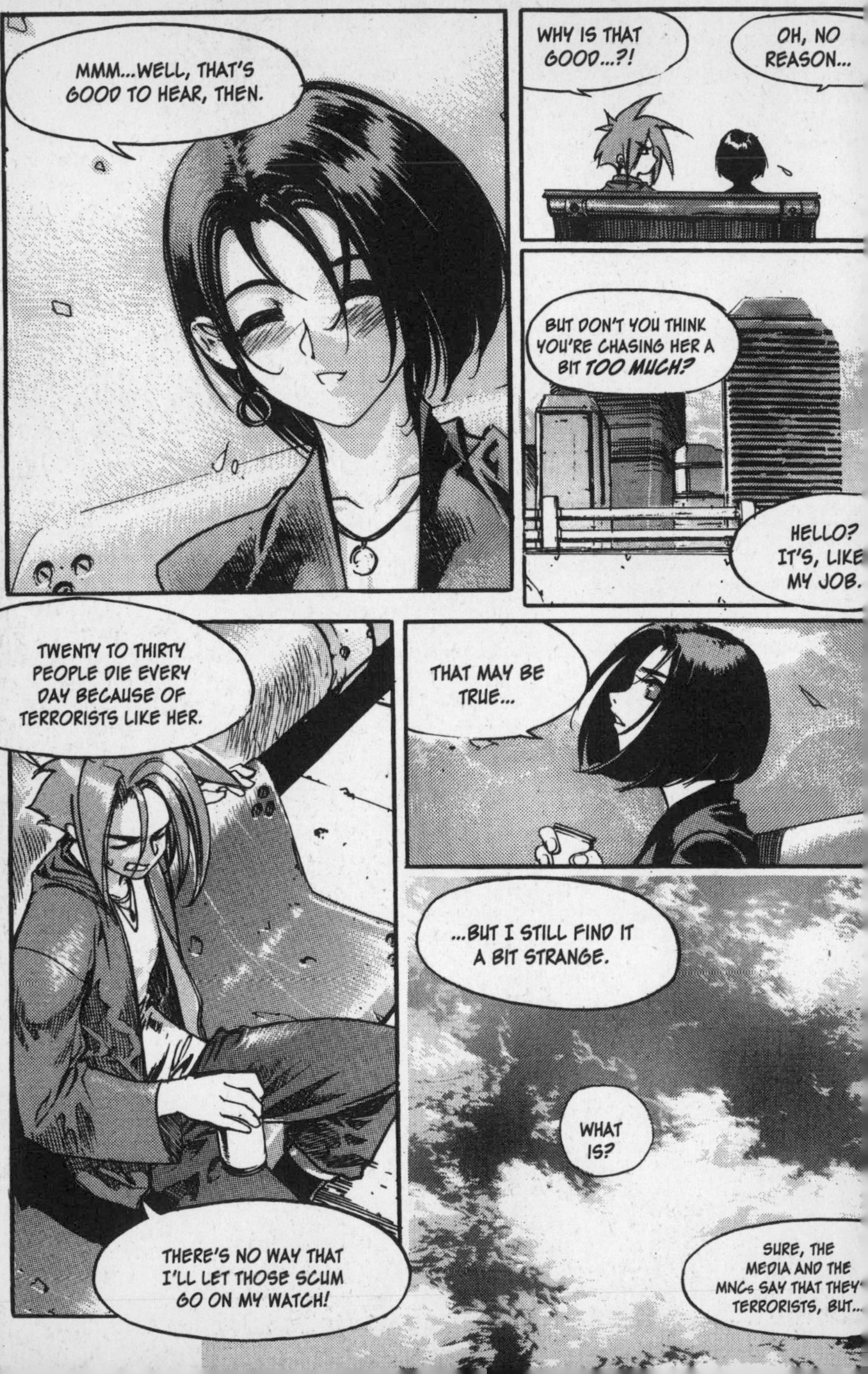
MMM...WELL, THAT'S GOOD TO HEAR, THEN.
WHY IS THAT GOOD...?!
OH, NO REASON...
BUT DON'T YOU THINK YOU'RE CHASING HER A BIT TOO MUCH?
HELLO? IT'S, LIKE MY JOB.
TWENTY TO THIRTY PEOPLE DIE EVERY DAY BECAUSE OF TERRORISTS LIKE HER.
THERE'S NO WAY THAT I'LL LET THOSE SCUM GO ON MY WATCH!
THAT MAY BE TRUE...
...BUT I STILL FIND IT A BIT STRANGE.
WHAT IS?
SURE, THE MEDIA AND THE MNCs SAY THAT THEY' TERRORISTS, BUT...

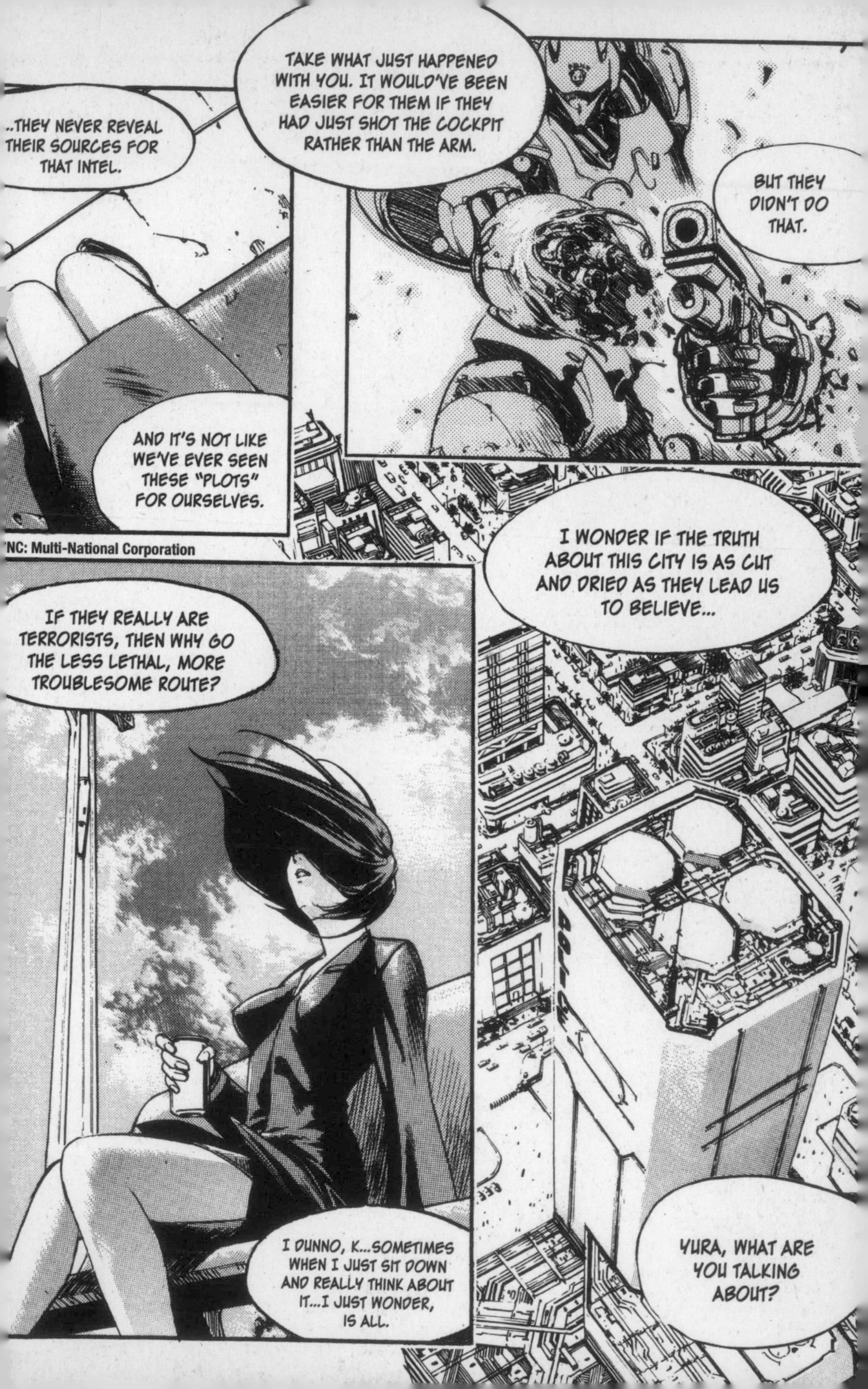
..THEY NEVER REVEAL THEIR SOURCES FOR THAT INTEL.
TAKE WHAT JUST HAPPENED WITH YOU. IT WOULD'VE BEEN EASIER FOR THEM IF THEY HAD JUST SHOT THE COCKPIT RATHER THAN THE ARM.
BUT THEY DIDN'T DO THAT.
AND IT'S NOT LIKE WE'VE EVER SEEN THESE "PLOTS" FOR OURSELVES.
MNC: Multi-National Corporation
IF THEY REALLY ARE TERRORISTS, THEN WHY GO THE LESS LETHAL, MORE TROUBLESOME ROUTE?
I WONDER IF THE TRUTH ABOUT THIS CITY IS AS CUT AND DRIED AS THEY LEAD US TO BELIEVE...
I DUNNO, K...SOMETIMES WHEN I JUST SIT DOWN AND REALLY THINK ABOUT IT...I JUST WONDER, IS ALL.
YURA, WHAT ARE YOU TALKING ABOUT?

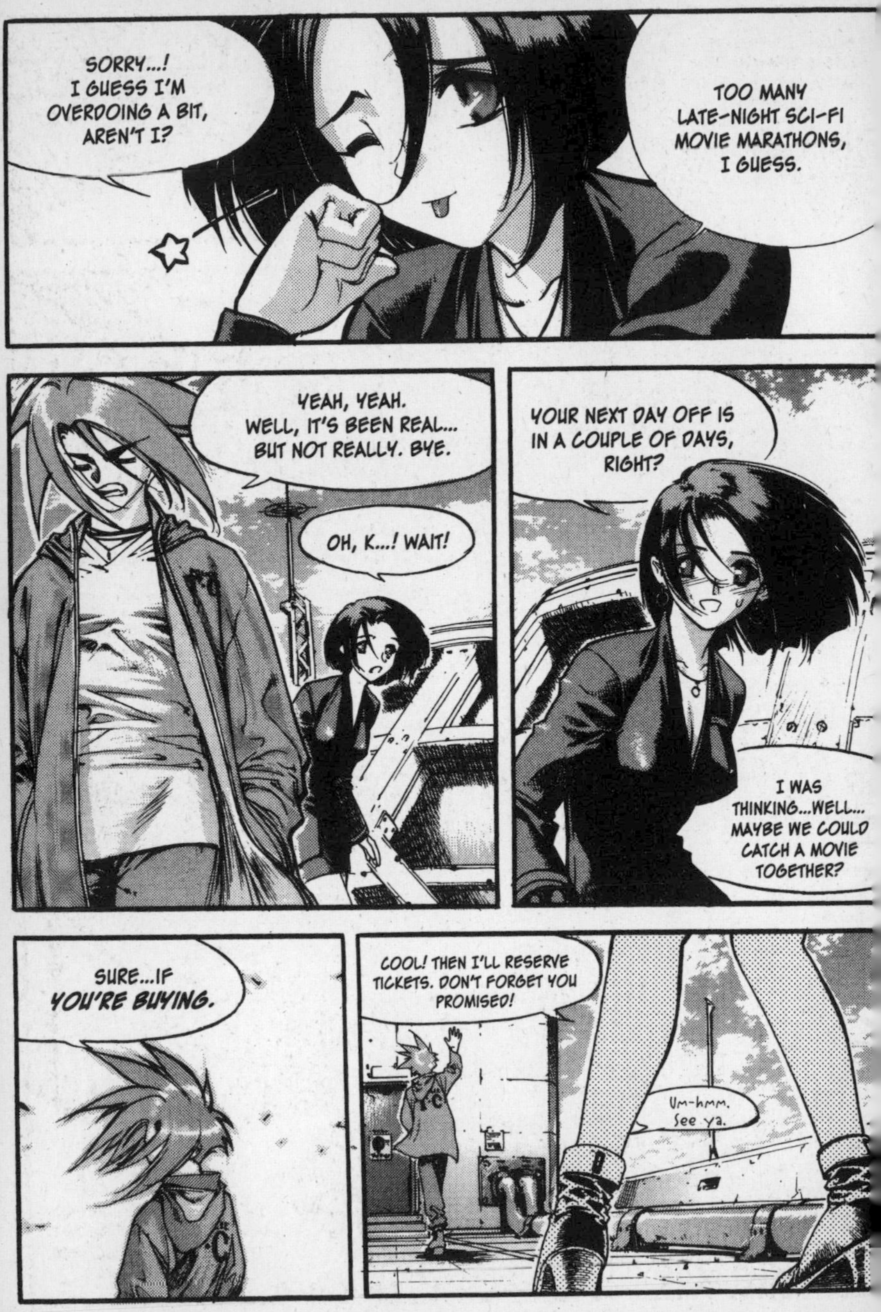
SORRY...! I GUESS I'M OVERDOING A BIT, AREN'T I?
TOO MANY LATE-NIGHT SCI-FI MOVIE MARATHONS, I GUESS.
YEAH, YEAH. WELL, IT'S BEEN REAL... BUT NOT REALLY. BYE.
OH, K...! WAIT!
YOUR NEXT DAY OFF IS IN A COUPLE OF DAYS, RIGHT?
I WAS THINKING...WELL... MAYBE WE COULD CATCH A MOVIE TOGETHER?
SURE...IF *YOU'RE BUYING.*
COOL! THEN I'LL RESERVE TICKETS. DON'T FORGET YOU PROMISED!
Um-hmm. See ya.

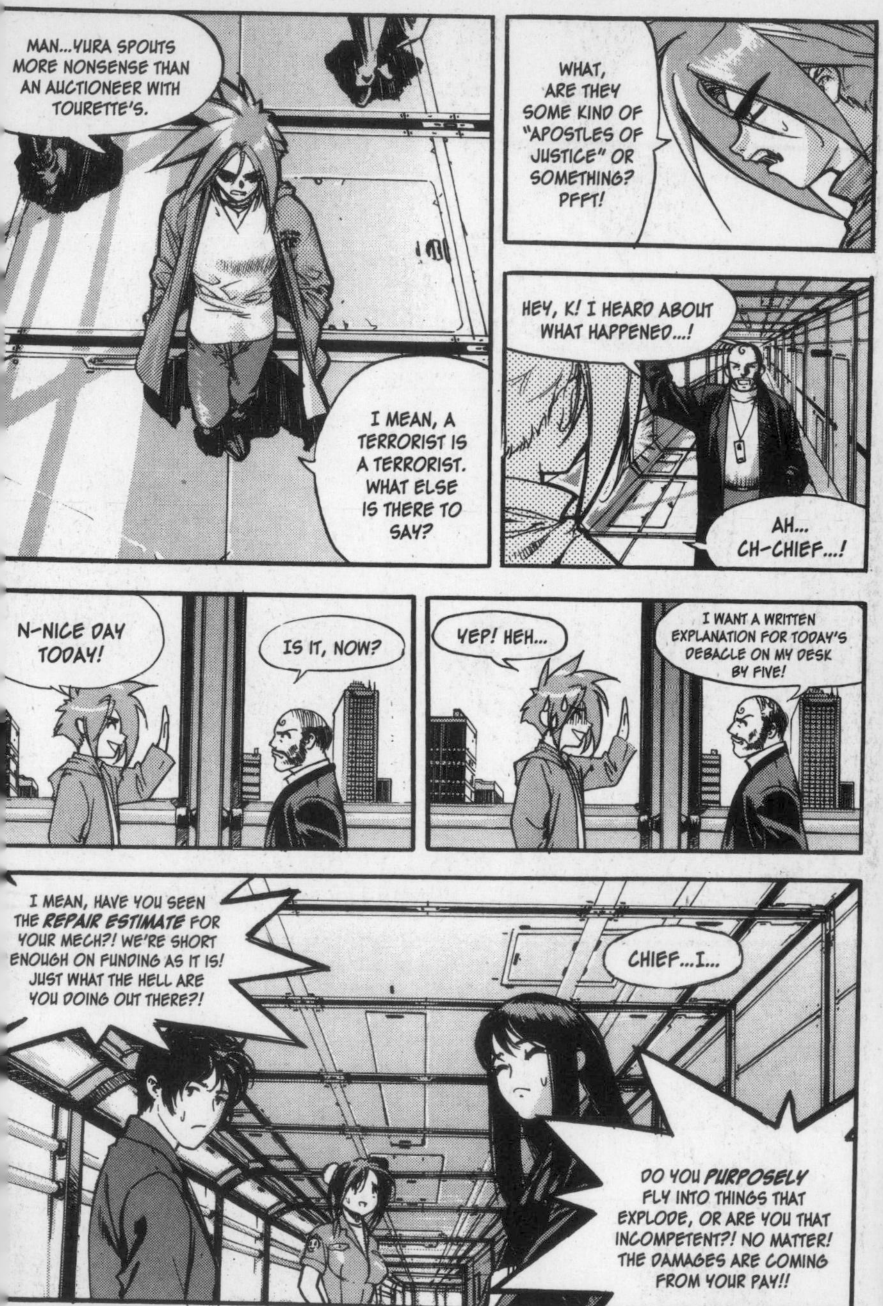
MAN...YURA SPOUTS MORE NONSENSE THAN AN AUCTIONEER WITH TOURETTE'S.
I MEAN, A TERRORIST IS A TERRORIST. WHAT ELSE IS THERE TO SAY?
WHAT, ARE THEY SOME KIND OF "APOSTLES OF JUSTICE" OR SOMETHING? PFFT!
HEY, K! I HEARD ABOUT WHAT HAPPENED...!
AH... CH-CHIEF...!
N-NICE DAY TODAY!
IS IT, NOW?
YEP! HEH...
I WANT A WRITTEN EXPLANATION FOR TODAY'S DEBACLE ON MY DESK BY FIVE!
I MEAN, HAVE YOU SEEN THE ***REPAIR ESTIMATE*** FOR YOUR MECH?! WE'RE SHORT ENOUGH ON FUNDING AS IT IS! JUST WHAT THE HELL ARE YOU DOING OUT THERE?!
CHIEF...I...
DO YOU ***PURPOSELY*** FLY INTO THINGS THAT EXPLODE, OR ARE YOU THAT INCOMPETENT?! NO MATTER! THE DAMAGES ARE COMING FROM YOUR PAY!!

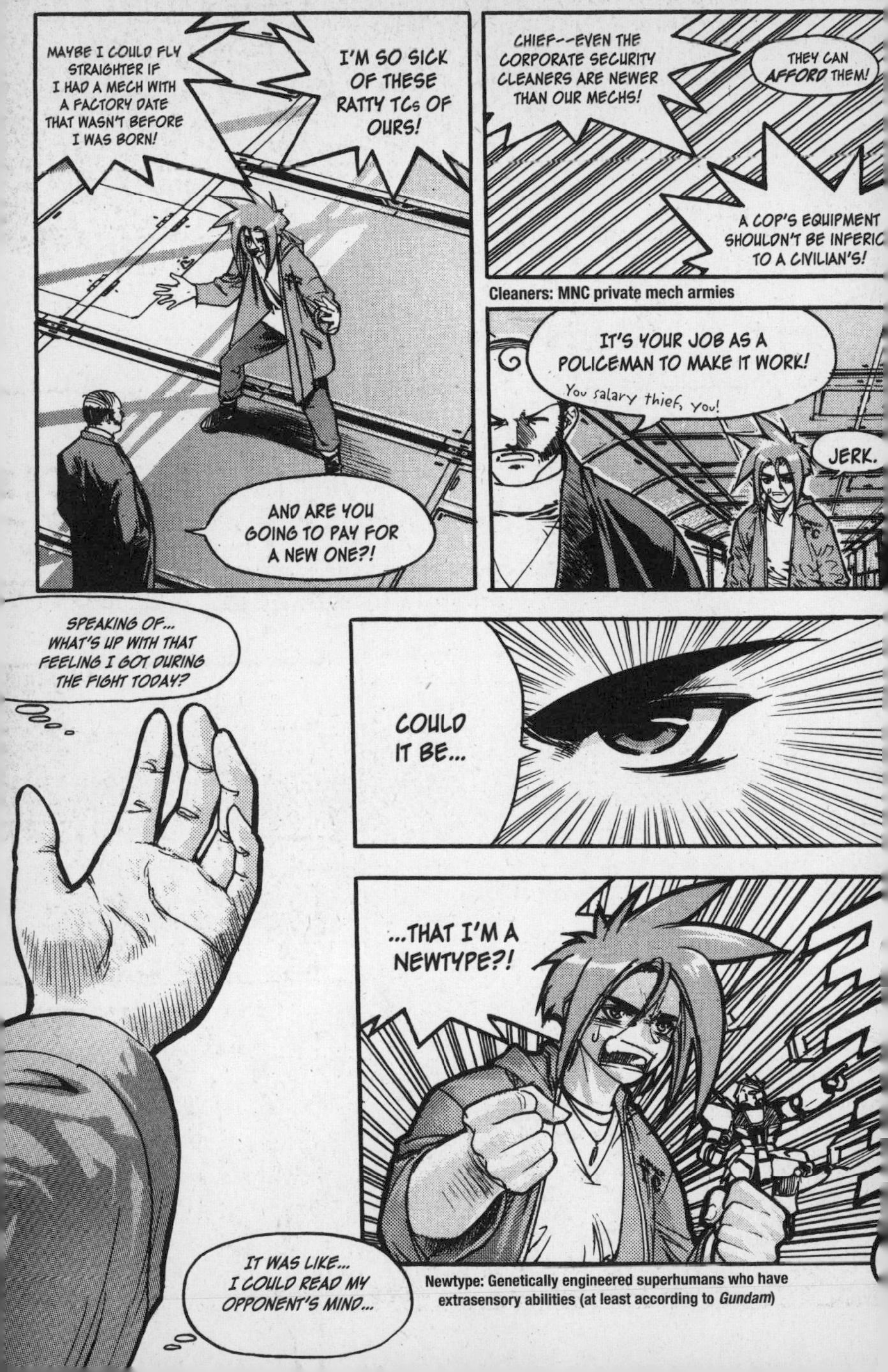
MAYBE I COULD FLY STRAIGHTER IF I HAD A MECH WITH A FACTORY DATE THAT WASN'T BEFORE I WAS BORN!
I'M SO SICK OF THESE RATTY TCs OF OURS!
AND ARE YOU GOING TO PAY FOR A NEW ONE?!
CHIEF--EVEN THE CORPORATE SECURITY CLEANERS ARE NEWER THAN OUR MECHS!
THEY CAN AFFORD THEM!
A COP'S EQUIPMENT SHOULDN'T BE INFERIC TO A CIVILIAN'S!
IT'S YOUR JOB AS A POLICEMAN TO MAKE IT WORK!
You salary thief, you!
JERK.
SPEAKING OF... WHAT'S UP WITH THAT FEELING I GOT DURING THE FIGHT TODAY?
IT WAS LIKE... I COULD READ MY OPPONENT'S MIND...
COULD IT BE...
...THAT I'M A NEWTYPE?!

Cleaners: MNC private mech armies

Newtype: Genetically engineered superhumans who have extrasensory abilities (at least according to *Gundam*)

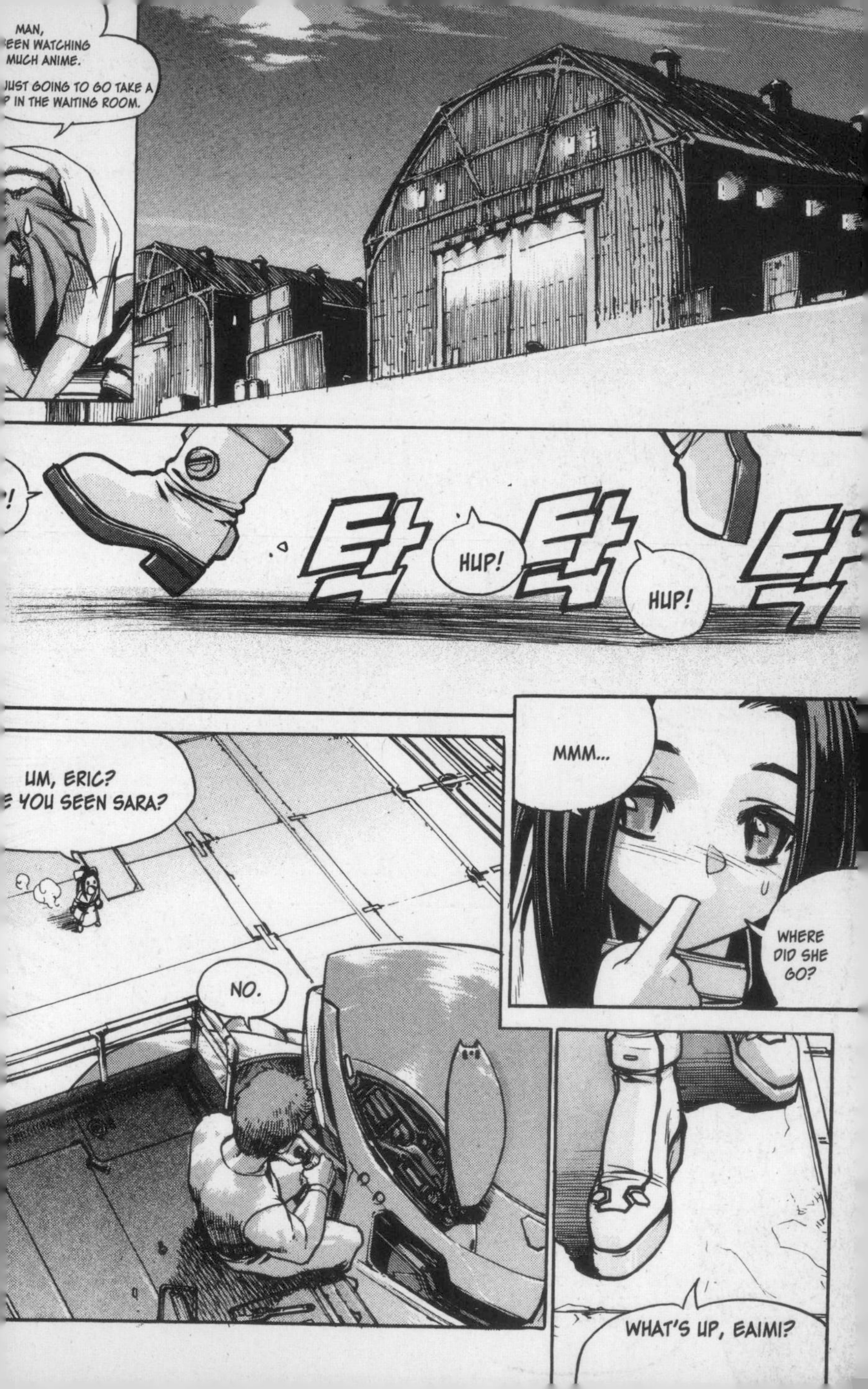
MAN,
EEN WATCHING
MUCH ANIME.
UST GOING TO GO TAKE A
P IN THE WAITING ROOM.
탁
HUP!
탁
HUP!
탁
UM, ERIC?
E YOU SEEN SARA?
NO.
MMM...
WHERE DID SHE GO?
WHAT'S UP, EAIMI?

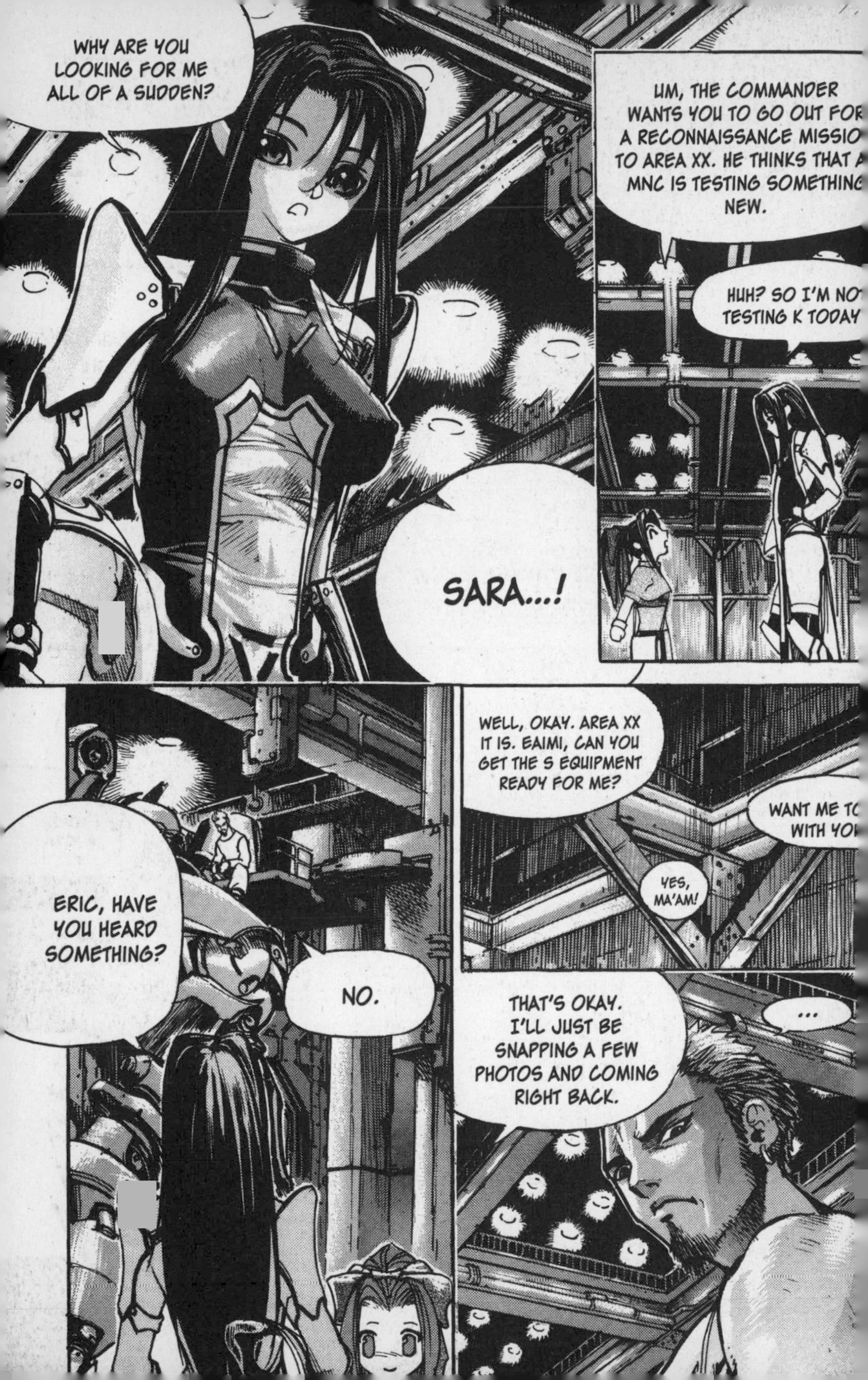
WHY ARE YOU LOOKING FOR ME ALL OF A SUDDEN?
SARA...!
UM, THE COMMANDER WANTS YOU TO GO OUT FOR A RECONNAISSANCE MISSIO TO AREA XX. HE THINKS THAT A MNC IS TESTING SOMETHING NEW.
HUH? SO I'M NOT TESTING K TODAY
ERIC, HAVE YOU HEARD SOMETHING?
NO.
WELL, OKAY. AREA XX IT IS. EAIMI, CAN YOU GET THE S EQUIPMENT READY FOR ME?
WANT ME TO WITH YO
YES, MA'AM!
THAT'S OKAY. I'LL JUST BE SNAPPING A FEW PHOTOS AND COMING RIGHT BACK.
...

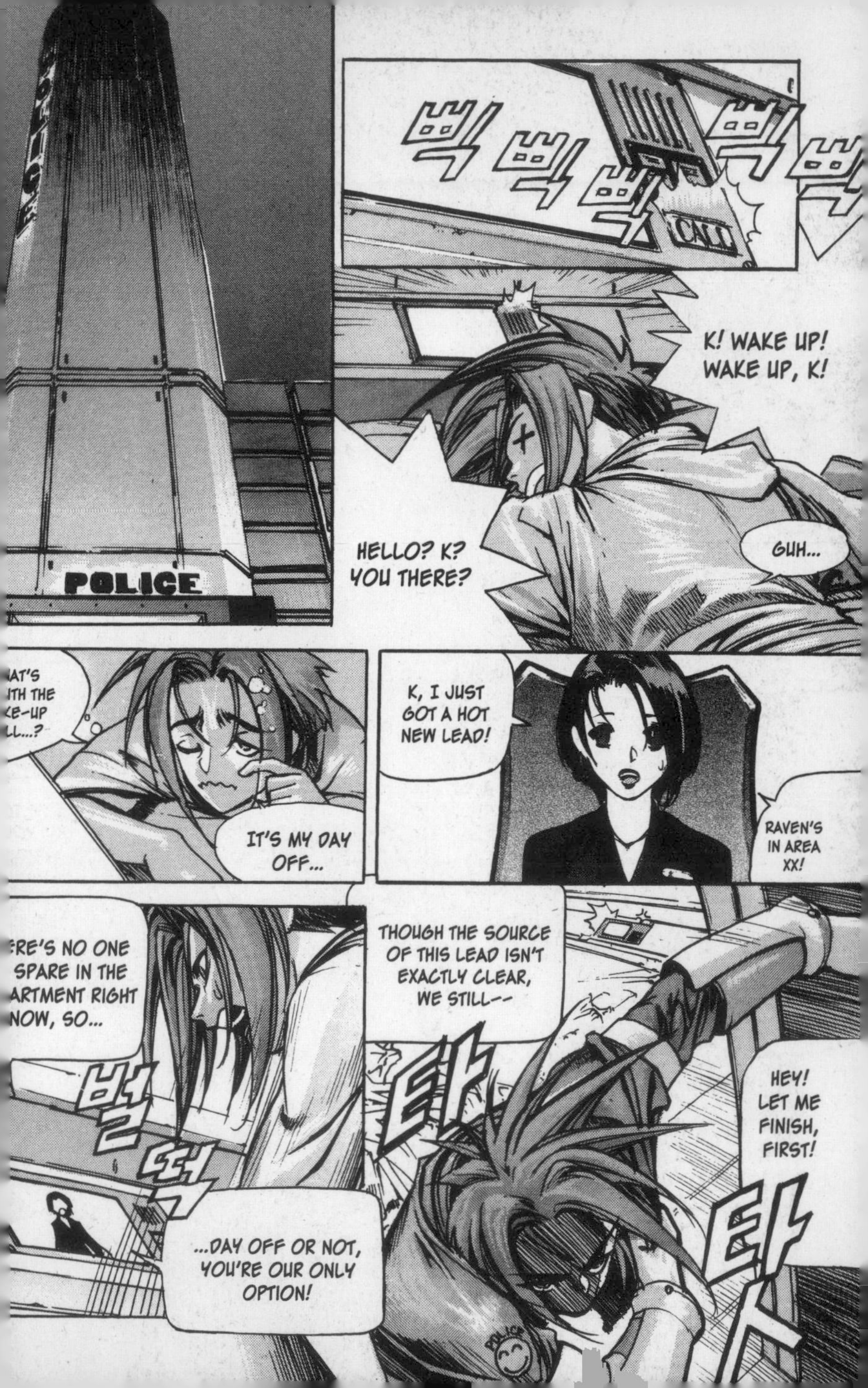
POLICE
POLICE
삑 삑 삑
CALL
삑 삑
K! WAKE UP! WAKE UP, K!
HELLO? K? YOU THERE?
GUH...
AT'S ITH THE KE-UP LL...?
IT'S MY DAY OFF...
K, I JUST GOT A HOT NEW LEAD!
RAVEN'S IN AREA XX!
ERE'S NO ONE SPARE IN THE ARTMENT RIGHT NOW, SO...
THOUGH THE SOURCE OF THIS LEAD ISN'T EXACTLY CLEAR, WE STILL--
벌떡
탁
...DAY OFF OR NOT, YOU'RE OUR ONLY OPTION!
HEY! LET ME FINISH, FIRST!
탁

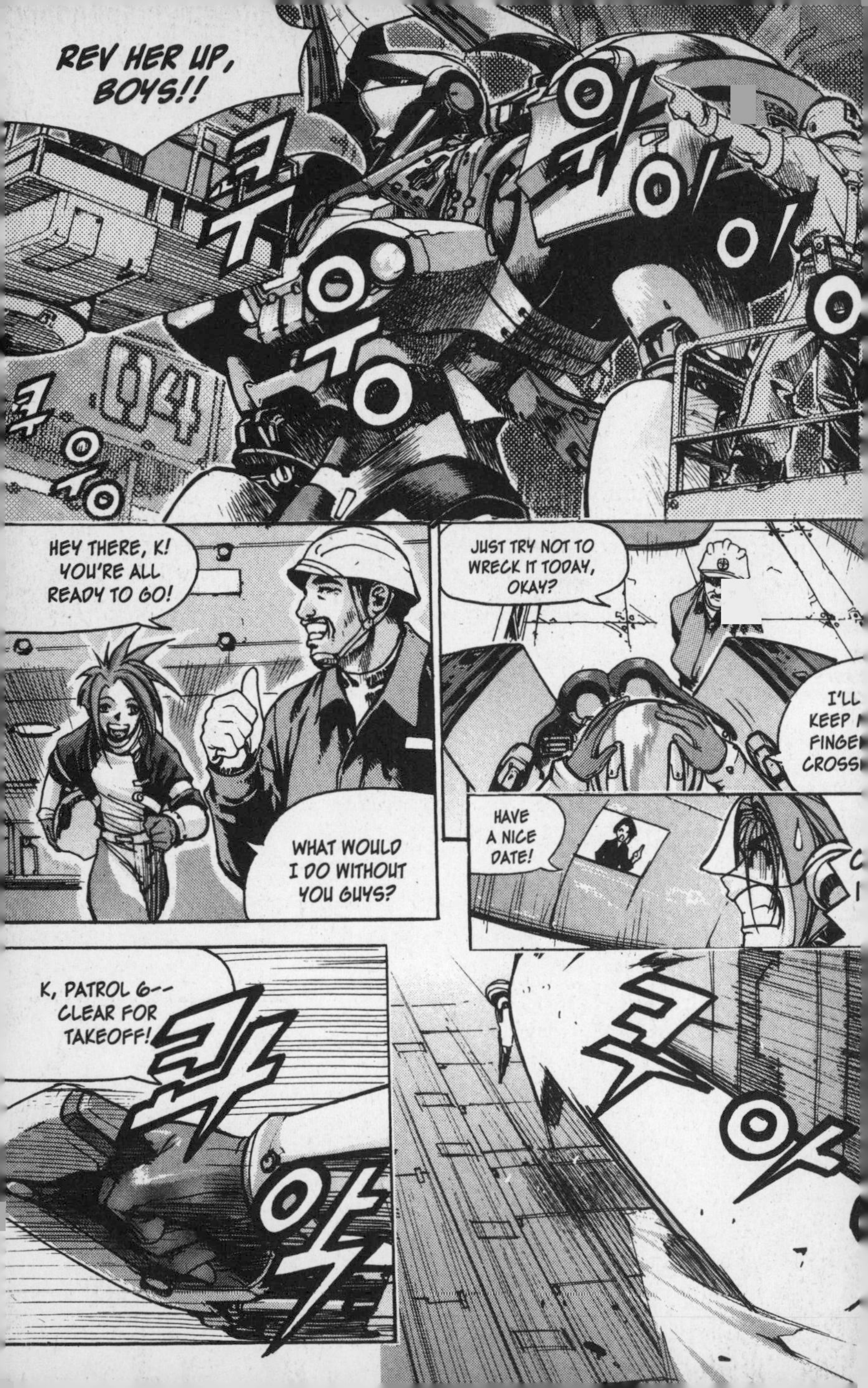
REV HER UP, BOYS!!
HEY THERE, K! YOU'RE ALL READY TO GO!
WHAT WOULD I DO WITHOUT YOU GUYS?
JUST TRY NOT TO WRECK IT TODAY, OKAY?
I'LL KEEP
HAVE A NICE DATE!
K, PATROL 6-- CLEAR FOR TAKEOFF!

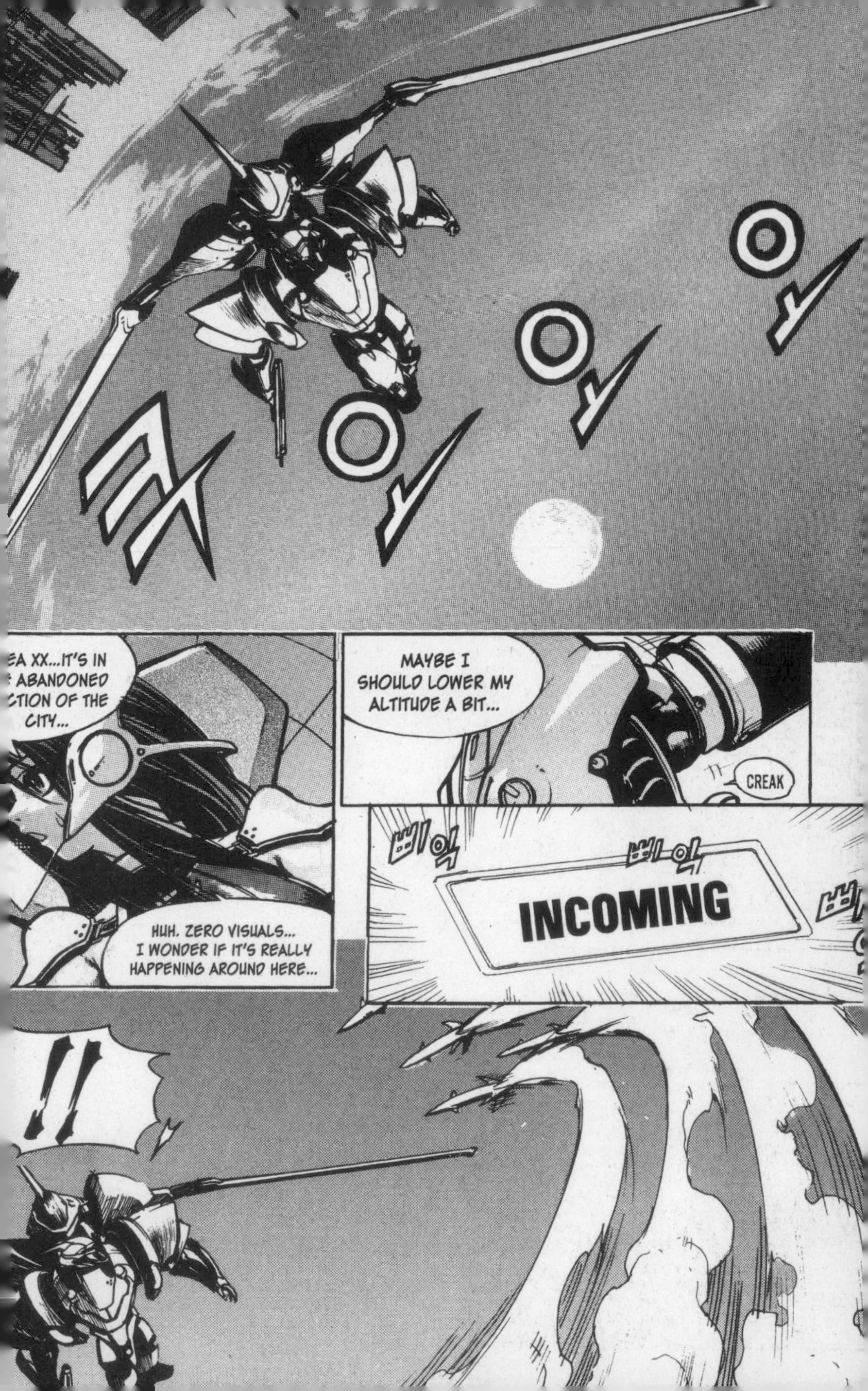
EA XX...IT'S IN
E ABANDONED
CTION OF THE
CITY...
HUH. ZERO VISUALS... I WONDER IF IT'S REALLY HAPPENING AROUND HERE...
MAYBE I SHOULD LOWER MY ALTITUDE A BIT...
CREAK
삐익
삐익
INCOMING
!!

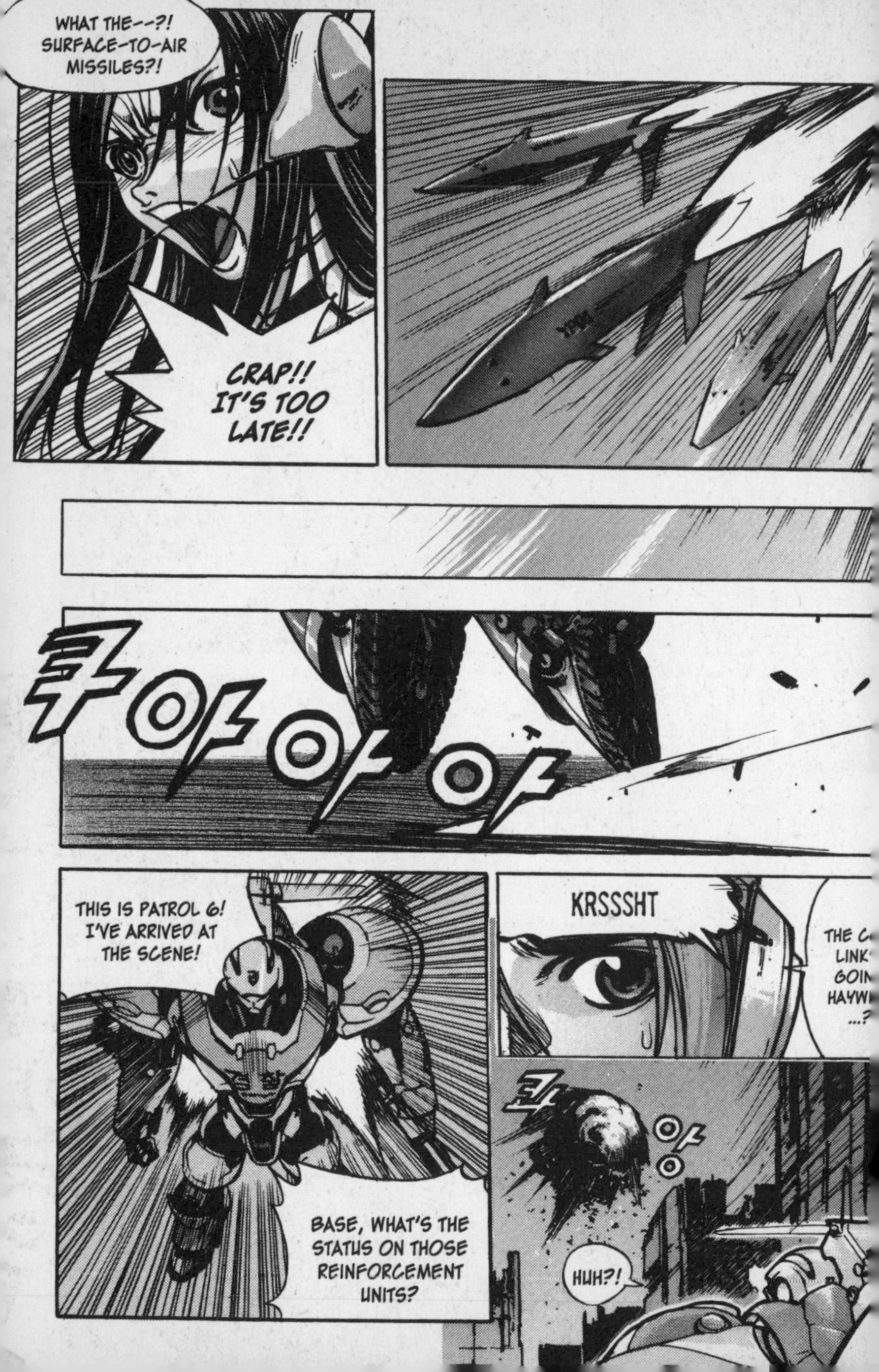
WHAT THE--?! SURFACE-TO-AIR MISSILES?!
CRAP!! IT'S TOO LATE!!
THIS IS PATROL 6! I'VE ARRIVED AT THE SCENE!
BASE, WHAT'S THE STATUS ON THOSE REINFORCEMENT UNITS?
KRSSSHT
THE C LINK GOIN HAYW ...?
HUH?!

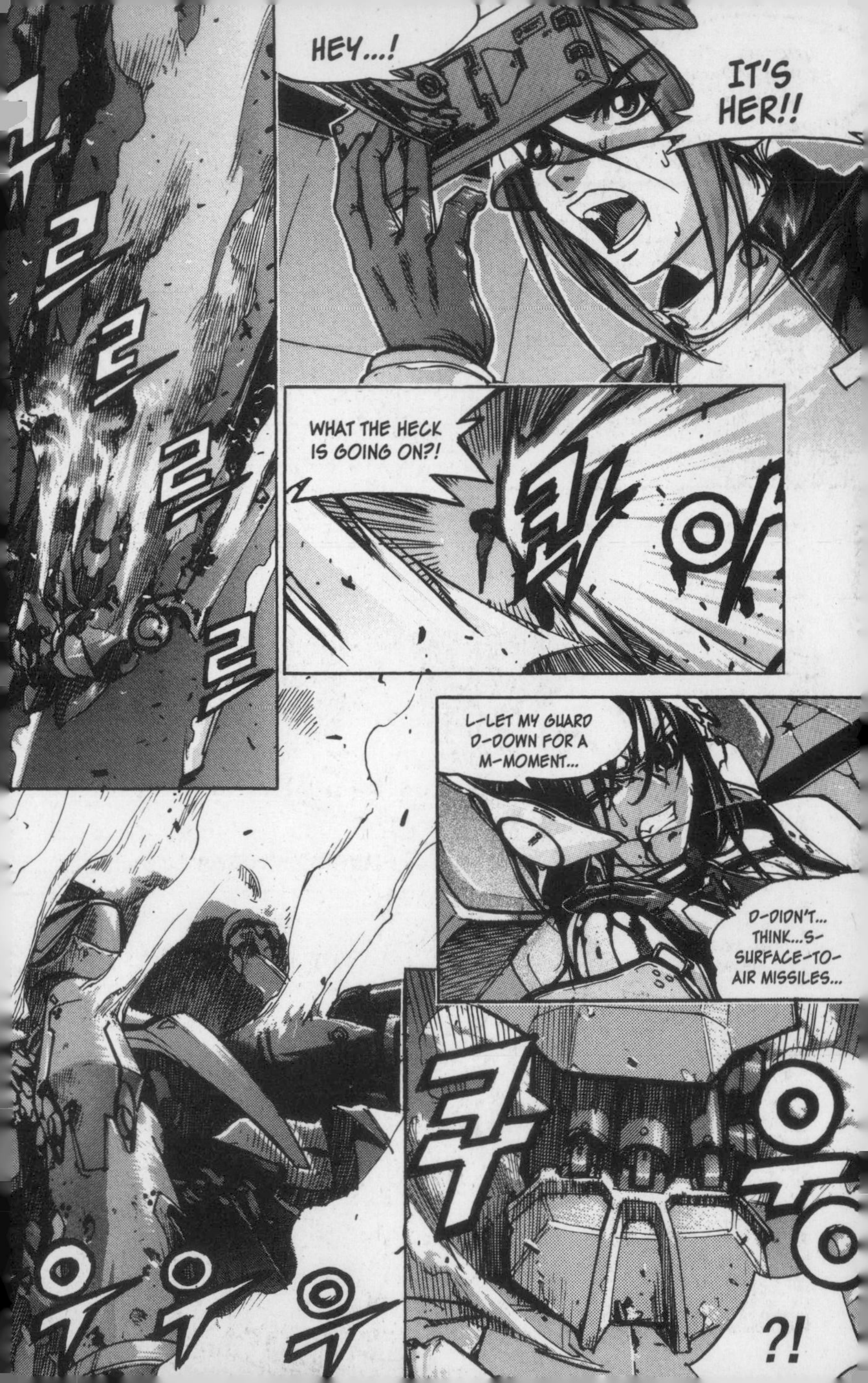
HEY...!
IT'S HER!!
WHAT THE HECK IS GOING ON?!
L-LET MY GUARD D-DOWN FOR A M-MOMENT...
D-DIDN'T... THINK...S-SURFACE-TO-AIR MISSILES...
?!

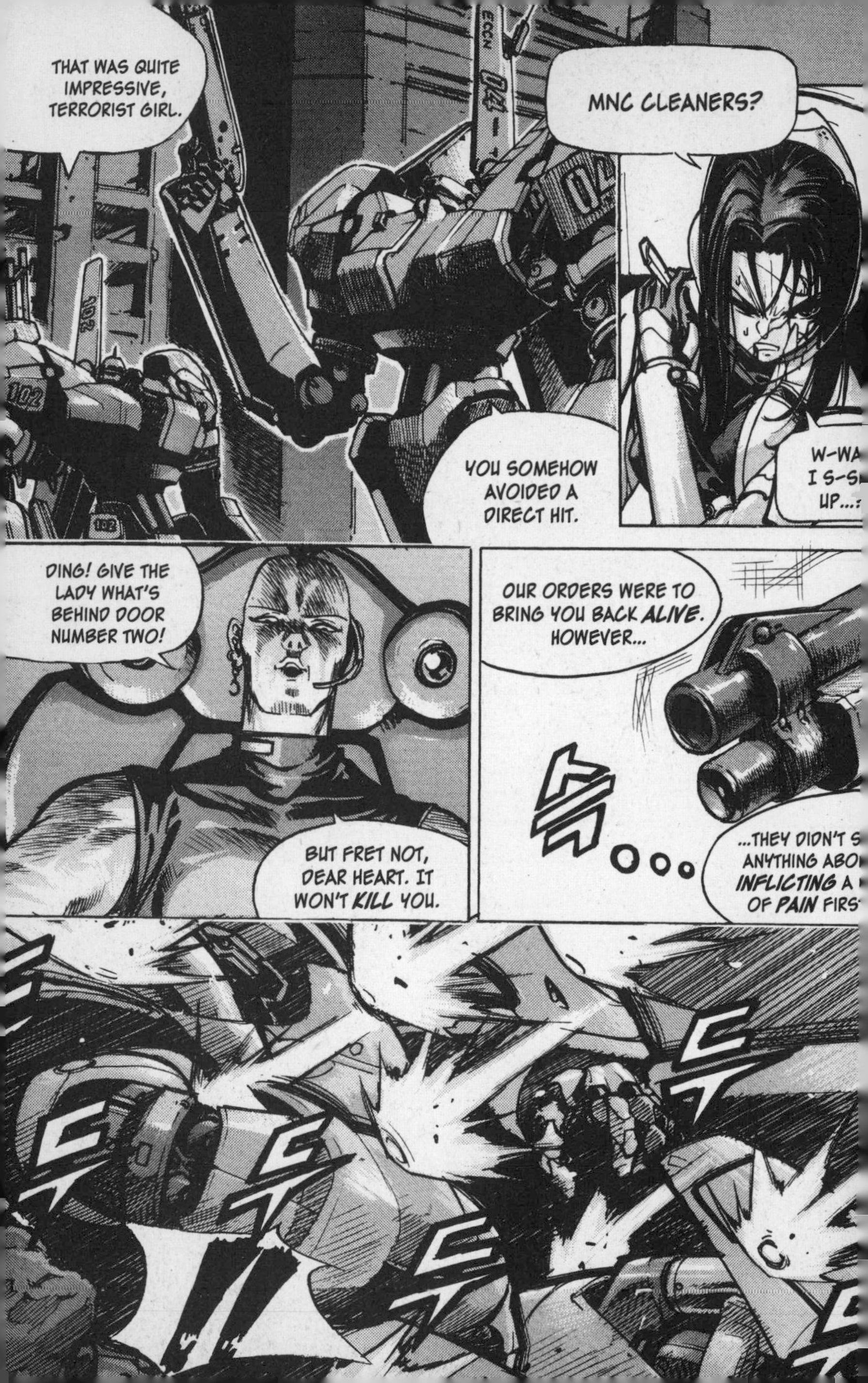

THAT WAS QUITE IMPRESSIVE, TERRORIST GIRL.
YOU SOMEHOW AVOIDED A DIRECT HIT.
MNC CLEANERS?
W-WA I S-S UP...
DING! GIVE THE LADY WHAT'S BEHIND DOOR NUMBER TWO!
BUT FRET NOT, DEAR HEART. IT WON'T KILL YOU.
OUR ORDERS WERE TO BRING YOU BACK ALIVE. HOWEVER...
...THEY DIDN'T S ANYTHING ABO INFLICTING A OF PAIN FIRS

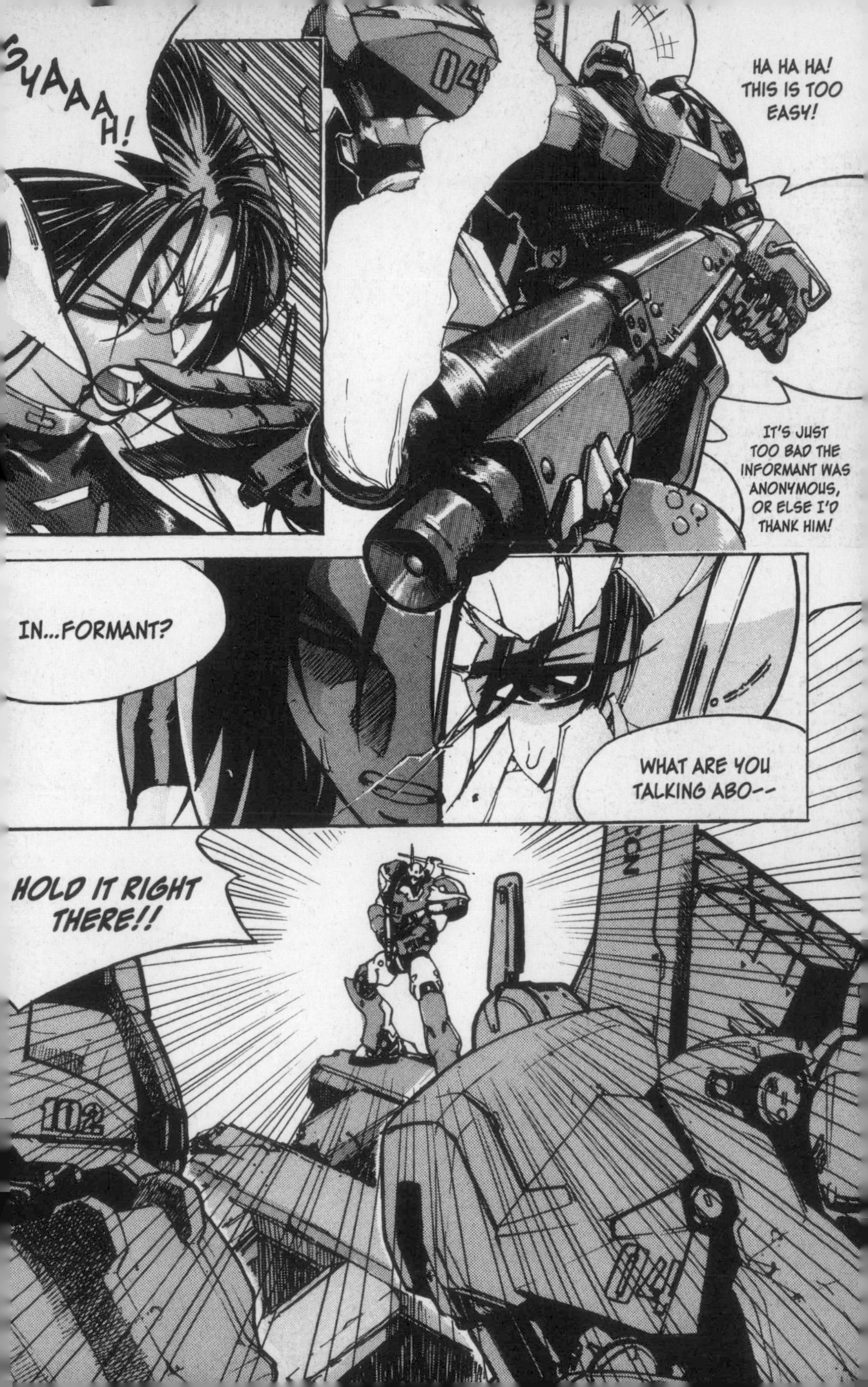

GYAAAAH!
HA HA HA! THIS IS TOO EASY!
IT'S JUST TOO BAD THE INFORMANT WAS ANONYMOUS, OR ELSE I'D THANK HIM!
IN...FORMANT?
WHAT ARE YOU TALKING ABO--
HOLD IT RIGHT THERE!!

pause

If you've been enjoying the unforgettable left-to-right read experience, we invite you to jump to the back of this book more cutting-edge manga…this time from Japan!

Or, if you've just soaked up the hottest manga from Japan, need to turn to the front of **this book** for some of TOKYOPO originally created manga and other cool articles.

LEFT-TO-RIGHT OR RIGHT-TO-LEFT — WI GOT MANGA COVERED IN ALL DIRECTIO

Finally, if you're blown away by what you've been readin then e-mail your friends, call your loved ones, and write president—tell them all about the Manga Revolution!

We now return you to your regularly scheduled manga.

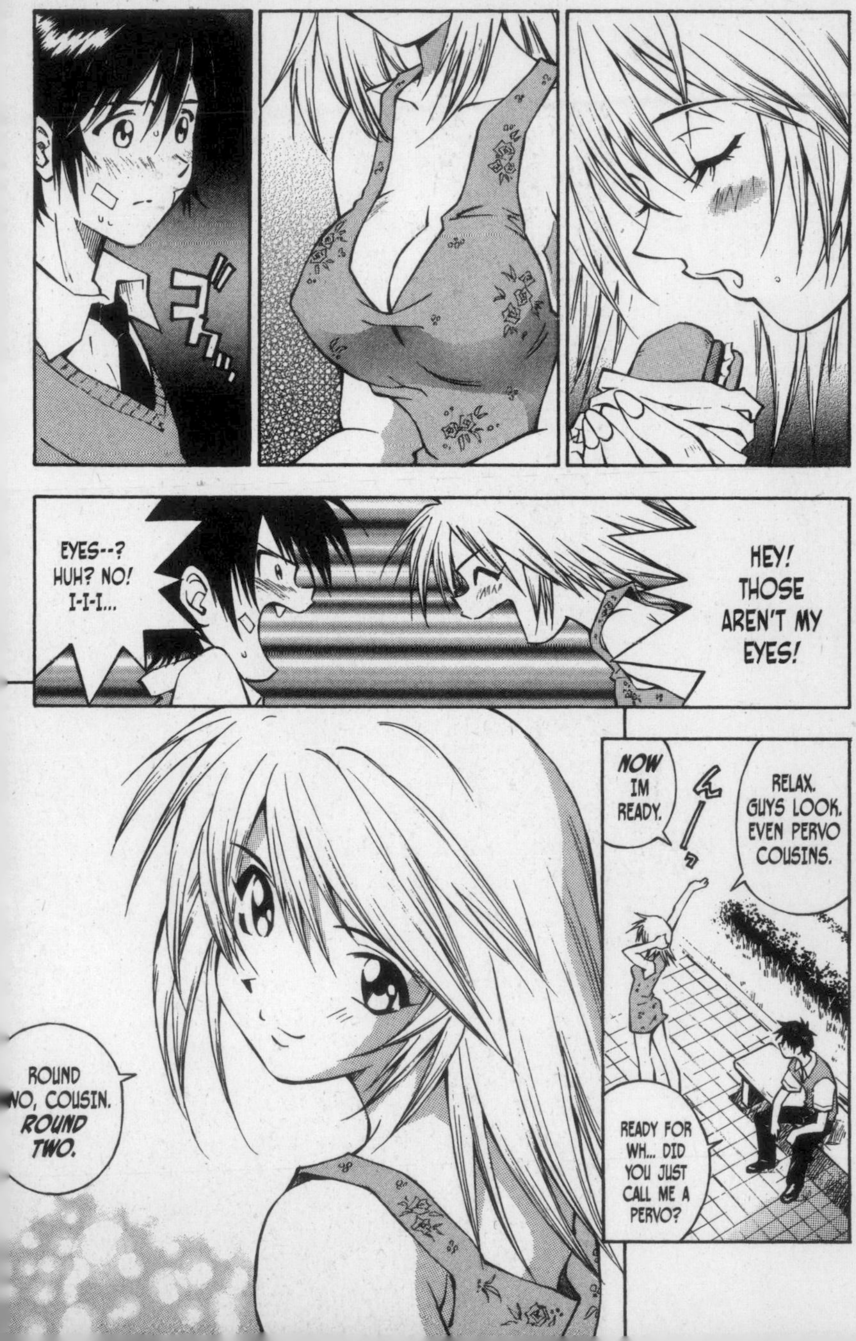
EYES--? HUH? NO! I-I-I...
HEY! THOSE AREN'T MY EYES!
ROUND WO, COUSIN. *ROUND TWO.*
NOW IM READY.
RELAX. GUYS LOOK. EVEN PERVO COUSINS.
READY FOR WH... DID YOU JUST CALL ME A PERVO?

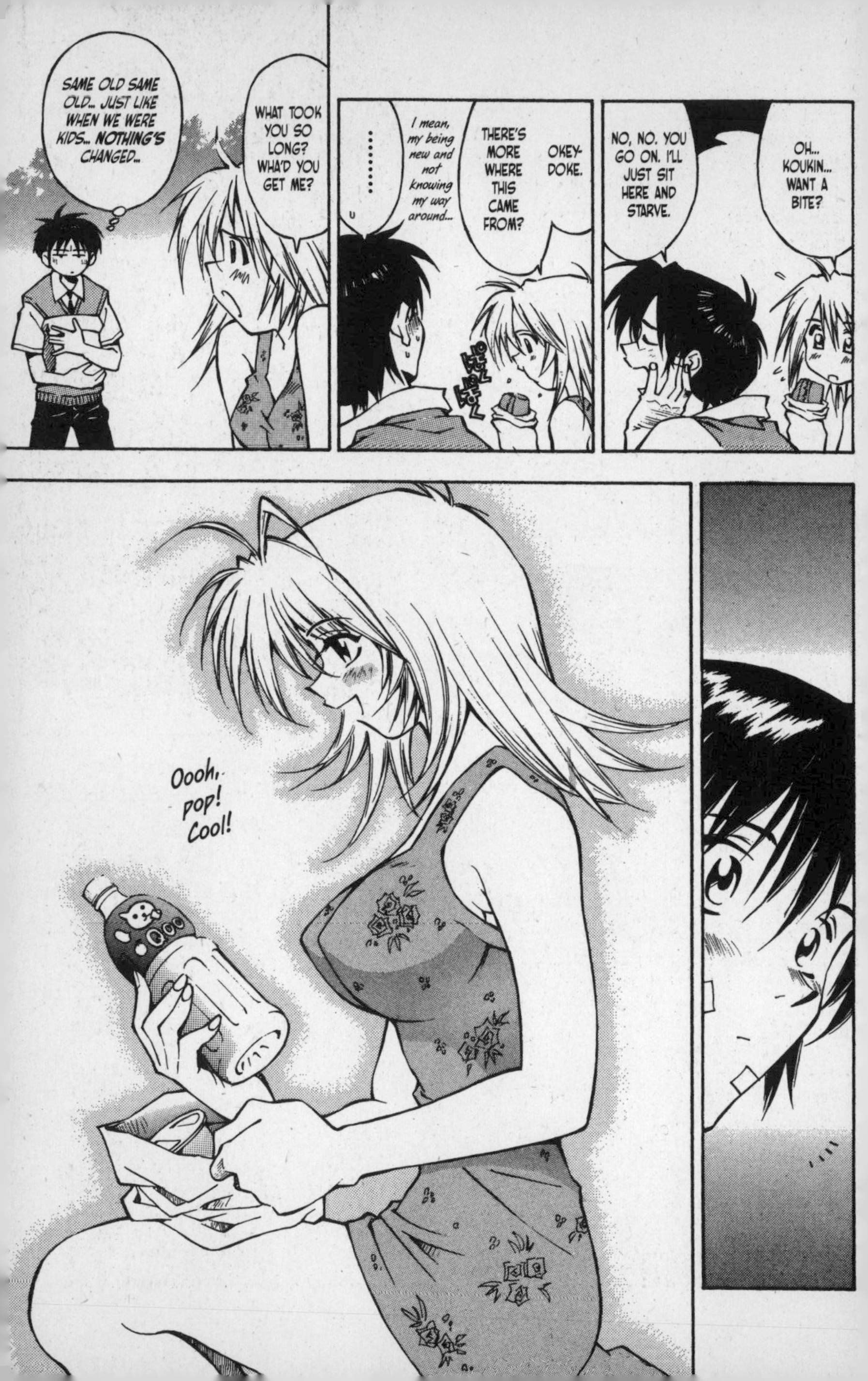
SAME OLD SAME OLD... JUST LIKE WHEN WE WERE KIDS... NOTHING'S CHANGED...
WHAT TOOK YOU SO LONG? WHA'D YOU GET ME?
......
I mean, my being new and not knowing my way around...
THERE'S MORE WHERE THIS CAME FROM?
OKEY-DOKE.
NO, NO. YOU GO ON. I'LL JUST SIT HERE AND STARVE.
OH... KOUKIN... WANT A BITE?
Oooh, pop! Cool!

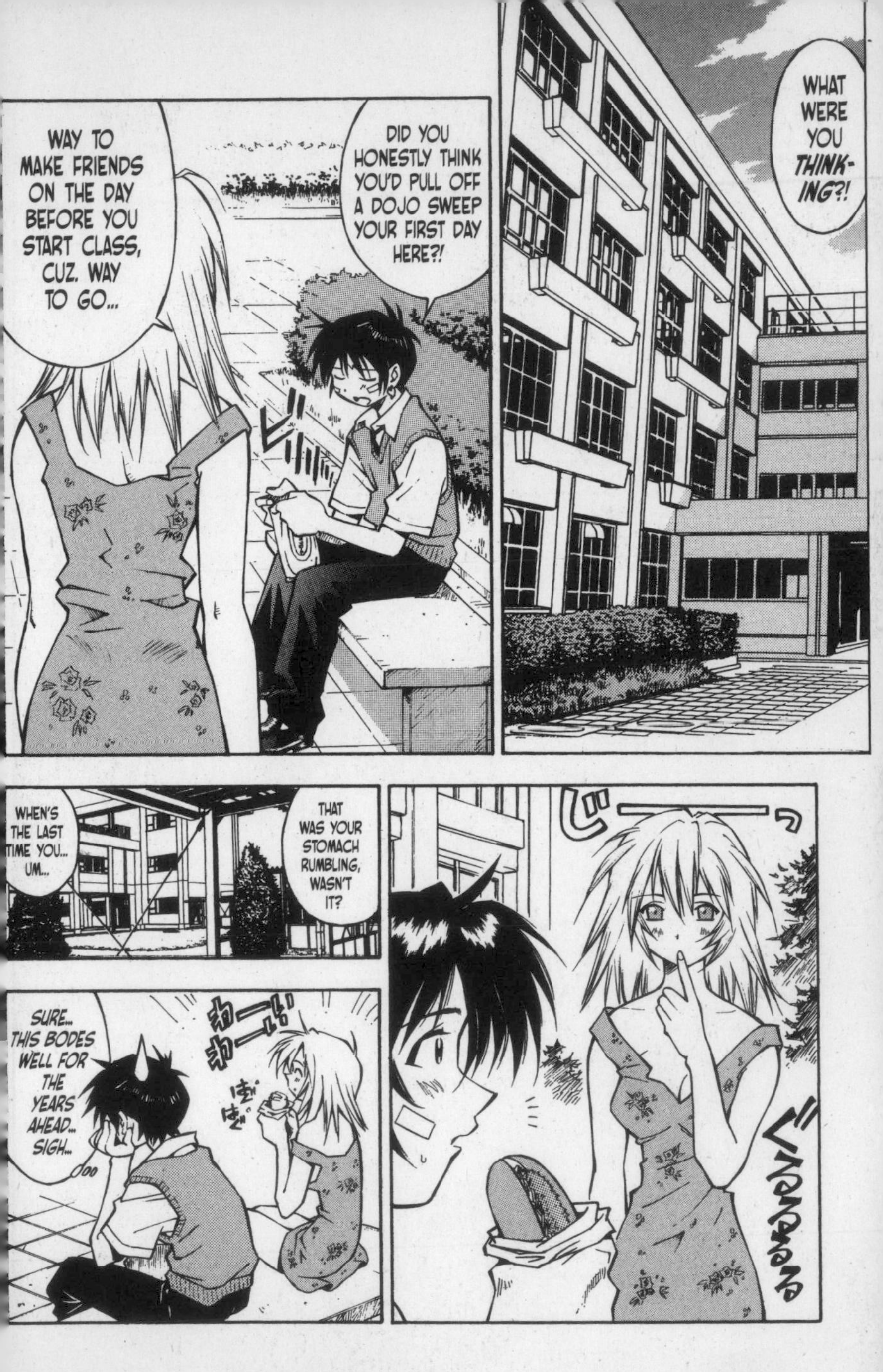
WAY TO MAKE FRIENDS ON THE DAY BEFORE YOU START CLASS, CUZ. WAY TO GO...
DID YOU HONESTLY THINK YOU'D PULL OFF A DOJO SWEEP YOUR FIRST DAY HERE?!
WHAT WERE YOU THINKING?!
WHEN'S THE LAST TIME YOU... UM...
THAT WAS YOUR STOMACH RUMBLING, WASN'T IT?
SURE... THIS BODES WELL FOR THE YEARS AHEAD... SIGH...

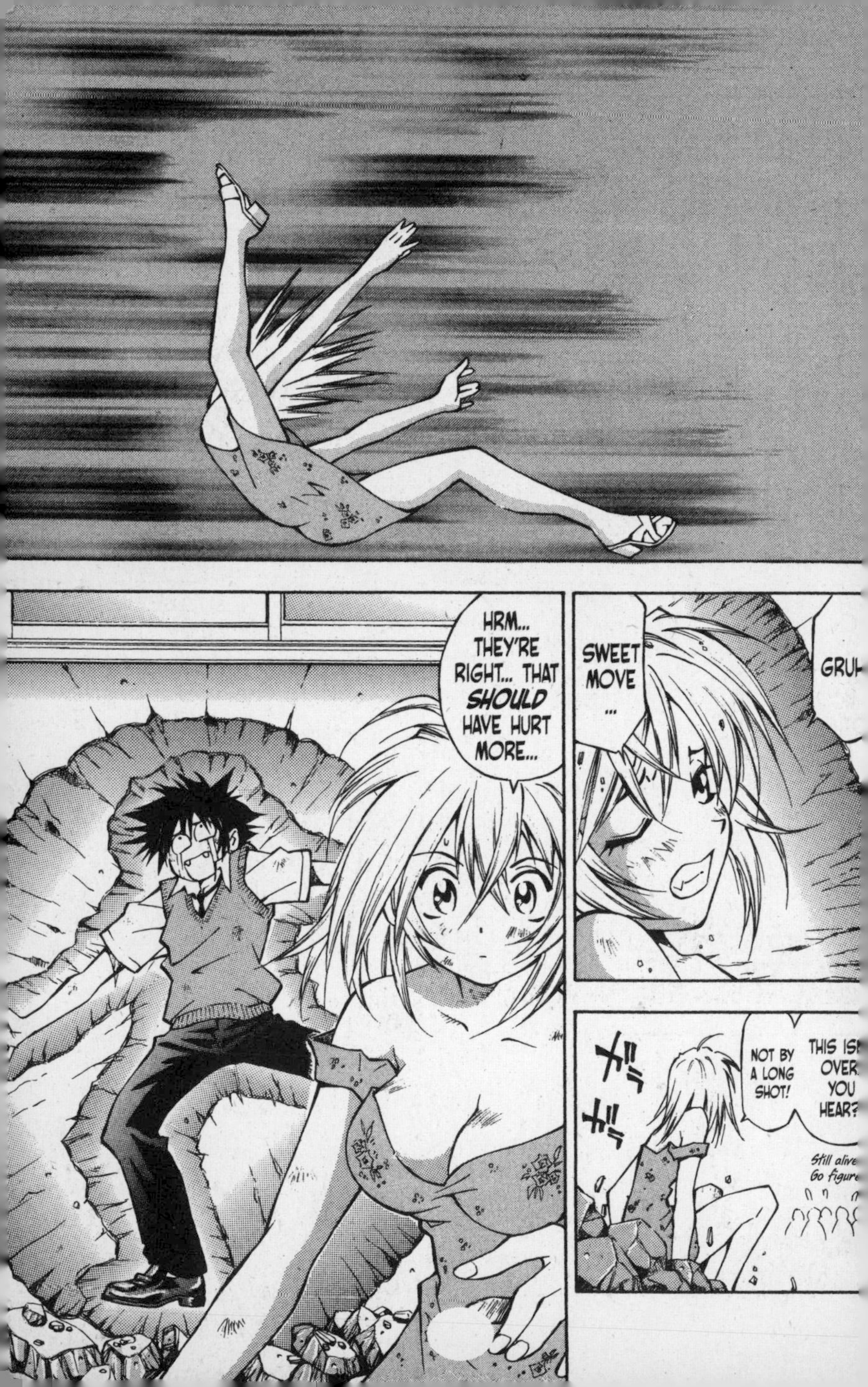
HRM... THEY'RE RIGHT... THAT *SHOULD* HAVE HURT MORE...
SWEET MOVE ...
GRUH
NOT BY A LONG SHOT!
THIS IS OVER. YOU HEAR?
Still alive Go figure

CHOOSE YOUR OPPONENT. NOT THE OTHER WAY AROUND.

WORD TO THE WISE, LITTLE GIRL...

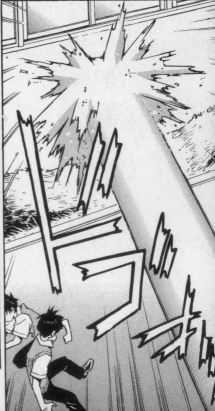

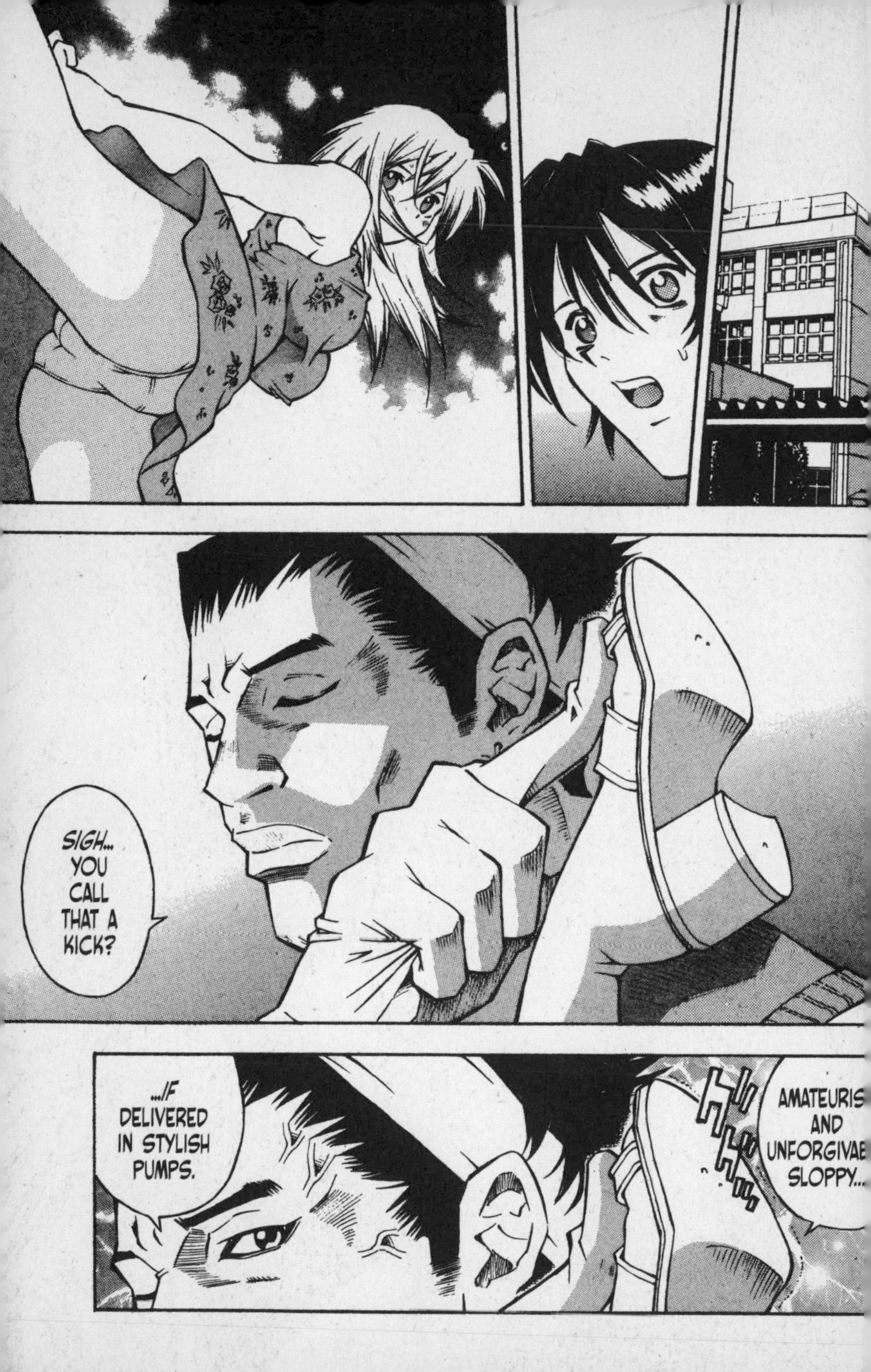
SIGH... YOU CALL THAT A KICK?
...IF DELIVERED IN STYLISH PUMPS.
AMATEURIS AND UNFORGIVAB SLOPPY...

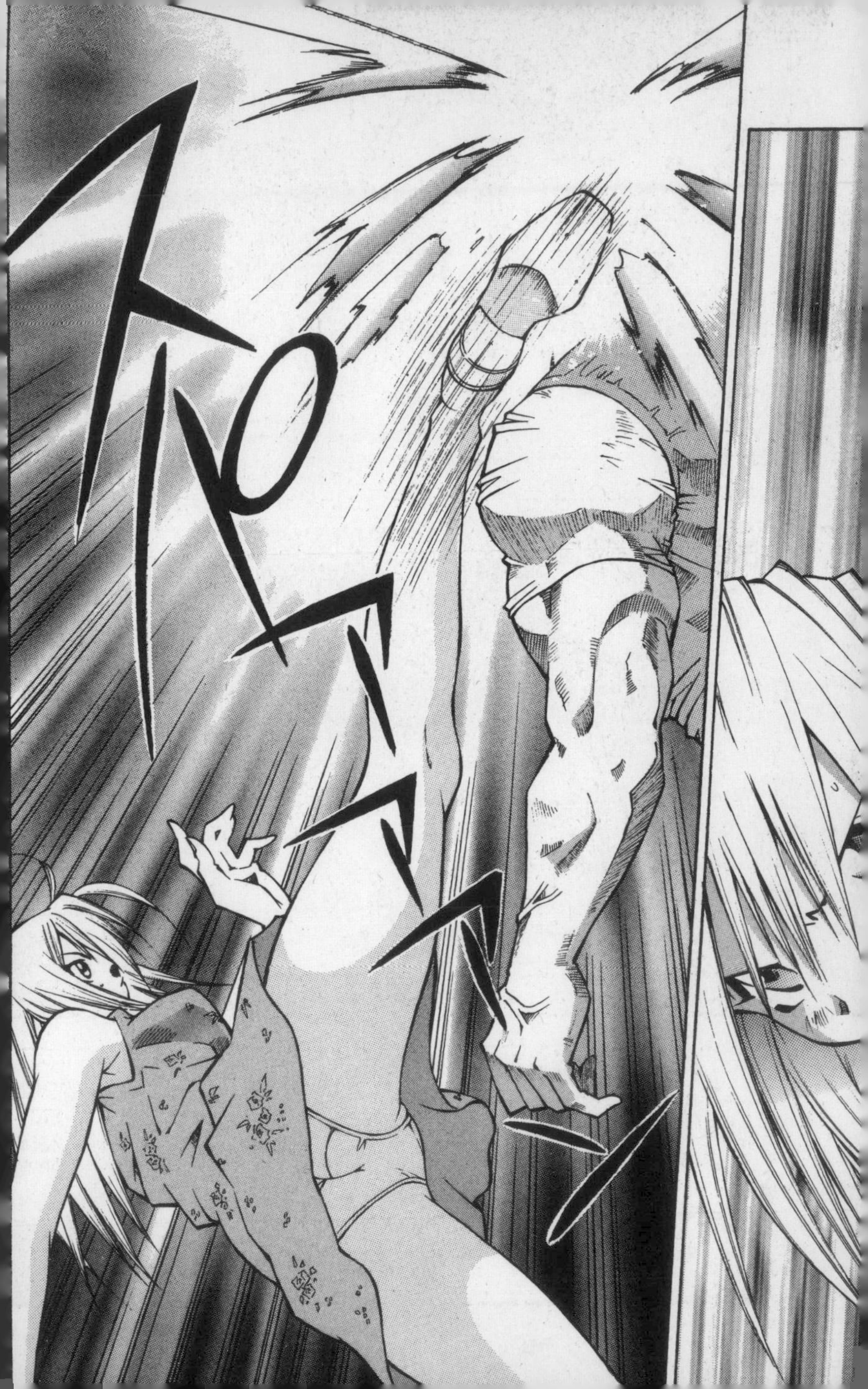

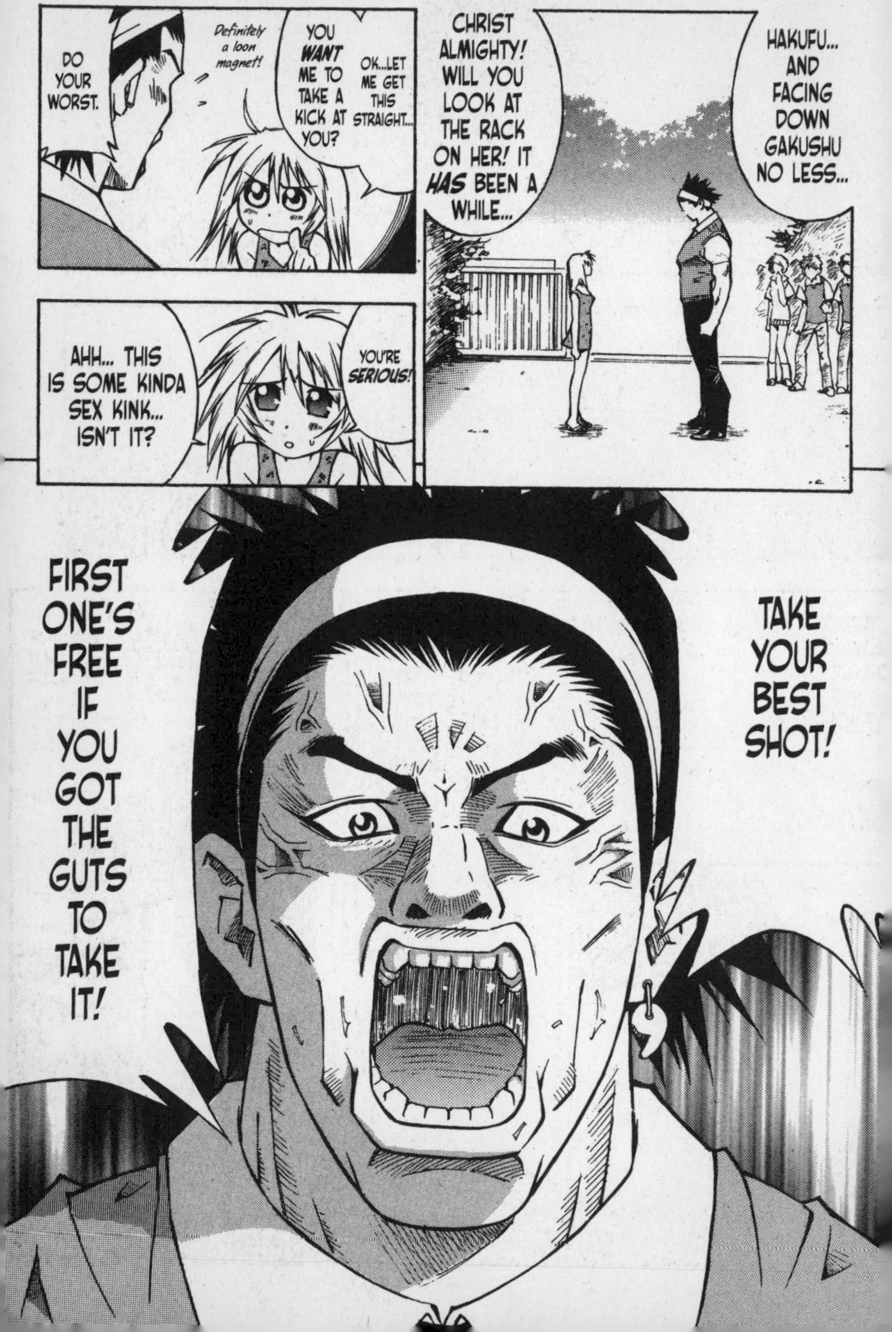
DO YOUR WORST.
Definitely a loon magnet!
YOU WANT ME TO TAKE A KICK AT YOU?
OK...LET ME GET THIS STRAIGHT...
AHH... THIS IS SOME KINDA SEX KINK... ISN'T IT?
YOU'RE SERIOUS!
CHRIST ALMIGHTY! WILL YOU LOOK AT THE RACK ON HER! IT HAS BEEN A WHILE...
HAKUFU... AND FACING DOWN GAKUSHU NO LESS...
FIRST ONE'S FREE IF YOU GOT THE GUTS TO TAKE IT!
TAKE YOUR BEST SHOT!

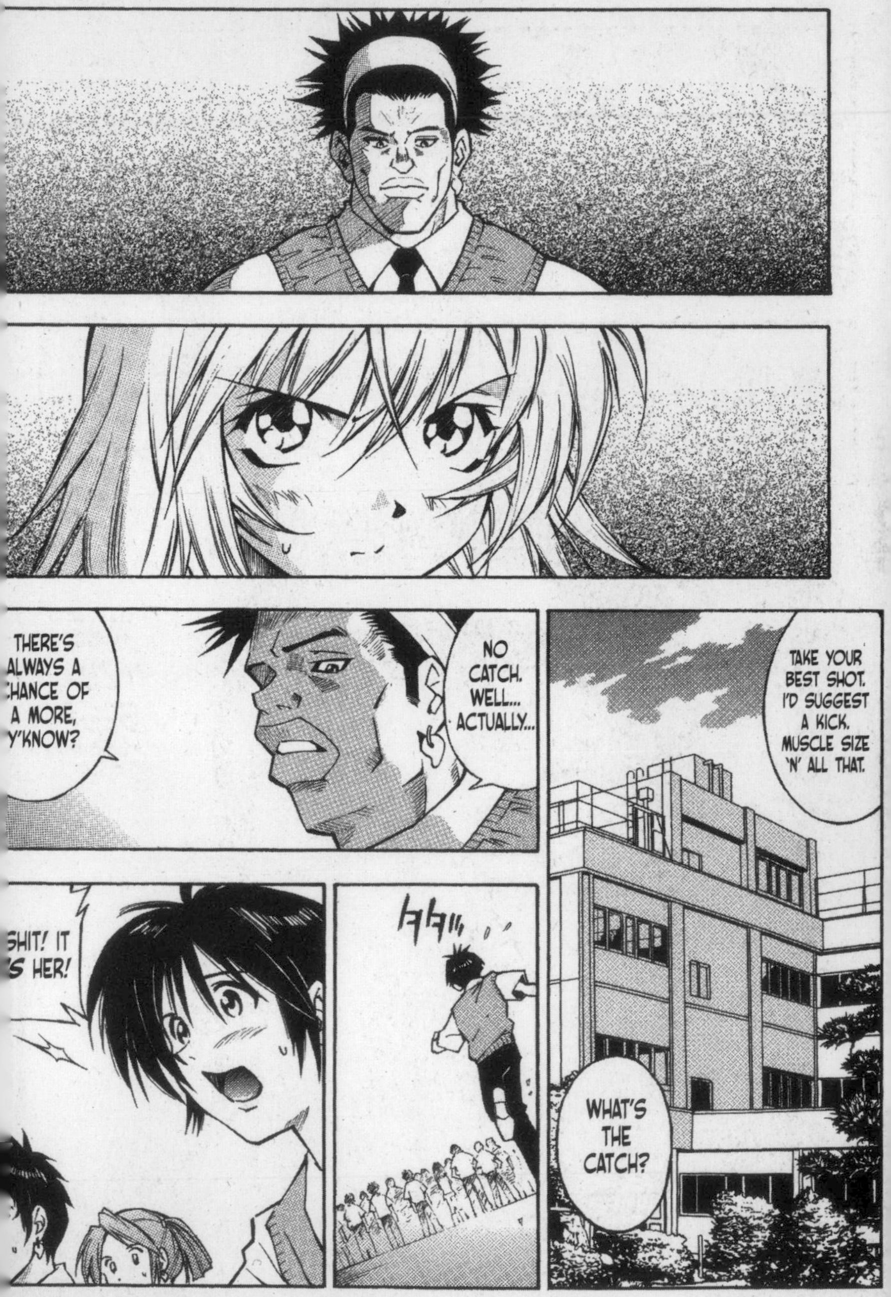
THERE'S ALWAYS A HANCE OF A MORE, Y'KNOW?
NO CATCH. WELL... ACTUALLY...
SHIT! IT S HER!
TAKE YOUR BEST SHOT. I'D SUGGEST A KICK. MUSCLE SIZE 'N' ALL THAT.
WHAT'S THE CATCH?

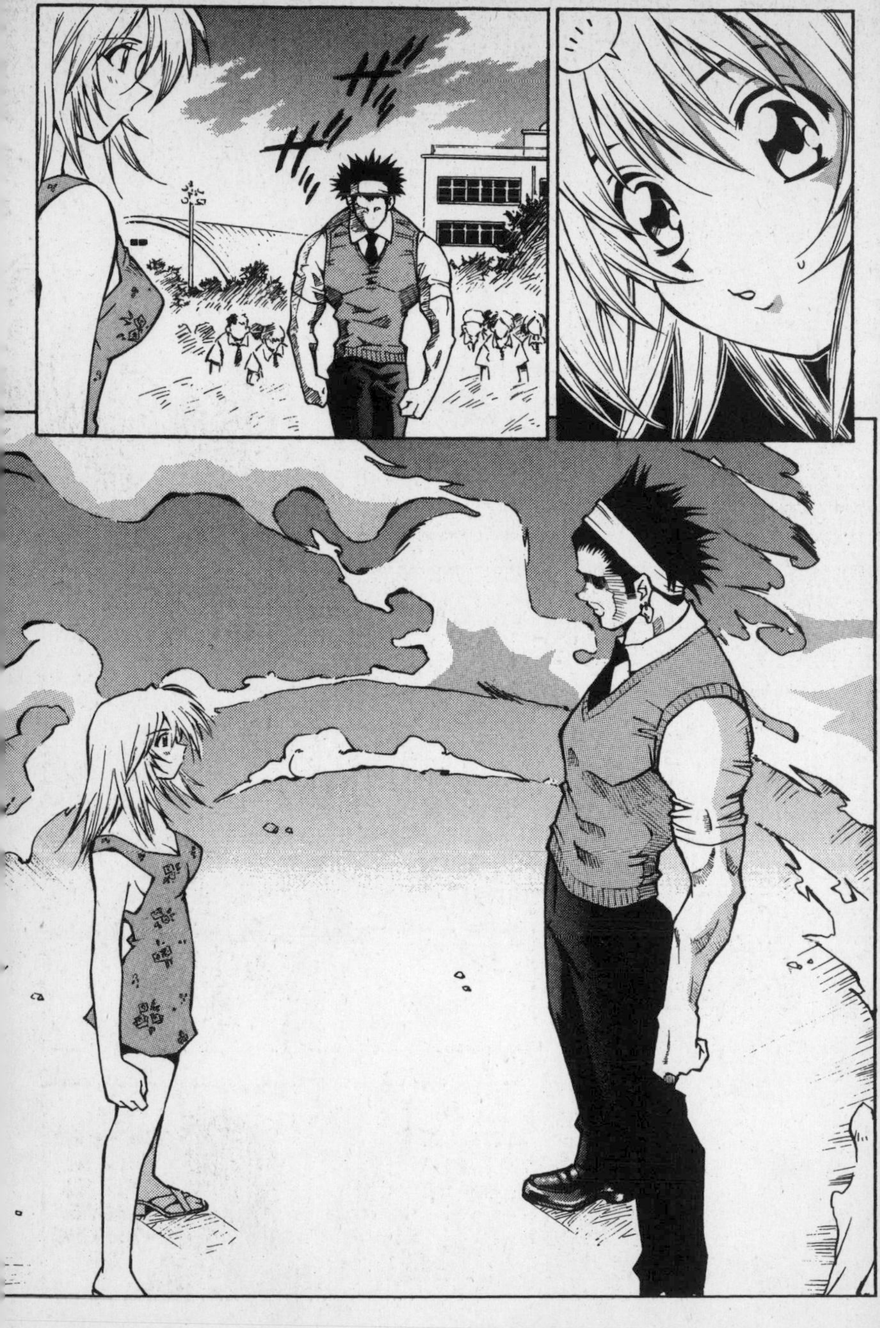
…

ONE MORE TO GO...

OR IS IT TWO? DAMN! I LOST COUNT!

BETTER MAKE IT THREE TO BE SURE.

MOST DEFINITELY NOT GOOD. WE BETTER TELL MR. ENJUTSU WHAT'S GOING DOWN.

TELL HIM WHAT?! THAT *ONE* GIRL'S WIPING THE FLOOR WITH US?

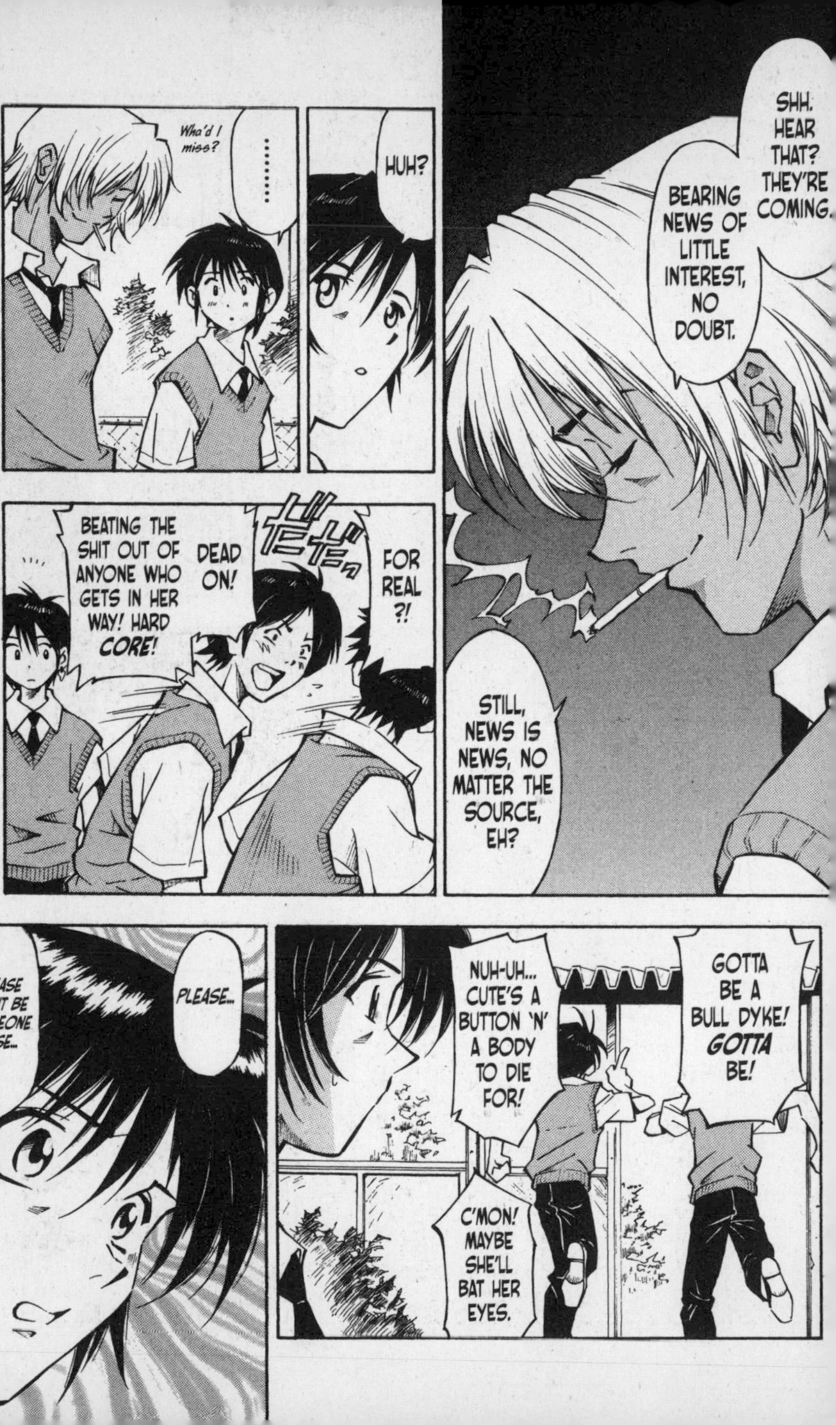

Wha'd I miss?
......
HUH?
BEATING THE SHIT OUT OF ANYONE WHO GETS IN HER WAY! HARD CORE!
DEAD ON!
FOR REAL?!
SHH. HEAR THAT? THEY'RE COMING.
BEARING NEWS OF LITTLE INTEREST, NO DOUBT.
STILL, NEWS IS NEWS, NO MATTER THE SOURCE, EH?
PLEASE LET IT BE SOMEONE ELSE...
PLEASE...
GOTTA BE A BULL DYKE! GOTTA BE!
NUH-UH... CUTE'S A BUTTON 'N' A BODY TO DIE FOR!
C'MON! MAYBE SHE'LL BAT HER EYES.

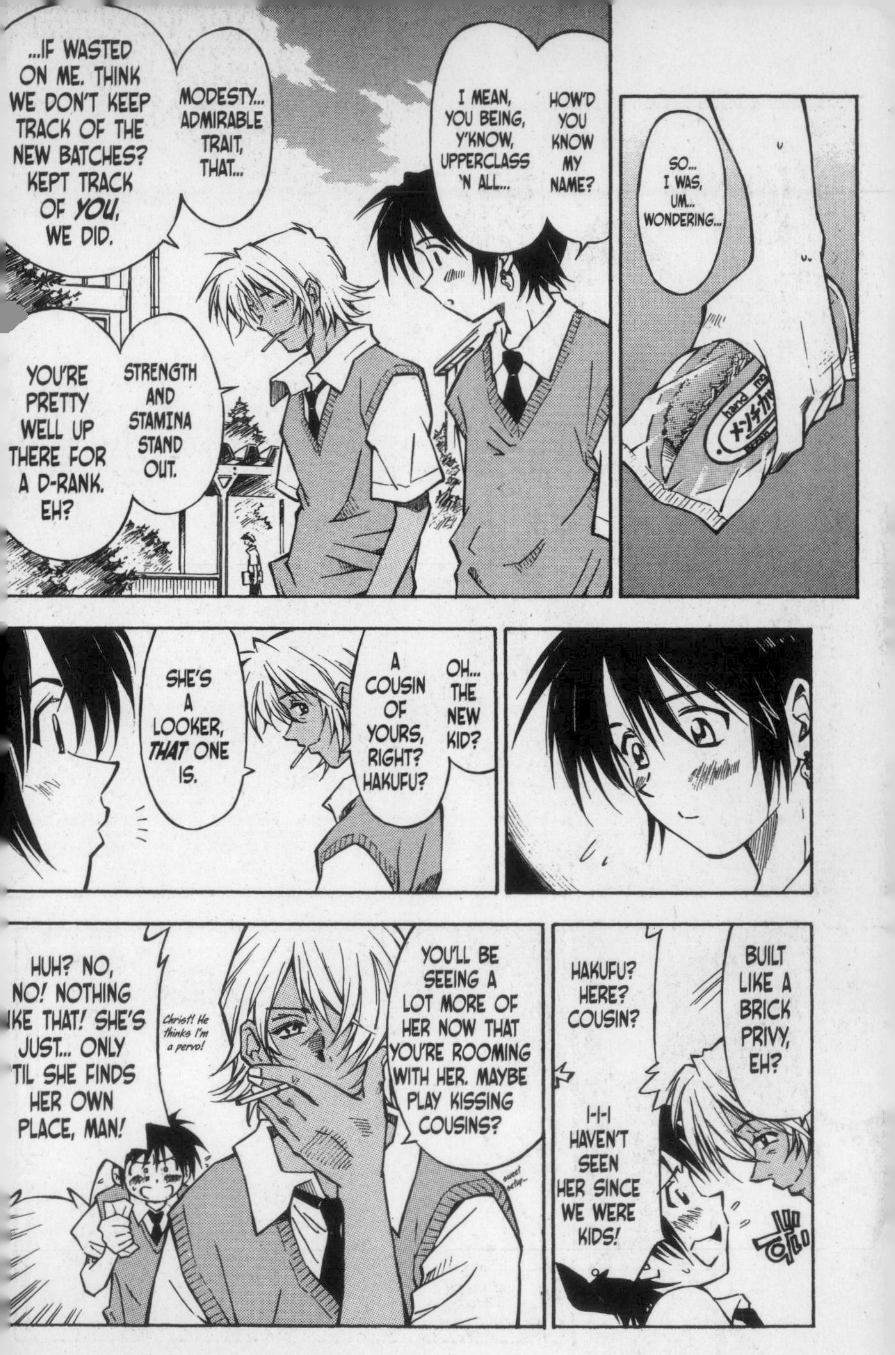

...IF WASTED ON ME. THINK WE DON'T KEEP TRACK OF THE NEW BATCHES? KEPT TRACK OF *YOU*, WE DID.
MODESTY... ADMIRABLE TRAIT, THAT...
I MEAN, YOU BEING, Y'KNOW, UPPERCLASS 'N ALL...
HOW'D YOU KNOW MY NAME?
YOU'RE PRETTY WELL UP THERE FOR A D-RANK. EH?
STRENGTH AND STAMINA STAND OUT.
SO... I WAS, UM.. WONDERING...
SHE'S A LOOKER, *THAT* ONE IS.
A COUSIN OF YOURS, RIGHT? HAKUFU?
OH... THE NEW KID?
HUH? NO, NO! NOTHING IKE THAT! SHE'S JUST... ONLY TIL SHE FINDS HER OWN PLACE, MAN!
Christ! He thinks I'm a pervo!
YOU'LL BE SEEING A LOT MORE OF HER NOW THAT YOU'RE ROOMING WITH HER. MAYBE PLAY KISSING COUSINS?
sweet setup...
HAKUFU? HERE? COUSIN?
BUILT LIKE A BRICK PRIVY, EH?
I-I-I HAVEN'T SEEN HER SINCE WE WERE KIDS!

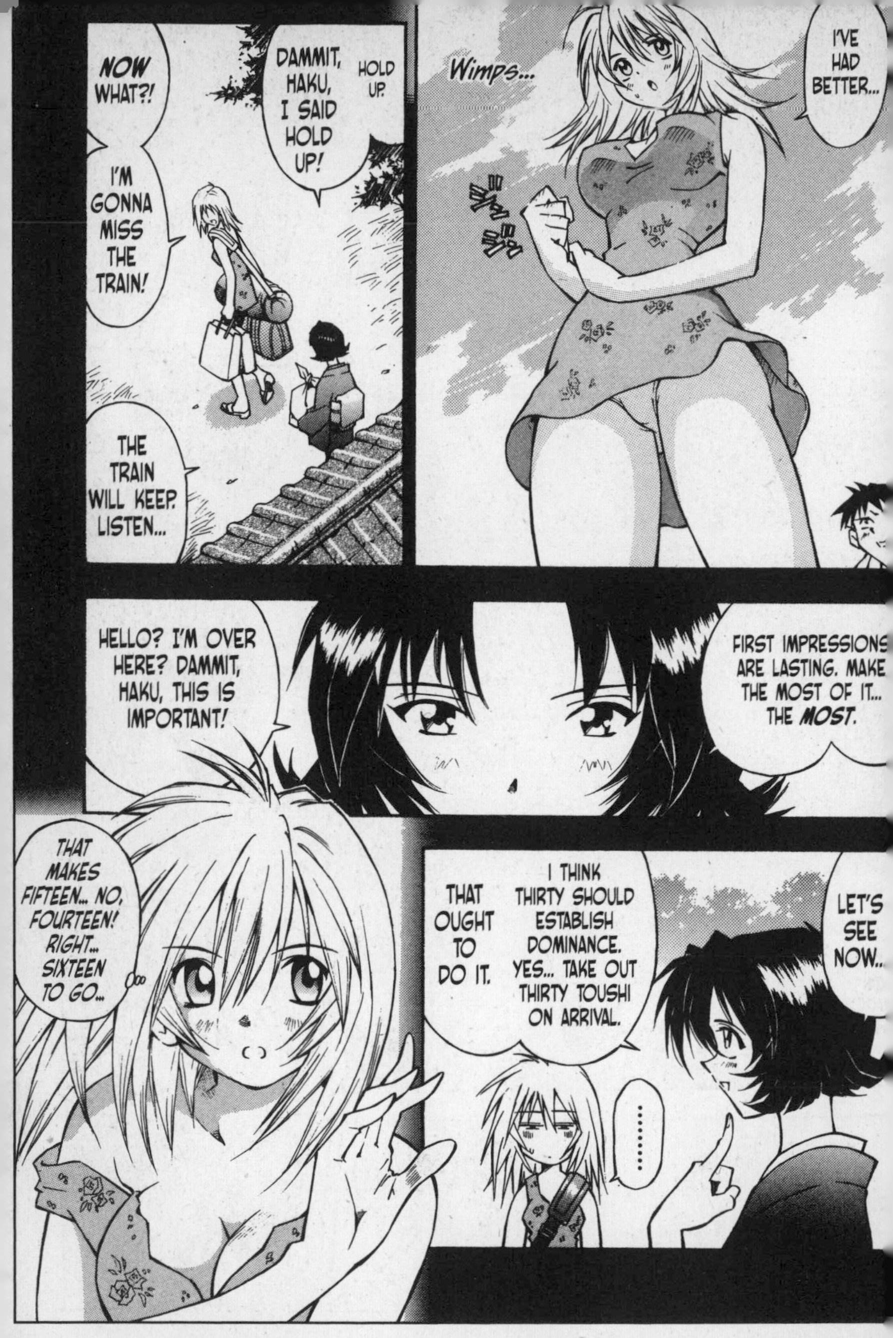
NOW WHAT?!
DAMMIT, HAKU, I SAID HOLD UP!
HOLD UP.
I'M GONNA MISS THE TRAIN!
THE TRAIN WILL KEEP. LISTEN...
Wimps...
I'VE HAD BETTER...
HELLO? I'M OVER HERE? DAMMIT, HAKU, THIS IS IMPORTANT!
FIRST IMPRESSIONS ARE LASTING. MAKE THE MOST OF IT... THE MOST.
THAT MAKES FIFTEEN... NO, FOURTEEN! RIGHT... SIXTEEN TO GO...
THAT OUGHT TO DO IT.
I THINK THIRTY SHOULD ESTABLISH DOMINANCE. YES... TAKE OUT THIRTY TOUSHI ON ARRIVAL.
LET'S SEE NOW...
....

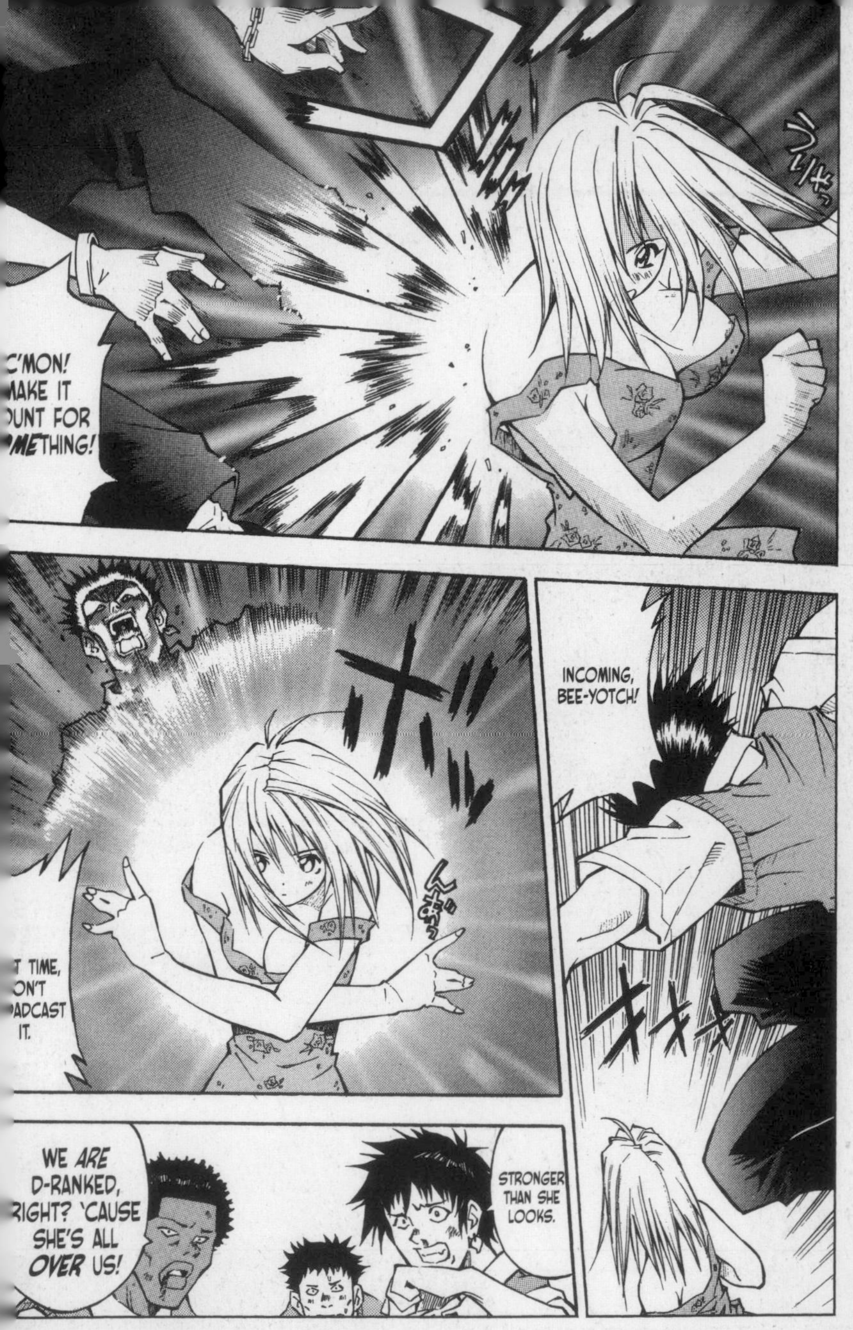
C'MON! MAKE IT
OUNT FOR METHING!
T TIME, ON'T ADCAST IT.
INCOMING, BEE-YOTCH!
WE ARE D-RANKED, IGHT? 'CAUSE SHE'S ALL OVER US!
STRONGER THAN SHE LOOKS.

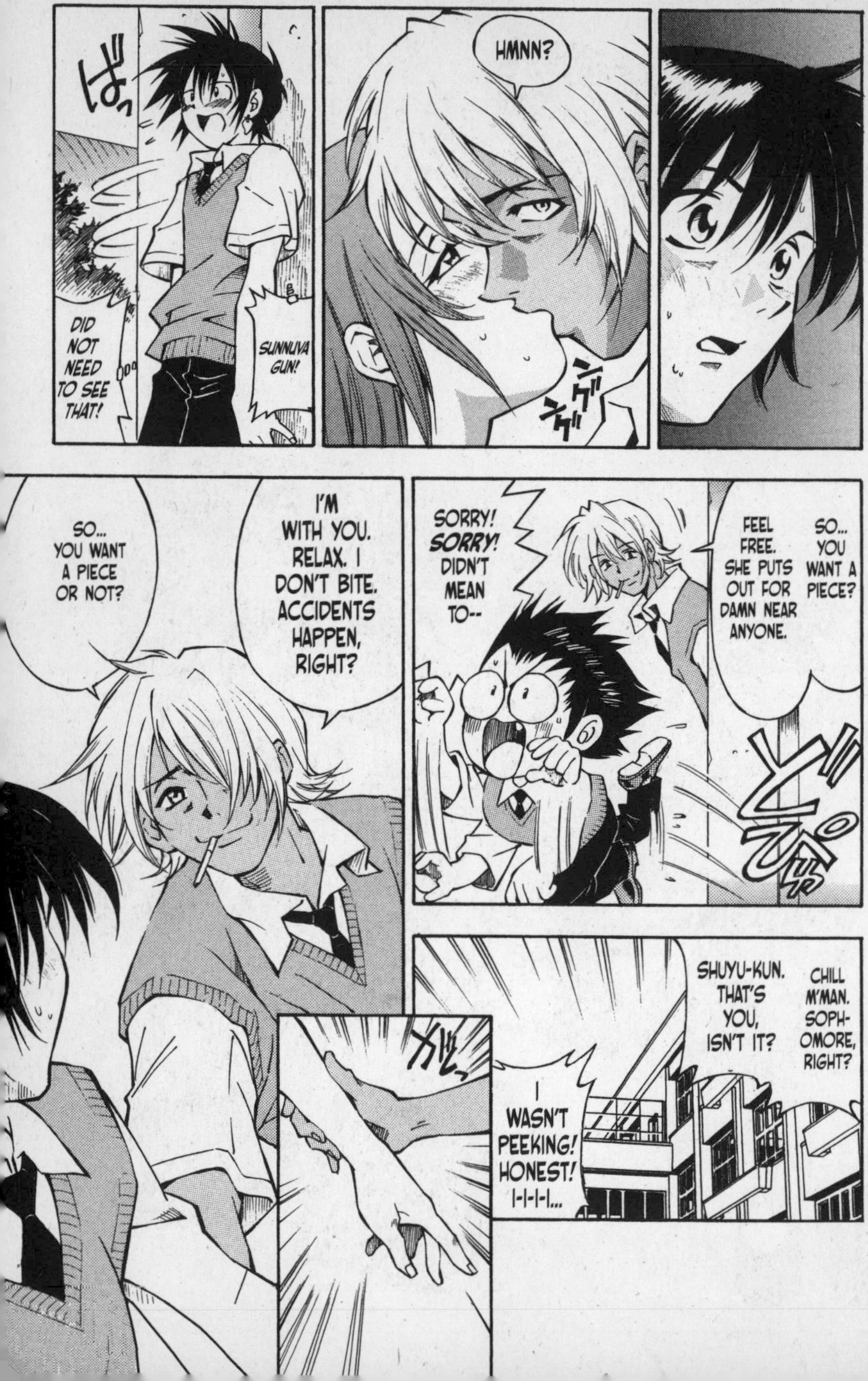
ばっ
DID NOT NEED TO SEE THAT!
SUNNUVA GUN!
HMNN?
SO... YOU WANT A PIECE OR NOT?
I'M WITH YOU. RELAX. I DON'T BITE. ACCIDENTS HAPPEN, RIGHT?
SORRY! ***SORRY!*** DIDN'T MEAN TO--
FEEL FREE. SHE PUTS OUT FOR DAMN NEAR ANYONE.
SO... YOU WANT A PIECE?
SHUYU-KUN. THAT'S YOU, ISN'T IT?
CHILL M'MAN. SOPH-OMORE, RIGHT?
I WASN'T PEEKING! HONEST! I-I-I-I...

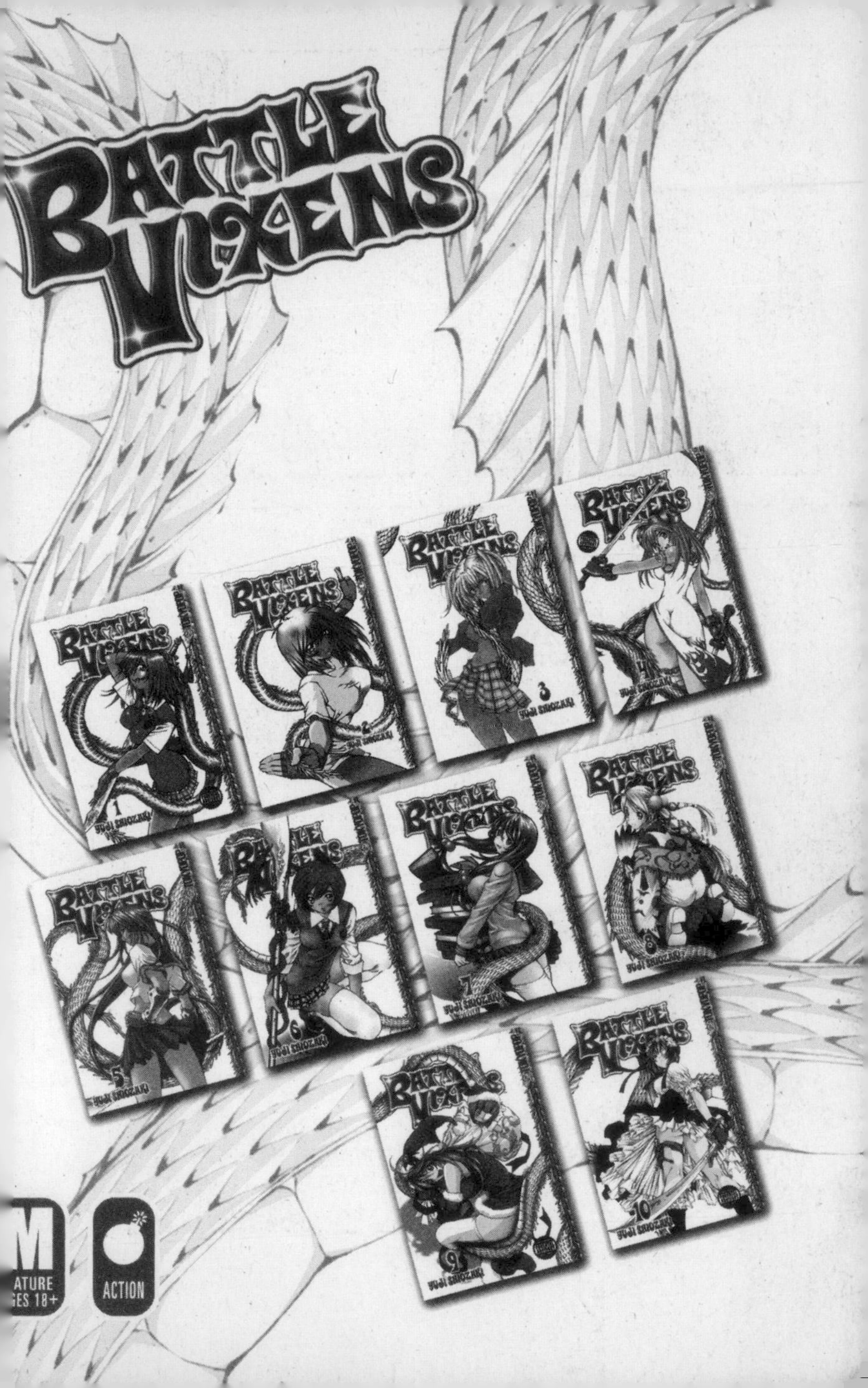
BATTLE VIXENS
M
ATURE
GES 18+
ACTION

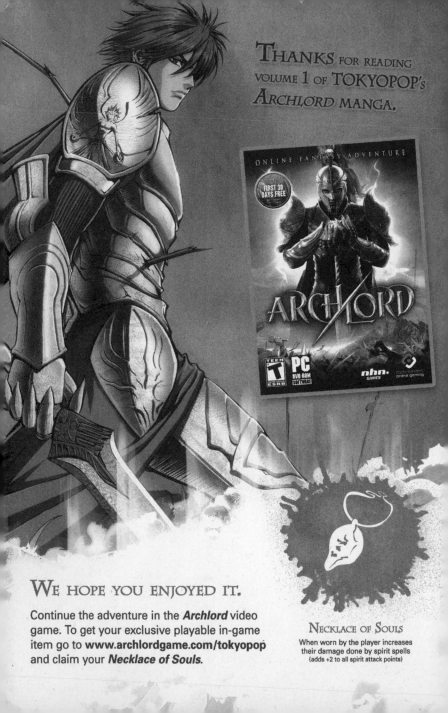